The Crafts Business Encyclopedia

The Modern Craftsperson's Guide to Marketing, Management, and Money

---

REVISED EDITION

by Michael Scott

As Revised by Leonard D. DuBoff

A HARVEST ORIGINAL

HARCOURT BRACE & COMPANY

San Diego   New York   London

Requests for permission to make copies of any part
of the work should be mailed to: Permissions Department,
Harcourt Brace & Company, 8th Floor, Orlando, Florida 32887.

Thanks to the following organizations for their permission
to use material from their publications: The American Craft Council,
the New York State Bar Association, The Crafts Report Publishing Co., Inc.,
and Van Nostrand-Reinhold Company for the use of quotes from
Selling Your Crafts by Norbert Nelson, © 1967
by Litton Educational Publishing, Inc.

Library of Congress Cataloging-in-Publication Data
Scott, Michael, 1924–1989
The crafts business encyclopedia: marketing, management, and money.
—Rev. ed., 2nd Harvest ed./by Michael Scott, with revisions by Leonard DuBoff.
p.   cm.—(A Harvest book)
Includes bibliographical references.
ISBN 0-15-622726-6
1. Small business—Management.   2. Handicraft—Management.
3. Handicraft—Marketing.   I. DuBoff, Leonard D.   II. Title.
HD62.7.S395   1993
745.5'068—dc20   93-12997

Designed by Camilla Filancia
Printed in the United States of America
Revised Harvest/HBJ edition 1993
A B C D E

To Sheila, Janie, and Tim for making
the circle of the late Michael Scott's rich
and fulfilling life complete; to the late
Michael Scott, founding editor of *The
Crafts Report*, for his friendship and
significant contributions to the field;
to his wife, Sheila, for her friendship,
support, and encouragement with this
revision; and to my brother Michael—
the lawyer who encouraged me to join
his profession—and his wife, Diane,
an artist with exceptional talent.

—LEONARD D. DuBOFF

Contents

The subjects that appear alphabetically in this encyclopedia are grouped here under general categories for easy reference.

Bookkeeping

Credit

Financial Management
(See also: Accounting, Banking, Bookkeeping, Credit, Pricing, Taxes.)

Insurance

Labor and Employees

Legal

Management

(See also: Accounting, Financial Management, Insurance, Legal, Production, Selling and Marketing, Taxes.)

Balance Sheet

Bankruptcy

Budget

Bulk Buying

Business Forms

Business Trips

Capital

Cash Flow

Collateral

Collection Problems

Contracts

Cooperatives

Corporation

Credit

Depreciation

Employees

Equity

Expenses

Fire Prevention

Income

Insurance

Inventory

Investment

Lawyers

Lease

Loans

Marketing

Market Planning

Market Research

Mortgage

Orders

Overhead

Pensions

Pricing

Product Line

Product Research

Profit

Record Keeping

Safety

Sale

Sales Cost

Sales Terms

Security

Suppliers

Systems

Telephone

Turnover

Miscellaneous

Books

Design

Education

Exhibitions

Fine Art

Grants

Industrial Design

Metric System

Periodicals

Politics

Writing

Zoning

Organizations

American Craft Council (ACC)

Better Business Bureau (BBB)

Chamber of Commerce

Government Activities

National Endowment for
    the Arts (NEA)

Selling and Marketing

Advertising
Architects
Back Order
Business Trips
Buyers
Cash Discounts
Catalog
Collection Problems
Collectors
Commission
Consignment
Consumer
Cooperatives
Customer
Direct Mail
Discounts
Display
Exclusive Rights
Exhibitions
Expense Accounts
Gallery
Guarantee
Industrial Design
Interior Decorators and Designers
Loss Leader

Mail Order
Marketability
Marketing
Market Planning
Market Research
Memo
Minimum Orders
Museum
Orders
Portfolio
Pricing
Product Line
Product Research
Rented Crafts
Retailing
Returns
Sales Cost
Salesmanship
Sales Representatives
Sales Terms
Samples
Seconds
Shows and Fairs
Turnover
Wholesaling

Shipping

Bill of Lading
Common Carrier
Customs
Free on Board (F.O.B.)
Freight Allowance
Freight Collect

Freight Prepaid
Net Weight
Packing
Post Office
Shipping
United Parcel Service

Tax
(See also: Accounting.)

Capital-Gains Tax
Depreciation
Estimated Tax

Excise Tax
Expenses
Income Averaging

Income Tax—Business   Sales Tax Exemption
Income Tax—Personal   Social Security
Inventory   Tax
Property Tax   Withholding Tax
Sales Tax

Appendices

Preface to the Revised Edition

It is important for an artist or craftsperson to continue to hone creative skills and to develop new ideas or concepts. Artistic growth is essential for aspiring artists who desire to have their work accepted or for established ones who wish to continue receiving their well-deserved recognition. Yet, artistic quality is not enough to ensure success. It is also important for the craftsperson to be aware of the business norms and rules which govern our profession.

As a teacher, I am constantly advising my students to learn the business skills necessary to function effectively. I have learned that lack of business knowledge can be extremely harmful to one's career. As a professional artist, I have developed a healthy respect for business knowledge, and I have recognized the importance of being aware of business standards.

The Crafts Business Encyclopedia provides an easy, readable text containing most of the basic information a crafts professional needs to participate in the crafts business. It is a valuable tool for any serious professional and one that should be on every craftsperson's bookshelf.

Leonard DuBoff, a professor of law who pioneered the field of art law, devoted his vast experience in that discipline to revising this text, which was originally written by Michael Scott, founding editor of *The Crafts Report*. This accurate, up-to-date, and useful book provides the reader with the kind of information in a digested form that is not otherwise readily available. The explanations, forms, and examples help the reader understand technical business issues and make the business aspects of crafts comprehensible. It is important to emphasize the need for business savvy, and this book will help you to obtain that knowledge.

—DAN DAILEY

Crafts artist and professor of fine art
and founder of the glass program
at the Massachusetts College of Art
School of Design, 1993

Foreword to the Revised Edition

The need for a comprehensive encyclopedia of terms and concepts that are important to crafts artists was recognized more than a decade ago by Michael Scott, the founding editor of *The Crafts Report*. His pioneering work filled an educational void in the industry: For the first time, crafts artists had a convenient and readable source within which to learn about essential business, legal, and marketing concepts.

Times and business practices change and so do many laws. *The Crafts Business Encyclopedia* kept pace with current developments through the years.

After Michael Scott's untimely death, it became clear that there was still a strong demand for this book and that a revision would be necessary. The business of crafts had taken many significant leaps forward since the last edition.

In this revised edition, Leonard D. DuBoff, an attorney who pioneered and developed the field of crafts law, follows the tradition of quality established by Michael Scott. It is understandable, since the two were good friends during Michael's lifetime and he often called upon Len for assistance with legal questions.

In this edition, Leonard DuBoff, a professor of law and author of numerous other works on the crafts industry, presents in the clearest of prose an encyclopedic discussion of the host of business concepts encountered by crafts artists. He has also added several extremely useful appendices.

As the wife of a professional artist for more than fifty years, I recognize the importance of producing quality work, yet, even the most skilled artist cannot succeed in today's competitive world without having a grasp of the rules of business.

My work on the International Year of American Crafts has underscored the importance of business education for crafts artists. As we guide consumers toward an awareness of the significant role played by the crafts in the world, crafts artists will inevitably receive more attention; their professional knowledge and business practices must keep pace with the increasing visibility of their field.

This book is a convenient, readable, and accurate source of information for crafts artists on the host of business issues important to the crafts industry.

—HORTENSE GREEN
*Crafts advocate and coordinator
of affiliate relations for the
American Crafts Council, 1993*

Acknowledgments

It is now more than fifteen years since Michael Scott, the late editor and founder of *The Crafts Report*, first contacted me and asked whether I would be willing to refocus some of my art-law research to benefit craftspeople. What resulted was a series of articles that ultimately evolved into a regular column on crafts law in *The Crafts Report*. In addition, I was asked to participate in numerous conferences and seminars that also featured Michael Scott. We thus became colleagues and good friends.

In 1990 Michael Scott died, and his wife, Sheila, asked me to revise this text. I was flattered and challenged. I did not want to lose any of Michael Scott's humor, yet it was necessary to update the material in order to reflect the numerous changes that have occurred in business, law, marketing, and tax. It was, therefore, my goal to try to preserve the essence of Michael Scott's groundbreaking *Crafts Business Encyclopedia* while making the text as accurate and up-to-date as possible.

In accomplishing this task, there have been several colleagues and friends who have been extremely helpful. I would, therefore, like to thank my research assistants Patrick Maloney, J.D., Lewis and Clark Law School, 1991; Michael Cragun, J.D., Lewis and Clark Law School, 1992; and Christy King, J.D., Lewis and Clark Law School, 1992, for their help in researching the myriad changes that have occurred since the original text was published. Extreme thanks are also due Lynn Della, my former legal assistant and longtime friend, for all of her help with this revision. Lynn has provided significant contributions to the quality of this book and the accuracy of its contents.

I would also like to thank the staff of *The Crafts Report*—in particular, Joy Laster, news editor; Judy Wilson, circulation and advertising editor, and the new editor, Marilyn Stevens. All were helpful in providing me with updated information on crafts organizations. My thanks also to the staff of *Niche Magazine* for the information they provided to me on crafts marketing. In particular, I would like to express my appreciation to Laurie Rosen, editor, and Rebecca Casen-Oats. Mary Hujsak, librarian, American Crafts Council, was very helpful in assembling the bibliography.

The arduous task of transcribing my illegible scrawl, cryptic notes, and unreadable interlineations into a publishable manuscript has once again been miraculously accomplished by Lenair Mulford of the Lewis and Clark Law School staff. Words cannot express my appreciation to her.

I would also like to thank my children, Colleen Rose DuBoff, Robert Courtney DuBoff, and Sabrina Ashley DuBoff, for their help with this book and for their understanding. There were many occasions they attended school outings or community functions with one parent since I was closeted with this project.

I would also like to express my sincere appreciation to Sheila Scott for her confidence. In addition, I would like to thank my editor, Vicki Austin, of the Harcourt Brace & Company staff, for her suggestions and support while I revised this book. I would also like to acknowledge Thea DeHart, copy editor on this edition of the text. Her queries assisted in focusing the text.

I would also like to thank my friends in the crafts community for their help and valuable recommendations regarding the contents of this revised text. They have helped me to sharpen my focus and create a book that hopefully continues to fulfill its mission by being useful to the crafts community.

Last, but certainly not least, I would like to acknowledge the person who has contributed the most to my career and who has had the most profound effect on the work I have done throughout my career: my wife for more than a quarter of a century, Mary Ann Crawford DuBoff.

—LEONARD D. DuBOFF
Portland, Oregon, 1993

Introduction

This book was written for anyone who makes craft objects for sale, whether as a part-time activity or a full-time profession. The key word is *selling*, because once you sell, even on a very limited basis, you're "in business" and entitled to some tax benefits and you are subject to certain legal obligations. Whether you succeed or fail, whether you make money or lose money, depends in great measure on how well you run your affairs, manage your money, find your markets, and understand your problems.

The word *business* often raises hackles when it is mentioned in the presence of artists and craftspeople. Many creative people are suspicious of anything associated with the impersonal business world. Indeed, a craftsperson's very work is the antithesis of the mass production and mass marketing that have become synonymous with business today.

But let's face it: Much of our life is ruled by laws that govern business activities. Taxes, banking, labor, accounting, copyright, licenses, even so simple a contract as renting space at a craft fair—all these are governed by law. To ignore this fact is to invite economic and legal problems.

Similarly, the techniques of mass production brought forth numerous sales techniques that can, without violence to the conscience, be adapted to craft selling. Just because some of these techniques have, on occasion, been used by unscrupulous businesspeople to fleece the public is no reason to throw out the baby with the bathwater. Would anyone suggest that we abolish the use of electricity simply because electricity was invented to power the emerging industrial machine of the nineteenth century? No, we use that same electricity to turn our potter's wheels, fire our kilns, illuminate our workrooms, power our tools.

Let us explore what is useful, discard what is objectionable, and turn the techniques of marketing, merchandising, management, selling—yes, *business*—toward implementing and supporting our major purpose as craftspeople; namely, to produce work that represents our best creative talents and allows us to survive and prosper.

This book is not designed primarily for the fine artist whose work finds its way into rich folks' collections, although many of the business principles discussed here apply as well. Our concern is the craftsperson who makes a living (or hopes to) by producing and selling quality craftwork.

What is the difference between fine art and craft? There have been many thoughtful articles criticizing the distinction and emphasizing the unity of so-called "fine art" and "crafts," yet the law still distinguishes between the two for many purposes and, despite a preference for unity among creative people, it is necessary to preserve the separation of "fine art" and "crafts" in this book. Aside from investment and legal considerations, fine art normally has a purely aesthetic value; craftwork usually has both aesthetic and functional values.

The boundaries between the two are often indistinct. Weaving, for example, is a craft that was born of the need to make things to keep people covered and warm. Weaving today has gone far beyond that elementary utilitarian purpose. An exquisite wall hanging uses the same craft technique, but its basic function is aesthetic. However, even the magnificent rugs and tapestries in old castles served to keep the drafty places warm.

There was a time when no distinction was made between art and craft. Ancient languages had only one word to describe both functions; note the similarity between *artist* and *artisan*. For many centuries, the limits of technology and resources required that everything made by human hands be useful. But the human spirit is such that everything also had to be made as beautiful as circumstances and talent would allow. It was simply unthinkable to produce a useful object without grace and beauty or to produce an object whose only function was to be beautiful.

The industrial age brought the mass manufacture of goods for which utility and economy of production were the only important factors. If they also happened to look good, that was a coincidence.

When advertising became a major mover of goods, design again became a factor. But it was less a matter of beauty than an item's salability; it had to look different from similar products.

The aesthetic emptiness of mass-produced merchandise, the void of the "plastic society," has sparked a remarkable increase in public awareness of crafts in recent years. The fact that an object was made by human hands, that its appearance expresses the human spirit, and that there is no other object precisely like it fills a need at a time when individuality and personality are being drowned in a sea of impersonal mass marketing.

But craftspeople cannot be hermits. While no authority can dictate our creative integrity, all of our other activities are subject to the regulations of the society in which we live. We must understand those regulations if we want to survive economically without compromising our artistic and creative standards.

The pages that follow explain not only what happens on the business side of crafts, but why it happens; not only what you can do about it, but also why. Thinking people need to know the reasons behind events so that future events can be handled with greater understanding and competence.

This book is not intended to turn craftspeople into lawyers or accountants or even business specialists. But it will help steer you through the maze of regulations that society has formulated (for better or worse); to serve as a ready reference whenever a problem arises in the areas of marketing, management, and money; and to be a guide toward a more productive and more satisfying experience by taking the mystery out of the business aspect of crafts.

The entries are listed alphabetically, with cross-references to related subjects indicated at the end of each entry. The contents pages list entries under general categories such as selling, production, banking, pricing, taxes, legal, and so on.

This is not a book designed to be read once, like a popular novel. Rather, it is hoped that this volume will find a permanent place in the workshops and studios of all craftspeople who love their craft and want to make it an important part of their life's work.

If any errors have found their way into these pages, they are my responsibility. If anything has been left out, readers are cordially invited to let me know so that future editions can be revised to reflect greater accuracy and be of greater service to the crafts profession.

—MICHAEL SCOTT, *1984*
as revised by
Leonard D. DuBoff, 1993

The Crafts Business Encyclopedia

Accounting

Accounting is a professional activity concerned with the financial records and activities of a business or an individual. There is a significant difference between bookkeeping and accounting: Bookkeepers maintain the records, accountants use and interpret them.

There are several levels of accountants. Some are licensed tax preparers; some are certified public accountants (CPAs), who have passed rigid examinations to determine their qualifications. There are practitioners who range from no degree to postgraduate degrees in accounting.

Proper financial records, properly kept, are required for various legal reasons, such as calculating taxes. But equally important is the interpretation of those records to help a crafts business analyze its strengths and build on them or to discover its weaknesses and correct them. This is called financial management.

Many small-business enterprises that seem to have all the ingredients for potential success—a good product, a hardworking owner—nonetheless operate far below their potential or even fail because of inadequate financial records or the inability to interpret records properly. A set of books can be compared to a roll of exposed film. All the ingredients are there, but it must be developed before you can see the picture.

That's where the accountant comes in. Even the most uncomplicated business activity should periodically utilize the services of an accountant—first to set up a system of financial record keeping when the business is started and thereafter, at least once a year, to prepare tax returns, furnish an annual statement, and analyze the financial condition of the business.

Every business has its own situations and problems, so each set of books has to be created to suit the particular need. Most systems include the following basic categories:

1. *Cash receipts:* To record cash coming in.
2. *Cash disbursements:* To record expenditures.
3. *Sales:* To record and summarize monthly income.

4. *Purchases:* To record the purchases of merchandise bought for processing, resale, or business operations.
5. *Payroll:* To record wages and deductions such as taxes and Social Security.
6. *Equipment:* To record capital assets such as machinery, equipment, furniture, automobiles.
7. *Inventory:* To record investment in stock (and arrive at a true profit picture).
8. *Accounts receivable:* To record what is owed to the firm.
9. *Accounts Payable:* To record what the firm owes its creditors and suppliers.

The books need not be ledgers maintained by someone wearing a green eyeshade. Today, most "books" are actually maintained on computer systems. There are a number of good bookkeeping and accounting software programs available for personal computers. These include, for example, Quicken and Peachtree for accounting, and Turbo Tax for taxes.

The more extensive and involved the financial records and activities become, the more necessary it is to engage the services of an accountant on a regular basis. Many businesses use an accountant on a monthly or quarterly schedule to balance the books, check on the proper maintenance of the records, prepare periodic tax returns, and furnish other professional services. This is especially important for incorporated businesses.

An accountant's most important contribution to a large or small business firm may be in the area of taxes, not only in preparing tax returns but in providing advice—based on experience and continuing study of current tax laws—on how to organize financial activities for the best tax advantage.

Literally hundreds of decisions that involve money or management can benefit from an accountant's advice. Should you, for example, buy that new piece of equipment in November, or can you get a tax break if you wait six weeks and buy it in the next tax year? Will a move to bigger quarters at more rent be justified by the expected return? Which of your activities are profitable, which are not, which can be made profitable, and which should be abandoned? Applications for business loans from a bank usually require that the applicant furnish a financial statement prepared by a certified public accountant (CPA), who has passed rigid examinations to determine his or her qualifications.

A competent accountant is as important to a business activity as a competent lawyer, both to prevent and to solve problems. The proper use of an accountant's services requires a sense of trust and confidence and also requires that you lay all your financial problems on the table. Seek out accountants experienced in financial matters of a small business (your bank or business acquaintances can probably make recommendations), choose carefully, and feel free to discuss fees in advance. *(See also: Accrual Basis, Balance Sheet, Bookkeeping, Cash Basis, Cash Flow, Computers, Income Statement, Inventory, Pricing, Tax)*

Accounts Payable

In four little words: *what you owe others.*

A current bill that is due to be paid—from a supplier, the phone company, rent, taxes—but not long-term obligations such as bank loans. Accounts payable are shown on your balance sheet as liabilities. *(See also: Balance Sheet, Liabilities)*

Accounts Receivable

Simply put: *what others owe you.*

When you send out a bill and it isn't paid, it is carried on your books as an account receivable and is shown on the balance sheet as an asset. It is almost an axiom in the business world to keep accounts receivable as low and as current as possible. The older such accounts get (the longer it takes to get the money), the more difficult they become to collect. Meanwhile your creditor is working with your money without paying any interest. Accounts receivable should be carefully followed up. *(See also: Assets, Balance Sheet, Collection Problems)*

Accrual Basis

An accounting method used for tax purposes in which items of income and expense are charged against the tax period in which they are incurred, regardless of whether the money was actually received or spent during that period. For example, if you order a quantity of clay at the end of one year but do not receive the bill or pay for the clay until the next year, under the accrual basis of accounting you would list the expenditure for the year in which you ordered the clay. Similarly, an invoice you send to a customer for a dozen pots is credited as income on the date the invoice is sent, not the date you receive the money.

The accrual method is not generally used by small businesses such as crafts; for most craftspeople the cash basis is much simpler. However, if you carry a large inventory of unsold work, the accrual basis may give you a better picture of your financial condition and may also provide tax advantages, because the costs incurred in producing the unsold work can be charged against that work, regardless of when it is sold. *(See also: Cash Basis)*

Advertising

Advertising is any form of mass communication for which you pay money. It differs from other types of publicity that may be free but over which you exercise relatively little control.

Advertising can appear in newspapers, magazines, radio, television, billboards, handbills, direct mail. Within certain limitations you are in complete control of what you want to say, how you want to say it, and to whom it is said.

One of the major limitations to advertising is money. Craftspeople who do no retail selling except at crafts shows rarely have occasion to advertise. But even if your retail operation is limited to sales at your studio or workshop only twice a year, you have to bring customers in. The simplest method for that purpose may be a mailing piece you send to a list of former customers. It may not be the least expensive on a cost-per-customer basis—printing and postage can add up to fifty cents or more per piece—but on the basis of the business you get it may be the most economical.

In selecting where and how you advertise, cost is not the only consideration. The returns are equally important. One hundred dollars' worth of advertising space in the *Ladies Home Journal* may reach millions of readers at a fraction of a cent per reader. But those readers are useless to your business unless you have a hot item they can buy through the mail. You certainly don't expect them to travel thousands of miles to visit your studio to buy a ten-dollar piece of pottery. Your money would be better spent by advertising in the community weekly that reaches the audience you can reasonably expect at your studio or shop.

The first task, then, is to determine what medium can carry your message to the right audience at the right price. To do that, make a list of all the available publications that circulate among your potential customers. If you are in a resort area, the weeklies or the publications placed in hotel rooms may be ideal during the tourist season. In large cities that have their own city-oriented magazines, a classified ad in the proper section may bring good results.

Study the publications to see who else advertises, what type of audience they appeal to, whether your ad will be in the right company. You wouldn't advertise Beethoven in a rock magazine—no matter how inexpensive the space or how wide an audience the magazine reaches. The same principle applies to craftwork.

Testing Results

The next task is to judge the results. Keep track of each advertisement, whether it's a display ad of ten inches on two columns, a classified ad, a handbill, postcard, or whatever. In the beginning it is best not to run more than one type of ad at a time, which makes it easier to test results. Does one newspaper produce better results than another? Dollar for dollar, does a mailing piece produce more sales than a magazine? (This is not to suggest a specific sequence but only an approach to testing various media.) Since advertising is an expensive proposition, it pays to keep records of results so that you can concentrate on the more effective methods.

Cost should be a factor only as it relates to results. A one-hundred-dollar ad that produces one thousand dollars' worth of sales is often more productive than a fifty-dollar ad that produces five hundred dollars' worth of sales, though the ratio is identical. Your overhead and the cost of preparing the ad remain fairly constant no matter how much or little you sell. In the above situation, then, it is more profitable to produce nine hundred dollars above the cost of the ad instead of $450. On the other hand, if the fifty-dollar ad produces eight hundred dollars' worth of sales, it is probably wasteful to spend another fifty dollars simply to produce another two hundred dollars in sales. Each situation is specific, and each result must be judged by the advertiser's particular needs and objectives.

When noting results, take into consideration special conditions. If there was a severe snowstorm the day after an ad ran and customers couldn't make it to your shop or studio, that should be taken into account when measuring the advertisement's results. Similarly, an ad offering a half-price sale should not be compared with an ad for a gallery showing.

A good way to record the effectiveness of ads and other promotional materials is to paste them into a scrapbook and make notes of the results next to them. Include not only the cost of the ad and what it produced but also weather and other influences. Keep both the good and the bad so that you can repeat your successes and avoid your failures.

Effectiveness depends in large measure on the ad itself. Several ingredients contribute to results: (1) where the ad runs; (2) what the ad looks like (whether it will be read); and (3) the nature of the offer.

Simplicity is key. This is particularly true in small-space advertising. That small space has to stand out among all the other ads and articles appearing on the same page. Your advertisement has to compete for attention, and everything in the ad should help toward that end; nothing should detract from readability. Plenty of white space, a catchy headline that grabs the reader's attention, brief but explicit copy, and an uncomplicated illustration all contribute to readability.

Let's briefly examine some of these factors.

White Space

When you buy advertising space—whether it's two inches in a newspaper, an 8½ × 11-inch sheet of paper, or a huge billboard on the highway—what you are really buying is empty space. You must fill it with your message. Don't fill it too full. If you cram ink from one border to the other, the eye won't know what to look at first. Keep a little white space—breathing space—in the ad. Properly used, white space is not wasted because it helps direct the eye to the written and illustrative material.

The Headline

A catchy headline need not be clever. *All Jewelry Half Off* is catchier to most readers than *A Jar of Jangling Jewelry* or *We Have Many Surprises*. Put yourself in the reader's shoes. Does the headline include some benefit, some reason to read the rest of the ad? McDonald's We Do It All for You slogan was a perfect example of expressing a customer benefit. (If only their hamburgers were as good as their slogans.)

Body Copy

This is the text of your advertisement. The same principle of reader benefit applies. Describe what you are offering from the reader's point of view. Not *I've Made a Roomful of Mugs* but *You'll Find Mugs of Every Size, Color, and Description to Fit Every Taste and Every Budget*. The reader couldn't care less how many mugs you made; what he or she wants to know is whether there's likely to be one he or she likes and can afford.

Keep the copy brief. One advertising copywriter has this dictum posted over his desk: Write It Down, Cut It in Half, and It's Still Too Long. If you're using a small space, don't try to tell the whole story. Strip it down to the bare essentials that will excite the reader.

In maiil-order or catalog advertising, of course, you may have to be more specific and list all sizes and colors. But even here brevity is usually the better part of wisdom.

Illustrations

Simplicity applies here as well. Better to use a small, dramatic drawing that reproduces clearly than a cluttered photograph that can barely be deciphered and comes out a gray glob on the newspaper page. Photos may be necessary in catalogs, but they are generally inadvisable in small-space newspaper advertising. Finally, every piece of printed material, every advertisement, must include your name, address, telephone number, and directions if you're located in some out-of-the-way place.

The Nature of the Offer

All advertising falls into two basic categories: immediate response or long-range impact. Immediate-response advertising is expected to produce quick results. Included in this category are announcements of sales, shop openings, gallery events, mail-order items, and offers of specific products.

Immediate-response advertising is relatively easy to measure. It either brings results at once or it doesn't. A sale ad generally brings large crowds though it may bring smaller profits. But when you do have a sale, the size of the crowd is an important factor in its success. A mail-order ad is the easiest of all to measure: You simply count the coupons. There's no confusion as to the source of the order or what brought the customer in.

Long-range impact is created through advertising expected to bring the craftsperson's or shop's name to the attention of the public and keep it there so that potential buyers will remember it when they are ready to buy a craft item. This type of advertising would emphasize craftsmanship, artistry, exclusiveness, or whatever other attribute makes the shop or craftsperson distinctive.

Several other considerations enter into long-range-advertising planning. One concerns repetition. Should you repeat the same ad? That question does not arise, of course, with ads for special sales or events. But advertising specialists generally agree that an "institutional" ad, one that sells your shop or your line on a long-range basis, works best when the ad is repeated several times in the same publication. The cumulative effect often pays off better than running a different ad each time.

Even where ads are different, they should have a family resemblance. That's noted best in department-store advertising. You could probably identify the ads of several local department stores even if the names were removed simply because they have a similar appearance each day although the specific content of each ad is different. Stick to the same style of illustrative device, the same typeface for the headline and text, the same signature for your name and address. Familiarity, in this case, breeds recognition.

Your local newspaper is usually equipped to supply ready-made artwork and other advertising-prepartion services for ads that run in that paper, often at no extra charge. Don't hesitate to ask for help.

Everything mentioned so far is based on the concept that your advertising needs and budgets are limited. If you have a retail store or are engaged in extensive mail-order selling, the picture changes somewhat. You have a constant need for advertising to bring in the customers and the orders. The same principles of effectiveness and measuring results apply, but you are in a bigger league and probably need the services of an advertising agency.

Agencies come in all sizes and various specialties. Their services are concentrated in two important areas: selection of the media in which you advertise and preparation of your advertisement. In addition, agencies have two primary sources of income: a 15 percent commission they are paid by the newspapers or magazines in which the advertisements appear and the fees they are paid by the advertiser for such special services as preparing artwork and text for printing purposes.

The more complicated an advertising program is and the larger the budget becomes, the more useful it is to engage the services of advertising specialists. On a small budget, a one-man agency or a friend who works as an art director for a large agency may be enough to fill the need. But a retail store with an annual volume of one hundred thousand dollars may spend as much as ten thousand dollars on advertising. If you are in that category, take your business to professionals who are as experienced in creating effective advertising programs as you are in creating beautiful craftwork.

A suitable advertising agency is found in the same way as any other professional service. Ask other businesspeople who advertise extensively. Interview several agencies. Tell them what you hope to accomplish and what your budget estimates are. Ask them to make a brief outline of their approach to your advertising problems. Find out what they've done for others in similar situations.

The bigger the agency, the more likely it is that they have a variety of talent and expertise to serve you. But in choosing an agency it is sometimes better to be the big fish in a small pond than the small fish in a big pond. The more important you are to an agency's annual income, the better the service you receive.

Look to advertising, however, to serve one purpose only: to communicate quickly with large numbers of people. If your product is wrong or your price too high or your reputation for delivery poor, no amount of advertising will save you. *(See also: Catalog, Press Release, Publicity, Public Relations)*

Agents *(See: Sales Representatives)*

American Craft and Retailers Association (ACRA)

The American Craft and Retailers Association (ACRA) was a nonprofit, educational association dedicated to promoting the highest standards of business practices among artists and retailers and to encouraging appreciation of American crafts. This nongovernmental organization created a certification mark in red, white, and blue depicting a hand within a circle, bearing the legend *Handmade in the USA*, to be used on handmade American crafts. ACRA also worked to promulgate an ethical code for the crafts industry and sponsored numerous seminars devoted to topical issues in the industry. In 1992, ACRA merged with the American Craft Association.

American Craft Association (ACA)

The American Craft Association (ACA) was organized by the American Craft Council as part of its most recent reorganization. ACA is one of the programs of the American Craft Council but is a separate corporation operating within the guidelines of a trade and professional association. Its board of directors is made up of members, individual craftspeople, and shop and gallery owners. ACA is a professional association for crafts retailers, artists, and others involved in the business of crafts rather than collectors. For further information, contact the American Craft Council (see Appendix D).

American Craft Council (ACC)

The American Craft Council (ACC) is a national nonprofit organization of approximately thirty-five thousand members that was founded in 1943 "to stimulate interest in contemporary crafts."

ACC publishes the bimonthly magazine *American Craft* as well as a variety of reference publications, books, and exhibition catalogs. Operating through the American Craft Information Center, ACC provides members access to a craft registry of more than two thousand craftspeople working in all media. It also provides computerized access to information about programs offering instruction and about newsletters and catalogs of national, regional, and local craft organizations, museums, galleries and shops. The center also provides a fax and photocopy service to answer inquiries. Contact ACC for procedures and fees.

ACC membership is open to anyone. Membership services include a subscription to *American Craft* magazine; free admission to the American Craft Museum (40 West 53rd Street, New York, New York 10019); reduced prices on selected crafts books, certain ACC events, and various conferences or seminars; and other benefits depending on membership category. (See Appendix D for more information.) *(See also: Organizations)*

Amortization

To amortize is to spread a particular cost over a long period of time. Financial obligations such as mortgages are amortized by making regular periodic payments. Capital investments such as equipment and tools are amortized through depreciation, which means they are carried on the books at a predictable annual reduction in value on the assumption that they will ultimately wear out. In simplest terms, a five-hundred-dollar loom with a life expectancy of ten years would be amortized at fifty dollars a year. This is important both for tax purposes and for establishing the current value of your fixed assets at any given time. *(See also: Assets, Depreciation, Loans)*

Apprentice

Before there was a system of formal education, apprenticeship was the only way to learn a craft or trade. Boys from ten to fourteen would go to work for a journeyman and earn no more than subsistence-level room and board doing all the unpleasant, dirty jobs around the shop at first and learning the craftsman's trade bit by bit.

Apprenticeship is still the term used for learners in such trades as printing and skilled construction work. Such apprentices are now paid salaries and other benefits that increase according to specific formulas as they learn their trade.

The resurgence of handcrafts had led to a rebirth of apprenticeship in that field as well. Although some basic techniques and principles can be learned by apprentices in the classroom, most find that their technical and artistic development depends to a great extent on working with an experienced crafts artist. This helps them not only to refine their skills but also to understand the production methods, operational procedures, and business problems of earning a living in crafts.

The old method of room and board in exchange for learning a craft is no longer common, although it does still exist. Nor is apprenticeship a lengthy process that extends over several years. Few apprentices today stay more than a year with the same crafts artist and, in almost all cases, money changes hands: Sometimes the crafts artist pays the apprentice a small sum, often the apprentice pays the crafts artist for the privilege of studying with him or her, and sometimes an outside source provides the funds.

A major problem encountered by some crafts artists in hiring apprentices involves state and federal labor laws, although there is no national policy specifically related to apprenticeships. Some crafts artists have been required to pay their apprentices the minimum wage, withhold income taxes, and meet a variety of other requirements demanded by the labor laws. In other cases, especially where the apprentice pays a fee to the crafts artist, the apprentice may be considered a student and thus not subject to the labor laws, even though no formal curriculum exists. These conditions have led some craftspeople—as a means of getting away from the employee connotation of apprentice—to propose the term *intern* for someone whose work is both productive and a learning experience. It is advisable to consult with state and federal labor departments about the specific conditions that would apply in each case.

The relationship between the craftsperson and the apprentice is a special one. Careful thought should be given to whether the crafts artist and the apprentice are personally compatible, whether the crafts artist is emotionally and psychologically equipped to teach his or her craft with patience and understanding, and what the specific arrangements and working conditions will be. Will the apprentice, for example, work on the crafts artist's objects? Will the apprentice have an opportunity to work on his or her own work? Who pays for the materials for the apprentice's own work? Is there a clear understanding about work hours and the operation of the shop? Who is responsible for what particular chores?

The relationship between a crafts artist and an apprentice is a two-way street. The apprentice benefits from the learning experience; the crafts artist benefits from the apprentice's contribution to the production process. But these benefits are available only if the two people select each other carefully and understand their arrangements completely before they begin. A good source of information is *Apprenticeship in Craft* (see Appendix C). *(See also: Education, Employees, Organizations)*

Architects

Architectural and interior-design commissions can become a lucrative part of a crafts artist's income, especially in ceramics, metalwork, stained glass, woodwork, textiles, and similar media.

In the past, handcrafted woodwork, stained-glass windows, elaborate chandeliers, and intricately crafted metalwork or decorative accessories were basic elements of architectural design in castles, churches, even railway stations. The incorporation of major craftwork has become important again in recent times with the advent of vast expanses of glass or marble or cement that require some eye-pleasing interruption. Furthermore, the federal government and numerous state and municipal governments now require that a percentage of the remodeling or construction costs of government buildings must be spent for art- or craftwork in those buildings.

Architectural commissions are available through a number of sources. Perhaps the most effective way is to let architectural firms in your area know of your availability. Architects working on religious, university, or government buildings are particularly good prospects. Contact them with a brief résumé, some photos or slides of your work, and a request for an interview at which you can show your portfolio. The results will not be as immediate as an approach to sell a craft object to a retail store, but the ultimate results can bring satisfactory returns. Design competitions—especially for government buildings—provide occasional opportunities.

Since construction of a new building is a lengthy process that requires the approval of numerous government agencies, building departments, zoning commissions, and so on, it is not difficult to get in on the ground floor if you can find out where such information first becomes available in your locality (city clerk, county clerk, building department). You must, however, contact architects in the early stages of the process. When you see the hard hats digging a hole in the ground, it is usually too late. The architectural work has been completed, budgets are firmly established, and someone else may already have the commission you could have had.

Working with architects or interior designers usually requires a high degree of professional competence. Sketches, design proposals, color samples, even scale models are often required. There is usually a specific amount of money available, so it becomes necessary to calculate your costs and what you can do on the basis of the ultimate fee—architects do not normally take a percentage of the fee you are paid. The architect's requirements must be closely studied. If the craftwork becomes an integral part of the structure, as with a stained-glass window, it is necessary to work with the architect and the construction firm to coordinate the completion and installation of the craftwork with their schedules. *(See also: Commission, Customer, Interior Decorators and Designers)*

Arts Councils *(See: State Arts Agencies)*

Assets

A punster once observed that "assets make the heart grow fonder"—and for good reason. Assets are all the things you own, but accountants give them a slightly more restricted meaning; namely, all the things you own that can be measured in terms of money. Assets include real estate, personal property, intangible property, machinery and equipment, cash in the bank, inventory, raw materials on hand, even the money others owe you.

You may think that your own good name is your biggest asset, but unless it's *General Motors*, it is hardly likely that your good name, traits such as honesty, integrity, creative talent, or a great sales personality can be listed on your books as an asset. Along with your name, goodwill cannot be carried on your books as an asset unless it was actually purchased for value.

For accounting purposes, there are many kinds of assets. For craftspeople the following are the most common:

Fixed Assets: Such items as real estate, personal property, tools, equipment.

Liquid Assets: Such items as bank accounts, inventory, accounts receivable—in a word, the kind of assets that can readily be turned into cash to pay bills.

Tangible Assets: An asset that has physical properties and exists in the real world. Equipment, bank accounts, tools, raw materials, and inventory are all tangible assets.

Intangible Assets: Assets that have an obvious value far beyond their physical one. Lists of customers, for example, a well-established trade name, and a unique crafts process are all intangible assets.

Assets and liabilities appear together on a balance sheet, which should be drawn up at least once a year and sometimes more often. This is necessary for numerous purposes, including calculating taxes, getting approval for bank loans, revealing what—if any—profits you have made and what your business is worth in dollars and cents. *(See also: Balance Sheet, Liabilities)*

Audit

An audit is an examination of a set of books and financial records to determine whether they are kept properly, whether all financial transactions are entered according to accepted accounting and bookkeeping procedures, and whether all ingredients exist to evaluate accurately a company's financial condition.

Audits for small businesses are usually conducted by an accountant once a year. They may also be conducted by a government agency such as the Internal Revenue Service if tax problems arise. A financial statement or balance sheet is drawn up following an annual audit; it is required in almost all corporation bylaws and is usually necessary when applying for a major bank loan. *(See also: Accounting, Balance Sheet, Income Statement)*

Back Order

When an item that has been ordered cannot be shipped at once but is to be shipped at some future time, this is known as a back order. A notice should be sent to the customer stating this and requesting approval for the later shipping date. If part of the order is available, all the items in the original order should be listed on the invoice or packing slip, with the notation *back order* next to the items that are not included in the shipment. This indicates to the customer that the omission of such items is not an error in shipment and that it is not necessary to write a new order. Back order items are generally not billed until they are shipped. *(See also: Orders)*

Balance

This word represents the difference between two amounts, or what is left over after one amount is subtracted from the other. It has innumerable applications, including balance of trade, balance of power, and balance of payments.

For craftspeople it has four basic applications:

1. Your bank balance represents the amount that remains after all the checks are subtracted from all the deposits. If you deposited one thousand dollars and wrote checks for eight hundred dollars, your balance is two hundred dollars.

2. The balance on your account at a craft supply store is the amount you still owe after all your payments are subtracted from all your purchases. That shows up in your accounts payable. If you have overpaid, then all your purchases are subtracted from all your payments, and you have a credit balance.

3. If a customer leaves a ten-dollar deposit on a one-hundred-dollar item, the balance due you is ninety dollars. This is noted in accounts receivable.

4. At the end of the year, after all your expenses are subtracted from all your income, the balance—you hope—represents your profit.

The balance plus one amount must always equal the other amount. That's really what it's all about when you balance your checkbook or your accountant balances your ledger. *(See also: Balance Sheet, Bank Statement, Checking Account, Income Statement)*

Balance Sheet

Unlike an income statement, which summarizes the income and expense activity over a given period, the balance sheet (often called a financial statement) reports the financial condition of a business at a given point, usually on the last day of the year.

The balance sheet reports the assets (everything you own) and the liabilities (everything you owe) on the particular date. Subtracting the liabilities from the assets produces a figure that is the owner's equity, or the net worth of the business.

A balance sheet is prepared by an accountant and is used to inform the owners or stockholders of the condition of the business. It is also required with most applications for a bank loan. The bank generally wants to see a balance sheet that is less than three months old. Drawing up a new balance sheet involves an additional accountant's fee, so apply for a loan before March 31 if you can.

An imaginary balance sheet for an imaginary crafts business is illustrated here. In this example, the owner of Pot Luck Pottery finds that the net worth of the business—in effect, the value of what is owned—is $15,629.84. *(See also: Assets, Equity, Financial Statement, Income Statement, Liabilities, Net Worth)*

Bank Loans *(See: Loans)*

Bankruptcy

When you owe more than you can possibly pay and when there's no other way to settle your debts, you may wish to seek protection from your creditors by filing bankruptcy. Bankruptcy is a federal-court procedure whereby the court customarily appoints a trustee to administer your assets to pay your creditors. This usually involves selling your assets, in which case the creditors may receive only part of what is owed to them, but you are free from all further obligations. Your debts are wiped out, and you can start all over again.

There are some situations in which the bankrupt is allowed to reorganize its business affairs under the court's watchful eye. This happens when creditors have reason to believe that there's a real chance that the financial difficulty can be solved under the conditions imposed by the court. They do this in the hope that they'll collect more of the debt, even though they may have to wait longer to do it.

Bankruptcy can be either voluntary (as when you petition the court to declare you bankrupt), or involuntary (as when your creditors petition the

Pot Luck Pottery

Balance Sheet

December 31, 1991

Assets
Current Assets

Cash	$ 1,843.56	
Accounts Receivable	4,865.50	
Raw Material Inventory	1,116.46	
Finished Inventory	8,085.41	
Prepaid Expenses	340.80	$16,251.73
Less allowance for bad debts		97.30
Total Current Assets		$16,154.43

Fixed Assets

Building	$14,152.80		
Less Depreciation	2,100.00	$12,052.80	
Equipment	$2,629.44		
Less Depreciation	464.73	2,164.71	
Total Fixed Assets			$14,217.51
Total Assets			$30,371.94

Liabilities and Capital
Liabilities

Accounts Payable	$ 1,389.63	
Mortgage	10,400.00	
Loans	2,666.78	
Payroll Taxes Payable	285.69	
Total Liabilities		$14,742.10
Capital (Equity)		$15,629.84
Total Liabilities and Capital		$30,371.94

court to declare you bankrupt). Bankruptcy is certainly no crime, although for most people it is an embarrassment.

Some debts cannot be discharged in bankruptcy, however, including federal income taxes, certain student loans, and obligations incurred for intentional wrongful acts. *(See also: Collection Problems)*

Banks

Banking used to be a sedate affair shrouded in an otherworldly mystique, but it's tough competition these days. As with any competitive enterprise, banks will do all sorts of things to get your business and will offer a wide range of services to attract customers.

Some old-fashioned bankers would still like you to think you're in court or in church when you talk to them. But business is business, so it pays to understand precisely what the different banks offer and what they charge.

A bank is, essentially, a money store. Money is the product it buys and sells. The interest rate a bank charges on a loan is the price you pay for the use of the bank's product. Like renting a car, sooner or later you have to take it back. Meanwhile you pay rent for the use of it. Conversely, the bank has to buy its product—money—somewhere. You are the supplier—depositor—and you get paid for the use of your money just as a store pays you for your craftwork.

Like all successful enterprises, banks try to buy at the lowest price and sell at the highest. That's how profits are made, and that's why it always costs more to borrow money from a bank than you get paid for depositing money in a bank.

There are essentially two types of banks: commercial banks and savings banks or savings and loan institutions. As the name indicates, *commercial banks* deal primarily in business- and commercial-money transactions such as checks, credit cards, automobile loans, and foreign remittances. Savings banks deal primarily in a variety of savings accounts and long-term loans such as mortgages. A number of banking services, such as safe-deposit boxes, traveler's checks, Christmas and vacation clubs, education and home-improvement loans, are offered by both types of banks. Since banks are regulated by state and federal agencies, the specific services vary from state to state. In some states, for example, commercial banks can offer savings accounts and savings banks can offer checking accounts.

Fees for these banking services, however, can differ widely even within the same city. A government study found, for example, that home-mortgage-interest rates in New York ranged from 8.5 percent at one bank to 9.25 percent at another. Three quarters of a percentage point may not seem like much of a difference, but look at the end result: A twenty-year twenty-thousand dollar mortgage costs a whopping $2,306.40 more in interest at 9.25 percent than at 8.5 percent. Interest rates for home-improvement loans showed an even wider spread in the study, from 9.05 percent to 13.58 percent.

Craftspeople who conduct extensive business activities through their checking accounts will find that it pays to shop around even here. Some banks charge a fixed monthly fee plus fifteen cents to thirty cents per check. Others charge nothing for checks if a certain minimum is kept on deposit. Still others base their charges on an average monthly balance, and some banks even charge for the deposits that are made.

Minimum-balance accounts are sometimes advertised as "free." Although you do not pay directly for checking services, you do pay for them indirectly if you must maintain a minimum balance larger than the amount you would ordinarily keep in the checking account. If those excess funds were in a savings account, they would earn interest.

If you are required, for example, to maintain a minimum monthly balance of four hundred dollars but you need only fifty dollars to cover your checks at any given time, you would lose the interest you could have earned on the other $350. At a rate of 5 percent a year, you would lose $17.50. If the alternative were to maintain no minimum balance but pay one dollar a month for checking services, you would be $5.50 ahead at the end of the year. That's not a huge sum, but it's an example of how carefully every aspect of a banking relationship must be examined in terms of the final dollar result.

The same principle applies to the extra services. For example, most banks typically charge between fifteen dollars and twenty-five dollars if a check bounces. Others charge nothing. One bank charges four dollars for a stop-payment order; another only fifty cents. One bank charges $2.50 to certify a check; another charges only twenty-five cents.

As a savings-account depositor, you must understand where the best returns are. Savings banks pay a variety of interest rates. The lowest rate is on accounts from which you can withdraw at will. Certificates of deposit, which last from one to seven years, pay different rates: Customarily, the longer the term, the higher the rate. But you generally cannot convert them into cash before their maturity without a penalty, except in cases of extreme emergency such as death. Even the same interest rate may provide different returns in actual dollars, depending upon the basis on which the interest is calculated. The low-average-monthly-balance method is less favorable to the depositor than the day-of-deposit-to-day-of-withdrawal method.

As in every trade or profession, banking has its own language. Don't be afraid to ask questions, and don't hesitate to ask your neighborhood banker to explain what a particular transaction means in actual dollars and cents.

(See also: Bank Statement, Canceled Check, Cashier's Check, Certified Check, Checking Account, Cleared Check, Commercial Bank, Credit Union, Deposit, Endorsement, Installment, Insufficient Funds, Interest, Letter of Credit, Loans, Money Order, Mortgage, Overdrawn, Savings Bank, Traveler's Checks)

Bank Statement
Every month you receive a statement from your bank that lists all the checks that cleared—those that were paid by the bank from your account —all the deposits that were collected, any bank charges, plus the opening and closing balance.

It makes good sense to check the bank statement against your own records. The bank usually provides a form on the back of the statement to help you do this. Here's the procedure:

1. Note all the deposits that show up in your checkbook but are not shown on the bank statement because they were made after the statement was prepared. Add this amount to the final balance shown on the statement. This gives you the credit balance. (Remember that it takes three to ten days between the time you make a noncash deposit and when the bank collects it and credits it to your account.)

2. Total any bank charges shown on the statement. Enter this figure in your checkbook and subtract it from the last balance shown.

3. If the bank returns canceled—paid—checks with the statement, put them in numerical order. If the bank does not return canceled checks, it will usually list the paid checks in numerical order on the statement. Then go through your checkbook and mark all the stubs for checks that have cleared.

4. The stubs that are not marked indicate the checks that have not cleared. These are called outstanding checks. They are reflected in your checkbook balance but not on the bank statement. Add up the amounts of all the outstanding checks. This total is the debit balance.

5. Subtract the debit balance, or outstanding checks, from the credit balance—the bank balance plus recent deposits.

The final figure should agree with your final balance in your checkbook after any bank charges are subtracted. Often it doesn't. If you cannot reconcile your checkbook balance with the bank balance, carefully go over all the entries and totals. If it still won't work out, go to the bank and have them help you.

The bank statement has another important value: It signals a problem if a check you wrote long ago hasn't cleared. If you send someone a check in April and by July it still hasn't been paid by your bank, it's time to find out what happened. Perhaps it was lost in the mail.

Keep the bank statement and the canceled checks together in a safe place and in proper numerical order. If a question comes up about whether you've paid a particular bill, you can refer to that billing statement on which you've presumably indicated the number of the check you wrote when you paid it, and you can locate the canceled check with the recipient's signature, the endorsement, on the back to prove that the payment was made and the check cashed. *(See also: Checking Account)*

Better Business Bureau (BBB)

A Better Business Bureau (BBB) is a nonprofit organization of business establishments set up to aid business and the consumer. The BBB allows the business community to regulate itself by using the power of public opinion, rather than the law, to keep businesses on the straight and narrow in their relations with customers and with one another.

More than 150 local Better Business Bureaus throughout the country provide background information on local firms and merchants. Such information is free and available to anyone on request. Ideally, and in the hope of avoiding problems, the buyer makes use of the Better Business Bureau before making a purchase or signing a contract. However, the Better Business Bureau can also help the buyer if difficulties arise after the transaction is completed.

If a crafts artist scouts around to make a major purchase, such as a kiln or a loom, and finds an unknown source, it would be wise for him or her to contact the Better Business Bureau in the area where the unknown manufacturer or advertiser is located. The bureau's files should reveal how long the company has been in business, its record for reliability, how it deals with complaints, and any other information relevant to helping the craftsperson make an intelligent decision.

The Better Business Bureau is able to handle complaints that are put in writing. Though a Better Business Bureau has no legal clout, it often suceeds by exerting peer pressure on the offending merchant if investigation proves the customer's complaint to be valid. This tack may not always succeed. It does mean, however, that the bureau will have the complaint on file to discourage others from dealing with that firm in the future.

Most Better Business Bureaus also perform a great deal of work in the area of consumer education to help people make wise decisions before buying. But there are things a Better Business Bureau will not do:

1. Handle matters that require a lawyer, such as contract violations;
2. Make collections;
3. Give recommendations or endorsements;
4. Furnish lists of companies or individuals in a particular line of business;
5. Pass judgment—though the Better Business Bureau may indicate that a particular store has had complaints about its refund policy, for example, it will not say that the store is disreputable.

Although many major cities and states have a Better Business Bureau, not all do. Where no BBB exists, the local chamber of commerce can often be helpful in solving problems that arise between buyers and merchants.

Better Business Bureaus are supported by local businesspeople who pay annual dues, which vary from one BBB to the other. Craftspeople who conduct a mail-order business and advertise extensively may find membership in a Better Business Bureau particularly helpful. Mentioning such a membership in an advertisement or catalog adds to the advertiser's prestige and reputation for integrity and thus helps attract new customers. *(See also: Chamber of Commerce)*

Bill *(See: Invoice)*

Bill of Lading

When you ship by freight, the trucker or carrier gives you a bill of lading that specifies what is to be shipped, how it is to be shipped, and to whom it is to be delivered. The recipient of the shipped goods normally gets a copy of the bill of lading as notification that the goods have been shipped and as verification that he or she is authorized to receive the shipment.

Bills of lading come in various forms, including some that are negotiable. Such uses are rare for craftspeople. If you ship via freight, you normally get a straight bill of lading, which is not negotiable and authorizes delivery only to the person or company named on the document. *(See also: Shipping)*

Bookkeeping

Aside from being the only word in the English language with three consecutive double letters, bookkeeping is an essential operation in the conduct of any crafts business activity. It involves the recording of every financial transaction in the books of account, regardless of whether the craftsperson is an individual operating out of a downstairs workshop and serving as his or her own bookkeeper or a large operation in which a full-time bookkeeper is employed. Bookkeeping is not a matter of choice but of necessity. Your financial records are the basis on which your tax returns are prepared; they are used as suppporting evidence in tax matters, whether for income taxes, sales taxes, or other tax obligations.

When analyzed, properly maintained financial records can reveal where your activity is profitable and unprofitable, where you may be able to save money, where the price of your work needs to be adjusted, how to plan your cash flow, and many other factors that spell the difference between economic survival and economic disaster.

Many craftspeople seem scared of bookkeeping as if it were a deep, dark mystery. It need not be. Many high schools and colleges offer adult evening courses in simple bookkeeping specificially for people who keep their own records. A few hours invested in such a course can reap big dividends. Simple standardized bookkeeping materials are available in most major office-supply stores or by mail from such firms as Dome Publishing Company and Ideal System Company (see Appendix D).

Unless you are involved in complicated credit transactions, elaborate accounts-receivable operations, or other ultrasophisticated financial dealings, you'll find that the bookkeeping mystery really boils down to this simple principle: Keep track of every penny that comes in and every penny that goes out. This can usually be done in a simple ledger that an accountant or even an experienced bookkeeper can help you set up.

Bookkeeping differs significantly from accounting. The bookkeeper maintains the records. The accountant interprets and analyzes the financial information recorded on the books, prepares the tax returns based on a thorough knowledge of the tax laws, and furnishes you with useful advice and information based on professional training and experience. *(See also: Accounting, Double Entry, Single Entry, Systems)*

Books

It is doubtful that anyone has counted all the crafts books ever written. There are literally thousands, covering every conceivable crafts medium from every conceivable angle, for audiences ranging from rank beginners to top-notch professionals.

The library of books on the business side of crafts is extremely small, however. Many of the books specialize in one facet of the crafts business, with the main focus on selling. In addition, books on business subjects in general are too many in number to list here. Any good librarian can make some recommendations, depending on the reader's particular interest and background.

One particularly useful source of literature is the Small Business Administration (SBA), which has hundreds of marketing aids and management aids available—many free of charge. A list of these can be obtained from the nearest SBA field office (see telephone white pages under *U.S. Government, Small Business Administration*) or by writing to the SBA in Washington (see Appendix D). Another source is the American Craft Information Center of the American Craft Council (see Appendix D), which has published extensively on management and marketing subjects of specific concern to craftspeople.

The Agricultural Cooperative Service of the United States Department of Agriculture (see Appendix D) has published a series of excellent outlines on organizing and operating crafts cooperatives. One of the finest government publications is "Encouraging American Craftsmen" (see Appendix C). Other publications dealing with the business side of crafts include *The Law (In Plain English)*® *for Craftspeople; Business Forms and Contracts (In Plain English)*® *for Craftspeople; Legal Guide for the Visual Artist; Making It Legal: A Law Primer for Authors, Artists & Craftspeople; Art Law in a Nutshell; An Artist's Handbook on Copyright; This Business of Art; The Law (In Plain English)*® *for Small Businesses; The Handcraft Business Small Business Reporter; Tax Guide for Small Business; National Directory of Shops/Galleries/Shows/Fairs; Crafts Marketing Success Secrets;*

Creative Cash; Be Your Own Boss: The Complete, Indispensable, Hands-On Guide to Starting and Running Your Own Business. (See Appendix C for complete information on these titles.) *(See also: Periodicals)*

Break-Even Point

The point at which income and expenses match exactly is called the break-even point. You neither make money nor lose money at this point. It's a standoff. The name of the game, of course, is to move beyond the break-even point, because that's where the profits are. The losses are below the break-even point. Knowing your break-even point is not, however, an academic exercise. It can be an important tool in pricing properly, controlling costs, and scheduling production.

Finding the break-even point is not complicated once the principle is clear. Two things must be known: the price at which you plan to sell an item and your costs.

For example, you want to make copper bowls this week to sell for ten dollars each. You have two cost factors to consider: the *fixed* cost (rent, overhead, and so on), which remains the same whether you make one bowl or one hundred, and the *variable* costs (copper, polishing supplies, labor, and so on), which change in direct proportion to the number of bowls you make.

The fixed costs for this example are set at one hundred dollars and the variable costs at three dollars per bowl. Each ten-dollar bowl contributes three dollars toward its own cost of production, which leaves seven dollars for fixed costs. Without drawing any charts or graphs it is clear that you have to make more than fourteen bowls just to cover the fixed costs (14 × $7 = $98). No profit yet. That is the break-even point.

If you can make only twenty bowls a week, you'll spend the bulk of your time working for the landlord and the telephone company. In other words, fourteen bowls is not a good break-even point. Of course, if you can make and sell fifty bowls, you're way ahead—seven dollars on each of thirty-six bowls, or $252.

At this point make a chart that shows the break-even point at various price ranges, with the same fixed and variable costs:

Price per bowl	Variable cost per bowl	Part of fixed cost per bowl	Total fixed cost	Break-even number of bowls
$10	$3	$7	$100	14.3
$12	$3	$9	$100	11.1
$15	$3	$12	$100	8.3

GRAPH A

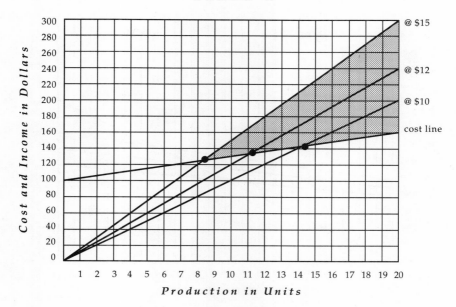

The shaded area above the break-even points is profit.
Note the greater profit area at fifteen dollars each than at twelve dollars or ten dollars.

According to this chart, you could do quite well if you were to make twenty bowls to be sold at fifteen dollars apiece. But suppose you can't increase the price. Perhaps you can cut costs. If the total fixed costs, for example, could be reduced to ninety dollars, you would reach the break-even point (at the ten-dollar price) with the thirteenth bowl (13 × $7 = $91). If you were also able to reduce the variable expense to $2.50, which would leave $7.50 toward the fixed cost of ninety dollars, you would reach the break-even point at twelve bowls (12 × $7.50 = $90).

To save all this arithmetic, a graph comes in handy. In Graph A one curve indicates costs, and three lines indicate production of twenty pieces at different prices: ten dollars, twelve dollars, and fifteen dollars each. The cost curve starts at a fixed cost of one hundred dollars and adds three dollars in variable costs for each bowl, up to sixty dollars for twenty bowls for a total of $160. Note where the curves intersect, and note how much bigger the cone-shaped profit area above the break-even points gets as the price per bowl goes up.

In Graph B the production curve is constant at the ten-dollar price level, but costs are lower. The cost curve now indicates total costs of $120, $140, and $160. Note how the break-even point changes even though the cost per bowl on all twenty bowls has been reduced by only one dollar each time.

GRAPH   B

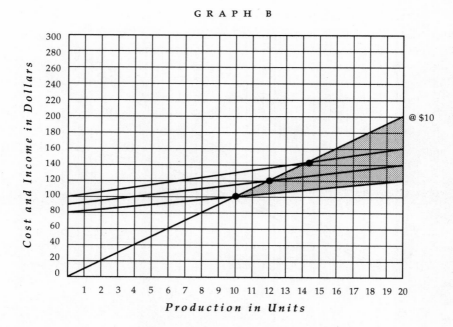

Fixed price (ten dollars each) with variable cost curves.
Profit is greatest when total costs are lowest, here $120.

If you find that the break-even point is satisfactory, fine. If it is unsatis-
factory, you have five options: lose money, raise prices, cut costs, increase
production, cease production.

Be careful, however, when raising prices or increasing production. If you
can't sell your work at the increased price or if you can't sell the greater
quantity, you are left with only two options: cut costs or stop production.
The break-even point is based on the assumption that you'll sell everything
you make.

Brochures *(See: Advertising, Printed Materials)*

Budget
A budget is simply a plan—a realistic plan or it won't work—that outlines
expected income and expenditures during a given period in the future. It
helps to anticipate future needs and to decide how to meet them. A variety
of budgets exist in the business world, but two are of interest to a small
enterprise such as a crafts business.

The *capital budget* concerns itself with the purchase of equipment and
major outlays that are not immediately used up in the production of craft-

work. Preparing such a plan for the coming year, for example, indicates not only what you expect to buy and when but also how you expect to pay for it—whether through loans, savings, income, or a partnership.

Much more important to the success of a small business is the *cash budget*. This should indicate, on a monthly basis for six or twelve months ahead, what you expect to take in as a result of sales and what you expect to pay out in order to operate. The number of entries can be as brief or as elaborate as necessary in order to forecast properly and check up on yourself later. Under *Income*, for example, it might be sufficient to have three lines: *Wholesale*, *Shows and Fairs*, *Other*. If you operate your own store, *Retail* would be a fourth line. Under *Expenses* it may be sufficient to enter just a few categories: *Raw Materials*, *Rent and Utilities*, *Selling Expenses*, *Payroll*, *Taxes*, and *Miscellaneous*.

At the beginning, when some of this may be no more than guesswork, it is useful to create two columns next to each line. In the first column you enter the budget figure—how much you estimate the income or expense for that item will total. Leave the second column blank. When your accountant has worked up the actual figures, enter them in the second column. You will see at a glance where your budget has been accurate, where it needs amending for the future, where the weak spots and the strong points are. As a result of the comparison, your next budget will be more realistic.

By pinpointing the periods of high expense versus low income that happen in almost every business, the cash budget can also reduce the need for borrowing money or predict more accurately how much should be borrowed or how much should be held in reserve. Budgeting, in other words, is not simply a bookkeeping exercise. It is an indispensable tool in avoiding costly mistakes and correcting errors of judgment. *(See also: Cash Flow)*

Bulk Buying

Despite the penchant for independence that is almost inbred in craft producers, more and more craftspeople have found that buying materials and supplies together can save substantial sums of money because the greater the quantity ordered the lower the cost. That's known as bulk buying. It may not always be possible to buy specific crafts materials such as clay or yarn if the crafts media of the participating craftspeople are different, but there is always the possibility of bulk buying packaging materials, office supplies, and other items. *(See also: Suppliers)*

Bulk Sale *(See: Collection Problems)*

Business Expenses *(See: Accounting, Expenses, Overhead, Sales Cost, Shows and Fairs, Wages)*

Business Forms

Once upon a time there was a theory that the more paperwork you did the more efficient you were. That theory may have been a great boon to printers and it still enjoys considerable prestige in government and industry, but some doubt has been cast on the notion elsewhere. However, a minimum of paperwork is required, no matter how much we may loathe it or how large or small our operations may be.

It is necessary, occasionally, to write to a customer or supplier, send out invoices, fill out a bill of lading or an order form, mail a past-due notice, furnish expense accounts for tax purposes, and so forth. You may want to have frequently used forms, such as letterhead stationery, envelopes, invoices, and order blanks, printed to your specification. You can save considerable sums of money by using a preprinted form (stock form) with your name and address either imprinted or rubber stamped on it. Such stock forms are available through local printers, stationery supply stores, or by mail from a manufacturer, and they include virtually every type of form you might use.

Letterheads, envelopes, and business cards, as well as a variety of forms, are often less expensive when ordered by mail, but they may not always be as personalized as something you can order from your own printer.

Even the formality of a letter on a letterhead is being replaced on many occasions by forms known variously as speed letters, speed memos, or read-and-reply speed messages. These are preprinted forms that come in sets of two to four parts with carbons or carbonless. You write your message on one half of the form, send two copies to the person with whom you're communicating, and that person writes his or her answer on the other half and sends one copy back to you. This not only speeds up the letter writing at both ends, but you have your original question at hand when you receive the answer and need not dig for it in your files.

In addition to preprinted forms, there is a book entitled *Business Forms & Contracts (In Plain English)® for Craftspeople* (see Appendix C). This book contains most of the forms a craftsperson will need along with an explanation of what each clause in the form means and how the form is supposed to work.

Business Name *(See: Trade Name)*

Business Tax *(See: Income Tax—Business)*

Business Trips

When you go out of town to a crafts fair at which you've rented a booth or when you go on the road to sell your work to stores, it's a business trip and, therefore, tax deductible. The important thing isn't how much you sold at the show or how successful the trip was but that it was for business reasons.

If the trip is primarily for business, all reasonable and necessary business-related expenses are deductible. If the trip is primarily for pleasure or personal reasons, then expenses are not deductible—although expenses directly related to the incidental business activities may be deducted.

A business trip extended for pleasure or a nonbusiness side trip does not qualify for business deductions. There are many combinations, of course. If you take a trip to Colorado for a crafts show and then spend another week skiing, your travel expenses are covered as well as the expenses during the crafts show. Only the ski week is not deductible.

Expenses for your spouse and family have to be treated carefully. If your spouse is an active participant in your craft business, helps you sell at the show, and so on, the expenses are deductible. But even if your kids run a few little errands for you, you'll have a hard time proving to the tax collector that they are essential to your business. Car expenses, of course, are usually totally deductible. For more information, contact your local IRS office and request their pamphlet on auto expense deductibility. They don't change whether you're driving alone or moving the whole family.

You can take several precautions to be able to prove to the Internal Revenue Service that your trip was for business purposes. First, set up an itinerary that spreads your business contacts along the whole route of the trip. This is not necessary when you travel to a crafts show, because your booth at the show is in itself sufficient reason to go that distance. Next, write to all the business contacts you plan to see. Tell them when you want to see them and what you want to discuss. Keep copies of your letters on file as proof of your intentions. Make a note of all the business calls you make during the trip, whom you saw, when and where, what the results were. Finally, keep an accurate record of all expenses. *(See also: Expense Accounts, Sale, Shows and Fairs)*

Buyers

Although any customer is a buyer in the dictionary sense of the term, in retail commerce a buyer is the person who does the buying for a store. In small stores that person is usually the owner. In large establishments such as department stores particular merchandise lines are represented by numerous buyers such as a gift buyer, a home-furnishings buyer, a boutique buyer. Major departments of the largest department stores often have several buyers, some of whom are assistant buyers.

To sell craftwork to a department store, it is necessary to contact the right buyer for your particular product. For ceramics that might be the gift buyer, for leather belts the menswear buyer, for jewelry the jewelry buyer, and so on. Most department-store buyers have specific days or hours in which they see vendors—that's you. Their time is usually limited, so it is best to be prepared for a brief presentation with a few samples. Also be prepared to leave a sample so that the buyer can think about it, discuss it with other store executives, and determine whether an order should be written and for what quantity.

Store buyers are under considerable pressure to perform, so they may be demanding in terms of price, quality standards, delivery schedules, and sales conditions. They must be sure, for example, that the order you deliver will match the sample and that you will make delivery when specified.

The better buyers attend wholesale days at crafts fairs to find new sources of supply. Remember that they need you as much as you need them, except that there are more craftspeople than store buyers, so they can pick and choose what they think will sell best in their stores.

That decision involves a bagful of ingredients: design, price, competition, customer appeal, existing stock, and sometimes pure intuition. What will sell in a fashionable Fifth Avenue store may not appeal to customers in a popular-price small-town store and vice versa. That doesn't make one store a better sales venue than the other, just a different one.

Most buyers will look for items that are not sold in another store around the corner, especially for such unique merchandise as craftwork. But they will often be impressed that other stores in other cities already stock your work and have reordered a number of times. Someone else's positive experience with your work can help a buyer make a decision by reducing the risk factor.

Some stores find that staging events in connection with a particular line of merchandise helps bring customers in and make sales. The public enjoys watching a crafts artist at work. If you have a craft that can be easily demonstrated and explained and you have the stage presence to do it, a store buyer may react positively to the suggestion that you demonstrate your craft for an hour or two every afternoon for several days. That gives them a peg for advertising you and your merchandise. Try it out on a major store in your area. Your costs are almost nothing—except for time—and the results, both in sales and publicity, may be excellent. *(See also: Retailing, Samples, Wholesaling)*

Buying Habits *(See: Buyers, Customer, Mail Order, Marketability, Salesmanship)*

Canceled Check

A check that you have issued and that your bank has paid from your account is called a canceled check because its function is over and it cannot be used again. There was a time when little holes were punched into such checks, but today other forms of cancellation accomplish the same purpose. A check that has gone through this procedure is often referred to as a check that has cleared.

Canceled checks are returned to you with your monthly bank statement or kept on file at the bank. They serve two important purposes: to enable you to double-check the bank statement and to prove that you have made payment. Because checks have to be endorsed by the person or firm to whom they are issued before they can be cashed or deposited, a canceled check is your best evidence if a dispute about payment arises. If you keep your own canceled checks, organize them numerically. Mark the bills you pay with the check number and date of payment, and it will be easy to locate the check as proof if a question comes up later.

The other side of the coin is a situation in which your records don't show that you have been paid, but your customer claims to have the canceled check. In that case, ask to see the check or a photocopy (of both sides so that you can see whether you endorsed it). Perhaps it's a simple bookkeeping error. Then again, perhaps the check was lost or stolen and someone forged the endorsement. *(See also: Bank Statement, Checking Account, Endorsement)*

Capital

This word has two meanings in business. One definition refers to the total worth of a business in terms of all its assets. The accountant's definition, which is of more immediate interest, refers to the investment in a business expressed in terms of money. This includes not only the cash put up by the owner of the business but also other sources such as loans, trade credit, equipment, or real estate.

Capitalizing a new business often draws on a combination of resources. Suppose you and a partner want to open Pot Luck Pottery. You calculate that you'll need five thousand dollars to get started. Where do you get that capital? Partner A invests in a kiln, a wheel, and other equipment worth twelve hundred dollars and puts up three hundred dollars in cash. Partner B puts up fifteen hundred dollars in cash. You're still two thousand dollars short, so you go to the bank or your mother-in-law to borrow the balance, and you're in business.

The initial investment is not the only source of capital. The income earned by your business increases the company's capital if some of it is invested in new equipment. Similarly, if you borrow money in order to expand several years after you've started, that also counts as capital. *(See also: Equity, Loans)*

Capital-Gains Tax

Suppose you own a woodworking shop, including the building, tools, and equipment. You decide you want to move to some other part of the country, so you put the shop up for sale, and you sell it at a profit. That profit is known as a capital gain—your capital investment has increased in value, and you realized the increase in dollars and cents.

The capital gain becomes part of your income for tax purposes. Under current tax law, capital gains are taxed at the same rates as ordinary income, limited to a maximum of 28 percent. Prior to the 1986 Tax Reform Act, capital gains were taxed at significantly lower rates than ordinary income—a practice that many believed would encourage capital investment and thus expansion of the economy. Even now, many in Congress would like to amend tax laws to return to favorable capital-gain tax rates. The capital-gain tax applies to the profit on the sale of any capital asset, including corporate stocks, buildings, equipment, and similar capital investments.

Cash Basis

An accounting method used for tax purposes in which items of income and expense are charged against the tax year in which the money actually changed hands, regardless of when an invoice was sent or a bill was received. Unless there is a large inventory of unsold work, this is the most common method used by small businesses such as crafts. Accrual basis is the other type of accounting procedure; you need permission from the Internal Revenue Service to switch from one method to the other. *(See also: Accrual Basis)*

Cash Discounts

The term *2/10-net 30*, which you often see on a bill, means that 2 percent can be deducted from the stated amount if the bill is paid within ten days and that the entire amount is due within thirty days. That 2 percent amount is known as a cash discount. It is used as an inducement for prompt payment of bills.

When you take 2 percent off a bill sent by a supplier, you are reducing the cost of the merchandise you bought by 2 percent. If you buy two thousand dollars' worth of supplies in a year, you save forty dollars. You'd probably have to sell more than two hundred dollars' worth of craftwork to clear forty dollars.

If you allow a 2 percent cash discount to your customers, you are reducing your income by 2 percent on all amounts paid within ten days. If your cash flow depends on prompt receipt of bill payments, that may be worthwhile, particularly if the alternative is to borrow money at a rate of between 12 and 15 percent. *(See also: Sales Terms)*

Cash Flow

It has been said that cash is the fuel that runs your business.

This cash is not the original investment that got you started but the cash

that's needed every day to keep you going to pay for materials, rent, telephone bills, and the hundred other expense items. It's much like owning
an automobile. Buying the car is the original investment, but you have to
keep it supplied with gas or it won't take you anywhere. Cash flow, then,
is simply the manner in which cash comes in and goes out of your business.

Some craftspeople may protest that they are "too small" to worry about
cash flow. But there's no such thing as too big or too small, unless you're
independently wealthy.

Controlling your cash flow has two important functions: to make sure
you have cash on hand to pay bills when they are due; and to plan ahead
for expansions, promotions, crafts-show costs, and similar expenses you may
want or need to incur in the future.

It is essential to understand your cash-flow situation if you experience
soft spots in your crafts activity—certain times of the year when money is
slow coming in but regular expenses keep on going. Knowing what your
cash needs will be helps you to put money away to pay the bills during the
slow periods.

Handling the cash flow so that you keep out of financial trouble involves
two basic operations: Knowing what you need to spend and when you need
to spend it and controlling how the money comes in.

Current Cash Flow

Even the simplest set of records will tell you what your regular obligations
are: rent, utilities, telephone, wages, loan payments, taxes, cost of materials.
The most accurate reflection is a balance sheet, which an accountant can
prepare periodically; but for a business that involves only one or two people,
this isn't essential. You can add these expenses up yourself.

You need to know not only what you must spend each month but also
when you must spend it. Your budget, therefore, should indicate how much
rent is due on the first of the month, how much you have to pay on a bank
loan on the tenth, and so forth.

Now you have some idea how much money you must have available at
various times of the month to pay those bills. You may not be able to do
much about timing your expenses, but you can exert considerable control
over your income. For example, if you know you must have cash in the
bank to meet a sizable bill on the fifteenth of every month, send out your
invoices to customers sufficiently far in advance so that you can reasonably
expect the money to reach you by then. Sending a bill on the first may be
too late—unless you offer a cash discount for paying within ten days and
your experience tells you that customers take advantage of a cash discount
for promptness.

Some expenses are also within your control. Your own wages, for example. If your cash receipts are fairly steady throughout the month but your expense peaks come on the first and the fifteenth, then time your own paycheck to the tenth and the twenty-fifth.

Ideally, you should have an expense plan and an income plan for twelve months ahead. You may find that the income plan reveals several strong sales periods: a couple of specific craft shows during the summer or perhaps a heavy volume just before Christmas. Compare this with your expense plan. Are there any heavy expense items that you could shift to these periods?

There are, of course, unforeseen circumstances for which you either have to delay payment of bills or accelerate income. Knowing your cash-flow situation enables you to discuss with a supplier why you need a little extra time and when you can pay the bill. The telephone company usually won't wait, but your landlord might, especially if you've always paid the rent on time.

By the same token, you can ask a customer who owes you money to send the check a little ahead of the normal payment schedule. It may be worth your while to offer a cash discount of between 4 and 5 percent instead of 2 percent for immediate payment. It's certainly cheaper than borrowing from the bank.

Long-Range Cash Flow

On the assumption that nobody stands still, a craftsperson needs to plan ahead. There will come a day when you want to buy a new kiln, another loom, a certain set of tools; or you may want to print and mail a brochure, go on an extensive sales trip, buy your own workshop building. None of these expenses can be paid reasonably out of current income. Some will have to be financed with long-term loans, such as a real-estate mortgage. Remodeling a shop may require a short-term bank loan. But others can be financed by setting aside a specific portion of your income for those purposes. A sales trip or brochure, for example, can be expected to produce specific sales results, even though the actual income may not appear until six months later.

Anticipating cash-flow needs for growth expenses is an integral part of cash-flow planning. Consequently, those growth expenses may well require some new planning for income cash flow.

Having moved into a larger shop and installed another wheel and a bigger kiln, it is safe to assume that you hope to produce more pots. Producing more pots means that you'll have to buy more clay, pay a bigger electric bill, perhaps hire a helper. Is your cash-flow projection sufficiently detailed to indicate whether there will be enough income to keep such commitments?

No blueprint is available for an exact cash-flow plan. Every crafts producer has his or her own needs, work methods, resources, collection techniques, supplier relations. Your only guidelines are to maintain an adequate cash supply to meet your obligations and to plan ahead so that the cash supply remains adequate.

Cashier's Check

Most checks are written by depositors against their bank checking accounts. A cashier's check is written by the bank against its own funds. This is done mainly for the convenience of savings-account customers who wish to withdraw their money in the form of a check rather than cash.

Most crafts professionals have a regular checking account at a commercial bank. However, you may need to transfer a sizable sum from your savings account to your checking account to pay for a major equipment purchase, and it is safer to do this with a cashier's check rather than cash. A cashier's check can also be made out to someone else and used like any other check in payment of a bill. The only drawback is that you don't have a canceled check as proof of payment. You do have a carbon copy of the cashier's check, but only the bank can determine how, when, and by whom the cashier's check was cashed if a problem should arise.

Although a cashier's check and a certified check are similar in that the bank is responsible for payment in both cases, they differ in that a certified check is drawn against the depositor's own account and a cashier's check is drawn against the bank's account. A cashier's check is often considered as reliable as a certified check. *(See also: Banks, Certified Check, Money Order)*

Catalog

A catalog is a fairly expensive promotional device that few individual craftspeople can afford to produce, though craftspeople have joined together successfully to produce a common catalog.

Since the initial costs of preparing a catalog, especially the photography and printing, are high, they can be justified only if the catalog is produced in a sizable quantity. In addition to the expense of production, the cost of a reliable and effective mailing list and postage must be considered. The crafts producer also should be sure that the potential demand can be satisfied. The crafts objects shown in the catalog, in other words, must be reproducible in quantity, and the crafts producer must be willing to produce, pack, and ship in small quantities to large numbers of customers.

Some retail stores that produce their own catalogs ask manufacturers whose work is shown to share in the cost. That can be legitimate if the price is right. However, if the crafts producer has already sold the craftwork to the store at 50 percent off the retail price, then he or she should not also be expected to pay part of the promotion cost. If a cooperative arrangement is sought by a retailer, then a different price structure should be agreed on so that the crafts producer's share of the cost is not taken out of his or her wholesale profit.

Catalog sheets are another matter. These are single sheets, usually letter size (8½ × 11 inches), three-hole punched to fit into a loose-leaf book. They can be used by a sales representative or a retail store that may not be able to carry your whole line but can sell to prospective customers by showing some samples of your work and then referring to the catalog sheet for details on other sizes, colors, styles, or similar products. The pieces would then be individually ordered from the crafts producer.

Where a retailer sells from a catalog sheet, sends the order and the whole-sale price to the crafts producer, and expects shipment to be made directly to the retailer's customer, a special price arrangement should also be made to cover the shipping and packing costs. Either the wholesale price should be somewhat higher or there should be a basic packing and shipping charge of a dollar or two, depending on the particular type of craftwork. There should also be a minimum charge so that all the profits are not eaten up in filling orders.

This margin is covered, of course, when a crafts producer fills orders at the retail price from his own catalogs or catalog sheets, although even here a minimum order or a packing and shipping charge is often required.

Selling through a catalog requires three basic ingredients: explicit illustrations; explicit descriptions of the items, including colors and sizes; and explicit ordering instructions. Study some of the catalogs you get in the mail. See how they handle the illustrations and descriptions. Note that every item generally has an identifying number to avoid misunderstandings on the order form. Note particularly how the order forms are designed to make it as easy as possible for the cutomer to write the order and for you to understand it. *(See also: Advertising, Direct Mail, Mail Order, Minimum Orders, Printed Materials)*

Certified Check

A certified check is as good as cash. When a check is certified, it means that the bank has confirmed that the person who writes it is a depositor and that the money has been set aside to pay that particular check. The bank becomes responsible and liable for payment, and the depositor has no further access to that money. There is no such thing as a bad certified check; it will never bounce and cannot be stopped.

To have a check certified, you present it to the bank on which it is drawn (where your account is kept). An officer rubber-stamps the certification across the face—the front—of the check and adds his or her signature. A check is normally presented for certification by the person who writes it, but this can also be done by the person who receives it. For instance, when a person is paid by check to perform a service in the future, he or she might have the check certified and cash it only after the job is done.

Certified checks are often required in substantial or irrevocable transactions, such as the transfer of real estate. *(See also: Cashier's Check, Checking Account)*

Chamber of Commerce

A chamber of commerce is a group of businesspeople and companies whose purpose it is to reflect the views of the business community. They are organized on local, state, and national levels and occasionally even within certain industries. Chambers of commerce are supported by dues payments from members and engage in a variety of activities. Since they represent a diversity of business interests, one of their major functions is to bring various businesspeople together to exchange ideas and support each other.

Some chambers of commerce have given support to artists and craftspeople by sponsoring local crafts fairs. Others are involved in attracting tourists to their areas and occasionally include listings of local crafts outlets and crafts activities in their literature. More would probably do so if approached by local crafts artists.

Craftspeople who intend to relocate to another area of the country often find that information from the local chamber of commerce about business conditions, taxes, facilities, and other details can help them make a decision. In this connection, remember that a chamber of commerce rarely, if ever, mentions any negative aspect of its community. *(See also: Better Business Bureau)*

Chattel Mortgage *(See: Mortgage)*

Checking Account

The first thing to do after you have established your crafts business is to open a checking account. Unless you operate on an extremely small and part-time basis, a business checking account is the only safe method for keeping your business income and expenses separate from your personal income and expenses.

A check is simply a piece of paper by which you transfer money to someone else. It represents money in your account at the bank whose check you are using. The recipient of the check presents it to his or her bank, which in turn presents it, through banking channels, to your bank. Your bank withdraws the money from your account and transfers it to the recipient's account at his or her bank, again through banking channels. When all that is done, your balance is adjusted and the canceled check is returned to you or kept on file at your bank as proof that the transaction has been completed.

Bankers call a check a negotiable instrument, but its negotiability is limited. Only the person or firm to whom you write a check is entitled to cash it or pay it over to someone else. To cash a lost or stolen check requires forgery, which is a crime. A forged check may not be charged against your account, but if this should happen, the bank must credit your account upon discovery.

It is easiest to open a checking account at a bank that knows you, perhaps where you have your personal checking account. If you want to open an account in the name of a company rather than in your name, you will have to furnish the bank with a corporate resolution, if your business is incorporated, or with a d/b/a (doing business as) document. You receive this document from the state or local agency where you register your business as one conducted under an assumed name. Bank accounts cannot be opened under fictitious names unless those names are properly registered with the authorities as assumed business names (abn) or d/b/a names.

Checks are valid only if they are signed by the person or persons whose signatures are on file at the bank. In a joint account, for example, both partners can have their signatures on file, and either signature can make the check valid. Business accounts for enterprises in which a number of participants are involved often require that each check be signed by two people on file.

The bank will furnish deposit slips and checks, usually with the account's name imprinted. Charges for checking accounts vary, and it pays to shop around. Some banks offer no-charge checking for business accounts as long as a specified minimum balance is maintained. Others charge a fee based on the average balance in the account during the month. On so-called special checking accounts, which many people use for their personal banking affairs, a minimum balance is not required, but there is a fixed monthly fee to maintain the account, and, at many banks, a charge of between fifteen cents and twenty-five cents for each check that is written. It is in your interest, therefore, to find the bank that has the best arrangement based on the balance you intend to keep in your account and the number of checks you expect to write each month.

Checks come in many sizes, shapes, designs, and colors. For business checks, the only important consideration is that there be a section on the face—the front—of the check where you can indicate the invoice number or item for which the check is written. That isn't essential, but it helps the recipient identify the purpose of the check.

Two general precautions should be observed when writing a check:

1. Never sign a blank check that does not have the recipient's name and the amount written on it. If such a check is lost or stolen, anyone can fill in the empty spaces with his or her name and amount and cash it.

2. Write the check carefully so that it cannot be altered to increase the amount. Where you indicate the amount in figures, write the first figure as close to the dollar sign as possible. Where you indicate the amount in words, place a line in front of the first word so that no other word can be added. Following is an illustration of three checks, all for the same amount. The first one, A, was written improperly, making it possible to raise the amounts as shown in B. The last check, C, illustrates how a check should be written, leaving no blank spaces in front of the dollar figures or words so that it cannot be altered.

If you make an error in writing a check, tear the check up into little pieces, mark the stub *void*, and start again with the next check.

Keep a running balance on your check stubs. Subtract from the balance whenever you write a check, and add to the balance whenever you make a deposit. That way you'll always know how much money you have in the bank. It takes between three and ten days for a check deposit to clear. That means that a check you receive from someone else and deposit in your account will not actually show up on your cash balance for several days. You can write a check against your account figuring that deposit into your balance as long as you're certain the deposit will have cleared before the check you wrote returns to your bank for payment. But be careful if you're playing it tight. A check deposited to your account but that cannot be collected by the bank will throw a monkey wrench into your calculations.

A bad check, also known as a rubber check because it bounces, is one for which there isn't enough money in the bank account on which it is drawn. To write such a check intentionally can expose the writer to lawsuits. If you write such a check by accident or because your arithmetic was off when you figured your bank balance, you will probably receive an angry telephone call from the recipient. He or she deposited the check, but it was returned marked *insufficient funds*. That's embarrassing to you, but as long as your conscience is clear and you're sure that you now have enough money to cover the check, tell the recipient to redeposit it.

The only way to interrupt the payment of a check once you've sent it off is by giving your bank a stop-payment order. However, this can be costly and should be done only for good reason, such as a lost or stolen check. Stopping payment for frivolous reasons or to break a contract is illegal in most states. (*See also: Bank Statement, Canceled Check, Cashier's Check, Cleared Check, Collection Problems, Commercial Bank, Deposit, Endorsement, Insufficient Funds, Outstanding Check, Overdrawn, Savings Bank, Stop Payment, Traveler's Checks*)

Cleared Check

The transfer of money among banks based on the checks that are written by depositers is known as clearing. The term *cleared check* has come to mean

A

THIS CHECK IS DELIVERED FOR PAYMENT
ON THE FOLLOWING ACCOUNTS

DATE		AMOUNT
TOTAL OF INVOICES		
LESS ___ % DISCOUNT		
LESS FREIGHT		
LESS		
TOTAL DEDUCTIONS		
AMOUNT OF CHECK		

10

JAMES C. MORRISON
1765 SHERIDAN DRIVE
YOUR CITY, U.S.A. 07093

00-6789/0000

31 June 19 93

PAY
TO THE
ORDER OF Sam Adams $ 9.85

Nine —— 85/xx   DOLLARS

DELUXE CHECK PRINTERS
YOUR CITY, STATE 12345

NOT NEGOTIABLE
SAMPLE - VOID
DO NOT CASH!

John Hancock

⑆000067894⑆ 12345678⑈

B

THIS CHECK IS DELIVERED FOR PAYMENT
ON THE FOLLOWING ACCOUNTS

DATE		AMOUNT
TOTAL OF INVOICES		
LESS ___ % DISCOUNT		
LESS FREIGHT		
LESS		
TOTAL DEDUCTIONS		
AMOUNT OF CHECK		

10

JAMES C. MORRISON
1765 SHERIDAN DRIVE
YOUR CITY, U.S.A. 07093

00-6789/0000

31 June 19 93

PAY
TO THE
ORDER OF Sam Adams $ 69.85

Sixty Nine —— 85/xx   DOLLARS

DELUXE CHECK PRINTERS
YOUR CITY, STATE 12345

NOT NEGOTIABLE
SAMPLE - VOID
DO NOT CASH!

John Hancock

⑆000067894⑆ 12345678⑈

C

THIS CHECK IS DELIVERED FOR PAYMENT
ON THE FOLLOWING ACCOUNTS

DATE		AMOUNT
TOTAL OF INVOICES		
LESS ___ % DISCOUNT		
LESS FREIGHT		
LESS		
TOTAL DEDUCTIONS		
AMOUNT OF CHECK		

10

JAMES C. MORRISON
1765 SHERIDAN DRIVE
YOUR CITY, U.S.A. 07093

00-6789/0000

31 June 19 93

PAY
TO THE
ORDER OF Sam Adams $9.85

—— Nine —— 85/xx   DOLLARS

DELUXE CHECK PRINTERS
YOUR CITY, STATE 12345

NOT NEGOTIABLE
SAMPLE - VOID
DO NOT CASH!

John Hancock

⑆000067894⑆ 12345678⑈

---

that the transfer of funds has been completed: The recipient of your check deposited it in his or her bank, that bank presented the check to your bank, your bank paid it from your account, and the canceled check is kept on file or returned with your bank statement. *(See also: Banks, Canceled Check, Checking Account)*

Collateral

In financial terms, collateral is something of value that is pledged as security against the repayment of a loan. If the payments are not made, the bank or other lender can claim the collateral and sell it to satisfy the outstanding balance of the loan. As regards a real-estate mortgage, for example, the real estate itself is the collateral. *(See also: Loans, Mortgage)*

Collection Agencies *(See: Collection Problems)*

Collection Problems

Making a sale is only half the battle; collecting for it can often be the other half. Don't be so anxious for the sale that you don't take proper precautions. A sale for which you don't get paid is no sale at all and, in fact, costs you the price of the item for which you were not paid.

Collection problems fall into three major catagories:

1. Payments by check;
2. Transfer or liquidation of a business;
3. Slow payers.

Cash Sales if Payment Is Made by Check

There's not much of a problem when you're face-to-face with a cash customer, as in a store or at a crafts show, but if that customer wants to pay with a check, you should protect yourself by following a few simple rules:

1. Before you accept a check as payment, ask for identification that includes the person's signature (driver's licenses and major credit cards are best) and double-check the signature. On the back of the check, mark the driver's-license number and the customer's address and telephone number if they do not appear on the face of the check. Do not accept business cards, bankbooks, library cards, social-security cards, and the like as proof of identity. Some states make it an unlawful business practice to write down the credit card number and expiration date when verifying identity.

2. Accept a check for payment only if it is made out to you and in the exact amount of the sale. Don't accept a check for twenty dollars if the sale is for fifteen dollars and you have to give five dollars in change.

3. Never cash a check for someone you don't know.

4. Don't accept third-party checks; that is, checks made out to someone else and endorsed to you. They only add another element of potential trouble. If you don't know the person who wrote the check originally, it could be stolen.

5. Mark all checks *for deposit only* the moment you receive them. Don't

wait. This makes it impossible for a thief to cash them. The extra few seconds you spend on this precaution can save a lot of grief down the line.

None of this guarantees that a check won't bounce, but at least you'll be more likely to find the maker of the bad check. You'll also protect yourself from being known as an easy mark. An ounce of prevention, in this case, is definitely worth the pound of cure involved in trying to collect a bad check or prosecuting its passer. Remember, if you get stuck with a bad check, it comes out of your profit.

It can happen, even with the best of intentions, that a check is returned to you because there were insufficent funds in the maker's account. Sometimes a deposit hasn't cleared in time to make money available to cash a check. In that event it is best to make polite contact with the customer, who will usually tell you to redeposit the check. In almost all cases the check clears the second time. If it bounces again, take legal action. Your bank won't accept a redeposit more than once.

A stop-payment order on a check made payable to you is another matter. If you haven't delivered the merchandise, just forget about the sale. It may not be worth the trouble to pursue the matter. But if the customer has the merchandise and doesn't have a good reason for stopping payment, you may have to prosecute for theft or breach of contract.

When a Store Changes Hands or Goes out of Business

This can create situations in which your original customer may no longer consider him- or herself liable for what is owed you or may not have the money to pay you. There are four common ways this can happen, and in times of economic distress, problems such as bankruptcy become more common.

1. *Bulk sale.* When a business with inventory is sold, the creditors—that's you—of the selling business have a continuing claim on the sold assets, even after the buyer of the business has paid for it. Very often the sales contract stipulates that the buyer takes over all assets and liabilities of the business. When that doesn't happen—and often even when it does—the creditors have to be notified.

Laws vary from state to state, but generally the basic requirement is that a ten-day notice of sale must be given to all creditors before the sale closes. This allows creditors to make their claims, find out when and how they will be paid, and take legal action if they are not satisfied with the terms. Prompt action is necessary.

2. *Common-law composition.* This is the most flexible and least formal way for a business that owes more than it can pay to liquidate in a manner equitable to its creditors or to continue in business. The debtor offers a proportion of the amount owed to all creditors who agree to accept that

amount as full payment. Since the legal costs are low, there is usually no point in rejecting such an offer if you are satisfied that the debtor is acting honestly and that no other creditors are being treated better than you are. If a check for the proposed settlement is enclosed with the notice, remember that depositing, cashing, or even just keeping the check may be considered acceptance of the plan.

3. *Assignment for benefit of creditors.* This is a more formal way of liquidating a business, but it is less formal and less expensive than bankruptcy. An assignment is a state-court proceeding in which all the assets of a business are turned over to a court-appointed assignee, who sells them off, usually at auction. The proceeds are distributed to the creditors in proportion to their claim after taxes, the assignee's fee, and other expenses have been paid. It is important to file a claim on the proper form when you receive a notice of assignment.

4. *Bankruptcy.* This is like an assignment, except that the proceeding is held in federal bankruptcy court and costs are usually higher. In a bankruptcy proceeding, if the debtor has given preferential treatment to some creditors, they can be made to return what they got so it can be divided among all the creditors. The court clerk notifies creditors of a bankruptcy; timely filing of your claim is essential. If you have a meaningful amount of money at stake, legal advice for your particular circumstances is a worthwhile investment.

Many states have special laws protecting artists and craftspeople from the loss of their consigned work when a gallery becomes insolvent or files for bankruptcy. Refer to *The Law (In Plain English) for Craftspeople* (see Appendix C) for further details. *(See also: Consignment)*

Slow Payers

This is probably the most common collection problem. It's not serious in times of prosperity, but when the economic going gets rough, bills are often left unpaid for sixty, ninety, or more days, even by reputable firms.

The reasons are simple. If a firm is temporarily short of cash, it can pay its bills by borrowing money from the bank at between 15 and 25 percent interest. When a firm leaves bills unpaid, the net effect is that it uses your money—borrows it, if you like—without paying any interest.

A basic principle in money management is "the older a bill gets, the harder it is to collect." A good follow-up procedure for collecting unpaid bills is absolutely essential.

Let us assume that you have checked the customer's credit rating and found it satisfactory. (If the credit rating is poor, you can expect serious collection problems. A poor credit rating reflects collection problems already experienced by others with the same account.) Most orders specify when payment is due. To encourage customers to pay their bills quickly, many businesses allow a 2 percent discount if the bill is paid within ten days. The entire amount is due within thirty days. In recent years, some firms have added a 1 or 2 percent per month surcharge if the bill is paid later than thirty days.

Some customers, especially large stores, pay their bills once a month, regardless of when they receive them during the previous month. You may also have to allow for slow mail delivery. But if you haven't been paid thirty-five to forty-five days after you send the bill, mail a courteous reminder. If you still don't have your money ten or fifteen days after that, send another reminder—this one more insistent. In most cases, sixty days should be the outside limit for your final reminder. That one should alert—not threaten—the customer that you plan to take further action if the bill is not paid immediately. If that doesn't bring results, turn the bill over to a collection agency, especially if the customer has not even had the courtesy to contact you and explain what the difficulty is.

There are always exceptions. If a customer who has paid promptly in the past suddenly falls behind and explains that he's had a fire in his store and needs a few extra weeks to get back on his feet, it is usually wise to cooperate. But a customer's good track record is no guarantee that his or her store can't get into trouble. Judge each situation on its own merits. If you have any real reason to worry, activate your collection effort promptly.

Follow-up

Several systems can be used for collection follow-up. Note that you should keep at least one copy of every bill you write. If you don't do much billing, keep a duplicate in a follow-up file and check that file every week to see who's late. When you send a follow-up bill, mark your copy to indicate the date the follow-up was sent. That will help determine when the next follow-up needs to be sent.

If you do an extensive amount of billing, it is often most economical to have bills made up in sets of four or five copies, with carbons (or carbonless forms) interleaved. You can purchase invoice sets imprinted with your name, address, and other information from most good business-form suppliers (look under *Business Forms* in the telephone yellow pages), and you can include the follow-up messages on the appropriate copies: *A friendly reminder that this invoice is past due* on the first reminder; *Please remit promptly on this past-due invoice* on the second reminder; and on the last, *This invoice is more than sixty days old. We will have to turn this over for collection if we do not receive payment by return mail.*

The initial cost of such forms may seem expensive, but they save you from writing and typing individual follow-up notices and provide an effective and businesslike way to collect the money that is owed you. Most business-people find that enclosing a reply envelope (even without a stamp) helps speed up bill payments. Use of reply envelopes may also help streamline receipt and processing of payments because they are readily distinguishable from other incoming mail.

Collection Agencies

If all else fails, the services of a collection agency may be necessary. Collection agencies generally charge a percentage of the amount they collect; the smaller the bill, the larger the percentage. But it's worth the money if there's no way you can collect the bill on your own. Customers know that collection agencies turn their experience with bad debts over to credit bureaus, and you'd be surprised how quickly a Dun & Bradstreet sticker, for example, brings results.

Dun & Bradstreet is one of the better known collection services, with offices throughout the country. For a modest annual fee you receive forms and invoice stickers for two reminders and a ten-day free-demand period. That means if you turn a bill over to them for collection, they charge nothing extra if the bill is paid within ten days after they send a notice to the customer. Collection agencies such as Dun & Bradstreet perform various other services, including locating debtors and sending further demand notices and lawyers' letters if need be.

It is important to select a collection agency whose reputation is sound. Heavy-handed tactics can backfire on your own reputation and expose you to legal liability. Check with other businesspeople in your area to learn what their experience has been with particular collection agencies or to discover if they have other recommendations.

Collection problems that need a lawyer's services are another matter entirely. The size of the outstanding bill has to be balanced against the size of the lawyer's fee to determine whether a court case is worth the expense. *(See also: Small-Claims Court)*

Collectors *(See: Fine Art)*

Commercial Bank

This is a bank whose main function is to handle checking accounts. Its other banking functions include lending money and renting safe-deposit boxes. Although many commercial banks also offer savings accounts, the interest paid is generally lower than that offered by savings banks or credit unions. *(See also: Banks, Credit Union, Savings Bank)*

Commission

This word has many dictionary meanings, two of which are of interest to craftspeople:

1. The amount of money paid to a salesperson or agent, usually a percentage of the dollar value of the sale. The percentage a gallery retains on consignment sales is also called a commission. The specific percentage should be agreed on before the selling activity begins.

2. Commission is also a fancy word for order. The term does not usually apply to work that is resold, but it is generally used in connection with a large work made to certain specifications, such as a large tapestry incorporating a company theme for display in a corporate headquarters.

Such a commission should always state the details about the work in writing: how and when the customer approves the work; payment schedules (advances, and so on); completion date; installation responsibility, if any; what will happen if the artist or client dies before the work is completed; whether the crafts artist retains rights to the work if the customer finds it unacceptable. Most important, specifications of the work itself (size, materials, design style, subject matter, and so on) should be clearly defined to avoid later controversy or, worse yet, rejection. *(See also: Architects, Customer, Industrial Design, Orders)*

Common Carrier

Most of the craftwork you ship will move by common carrier; some orders even specify that. A common carrier is any business that publicly offers to transport goods for a fee and that the law defines as a *common carrier*. Truck companies, bus lines, railroads, and airlines are typical examples. They are regulated by the government, operate on a franchise, and are required to charge the same fee for the same service to all customers. Common carriers have the responsibility for transporting the goods safely, speedily, and correctly and are legally liable for most cases of loss or damage.

Local truckers—individuals or companies—who do not fall within the definition of common carrier and are not granted a franchise are called private carriers. They can charge anything the market will bear and pick and choose their customers. Their liability and responsibility is much less clearly defined. Private carriers are not subject to the same regulations as common carriers, though they are subject to certain technical rules.

The common carrier franchise grants the carrier certain privileges not otherwise available. For example, franchises provide a limited monopoly on designated routes and, as a result of the lack of competition, rates are governmentally fixed. *(See also: Freight Allowance, Shipping)*

Computer Hardware

This term describes the physical equipment needed to perform computing functions and interact with software. Computer hardware usually comprises a central processing unit (CPU), hard drive, keyboard, mouse, monitor, and printer. *(See also: Computers, Computer Software)*

Computer Software

Software refers to computer programs, which are generally stored on floppy disks or diskettes. A wide variety of software is available to handle word processing, data-base management, bookkeeping, and a host of other business functions. *(See also: Computers, Computer Hardware)*

Computers

As the name indicates, these devices were originally invented to perform computation tasks. As a result of numerous innovations, however, including the invention of the silicon chip, computers have become popular for a variety of business tasks. Prices on computers have dropped dramatically in recent years, and today most small businesses are computerized.

Computers can be used for bookkeeping and accounting, check writing, maintaining customer and supplier lists, inventory control, and even some design functions. At one time, special programs had to be designed to accommodate the needs of individual businesses. Today, computer programs (software) are available for most small business needs. Crafts businesspeople who desire specific programs for their unique needs can work with systems analysts. These individuals either write the necessary software or work with software programmers to create a program that, when properly implemented, can save a crafts artist countless hours by performing many of the tasks necessary to running his or her business. *(See also: Computer Hardware, Computer Software)*

Consignment

One of the common selling techniques in crafts—and increasingly common in other areas of merchandising—is consignment selling. It is frowned upon, even denounced, by many crafts-marketing experts yet practiced by many craftspeople.

The difference between wholesaling and consignment is essentially this: When you sell a crafts object to a store, the store pays for it, and it becomes the store's property. When a store takes your work on consignment, it remains your property, and you don't get paid for it until after it has been sold (if it is sold).

Among the questions raised about consignment selling are:

1. Why should you, the craftsperson, make an investment in the store's inventory?

2. If the store doesn't have enough capital to stock its shelves, can it be a sound business operation?

3. If the store doesn't have enough confidence in your work to buy it outright, how effective or enthusiastic will its efforts be in selling your work on consignment?

4. Who pays for insurance while your work is on the store's premises? What happens if your craftwork is returned to you six months later and is no longer in salable condition?

5. What happens if a store goes bankrupt? Will you be able to establish your property right to the consigned merchandise?

6. Are you ready for additional paperwork?

Although it is generally thought that retail stores prefer consignment selling because they don't have to invest their money in merchandise, many enlightened shop and gallery owners have come to consider consignment an archaic way of selling. Norbert Nelson says in *Selling Your Crafts* (see Appendix C) that "there should be almost no exceptions to the 'no consignment' dictum."

Consignment may be rational for unknown craftspeople just getting started, but even then it should be with the understanding that as soon as the worth of their work has been established, the store will buy the items on a regular wholesale basis. Unfortunately, some galleries will deal only on a consignment basis; if you want them to handle your work, your choices are limited.

As long as consignment exists, take steps to protect yourself. Before entering into a consignment arrangement, it is imperative that an agreement be signed to avoid pitfalls and misunderstandings. Following are five major points that should be included in every written consignment agreement:

1. *Description of Products.* Every time you ship goods on consignment, describe the items in detail. Don't simply sign a blanket consignment agreement that fails to specify the merchandise being consigned. The best way to protect yourself is to have the consignment agreement refer to an appendix or exhibit listing merchandise. Each time you consign additional merchandise or sell previously consigned merchandise, you merely update the appendix or exhibit.

2. *Term of Consignment.* Specify how long the items can remain unsold in the store's or gallery's inventory before you have a right to demand their return.

3. *Pricing.* The most common method is to establish the retail price for your work and to spell out the percentage of that retail price that you will receive if the work is sold. You can also agree to a specific dollar amount and let the shop set its own retail price, but that's recommended only in unusual circumstances.

Under no circumstances should the store be allowed to reduce the price on your craftwork without your permission. On high-priced one-of-a-kind gallery items it is sometimes useful to establish a minimum price and allow the gallery to negotiate a sales price at or above the minimum. In all instances you should get the stated percentage on the ultimate sales price, not the minimum. This kind of relationship requires a high degree of confidence in the integrity of the shop or gallery.

4. *Method of Payment.* This depends on the nature of the items. Where a relatively large number of low-priced items is involved, monthly payment for sales is logical. For high-priced items that sell in small numbers, immediate accounting and payment when the item is sold make more sense. There are many variations on this theme. The important thing is to spell it all out in writing.

5. *Risk of Loss.* What happens if consignment items are damaged, stolen, or destroyed by fire? The consignment agreement can place this risk on the shop, but damage by fire or theft to property such as craftwork on consignment that the shop does not own may not be covered by the shop's insurance policies. Two solutions are possible: Craftspeople can carry their own inventory insurance, which includes items out on consignment; or stores and galleries can carry special insurance to cover consignment items.

These are just a few of the major considerations that should be included in every consignment agreement. Two additional points deserve emphasis: If substantial amounts of money are involved, consult an attorney; and among the most important elements of consignment selling are the integrity and solvency of the shop with which you do business.

Even with a contract, you may still lose your work if the gallery goes bankrupt, is sold, or merely gives its creditors a security interest in its inventory. Article 9 of the Uniform Commercial Code is designed to afford protection to the craftsperson in these situations. If you comply with the requirements of that law by filing a financing statement with the appropriate state office (usually the secretary of state or, in some states, the county clerk) and by giving written notice to the holders of any perfected security interest in the gallery's inventory before the gallery receives possession of your work, you will have established priority over a secured party who is or becomes a creditor of the gallery. This means that if any conflict arises concerning the ownership of the gallery's inventory, your claim to your work will take precedence over that of any other claimant, including a trustee in bankruptcy, if you have complied with the filing and notice requirements.

You can find the identity and address of any holder of a perfected security interest by contacting the appropriate government office. Such interests are kept on file and are available for public examination.

Note that although filing a financing statement will protect you if a bank or other creditor seizes a gallery's assets, it will not help you recover your work or your percentage of the sale price from customers of the gallery who have purchased it and are not aware of your interest.

Many states have responded to the problems faced by artists and crafts-people in consignment relationships by adopting artists' consignment laws. Typically, these statutes make a work of art placed on consignment *trust property* in the hands of the art dealer and the proceeds of its sale *trust funds* for the benefit of the artist (even if the dealer subsequently purchases the work for his or her own account) until the consignment price due the artist is paid in full. Trust-fund status imposes several well-defined legal duties on the art dealer (in the role of trustee and agent) and, more important, substantially protects the trust property and funds from claims, liens, and security interests of creditors of the art dealer-consignee.

Some consignment statutes require that a dealer and an artist write a contract and that a dealer pay the artist within a prescribed period after the sale of his or her work. Also, most consignment laws prohibit or severely restrict the consignor from waiving his or her rights and protections under the law. Those states that presently have artist-consignment laws in effect are listed in Appendix B, along with some significant features of their laws.

Consignment laws vary from state to state. You should consult your attorney about any specific rights and duties provided by your state's law. *(See also: Memo, Retailing, Salesmanship, Uniform Commercial Code, Wholesaling)*

Consumer

The consumer is the ultimate customer, the person who buys the craftwork for his or her own use and enjoyment, not for resale. *(See also: Buyers, Commission, Customer)*

Contracts

A contract is an agreement between two or more people, enforceable by law.

Simple? Not quite! Contracts involve all kinds of ramifications, a few of which are discussed here.

Whether you know it or not, you enter into contracts every day of the week. Every time you offer craftwork for sale and someone accepts the offer, a contract exists. Every time you buy supplies, you are entering into a contract that requires one party to deliver and the other party to pay.

Your mortgage, your lease, your relations with the telephone and electric companies, employees you hire, consignment agreements, the booth you rent at a crafts fair—all are contractual situations, and all are legally enforceable in the courts.

It is important to understand that to be enforceable, the persons involved in the making of a contract must meet *all* of the following four conditions:

1. *Competence.* The parties to the contract must be competent to enter into an agreement. Convicted prisoners and the insane, for instance, generally are not considered competent to make contracts in the legal definition of the term. Children may be able to make contracts, although they may be able to rescind them in some situations.

2. *Mutual agreement.* Both parties must agree on the terms of the contract. That's why there is often a great deal of negotiation before a contract is signed.

3. *Consideration.* The parties have to do something for each other. This is usually expressed in terms of money, although that's not always the case— it can be the performance of some service. But there has to be some balance. A contract that is obviously in favor of one party or the other may not meet the requirements of the law.

4. *Lawful purpose.* An agreement to do something illegal is no agreement at all. The courts won't enforce it.

The preceding four conditions can be used to check the following situations:

a. You promise your cousin that you'll make a pair of cuff links for him. Somehow you're always too busy. What can your cousin do?

b. A twelve-year-old girl admires a twenty-five-dollar necklace at your booth at a crafts show. "Here's a five-dollar deposit," she says. "I'll get the rest from my mother and be back in a little while." She comes back and says her mother won't let her buy the necklace and that she wants her five-dollar deposit back. Can you insist that she buy the necklace?

c. You pay the building inspector fifty dollars to overlook the kiln you installed in violation of the zoning laws. But he's an even bigger bandit than you are. He takes the money and reports you anyway. Can you sue?

d. You want a booth at a crafts show, and you are offered space at fifty dollars. You send the check, but when you appear at the show, there's no booth for you. Can you sue?

Consider the answers:

a. Your cousin may be sore, but he has no legal leg to stand on. There was no consideration involved, no agreement that he would pay for the cuff links or do something for you in return. The most he can do is never speak to you again.

b. A twelve-year-old could have completed the agreement; because of her age, however, she may rescind it. You'd better give her back the five dollars and sell the necklace to someone else.

c. A contract to commit a crime is not enforceable. You're probably better off to keep quiet about the whole deal and learn from your mistake.

d. Here's a perfectly good contract. Both you and the show management are competent to enter into a contract, you both agreed on the terms, the activity is perfectly legal, and you upheld your end of the bargain. You can sue.

A contract does not have to be in written form. Oral contracts, even contracts that are created merely through the actions of people, are legally enforceable. However, it is always better to put an agreement in writing to avoid misunderstanding. The law does, in fact, require that certain contracts be made in writing: all real-estate transactions, and most contracts that extend over a long period of time (more than a year or, in some instances, more than a lifetime) or that involve large sums of money (five hundred dollars or more). This is a technical area. When in doubt, consult an attorney.

It is also wise to specify a starting date and a termination date for certain contracts, such as employment or consignment agreements. They can always be renewed if both parties agree.

Most ordinary, everyday contracts require no legal advice; you'd need a full-time lawyer to handle them all. But it is important that you read all the fine-print conditions. When you receive an order, read it carefully—front and back—so that you understand not only what was ordered but all the conditions attached. When you apply for a bank loan, read every clause and ask the bank officer to explain anything you don't understand. After all, the bank's lawyer drew up the form. You have a right to read and understand what you're signing.

When you come to more complicated contracts, such as those that may have significant impact on your rights, interests, or obligations, a lawyer's advice is absolutely essential. A real-estate sale or purchase, for example, should never be undertaken without a lawyer's review, nor should a partnership agreement or an incorporation. In fact, any long-term or out-of-the-ordinary contractual relationship should be signed only after consultation with a lawyer. Expensive as legal advice is, it is a lot more economical to hire a lawyer before you sign a difficult contract than it is to hire one to sue the other party or defend you if trouble develops later.

Remember that a contract does not obligate the other party alone. It also requires you to live up to certain commitments. Be sure you know the details of those commitments. *(See also: Consignment, Corporation, Employees, Lawyers, Lease, Loans, Partnership, Shows and Fairs)*

Cooperatives

"A cooperative is a business formed by a group of people to obtain certain services for themselves more effectively or more economically than they can obtain them individually." That is the nutshell definition in *The Cooperative Approach to Crafts,* prepared by the Agricultural Cooperative Service of the United States Department of Agriculture (see Appendix C). The service has been deeply involved in helping crafts cooperatives get started, particularly in rural areas.

Most cooperatives are organized because their members have a need for centralized marketing services. But many have gone beyond that to buy supplies at quantity discounts for their members, to develop technical-assistance programs, and to purchase group insurance, among other services.

Though cooperatives generally are incorporated and follow established business procedures, they differ from the usual corporation in a couple of significant ways. First, they are not organized for profit; providing service at cost is a cooperative's basic purpose. Getting a return on their investment is not the major reason why people join a cooperative. If there is a profit at the end of the year, it is usually distributed among members according to a formula based on patronage, resource or labor participation, or some other basis.

The other major difference is that a cooperative is democratically controlled by its members. Unlike the normal corporation, in which stockholders vote according to the number of shares they own, most cooperatives operate on a basis of one vote per member. The members elect a board of directors and employ specialists in business administration or marketing to conduct the business affairs of the cooperative.

Since most crafts cooperatives consider marketing their primary purpose, members usually use their time to produce craftwork. The staff specialist takes care of the marketing, purchasing, and so forth. Knowing the market conditions and what will sell, the marketing specialist often makes useful design suggestions to the members of the cooperative.

Some crafts retail stores are also organized on a cooperative basis. In those cases, members obligate themselves to spend a specific amount of time working in the store.

The membership-fee structure of cooperatives, especially those in depressed rural areas, is modest. Many such co-ops are launched with long-term loans and even with federal assistance under various economic-development programs.

Several excellent booklets on the principle of cooperatives and how to organize them have been published by the Agricultural Cooperative Service of the United States Department of Agriculture (see Appendix D). Included among these are "The Cooperative Approach to Crafts" (CIR 33); "How to Start a Cooperative" (CIR 33); and "Cooperative Approach to Crafts for Senior Citizens" (PA 1156) (see Appendix C).

Copyright

A copyright is the exclusive legal right by which the creator of an artistic, literary, or musical work controls how that work is used and exploited. When you claim copyright in a crafts object you've made, you're telling the world that you have certain rights with respect to that object. That doesn't mean that no one else can use your work; it only means that no one else can copy your work or make derivative works without your permission and under arrangements—financial or otherwise—that are agreeable to you.

Generally, a copyright belongs to the artist who created the work. However, there are some notable exceptions. One of these is the so-called work-for-hire doctrine, which provides that when a work is created by an employee within the scope of his or her employment, the copyright belongs to the employer. If the work is created by an independent crafts artist, then the work will be a work for hire only if it is "specially ordered or commissioned for use as a contribution to a collective work, as a part of a motion picture or other audiovisual work, as a translation, as a supplementary work, as a compilation, as an instructional text, as a test, as answer material for a test, or as an atlas" and the parties expressly agree in a contract that the work shall be a work for hire.

It is a common misconception that copyright applies only to printed materials. This may trace back to the original language written into the United States Constitution (Article 8, Section 1), which gave Congress the power to "promote the progress of science and the useful arts by securing for limited times to authors and inventors the exclusive right to their writings and discoveries." It was under that constitutional provision that the Copyright Office and the Patent Office were established. To this day, the Copyright Office uses such words as *published* and *author* to refer to all types of work and its creators, including artists and craftspeople.

Some important changes were made when the current law, known as the Copyright Revision Act of 1976, became effective on January 1, 1978; this was the first major revision of the law since 1909. Under the old law, copyright protection was available only to "published" works with the proper notice affixed. The present law provides much greater protection for the artist. In effect, a work is now protected by federal copyright law at the moment of its creation. Indeed, you don't even need to register your copyright unless the Copyright Office specifically requests it or you want to institute a lawsuit against someone who has copied your work without your permission or you wish to preserve your copyright for a work published without proper copyright notice prior to March 1, 1989, the effective date of the Berne Convention Enabling Act, a later amendment of the copyright law. The statute is codified in the United States Code at 17 U.S.C. §§ 101–602.

A special application (Form VA) is used to copyright pictorial, graphic, or sculptural works, including two- and three-dimensional works of fine, graphic, and applied art (that's the language of the Copyright Office). These forms are available without charge from the United States Copyright Office (see Appendix D).

Each registration costs twenty dollars and, if the author is a human being, is valid for the author's lifetime plus fifty years. If the author is a corporation, such as in a work-for-hire situation, then the period of protection is either one hundred years from creation or seventy-five years from first publication, whichever period expires first.

Copyright in a work of the visual arts protects the pictorial, graphic, or sculptural elements that, either alone or in combination, represent "an original work of authorship." In the case of crafts objects, which often have a utilitarian aspect, the design of a useful article is considered copyrightable "only if, and only to the extent that, such design incorporates pictorial, graphic, or sculptural features that can be identified separately from, and are capable of existing independently of, the utilitarian aspects of the article." In plain English, that means you cannot copyright a wooden bowl or a belt buckle as such, but only the pictorial or graphic design on, or unique shape of, that wooden bowl or belt buckle. The essential factor is the presence of "artistic craftsmanship." The Copyright Office exercises no aesthetic judgment over whether such craftsmanship is good or bad, and the dollar value of the work has no bearing on its eligibility for copyright protection.

Some of the things that cannot be copyrighted include individual words, titles, and slogans, as well as standard symbols, emblems, and other commonly used graphic designs (such as circles and other simple geometric forms, colors, or the stars and stripes of the flag). Although many of these are in the public domain, others may be protectable under the trademark laws, discussed under Trademark. Original combinations of such elements are, of course, the very essence of artistic craftsmanship and thus copyrightable.

A plain white tablecloth is not likely to qualify for copyright protection, but the moment you add a design element, via weaving, batik, embroidery, or whatever, you have copyright protection for the design because it can be "identified separately from, and is capable of existing independently of, the utilitarian aspects" of the tablecloth. Similarly, a plain gold wedding band is only a circle of gold. But when you etch a design into that circle, you have created a work of artistic craftsmanship under the terminology of the Copyright Office.

Ideas, no matter how original, can never be copyrighted, but the manner in which the idea is expressed or executed in a tangible form can be protected.

Copyright notice and registration ultimately is only as good as your determination to take legal action if your rights are violated. There are occasions when such action may cost you more than the damages you might collect. In almost all cases, however, copyright serves as a strong deterrent to theft of your creative work.

Even in the case of large one-of-a-kind pieces, copyright registration can be useful. Suppose someone "steals" your design and turns it into a bedspread, or uses it to illustrate a book. You may at first find it objectionable to have your design reproduced as a bedspread or a book illustration. But, even if you don't, shouldn't you get your share of the profits or at least be paid a fee? Changing the use to which your original work is put does not change its protection if it is copyrighted. If you make a pendant and someone steals the design to make belt buckles, you are still covered. It is the design, not how it is used, that is protected.

The Copyright Office does not act as an attorney, however, for any problems you may have. It also will not research your copyright application to determine whether someone else has registered a similar work previously—a service provided by the Patent Office for inventions. In fact, there's nothing to prevent different people from copyrighting similar or even identical works as long as they were created independently of one another and the artists can prove that if the matter ever goes to court.

The function of the Copyright Office is only to register claims and to verify such registration when the need arises. As a result, the procedure is quite simple. You file Form VA, send it along with samples or photographs and a check for twenty dollars; then several months later you will receive a copy of the document with the proper seals and signatures. Beyond this protection, you must seek expert legal help if need arises to sue someone for infringing your copyright by using your work without permission.

Specific procedures have to be observed for indicating copyright ownership and for registering that claim with the Copyright Office. For "unpublished" works—crafts objects that have been created but not offered for sale or otherwise displayed or distributed publicly—one copy of the work must be deposited with the Copyright Office. For "published" works—those that have been distributed or offered for sale or have otherwise received wider exposure—it is necessary to file two copies. In the case of three-dimensional objects or works that are one-of-a-kind, fragile, large, or valuable, the Copyright Office will generally accept photographs. Consult the Copyright Office before registering in this manner.

Registration of your work gives you the important advantage that if anyone infringes upon your copyright after the work is registered, then you can get statutory damages of not less than five hundred dollars nor more than twenty thousand dollars—unless you can prove that the infringement was willful, in which case the court can award damages of up to two hundred fifty thousand dollars. You can also collect attorneys' fees. If the work is registered within three months after first publication, the effective date of the registration is retroactive to the date of first publication.

If your work was published prior to March 1, 1989—the effective date of the Berne Convention Enabling Act—then to properly protect your work notice must have been affixed to your work when it was published. However, since the act's effective date, your work has been copyright protected, even without notice affixed. Unfortunately, if you do not affix notice to your work, then a person who relies in good faith on the omission of the notice will be characterized as an "innocent infringer." Under the law, innocent infringers may not be liable for damages and may, in fact, be permitted to continue copying if a court finds that to enjoin the copying would work an extreme hardship on the infringer. It is for this reason that you should use the copyright notice on your work after it is published if the work is subject to protection under the copyright law.

Proper notice consists of the word *Copyright*, the abbreviation *Copr.*, or the symbol ©, followed by the name of the copyright owner and the year of publication or creation. The following is an example of a valid copyright notice: © *Ima Potter 1991.* "The year date may be omitted where a pictorial, graphic, or sculptural work, with the accompanying text matter, if any, is reproduced in or on greeting cards, postcards, stationery, jewelry, dolls, toys, or any useful articles." One court even held that a piece of jewelry was protected merely by the symbol © and the jeweler's initials because the initials were a well-recognized trademark.

"Affixed to the work" can be subject to many interpretations. The law requires that notice may not be hidden or obscured, that it must be visible under normal circumstances, and that it be part of the work. A copyright notice that is printed on a label sewn into or printed on the selvage of a fabric (even though the selvage or margin is intended to be cut off and not included in any finished product) or etched in the margin of a stained-glass window or carved into the bottom of a salad bowl would qualify as being "affixed to the work." Similarly, copyright notice placed on the back, base, or bottom of a sculpture would be acceptable, as would a copyright notice on the dustcover of a painting. One court held the copyright notice valid, though printed on a removable hangtag attached to an item of jewelry, because the jewelry was so fine and delicate that it contained no space large enough to display a legible notice. If you print a catalog or an advertisement in which the copyrighted piece is illustrated but the notice is not visible, it is advisable to print a small notice to readers that the work is copyrighted.

There is no provision for securing blanket copyright on all your work. However, all works published together or, if unpublished, created within the same calendar year may be registered together on the same application.

A copyright can be conveyed only by a written contract, though an oral nonexclusive license to reproduce a work is valid. In other words, you continue to own the copyright in your work even when you sell the work —unless a written sales contract specifies otherwise. This applies to one-of-a-kind pieces as well. Though you no longer own the piece, the new owner of the work has no right to reproduce it or sell its reproduction rights without your permission—unless you've sold the copyright along with the piece.

Some rights, of course, are implied when you transfer the work. An important doctrine expressed in the 1976 version of the copyright law concerns itself with the display of copyrighted works. Selling a copyrighted crafts object to a retail store gives that store the right to display, advertise, and sell the work. It does not give the store the right to copy it. A gallery, museum, or private purchaser has the right to display your work without infringing your copyright, but it may do so only for people who are present where the work is on display. "Display" via slides, films, or television would be an infringement if you had not given your permission for such use.

The fair-use provisions of the law provide some exceptions to the right to make copies of certain copyrighted works. It is generally agreed that nonprofit educational use, such as by a teacher who makes a few photocopies of a page or two of a copyrighted book, is not a violation, provided such copying is spontaneous; but making thirty copies of a major portion of the book would most likely be an infringement.

How does that affect craftspeople? A few examples: If a news photographer were to take a picture of a copyrighted work on display at a gallery for use with a review, that would not be an infringement. If that same picture were then used to make postcards that were to be sold, it would likely be a violation and the craftsperson could sue.

If a visitor at a crafts show were to take a snapshot of a row of booths, one of which had a display of your craftwork in it, the fair-use doctrine would probably protect him. But if a commercial photographer came to your booth at that same show to take a close-up of your copyrighted pots, you could sue for any subsequent commercial use of that photo.

Among the questions that a judge must consider in any case involving fair use are the nature of the work; the nature of the use; the extent of the copying; and the effect on the market, particularly with respect to loss of sales by the copyright owner.

Additional information about copyright protection and registration procedures is available by writing to the United States Copyright Office (see Appendix D). (See also: Patent, Trademark, License)

Corporation

Incorporation generally provides a shield from liability for business debts; that is, the owners of a corporation will customarily not be personally liable for the obligations incurred by the corporation. A corporation is considered a separate legal person.

A corporation can have any number of shareholder-owners. There should be a shareholders agreement that defines what each gives to the business and what each gets from the business. If some of the shareholders are employees of the business and others are not, the agreement should also specify employment arrangements, compensation, and so on.

A certification of incorporation (called a charter in some states or articles of incorporaton in others) must be filed with the secretary of state in the state of incorporation, and a copy must be filed in every state where the corporation does substantial business—meaning where it has a permanent office or the like. Filing fees for incorporation vary widely—from approximately forty dollars to nine hundred dollars. In addition, there are annual fees, taxes, and other reports to be filed. All this involves legal and accounting expenses.

For small businesses—those with fewer than thirty-five individual shareholders—what is known as an S election may be made under the Internal Revenue Code to have the corporation taxed as if it were still a sole proprietorship or partnership. This means that the corporation is not a taxable entity and that the shareholder-owners will have to pay tax or may deduct losses as if the business were not incorporated. For all other corporations, known as C corporations, the Internal Revenue Code provides that the entity must pay its own corporate income tax, though the rates charged are different from those that are levied against individual income.

The rules for electing to be taxed as an S corporation are technical and some businesses—for example, those with more than one class of stock—may not qualify. For this reason, a new business form, known as a limited liability company (LLC), has been developed. LLCs, like S corporations, are not taxable entities, though there is more flexibility with this new business form. You should consult with your tax adviser to determine which method will best serve your situation. *(See also: Joint Venture, Limited Liability Companies, Partnership, Sole Proprietorship)*

Cost Accounting

Although simple accounting concerns itself with the accurate recording and interpretation of the financial activities of a business or individual, cost accounting analyzes those records in terms of the various costs involved in the production and distribution of goods and services.

The profitability of your crafts business, in the final analysis, depends on only two factors: increasing production and sales, and controlling costs. The only way to control these costs is to know precisely what the costs are and how they are incurred.

Most craftspeople engage in some form of elementary cost accounting every time they determine the price to be charged for a particular crafts item. You may not call it that, but whenever you take pencil in hand to figure the cost of raw materials, time, and overhead invested in an item, you are, in effect, engaged in cost accounting. When an accountant does that for you, it is more sophisticated and serves to pinpoint problems about which you may hardly be aware.

Cost accounting won't tell you how to solve problems, but rather what problems need solving. Why, for example, did it cost 10 percent more in September to produce a dozen pots than it did in May? Are you in a rut with your present supplier, who keeps raising prices? Perhaps you should go shopping. Or do you spend more time on cleaning and packing than on productive work? Maybe you should hire a part-time helper.

Cost accounting is also helpful in avoiding errors in pricing and in determining your real costs. For example, suppose you have determined that your annual sales costs are one thousand dollars. The simplest way to apply that cost is to break it down by the week (twenty dollars) or even by the hour (fifty cents) and apply that figure to the work you produce that hour or that week. In applying these costs, assume that you have a regular customer for whom you produce two hundred dollars' worth of items a month all year long. You spent $100 to make these sales and have hardly any further sales costs for the twenty-four hundred dollars you're going to produce in that year. On the other hand, you go to a crafts show, spend one hundred dollars on booth space, transportion, meals, and so on and sell six hundred dollars' worth of craftwork. Proper cost accounting would obviously apportion a larger sales cost to the show than to the one good customer. Averaging the sales cost would not be a true reflection of your real costs in this example, even though the totals come out the same at the end of the year.

Though raw materials—like clay for potters—and labor are usually simple to apportion to a specific item, expenses for supplies—like pencils and typewriter ribbons—equipment, selling, and overhead are not. That's where your profit can disappear. A good cost-accounting system helps you to determine what steps must be taken to improve performance and reduce expenses.

Having a professional do the cost accounting may be a luxury in a small crafts business in which the owner does all the work. But the greater and more varied the activities of the business, the more necessary it becomes to analyze the specific cost ingredients of everything that is produced. *(See also: Accounting, Balance Sheet, Pricing, Profit-and-Loss Statement)*

Cottage Industry

The cottage-industry system of craft production, which is fairly prevalent in such depressed rural communities of the United States as the Appalachian region, is based on a centralized marketing-and-management operation, with production of craftwork taking place in homes. Some cottage industries are organized as cooperatives or associations in which the members have a voice and share in the profits; others are private enterprises.

The central office generally specifies what is to be produced, sets the quality standards, and furnishes the models or samples as well as the material. The finished work is paid for on a piece-by-piece basis and sold by the central management.

A number of cottage industries have recently come under the scrutiny of the United States Labor Department to determine whether the craftworkers are employees, independent contractors, or truly members of a cooperative association. As a result, a number of so-called cooperatives have been required to pay additional taxes and higher wages to their workers in order to comply with minimum wage laws. *(See also: Cooperatives, Employees)*

Craft Emergency Relief Fund (CERF)
A nonprofit organization created to assist craftspeople when they experience extraordinary losses. It has provided assistance for crafts artists who were involved in the San Francisco earthquake as well as those who were financially injured by the devastating hurricanes of the early 1990s. CERF obtains its funds from donations as well as fund-raising events and provides those in need with outright grants of equipment, studio supplies and the like. It also loans the craftsperson money on flexible terms. *(See Appendix D.)*

Credit
This word, in all its meanings, traces back to the Latin root *credito*, meaning belief.

Credit is the ability to borrow money based on the lender's belief that the loan will be repaid. Credit is also the ability to purchase goods without cash on the seller's belief that the bill will be paid.

Good credit is considered a valuable asset in business as well as personal affairs. It means that the lender or seller believes the borrower or customer to be honest, trustworthy, reputable. Poor credit means that the lender or seller doesn't think much of the borrower's ability or reliability to repay.

Open credit or a credit line means that money can be withdrawn from an account, or purchases can be made, up to a certain amount. An adaptation of this principle is revolving credit—common for department-store charge accounts and with credit cards—for which a maximum credit line is established, and the balance of available credit changes as purchases and payments are made.

Credit also has an accountant's definition: An asset or a potential asset exists somewhere else in your name. For example, if you have overpaid your supplier's bill, you have a credit (the amount of the overpayment) with that supplier. Accounts receivable can be considered a credit. In fact, any asset that has not been collected is a credit. Similarly, some of your liabilities, such as bills that have not been paid, represent someone else's credit on your books. *(See also: Credit Card; Credit Reference; Debts, Bad; Ledgers and Journals; Revolving Credit; Trade Credit)*

Credit Card

A credit card, or charge card, has been called plastic money because it allows the user to buy goods and services without immediately paying cash. Almost anything—from a pair of slippers to a world cruise—can be charged on a credit card. For millions of credit-card holders it is an easy and convenient way to shop. It is not, however, without its problems.

The most widely used credit cards, Visa and MasterCard, are issued by banks and are honored at thousands of stores and other business enterprises. Other cards, such as American Express and Diners' Club, cover primarily travel, hotel, restaurant, and entertainment expenses, although most have moved into general use. Still others, such as gasoline and department-store credit cards, are even more limited, being honored at only the issuing stores or at the gas stations selling a particular brand of gasoline.

A bank credit card is relatively easy to obtain through a local bank, usually the one at which you do your other banking business. The bank will make a quick credit check and place a top limit on the credit available on purchases with the card. There is often a fee for a bank credit card. In addition to this charge the bank makes its money by charging the merchant a percentage of each credit-card sales slip and by charging the credit-card holder interest on the unpaid balance.

Department-store and gasoline credit cards generally do not charge customers for having the card but benefit by bringing repeat business to their establishments and by earning high interest on unpaid balances. A few cards, such as the American Express card, charge cardholders an annual fee and expect full payment of the outstanding balance each month, unless specific arrangements for three-, six-, or twelve-month credit is arranged for such major purchases as airline tickets.

The procedure for buying with a credit card is simple. The cardholder presents the card to the store when the purchase is made. The card is then run through a machine that imprints the card's name, number, and expiration date on the charge slip. If a so-called smart card is used, the same data is placed into computer memory from the card's magnetic strip, verified automatically, and printed onto a receipt. Your signature on the charge slip is your commitment to pay the bill.

The charge slip comes in three parts: one goes to the customer, one is kept by the merchant, and one is submitted to the bank or credit-card company, which pays the merchant and collects from the cardholder via a monthly bill.

When the cardholder gets the bill, it will show all the purchases made during the preceding month, plus any outstanding balance from the previous month. Some companies enclose copies of the original charge slip that the cardholder signed; if not, it is especially important that the cardholder keep his or her copies of all charge slips.

On many credit-card bills a minimum-payment amount will appear next to the total amount due. This is typically between 3 and 10 percent of the total. The cardholder has a choice: Pay the total amount, or pay the minimum amount or any amount higher than that and pay interest on the unpaid balance. The unpaid balance is, in effect, borrowed money, and the interest rates are high, ranging from 1 to 2 percent per month for an annual rate of between 12 and 24 percent. The interest rates vary according to state law and the amount of the unpaid balance.

This annual interest rate should be taken into account when paying a credit-card bill. Unless the credit card is used only when necessary and bills are paid promptly, the final cost may outweigh the card's convenience. It is certainly more economical to borrow the money at a lower interest rate or to take it out of a bank account to pay a credit-card bill in full than to run up high interest payments.

Note that in addition to varying interest rates on borrowed money, banks also compute the amount of money on which you pay interest in different ways. You should read the fine print to see how the interest is computed by the individual bank issuing your card. There are four basic methods: adjusted balance, previous balance, average daily balance excluding current transactions, and average daily balance including current transactions. Without going into extensive arithmetic, it is not at all uncommon for the amount of interest charged to be twice as high under the average-daily-balance method that includes current transactions than under the adjusted-balance method, even though the *rate* of interest is the same.

Since you are not required to have a credit card at the same bank where you do your other business, it pays to look for a bank card that bills under the adjusted-balance method. This is particularly important if you pay off your total monthly balance each month. Under the adjusted-balance method, you are, in effect, getting an interest-free loan for the entire period—from the time the purchase is made until the payment is due—which can be more than sixty days.

Credit-card purchases can be made by mail or over the phone. The cardholder furnishes the number and expiration date, and the merchant fills out the form and signs it with his name plus the initials *MO* (mail order) or *TO* (telephone order). One copy is sent to the customer and one to the credit-card company. The merchant's copy, which is attached to the original order, serves as authorization in place of the customer's signature on the charge slip.

Credit cards can also be used for actual cash borrowing. Some banks will make cash advances on presentation of a credit card, and others will, in addition, automatically cover any overdraw on a checking account—up to a set limit—by charging it to the credit card. Cash advances begin to accrue interest from the moment they are made. There is no interest-free grace period as with purchases.

The American Express card entitles holders to go to any American Express office, write their own check for up to one thousand dollars, of which two hundred dollars can be for cash and eight hundred dollars for traveler's checks. Credit cards are also often accepted as identification if you want to write a check for a purchase at a store that is not a credit-card merchant.

Now let's look at it from the other side of the fence. Once you have been authorized by a bank or credit-card company to accept credit-card payments for craftwork you sell, you will receive a card-imprinting machine as well as decals for the front door to your store. When a customer makes a credit-card purchase, you deposit your copy of the charge slip exactly as you would deposit your checks, except that a special deposit slip is provided. The bank immediately credits your account even though it has not yet collected from the charge customer. Note that you often have to maintain a minimum balance so that the bank can charge your account in case it cannot collect from the customer.

The fee the credit-card company, bank, or other institution charges merchants is generally between 2 and 10 percent of the charge slips. The amount depends on the size of each credit-card sale and your total volume of credit-card sales. Once a month your account is debited with the service charge.

The most important concern for a craftsperson who makes credit-card sales is to be sure the card is valid. The customer's signature on the back of the card should be compared with the signature on the charge slip. The expiration date should also be noted. If it has passed, the card is expired and the cardholder is no longer entitled to use the card. If a sale is made under those circumstances, the credit-card company cannot collect and will charge the merchant's account.

Some credit-card companies require that sales in excess of a certain amount, twenty-five dollars, for example, be checked by phone with the credit card's central office before the sale is made. It is always advisable, even when this is not required, to check the card number against the list of lost or stolen credit-card numbers that the card companies furnish periodically. Some even give an award for picking up such cards. Of course, a sale should never be made on a credit card if the number shows up on that list.

For the same reason, lost or stolen cards should be reported immediately by the cardholder. If the loss or theft of a card is not reported promptly, the cardholder may be held responsible for purchases made by others. *(See also: Credit, Loans, Revolving Credit)*

Creditor

A creditor is anyone to whom money is owed and who has a legal claim to payment. It may be a bank that has made a loan, a supplier who has shipped raw material, an employee who has worked in expectation of being paid, or the government wanting to collect taxes. If someone owes you money, you are that person's creditor.

Creditors can improve their chances of being repaid in the event the debtor defaults on a loan by requiring the debtor to pledge collateral or to have a cosigner. A security interest gives the creditor certain rights to possession of the collateral if the debtor defaults. If you borrow money from a bank to buy a car, for example, the car is the bank's security interest and the bank becomes your secured creditor when it files its security interest in the collateral with the secretary of state or other appropriate authority. The bank's security interest under the Uniform Commercial Code is then said to be perfected. The bank may then repossess your car and sell it if you fail to satisfy the rest of your loan.

In cases of failure to pay, the law provides for several types of creditors. A first mortgage, for instance, has prior claim over a second mortgage. That's one reason why the interest on a second mortgage is generally higher; the lender takes more of a risk. In bankruptcy proceedings, government claims for unpaid taxes normally take precedence over all other claims. Employee claims on wages usually come next, then secured creditors, and finally unsecured creditors. Among secured creditors, purchase-money secured creditors—those who purchased the collateral with the proceeds of the loan—have priority over nonpurchase-money secured creditors. *(See also: Credit, Uniform Commercial Code)*

Credit Reference

Most people like to get paid when they send a bill. But with a new customer, you don't know what to expect. How can you be sure you'll get paid? Conducting a credit check is an important precaution when a new customer such as a store or gallery wants to buy your work without paying cash. Getting credit information up front can avoid collection problems later. This isn't considered offensive by stores. After all, they conduct their own credit checks when their customers apply for credit.

If you know the customer well, either personally or by reputation, it isn't generally necessary to run a credit check. In other cases, however, there are many ways to find out how reliably the prospective customer pays his or her bills. Local credit bureaus and national credit-rating organizations such as Dun & Bradstreet are one source, but they require you to be a member, and that can be expensive for a small crafts business with only occasional need for credit checks. Your bank can be helpful as well. It has access to numerous sources of credit references. But don't abuse the privilege. Use it only if you have a prospective account on which you need a detailed and careful credit check.

The most direct way to get some idea of a prospective customer's credit rating is to ask him or her for references, generally one bank reference and three trade references—other firms from whom the customer has bought. While no bank or business will give you specific financial information about a customer, they will usually cooperate by telling you whether the customer is considered a good credit risk. Suppliers are willing to cooperate because they expect such cooperation in return when they run a credit check on a new customer.

To get such information write to the references, requesting that they advise what their credit experience with this customer has been. Enclose a self-addressed stamped envelope for their convenience in responding.

If you still have doubts about the credit risk, it is an acceptable business practice to ask for immediate payment on the first order. If it's any easier for you, tell the customer that your accountant insists on it. True, you may be taking a chance on losing a customer, but operating without such precautions is taking a much bigger chance. A customer who doesn't pay bills is a customer you can do without. *(See also: Collection Problems, Credit)*

Credit Union

Credit unions have increased in popularity as many banks and savings and loans have failed, mismanaged depositors' money, or gone out of business.

Credit unions offer many of the same services as commercial banks and savings banks, such as checking and savings accounts, various certificates of deposit, and loans ranging from small signature (unsecured) loans to residential second mortgages, and even first mortgage financing at some larger, stronger credit unions.

The major difference between a credit union and a bank is that a bank is operated as a for-profit business, whereas a credit union is member owned and operated not-for-profit. By operating not-for-profit, a credit union can maintain a tighter spread between the interest rates it pays its member-depositors and the rates it charges its member-borrowers. Thus it tends to pay slightly higher interest on deposits and charge slightly lower interest on loans.

Besides not having to generate a profit for its shareholder-owners, a credit union is operated for the benefit of its members via a board of directors selected from among its members. In this way the management of a credit union tends to be more member and service oriented than that of a commercial bank. Furthermore, the constituency or membership of a given credit union tends to be comprised of individuals such as teachers, government workers, and timber-industry workers who share an interest, such as working for the same employer or group of related employers. *(See also: Banks, Commercial Bank, Savings Bank)*

Customer

Anyone who buys something from someone else is a customer. For craftspeople there are basically two types of customers: the retail customer, who is the ultimate consumer or owner; and the wholesale customer, the store buyer or gallery that buys in order to resell to the ultimate consumer.

Most craftspeople sell to both types of customers. While the retail customer may bring a high profit per unit, the wholesale customer orders more merchandise and thereby can increase the craftsperson's total profit. A mix of the two approaches is the most common, however. Even craftspeople who do the bulk of their selling on a wholesale basis to retail stores attend a number of crafts shows and fairs where they sell at retail prices to the ultimate consumer.

Another group of customers—less common in terms of total sales but important to some craftspeople—are architects, interior designers, corporations, and the like. They buy craftwork created to particular specifications.

The prices and discounts vary according to the nature of any sale. Wholesale customers usually buy at 50 percent off the retail price; interior decorators normally buy at between 10 and 30 percent off the retail price. Architects buy at the full price since the work they order is one-of-a-kind and the price is negotiated after all the specifications have been examined. Consignment sales are usually paid for after the work has been sold at between 60 and 66 percent of the retail price. *(See also: Architects, Buyers, Commission, Consignment, Orders, Retailing, Salesmanship, Shows and Fairs, Wholesaling)*

Customs

Customs is the agency responsible for policing import and export. Almost every country has some customs organization. When the United States Constitution was first adopted, customs duties on imports were considered the principal source of government support. The customs agency also regulates exports; for example, strict controls are imposed on certain technical materials exported to unfriendly nations. All the suggestions, hints, and regulations outlined in "Packing" and "Shipping" sections apply to export shipments. In addition, there are the import regulations of all the various countries.

The simplest way to ship small packages worth less than fifty dollars out of the United States is via mail. No export declaration is needed. The Post Office supplies the customs declaration (Form 2966), the international parcel-post sticker (Form 2933), and a dispatch note (Form 2972), all of which you fill out and attach to the outside of the package.

For larger or more expensive shipments, the paperwork gets more complicated. There is the bill of lading and a packing list, which the recipient at the other end needs to claim the shipment and which is sometimes necessary for customs inspection. A consular invoice and certificates of origin are also needed. These differ from country to country.

An export declaration has to be filed with the collector of customs at the point from which the shipment leaves the United States. If the object being shipped will ultimately be returned to the United States—a craftwork on loan to a museum, for example—the details should be carefully noted on the export declaration so that no trouble develops in getting the item back into the country duty free.

Customs, it should be noted, works in two directions: import as well as export. If you are the recipient of a shipment from another country, you will have to clear it through customs. It is necessary to have the bill of lading, invoices, and other documents to bring the shipment into the United States.

Craftspeople who only occasionally ship overseas may find that a specialist's fees are worth the time and aggravation saved. Freight forwarders who specialize in overseas shipments, for example, can handle the whole export operation. To clear an incoming shipment through customs, however, a customhouse broker is often the most knowledgeable. These specialists are listed in the telephone yellow pages. Freight forwarders can be found in cities that have major ports and international air terminals.

Note that there is a procedure whereby a craftsperson can enlist the aid of the United States Customs Service in preventing the import into the United States of work that infringes the copyright, trademark, or patent rights of anyone whose intellectual property is properly registered in the United States.

For information about specific situations, the United States Customs Service can be consulted. The Service maintains offices at every point of entry into the United States, including border crossings, international air terminals, and ports. Their telephone number can be found in the white pages under United States Government, Treasury Department, Customs Service. Or you can write to the United States Customs Service (see Appendix D). *(See also: Intellectual Property, Packing, Shipping)*

Damage Insurance *(See: Property Insurance)*

Debit

A debit is an amount acknowledged as due and owing in the accounting records of a business and, as such, may be viewed as a charge to a particular entity, project, or account. Specifically, debit is a bookkeeping term for an entry on the left side (expenses or liabilities) of a ledger. It indicates an amount paid by the business. Used as a verb, to debit is to make such an accounting entry or charge. *(See also: Credit, Ledgers and Journals)*

Debts, Bad

There comes a time in every business when a customer simply doesn't pay a bill. No matter how many reminders you send, how many phone calls you make, the bill remains unpaid. When economic times are difficult, the problem increases. Customers go bankrupt. Stores go out of business. The trouble and expense of having a collection agency go after the account is rarely worth the effort in the crafts field if the uncollected amount is fairly small. But even if you use a collection agency, the day arrives—at least six months but not more than a year later—when you have to decide that it's a lost cause. At that point it becomes a bad debt.

Accountants make provision for bad debts on your books because they're tax deductible. The provision is based on estimates of prior experience in your business. Bad debts should not exceed 1 percent of your accounts receivable—the bills your customers haven't paid. If they are higher, examine how carefully you investigate credit references before you extend credit. *(See also: Collection Problems, Credit, Credit Reference)*

Deductions *(See: Accounting, Expenses, Income Tax—Business, Overhead, Sales Cost, Shows and Fairs)*

Deficit

When liabilities exceed assets or expenses exceed income, the difference is a deficit. A deficit is a shortage of money—as opposed to a profit, which is a surplus of money. A brand-new crafts business often runs at a deficit in the beginning. In the long run this is something to be avoided.

The word *deficit* is also used to describe any other shortage. If your books show fifty pieces of an item in inventory but there are only forty-eight, your inventory shows a deficit. *(See also: Profit, Surplus)*

Delivery Charges *(See: Post Office, Shipping, United Parcel Service)*

Delivery Methods *(See: Shipping)*

Deposit

This word has two meanings in the business world: making a partial payment in order to reserve the merchandise for purchase at a future time; and putting money in the bank, either by cash or check.

The two major types of bank deposits are demand and time. A demand deposit is one through which you can get your money out any time you want it, as in a checking account. With a time deposit the bank reserves the right to require notice that you want to withdraw the money. Savings accounts, for example, are time deposits, because most savings banks reserve the right, though they rarely use it, to be given thirty days' notice of withdrawal. *(See also: Banks)*

Depreciation

When you make a major capital investment, such as buying a building or a piece of equipment, the assumption is that it will last a number of years. These costs are, obviously, part of the cost of doing business and thus may be subtracted from gross income along with other deductions for purposes of determining net taxable income. However, since a capital investment is, in reality, a conversion of one type of asset (cash) into another (equipment, building, and so on), it is not realistic (nor do the tax laws permit) for you to deduct the total cost of such investments in one year.. After all, you'll be working in that building or on that piece of equipment next year, the year after that, and so on. Instead, you are permitted to deduct, as a business expense, a portion of the undepreciated cost (adjusted basis) each year you use the property in business, which corresponds, in theory, to the actual diminution in value of the property as it wears out.

Depreciation is the method used to determine what portion of capital investments you can deduct from your gross income as a business expense each year. The tax laws provide for a method of depreciation known as modified accelerated cost recovery system (MACRS). Under MACRS, every fixed asset is assigned to one of several property classes based on its class life (roughly, its expected useful life). The property classes are three-, five-, seven-, ten-, fifteen-, and twenty-year property. In addition, most real property is classified as residential rental or nonresidential real property.

In theory, two methods of calculating depreciation are used:

1. *Straight line.* The value of an item is reduced by a fixed amount each year. For example, if a kiln that costs one thousand dollars is expected to last ten years, it will be depreciated by the fixed amount of one hundred dollars per year ($1,000 ÷ 10 years = $100 per year). After one year, the kiln has a remaining undepreciated, or book, value of nine hundred dollars;

after two years, eight hundred dollars; and so on until after ten years the kiln is fully depreciated and thus has, theoretically, no remaining value— its adjusted basis is zero.

2. *Declining balance.* The value of an item is reduced by a fixed percentage each year. For example, the one thousand dollar kiln with an expected life of ten years would be depreciated at the fixed percentage rate of 10 percent per year (100% ÷ 10 years = 10% per year), or one hundred dollars the first year (to nine hundred dollars), ninety dollars the second year (to $810), $81 the third year (to $729), and so on. Note that under this method the remaining value never reaches zero since each year's depreciation is only 10 percent of the remaining value of the item.

In practice, MACRS specifies a method that is either a modification or combination of the classic straight-line and declining-balance methods, and it includes the half-year convention, which assumes that a given item of depreciable property was placed in service at the midpoint of the year (July 1, if your tax year is the calendar year), regardless of when it was actually placed in service. Consequently, the first year's depreciation is just half what the declining-balance method would otherwise determine. Another consequence is that the full depreciation and corresponding tax deductibility for an item actually span a period that is one tax year longer than the class life of the item, with a partial deduction in both the first and last years.

For property in the three-, five-, seven-, or ten-year class, use the double (200 percent) declining-balance method over three, five, seven, or ten years and the half-year convention. For property in the fifteen- or twenty-year class, use the 150 percent declining-balance method and the half-year convention. In other words, the classic fixed percentage is either doubled (200 percent) or multiplied by 1.5 (150 percent) to determine each year's depreciation.

Another modification for these classes of property is that you change to the straight-line method during the first tax year for which that method, when applied to the adjusted basis at the beginning of the year, will yield a larger deduction than the declining-balance method.

Depreciation is calculated as well when a fixed asset has both a business use and a personal use—such as a building that includes your residence and your shop or a car that is used for family as well as business purposes. Only that portion of the depreciation attributable to the business purpose can be deducted as a business expense. Of course, nonbusiness property is never depreciable for tax purposes.

Note too that if business property other than residential rental and nonresidential real property is sold for a price that exceeds its book value, any such gain must be claimed as ordinary income to the extent of depreciation previously taken on that property.

Depreciation not only helps you more accurately calculate your cost of doing business but establishes the value of your fixed assets at any given time. Note, however, that different methods of depreciation may be appropriate for a given asset: one for purposes of business valuation, credit worthiness, personal net worth, and so on; a different method for tax purposes. (See also: Accounting, Equipment, Tax)

Design

Everyone knows that design is an integral part of the creative process. But to ignore design as fundamental in the marketing process as well is to enter troubled waters.

Design for the sake of design, no matter how imaginative or innovative, may be fine for artists who are already so well established that they can sell whatever they produce or for artists who are independently wealthy—or don't care much about eating regularly. Others must consider design not only from the creative viewpoint but from the viewpoint of whether it will sell.

This does not mean that craftspeople should lower their standards or compromise their good taste. But the marketing process always involves at least two parties: buyers and sellers. Though you can influence your customers, you cannot dictate to them. Furthermore, taste and fashion change constantly. What a crafts artist designs must be in tune with the times and the mood of the marketplace or else it won't sell. If, for example, the fashion pages indicate that elegance is back in style, the successful crafts artist in jewelry will design earrings and necklaces that complement the current fashion.

Design inspiration can come from popular magazines or scholarly journals, from the daily newspaper—both the fashion pages and the front pages—or the current rage on television. Remember that ecology and peace both inspired crafts objects that combined excellence of design with popularity of appeal. The truly great designers are those who discern the mood of the marketplace and have the talent to interpret this mood into innovative and tastefully designed craftwork. (See also: Marketability)

Design Patents (See: Patent)

Direct Mail

This is a method of advertising that uses the mails to reach the public.

The advantage of direct mail over newspaper, magazine, radio, or television advertising is that prospective customers can be identified with greater certainty by using selective mailing lists. The disadvantage is its relatively high cost. Catalogs, mail-order promotions, and invitations to shows and sales are forms of direct mail.

(See also: Advertising, Catalog, Mailing Lists, Mail Order, Post Office, Printed Materials)

Disability Income Insurance

In the event of a serious illness or accident, a major economic disaster can befall an individual craftsperson who is not eligible for unemployment benefits and has no source of income other than his or her labor. Although medical and hospital insurance may cover the cost of treatment, the loss of income is not covered.

A craftsperson who has partners or employees in a successful enterprise may continue to receive income even while disabled, but lacking that, disability income insurance can be a wise investment.

The insurance allows you to choose a specific weekly or monthly income for the duration of the disability or for a specified period of time. Premiums are based on the type and amount of coverage requested. Savings in premiums can be effected with a deductible clause, which provides that no benefits are paid during the first week or month of a disability. Most people can make it through a short disability, and the savings are worth the deductible.

Disability income insurance generally cannot be bought in excess of normal income because it would become more profitable to be sick than to be healthy and able to work. *(See also: Insurance)*

Discounts

A discount is a legitimate reduction in price that is based on some stated reason and deducted before payment is made.

A common discount encountered by craftspeople is the 2 percent discount allowed when the invoice is paid within ten days. It's known as a cash discount and is usually stated as 2/10 = net 30 on the invoice. It means that an invoice for one hundred dollars, for example, is paid in full if you send a check for ninety-eight dollars within ten days. The full amount is due in thirty days.

When the craftsperson is the supplier, it is often necessary to extend similar terms, especially to wholesale buyers such as department stores. But be careful. Some customers try to take the 2 percent discount but don't pay the invoice within ten days. Bill them for the difference. The whole purpose of the cash discount is to bring in the money quickly. It's cheaper to allow a customer a 2 percent discount than to borrow from a bank at 10 percent—or more—when you need the cash because your money is tied up in goods that have been sold but not paid for.

Another common practice is the quantity or volume discount. This applies to the price if the number of items or amount of an item purchased exceeds a certain minimum. For example, one hundred vases may be 10 percent less expensive than ten vases.

A trade discount is a reduction from the normal retail price when the merchandise is sold to someone in the trade. A crafts professional, for example, can often buy materials at a crafts supply store at a lower price than a hobbyist can.

The word *discount* has taken on another meaning. *Discount* has come to mean any reduction in price, such as the savings offered at discount stores. Those are not discounts in the true sense of the word, since they are not based on some stated reason or qualification. That version of the word is simply a substitute for price-cutting. *(See also: Sales Terms)*

Display

"All the world's a stage," Shakespeare said, and we can easily apply this observation to crafts displays. The display, after all, is the stage upon which your craftwork acts its part by either delighting or boring its audience—your customers.

The first rule is to keep the stage as uncluttered as possible so that you can see the actors. It is not necessary to put everything you take to a crafts fair or that you have in a store out on the table or in the window at the same time. A good display will show enough to demonstrate the range of work available and allow the customer to browse but won't show so much that the customer gets confused and can focus on nothing.

The second rule is to create displays that are consistent with the type of product being shown. Fine filigree silver earrings show up better on black velvet than on raw pine. Rough-hewn pots, on the other hand, do well on unpainted shelving but look out of place on black velvet.

Lighting and color should be considered as well: They are important ingredients of good display. Neutral colors for table coverings and backdrops are normally most effective to show craftwork, especially when the object is colorful. Wild, colorful patterns generally conflict with the colors of the craftwork. But like all rules, this one is not inflexible. Macramé, for example, can be effectively displayed against a brilliant green or red background. As designers, many craftspeople can undoubtedly find numerous good ideas by studying the display methods and devices used in department stores, museums, and at crafts shows they visit.

As for lights, there's little to be done about this at an outdoor show. The sun will do the job, and there's rarely electricity available anyway. Indoors, it is not always safe to rely on overhead lighting. How much light you need is dictated by the type of work you show. A display case of fine jewelry, for example, should be well lighted so that the objects sparkle. The light can be built into the case or provided through an overhead spotlight.

While an eight-foot folding table is probably the craftsperson's most commonly used display unit, many exhibitors have developed display units that are easily assembled and disassembled, with pieces small enough to fit into a car or van. Such units not only help to properly display the craftwork under a variety of circumstances but make the display stand out from all the rest.

These units need not be elaborate or expensive productions. A dozen pieces of lightly stained two-by-fours with predrilled holes can easily be assembled with nuts and bolts into a striking three-dimensional display for hanging ceramic planters. Or several wooden boxes can be stacked upside down in various arrangements to display craftwork on several levels. The same boxes can be used to transport the craftwork to the show.

An excellent illustrated section on designing such original display units is included in George and Nancy Wettlaufer's *The Craftsman's Survival Manual* (see Appendix C). They describe, for example, how they adapted a child's swing set to create a dramatic display unit for their pottery.

Although many crafts-show managers provide signs for their exhibitors, more and more craftspeople find that their own signs—using distinctive approaches, color schemes, or logotypes—provide much better identification and recognition value. Often such signs become an integral part of a display unit or are fashioned in the medium of the exhibitor's craft, using, for example, a woven or wooden sign.

It may seem elementary, but neatness and cleanliness count wherever craftwork is shown. The work into which you have poured so much of your time and talent deserves better than a flea-market atmosphere. A crafts artist who shows so little respect for his own work as to display it in a messy or shop-worn setting can hardly expect a prospective customer to respect its quality or value. The nature of craftwork demands that it be displayed in an attractive setting. *(See also: Shows and Fairs)*

Distributors *(See: Sales Representatives)*

Dividend

In the literal sense, a dividend is a share in the dividing of profits. The most common dividends are those paid on the basis of stock ownership, insurance policies, and other investments. A dividend is the investor's share of the profits in proportion to the size of his or her investment. Dividends are generally paid on a regular basis: annually on insurance policies and quarterly on many stocks, though the size of the dividends may vary from period to period according to the profits of the company. Dividends must be declared as income for tax purposes.

Double Entry

A bookkeeping and accounting method by which every transaction is recorded twice. This is based on the premise that every coin has two sides: A sale, for example, is a delivery of goods and a receipt of payment. The delivery of goods would be recorded as a debit (it reduces your inventory), but the payment would be counted as a credit (it increases your bank balance). The two halves of double entry are always equal and offset each other to a net of zero. This procedure is rarely used in small enterprises such as most crafts businesses. *(See also: Bookkeeping, Credit, Debit, Single Entry)*

Education

Since it is generally agreed that talent cannot be created, only developed or refined, the education of a crafts artist is a lifelong process.

Most practicing craftspeople get their first taste of making beautiful things by hand when they are young. Almost all children draw and paint and work with clay or yarn. That's part of the fun of growing up. Most turn to other interests as they get older. Many, however, continue to find enjoyment in developing their skills as hobbyists, and some use their skills to earn a livelihood—or at least to develop a part-time vocation.

The traditional method of learning a craft through apprenticeship to a master craftsman dates back hundreds of years, and is still practiced today, even in highly industrialized countries of Europe. It is not common in the United States or Canada. More craftspeople, students, and educators, however, are coming to the conclusion that some combination of apprenticeship and formal education is a desirable goal.

Formal education in crafts art is a fairly recent development. Many colleges and universities today offer crafts courses, sometimes leading to a master of fine arts degree—particularly in ceramics. A formal education, however, does not automatically create a fine crafts artist, though it may help in developing an understanding of design and an appreciation of the history of the medium. Also, a degree is usually required for school or college teaching.

An extensive list of educational institutions and the crafts courses in their curricula is included in *Contemporary Crafts Marketplace* (see Appendix C). This book is available in many libraries.

Travel is another excellent educational experience at any level of a crafts artist's development, especially for those whose work has its roots in some specific geographic or ethnic environment. This is particularly true of the traditional crafts such as weaving, pottery, and silversmithing; these can be seen within comparatively easy travel distance in the Western Hemisphere in such places as New Mexico, Appalachia, Guatemala, or Mexico, as well as Europe, Asia, and Africa.

An immense body of literature—books and professional crafts publications—is available as well to craftspeople who want to continue their education. These works provide technical knowledge, new methods and processes, and design inspiration.

The plethora of workshops conducted all over the country provide still another important means of continuing education. Most are one- or two-day affairs; some run for several weeks during the summer. They offer an opportunity for craftspeople to meet and study with outstanding artists in their particular medium and to exchange opinions and experiences with other craftspeople. Workshops are generally conducted by crafts guilds or associations and by established educational institutions. A careful reading of such publications as *American Craft* or *The Crafts Report* provides a fairly thorough listing of upcoming workshops and seminars (see Appendix C).

A problem in the education of working craftspeople is the scarcity of business education. Several universities—notably Boston University with its program in artisanry—have recently begun to incorporate classes on business subjects of special concern to craftspeople into their curricula. Workshops, too, can be found at which experts discuss such subjects as taxes, bookkeeping, legal affairs, and other problems that confront craftspeople who sell their work.

Education expenses that are necessary for improvement in your field are normally tax deductible. This can include the purchase of crafts books, attendance at seminars and workshops—including travel expenses—as well as formal education. The key to tax deductibility of education expenses is whether you are already working in crafts as a livelihood. Education expenses that qualify you to become a working crafts artist, for example, are not deductible. *(See also: Apprentice)*

Employees

When you hire someone to help around the shop, you've signed up for a whole new ball game. The moment you become an employer, you assume responsibility for meeting a payroll; for considerable paperwork; for payment of social security, workers' compensation, and unemployment insurance; for collecting withholding taxes and paying them to the government; for the payment of nonproductive time such as holidays and vacations; and for a variety of other managerial functions. All is worth the effort, of course, if what the employees produce is worth more than what you pay them in wages and fringe benefits; that is, if they help you make a better profit.

The labor laws, both national and state, make no distinction between permanent and temporary employees, between wages and commissions, between employees who are paid by the hour and those who work on a piece-by-piece basis. In addition, they don't necessarily take into account where the work is done.

The United States Department of Labor defines the term employee as it relates to the enforcement of labor laws as follows:

Generally the relationship of employer and employee exists when the person for whom services are performed has the right to control and direct the individual who performs the services, not only as to the result to be accomplished by the work, but also as to the details and means by which the result is accomplished. That is, an employee is subject to the will and control of the employer not only as to what shall be done but how it shall be done. In this connection, it is not necessary that the employer actually direct or control the manner in which the services are performed; it is sufficient if he has the right to do so.

The right to discharge is also an important factor indicating that the person possessing that right is an employer. Other factors characteristic of an employer, but not necessarily present in every case, are the furnishing of tools and a place to work to the individual who performs the services.

In general, if an individual is subject to the control or direction of another merely as to the result to be accomplished and not as to the means and methods for accomplishing the result, he is not an employee.

The Labor Department also explains that it doesn't matter what you call the employee: partner, salesman, agent, independent contractor, or whatever. If the relationship meets the preceding definition, then it is an employer-employee relationship, and all the obligations and responsibilities imposed by the labor laws, tax laws, and so on apply.

If you hire a plumber to fix the pipes, for example, you direct him to do the repair work. How he does it, what tools he uses, where he buys the supplies, and so forth are his decision, not yours. Therefore, he is not an employee. On the other hand, if you engage a helper to make leather belts, and you buy the leather, you tell him where to punch the holes, what tools to use, when to be at work, and when to go to lunch, then you have an employee.

In the case of a corporation, the corporation is the employer, and everyone who works for it under the terms outlined above is an employee. That includes you, the president, if you work for the corporation and draw a salary. The size of a paycheck does not determine whether an employer-employee relationship exists.

Some ticklish situations have arisen regarding apprentices, cottage industries, and cooperatives, in which some Labor Department officials have determined that an employer-employee relationship exists and others have found no such relationship. In questionable situations each case is judged on the particular set of circumstances and can be appealed to higher authorities. The only exceptions that generally apply concern an individual owner's spouse and children under age twenty-one.

As an employer, it is important to keep abreast of the constantly changing labor laws. Aside from minimum wage and overtime provisions, which are discussed elsewhere, some of the key provisions of federal and most state legislation prohibit the employment of children under fourteen, regulate employment of children to age eighteen in certain types of occupations, and prohibit any form of discrimination in hiring, training, upgrading, and wages based on race, nationality, sex, age, disability, and other conditions not related specifically to the objective requirements of the job.

When you first become an employer, it is necessary to obtain a taxpayer identification number from the Internal Revenue Service and, in some states, a separate state identification number. This number appears on all forms, tax payments, and other documents you file as an employer. In filing most of these documents, it is advisable to obtain the regular services of an accountant so that tax payments are made properly and on time and so that payroll records and other books are kept in proper order for possible inspection. Be sure to consult your state labor department for the applicable rules and regulations that go into effect the minute you put the first employee on the payroll.

Aside from the rules and regulations there is the intangible problem of selecting the right employees. The first hurdle is knowing where to look. This depends to a great extent on what you're looking for. If you want an inexperienced potter whom you can train, a local crafts school may be the first place to look. If you're looking for a handyman-driver-packer, a classified ad in the local newspaper may be the best solution.

It is surprising, however, how many employers rush headlong into hiring someone without the necessary preliminaries. W. F. Rabe of San Fernando State College, writing in a *Management Aid* for the Small Business Administration (see Appendix C), put the problem in this perspective:

> The owner-managers of most small companies would not think of buying a piece of equipment until they had evaluated it systematically. They want to be sure that the machine meets specifications, can help pay for itself, and lasts for a reasonable length of time. However, when selecting personnel to operate the equipment, some owner-managers use no system. Little, if any, time and energy are spent trying to match

the applicant to the job. The result is waste. In the long run, mistakes in selecting employees may cost far more than the loss caused by selecting the wrong equipment.

It is prudent, therefore, to take these four steps:

1. Define in your own mind exactly what the job is and what qualifications, experience, and attitude you are seeking in a prospective employee;

2. Interview a number of applicants to determine how they meet those standards;

3. Check their references, if any, especially if they're going to handle money or if you have to leave them alone in your shop or studio;

4. Tell them they're being employed for a probationary period, perhaps four weeks, and evaluate your decision during that time.

The first few weeks are critical. Any new employee, no matter how experienced, will need a little time to function effectively in a new situation when working with unfamiliar people and under differing circumstances. As an employer it pays to keep a watchful eye on new employees to see how they fit in and how they perform. If you think you've made a mistake, don't compound it by wasting more time and money. Find someone else.

For most of us, the only thing more difficult than hiring is firing. After all, you're holding someone else's livelihood in your hands. Try to make it gentle. Don't fire someone in the presence of others. During the probationary period, dismissal notice or severance pay is not necessary. But if someone has been on your payroll for some time, two weeks' notice is generally expected, just as you would want two weeks' notice if someone were to quit. Many employers prefer to give a discharged employee two weeks' pay instead of two weeks' notice to avoid ill feeling or a demoralizing situation if there are other employees in the shop.

An employee may legally be fired for a proper reason such as theft or incompetence or, absent a contract, for no reason at all. It is unlawful, however, to fire a person for the wrong reason, such as dismissing a female employee because of pregnancy or a blind person because of your prejudice.

Finally, be certain that all employees understand the rules and regulations and that you uphold them equitably. It is not fair to allow one employee to get away with lateness every morning when you require others to be prompt. It is also wrong to penalize or even discharge employees for not observing rules you never told them about. Changing rules without giving employees an opportunity to reorient themselves is also poor practice. If you're going to change the working hours, for example, give sufficient notice; don't just tell everyone to show up half an hour earlier starting the next day. If possible, notify employees of expected overtime somewhat in advance, as they may have made other plans.

How you treat your employees has a significant effect on how effectively and enthusiastically they work for you. That in turn has an effect on your profits. You might occasionally ask yourself: Would I want to work for a boss like me? *(See also: Apprentice, Cooperatives, Cottage Industry, Minimum Wage, Unemployment Insurance, Unions, Workers' Compensation, Withholding Tax)*

Endorsement

When you want to cash or deposit a check made out to you, your signature has to appear on the back of the check. It has to be signed exactly as it appears on the face of the check. If that is different from the name you use on your bank account, sign it twice: first as it appears on the face of the check, then as it appears on your account. For example, if you receive a check made out to Mrs. Tom Jones, but your account is under the name of Susan Jones, endorse the check first as Mrs. Tom Jones, then as Susan Jones.

If you cash a check made out to someone else, the same principle applies. First have the other person endorse the check, then add your endorsement. If you don't know the person for whom you are cashing such a check, be sure you see satisfactory identification, preferably a driver's license, credit card, or other document bearing a signature for comparison. Note the document number on the back of the check as well as the person's address so that you can find him or her if something goes wrong.

It is poor practice to endorse a check and then leave it lying around. If it is lost or stolen, it can easily be cashed if someone adds a second endorsement. Any check that is to be deposited and any check on which you are the second endorser should have the words *for deposit only* and your bank-account number written right under your endorsement. That way it cannot be cashed by anyone else.

The endorsement, or reverse, side of the check can also specify other restrictions, such as making the check payable upon delivery of the goods or when a certain service has been performed. When the recipient of the check endorses it, he accepts those restrictions. *(See also: Checking Account, Collection Problems)*

Equipment

In the process of learning a craft, you become familiar with the basic equipment: a loom, a potter's wheel, a kiln, hammers, saws, vises, and all the rest. But when you go into business and start your own shop or studio, equipment and tools suddenly take on an entirely new dimension. What kind of production capacity do you foresee? What kind of investment are you able to make?

A kiln is a good example of the various problems and solutions. If the kiln is too small, you will not be able to fire enough pieces to keep you in bread and butter. If it is too large, you waste not only the original investment but the cost of energy to fuel it.

A small, used kiln might make sense if you're working alone and just beginning to produce pieces for sale. In another year or two you might hope to build or buy a larger, more efficient one. Then again, if you can share the cost with another potter and work out an agreeable schedule, a large kiln may be a wise investment. Occasionally you might even be able to rent or lease equipment from a crafts supply shop if a temporary need arises.

Since equipment is often a major expense, financing its purchase can become a problem. The best way, of course, is to plan ahead and save the money. That way you not only avoid paying interest on a loan but the savings themselves earn interest in the bank. Don't save in a checking account; it usually pays no interest and even those that do usually pay less than savings accounts. Even if the plan is to put away only one hundred dollars a month for six months in a 5 percent savings account, you'll earn almost eight dollars in interest.

If you must finance the purchase out of future earnings, the best source is a bank loan. Shop around. Interest rates and other conditions are not always the same among different banks.

Before you invest in a new piece of equipment or a tool that represents a considerable expense, sleep on it. Two nights are better than one. Two heads are also better than one, so discuss it with some friends, some other crafts artists. And avoid an instant love affair with a sensational invention that promises the sky. If you can afford it, by all means take a chance. Perhaps it will do all that it promises. But if you're going into hock for it, look it over twice as carefully as you would any other piece of equipment with which you're more familiar. Consider all the possibilities—positive and negative—of how this particular equipment will solve your specific problems in your particular operation. Actually, that's a good rule for any major equipment purchase. Just because it worked well for someone else does not necessarily mean it will work well for you.

Once purchased, maintaining equipment and tools in good working order is as essential to the production of fine craftwork as using good raw materials. The end result reflects both. *(See also: Credit, Loans, Tools)*

Equity

The value of the investment an owner has in a business is called equity. This value is determined by subtracting the total liabilities of the business from its total assets. Equity is not necessarily the amount of money the owner has invested. In a prospering business, the equity would most likely be higher than the original investment; in a failing business it may be zero, regardless of how much was originally invested.

In the case of a mortgage, the term equity is used to describe the owner's—the borrower's—share of the total value of the property. As the mortgage loan is paid off month by month, the owner's equity increases. Thus, if you buy a one-hundred-thousand-dollar house with twenty thousand dollars in cash and an eighty-thousand dollar mortgage, your equity is twenty thousand dollars. After you've paid off four thousand dollars of the mortgage, your equity has grown to twenty-four thousand dollars—plus any appreciation in the value of the house since the loan was initiated. This continues until finally your equity is 100 percent, and you throw a big party to burn the mortgage. *(See also: Capital, Mortgage, Net Worth)*

Escrow

In financial terms, escrow is an account into which money is placed for a specific purpose. The money is to be held by a third party until the purpose is accomplished. An escrow account, for example, may be established to put funds into a bank for payment of a large order if credit references are not satisfactory. The money cannot be withdrawn by the depositor or touched by the person for whom it is intended until the order is delivered.

An escrow account is also used by a bank to collect money for taxes, water bills, and other obligations of people to whom it has made mortgage loans. The bank then pays those obligations for the mortgagor, although it does not usually pay interest on this type of escrow account. *(See also: Mortgage)*

Estimated Tax

All income from which no payroll taxes are withheld is subject to estimated-tax payments. For craftspeople, such income generally results from the sale of crafts objects. Estimated-tax payments on the income of self-employed individuals are due April 15, June 15, September 15, and January 15.

A declaration of estimated tax (Form 1040ES) must be filed on or before April 15 of each year for the current year. Estimated taxes must be paid even if some of your income is subject to withholding taxes. Such a combination situation is quite common among craftspeople who earn part of their income as teachers or at some other job at which they are on a payroll and another part in their own studio or shop where they are self-employed.

The penalty for underpayment of estimated taxes is 20 percent. There are two ways to avoid paying penalties:

1. Pay the same quarterly estimated tax in the current year as in the last, less any payroll taxes that may have been deducted from wages or salary if you held a job in the current year but not in the last year.

2. If you pay lower estimated taxes because you expect your income to

be less in the current year than in the last, your total estimated-tax payments must be at least 80 percent of your final tax obligation, paid on an even quarterly basis. The balance of 20 percent or less is payable without penalty when you file the next tax return on April 15.

Suppose things change midyear? Suppose you suddenly ran into a selling streak after you filed your estimated-tax return last April and are, therefore, likely to have more income than at first expected. In that case you amend your return when the next estimated payment is due, and increase those payments.

The reverse is also true if your self-employed income falls below what you had expected. This can happen if you switch from self-employed to a salaried job in the middle of the year or if an illness puts you out of commission for an extended period. In that case you reduce your quarterly payments by amending your return.

Be careful, though, to avoid estimating too low. If your payments drop below 80 percent of what is due in any quarter, you'll owe the penalty on the shortage. If they fall far below, you may be subject to extra penalties for willful failure to pay the proper estimated tax.

If you have had any income subject to withholding, the amount withheld is figured into the 80 percent determination. If, for example, your self-employed income obligated you to pay one thousand dollars in estimated taxes and your salary was subject to one thousand dollars in withholding taxes, your total tax obligation would be two thousand dollars. If you paid only seven hundred dollars (70 percent) of the one thousand dollars estimated taxes, that payment would seem to fall below the 80 percent requirement. However, 80 percent of the two-thousand-dollar total is sixteen hundred dollars. The withholding-tax payment of one thousand dollars and the estimated-tax payment of seven hundred dollars total seventeen hundred dollars, which is above the sixteen-hundred-dollar requirement. In this example, you're safe.

The Internal Revenue Service also assumes that withholding taxes, even if only earned in part of the year, are spread over the entire year to meet the even-quarterly-payment rule. Social-security taxes on self-employed income have to be included in the estimated-tax declaration and quarterly payments. (See also: Income Tax—Personal, Social Security, Withholding Tax)

Excise Tax
When the federal government imposes a sales tax, it goes by a different name: excise tax. Such tax is imposed on products such as gasoline, cigarettes, and alcoholic beverages and are collected from the consumer at the point of purchase just as other sales taxes are. However, they are not cal-

culated separately but are part of the posted price. Craftspeople rarely, if ever, get involved in selling products subject to an excise tax. *(See also: Tax)*

Exclusive Rights

The more artistic, unusual, or salable a crafts object is, the more likely it it that the craftsperson will be asked to grant exclusive rights to a store. That means the store wants to be the only one in a specified geographic area to sell your work. The assumption is that the store will, therefore, exert more effort to sell your craftwork.

The store's desire for exclusive rights is understandable. There is a certain prestige to offering exclusive crafts objects, and competition or even price-cutting is eliminated. Although exclusive arrangements may be great in smaller towns, they may hamper your sales in a metropolitan area. A few precautions, therefore, are advisable:

1. Put the exclusive arrangement in writing. Include a termination date. At first it should be no more than six months or a year.

2. Specify the exact geopgraphic area that is covered.

3. Specify the exact nature of the crafts objects that are covered. If you make a line of dishes and a line of hanging pots, is all your pottery included in the exclusive arrangement?

4. Require the store to purchase or sell a certain minimum volume.

5. Spell out what advertising and other promotion activities the store will engage in to promote sales of your work.

6. Demand the right of approval on prices and promotions.

The store, in return, may want certain commitments from you. Can you, for example, produce an adequate supply? Will you maintain quality and price? Will you participate in an exhibit they may want to run?

Exclusivity may work very well for you, especially in opening up new markets. But examine each situation carefully, evaluate each store's reputation and track record, and be prepared to observe every clause in your agreement. *(See also: Consignment, Retailing)*

Exhibitions

As the status of crafts as an art form grows, so do the opportunities to participate in exhibitions sponsored by museums, galleries, organizations, universities, and other institutions.

Some exhibitions restrict participation to certain geographic areas, such as the periodic Seven State Art Exhibition at Eastern Illinois University, which is open only to craftspeople in seven midwestern states. Others concentrate on a particular medium, such as the Contemporary Glass Exhibition staged by Peters Valley Craftsmen of New Jersey. Some last for a few weeks, such as the Cooperstown, New York, event each summer; others go on year-long tours, such as the American embroiderers biennial stitchery exhibition.

Most exhibitions offer cash prizes or purchase awards, and many also provide opportunities for the purchase of works that are delivered to buyers after the exhibition is over.

The immediate rewards of winning a prize or making a sale, however, are not the only reasons for participating in an exhibition. Equally important to crafts artists is the recognition and prestige that result from acceptance in an important exhibition. Being part of the Smithsonian's regular Crafts Multiples show and being included in the show's handsome catalog, for example, are likely to bring rewards to the participating craftsperson far beyond the immediate sale of his or her work. Recognition as an outstanding crafts artist enhances the value and price of the crafts artist's future work.

Almost all exhibitions are juried by slides, and many also require viewing of actual work after the slides pass the jury. A reputable exhibition sponsor will give details of the conditions and responsibilities of handling the work. Under most circumstances, entrants are responsible for shipping the work to the exhibition and for insurance in transit. Thereafter the exhibition sponsor should be responsible for proper care, insurance, and ultimate return of the work. Slides and crafts objects that are not accepted should be returned to the entrant promptly after jurying. If this is not spelled out in the exhibition prospectus, ask questions.

A modest entry fee, usually fifteen dollars or less, is required by many exhibition sponsors to help defray the cost of the judging process. Craftspeople should not, however, be expected to help defray the cost of the exhibition itself or to provide the kitty from which the prizes are awarded. Note too that many exhibition sponsors take a commission, rarely more than 20 percent of the purchase price, when a work on exhibit is sold.

All entries, whether by slide or actual work, should be properly identified. Many exhibition sponsors provide forms for this purpose. Where special hanging or display instructions are necessary, the craftsperson should describe these clearly and send them along with the entry. Also accompanying the entry must be the price at which it may be sold. If the work is not to be sold, that too should be indicated.

An important ingredient of any exhibition from a crafts artist's point of view is the printed exhibition catalog. This enables prospective buyers to contact the artist to see other examples of his or her craftwork. If no catalog is planned, then the exhibition sponsor should at least provide all visitors with a list of names and addresses of participating crafts artists.

Unlike crafts shows and fairs, exhibitions do not require the presence of the craftsperson, only his or her work. A reputable exhibition can bring long-lasting rewards—and often even immediate sales. (*See also: Museum, Purchase Award, Shows and Fairs*)

Expense Accounts

These two words mean precisely what they say: to account for expenses. Since every business-connected expense is tax deductible, it makes good sense to record all such expenses completely.

The term expense account does not refer to items of expense that are billed and paid for by check and thus appear accurately on the books of the business anyway. The term applies more to the incidental, out-of-pocket expenses. They may seem small at the time, but they add up.

If you go to an out-of-town crafts fair, for example, the cost of the booth does not show up on the expense account since you've already paid for it by check. But the car mileage, tolls, meals, lodging, laundry, and similar expenses should be accounted for.

Keep a notebook handy, and jot down every item, including the quarter tolls and the telephone calls, as soon as the expense is incurred. Memory plays strange tricks, and four forgotten quarters make a dollar. Get as many receipts as possible to confirm the expenditure. Tollbooths on turnpikes give receipts. The more receipts you have, the easier it is to prove to the government that you spent the money you say you spent and that it was spent for a business purpose.

The Internal Revenue Service requires that all lodging expenses be supported by a receipt, as well as any meal expense that exceeds twenty-five dollars and all business-entertainment expenses. If you use a credit card, the sales slip will serve as a receipt. Details of the business nature of the expense—the person with whom you had lunch, for example—can be recorded on the back of the credit-card slip.

A special situation exists with regard to automobile expenses. You can, of course, keep a record of the gasoline you bought, the repairs and depreciation of the car over a year's time, and so on. However, the government allows a standard expense (28¢ per mile as of 1992), which includes all car expenses except parking and tolls. That way you simply keep track of the mileage and show it on your expense account multiplied by 28¢. This is the procedure applied to car expenses by most business travelers.

For purposes of record keeping, it is best to keep an expense account on the basis of a specific time period—perhaps weekly—or according to a specific business trip. Mark the top of each list with the time period or the activity it covers. Be sure every entry is dated. Attach all receipts to the list of expenses, indicate by date and check number how you were reimbursed, enter the transaction in your bookkeeping ledger, and file the whole thing away where you or your accountant can find it. (*See also: Accounting, Business Trips*)

Expenses

Anything you spend in order to make craftwork for sale is a business expense. This includes rent, raw materials, supplies, wages, utilities, sales costs, traveling expenses, shipping, and a great many other items.

Business expenses are generally tax-deductible. In the case of craftspeople who devote their full time to producing craftwork for sale, all such expenses are deductible, even if they exceed the year's crafts income. In the case of people who have other jobs but who work at their craft regularly in their spare time with the intent to sell, business expenses are deductible up to the amount of income realized from the sale of craft objects in any given year. In the latter category, it is important to observe the Internal Revenue Service (IRS) guideline that establishes a presumption that an activity is a business rather than a hobby if it makes a profit in three out of five consecutive years. People who pursue crafts purely as a hobby cannot deduct their expenses.

If the IRS questions your business deductions, a critical factor is your intent. In other words, did you really intend to make a profit? Did you really intend to run a business, even if only part-time? Your business intentions will be much easier to substantiate if you have kept a good set of financial records, and can show, for example, that you have invested in equipment, have a separate business bank account, and have stationery with your business name.

Under the three-out-of-five-year rule, life is much easier if you show a profit early during the five-year period. Profit is what shows up on your tax return. There's no law that says you must take deductions. There may come a time, especially in a year when income and expenses are close together, when you find it worthwhile to omit some expense items in order to show a profit that year. That will, in turn, allow you to take all the deductions in a year when expenses may be considerably higher than income.

But no matter what taxpayer category you're in, the most essential point to remember is that a sound and consistent method of recording every expense item is required if you are ever called upon to prove your expenses to the tax collector. (*See also: Accounting, Income, Overhead, Profit, Wages*)

Export (*See: Customs*)

Fees

Payments for such professional services as those of lawyers, accountants, and doctors are known as fees, as distinguished from wages and salaries. If a craftsperson serves as a consultant or speaker, payment for that service is also a fee. Other payments called fees include admissions to entertainment or sports events; the costs of crafts shows, some educational activities (such as seminars), official documents, licenses, and registrations; and charges established by law for the services of a public official.

Craftspeople are often asked to contribute their time and talent for free to commercial ventures. You may be asked, for example, to perform for an educational film made for a commercial sponsor. "There's no money," you are told, "but you'll get credit"—as though credit can be deposited in a bank. The people who produce a film are paid. The teachers who use the film in a classroom are paid. The commercial sponsor obviously has a profit motive. Why should craftspeople be expected to donate their time and talent?

Perhaps this reflects the popular misconception that such things as weaving and making pottery are only fun, and who ever heard of paying people to have fun? Unlike the people who do the asking, crafts artists are rarely on salary. Their time is literally their money. Asking for that time without payment is asking too much.

Unless a free appearance can be tied directly into sales or some other benefit is obtained, it should be turned down. Craftspeople also have bills to pay. They have a right to be proud of their skills, their talents, their artistry and creativity. That is not something to give away for someone else's profit.

Crafts artists give generously of their time, talent, and money to worthy causes of their choice. But when commercial interests try to use craftspeople for commercial purposes without payment, the time has come to say no.

Better yet, negotiate a fee. *(See also: Income)*

Financial Management *(See: Accounting, Balance Sheet, Banks, Bookkeeping, Budget, Capital, Gross, Income Statement, Investment, Loans, Tax)*

Financial Statement
Although small, individually owned enterprises do not usually get involved in this, a larger business and every partnership or corporation have their accountants draw up two types of financial statements at least once a year: an income statement and a balance sheet.

The income statement reports the income and expenses of the business over the period. The balance sheet reports the assets, liabilities, and equity at the end of the period. They complement each other because the income statement helps to indicate how you got to where the balance sheet says you are. *(See also: Accounting, Balance Sheet, Income Statement)*

Fine Art
This term is applied to such media as painting and sculpture, which are usually sold through galleries. Several crafts media such as woven wall hangings and some glass, clay, and metalwork have begun to cross over from crafts art to fine art, especially if the object has purely aesthetic value and bears no resemblance to any functional object.

The word *fine* need not be interpreted as a definition of the artistic quality of the work but only of its nonfunctional purpose. Fine art is generally purchased by collectors, some of whom view it as an investment that will grow in value or that can provide certain tax advantages. Under the tax laws, for example, a collector can donate an artwork to a museum and take a charitable deduction for the donation. This is a volatile area, and the amount of the deduction that may be taken for tax purposes will vary depending upon the identity of the recipient and whether the tax law in effect on the date of the donation will permit a deduction of the fair market value of the work or only its cost.

Fine-Arts Floater

Craftspeople often suffer losses due to breakage or theft while transporting or exhibiting their work at shows and fairs. Such losses are not always covered by the show management—certainly not transportation—nor are they covered by the usual property insurance that you may already have on your home or shop and its contents. Proper protection for what insurance companies describe as periods of "storage, transporting, and exhibiting" requires the addition of a fine-arts floater to your property-insurance policy.

To protect against theft from your car, the policy must be endorsed to include off-premises theft coverage. To protect work that is transported by such other means as parcel post, UPS, freight, or someone else's car, specific transit coverage must be added to the fine-arts floater. Rates for floater coverage depend on such variables as the type of storage area—home, shop, warehouse, garage—whether the vehicle has a burglar alarm, security conditions in the exhibition building, packing of items, and so forth. Some work is more fragile or is more tempting to thieves, and that can also affect the rates.

The only way to write this fine-arts floater is by adding it to an existing homeowner or tenant/homeowner policy. Floater premiums ordinarily are about five dollars per one hundred dollars of coverage, with a twenty-five-dollar minimum. If the risk is large enough, as with property valued at ten thousand dollars or more, it may warrant being underwritten separately. A fifty-dollar deductible per occurrence is usually part of the policy.

This type of coverage is offered by all casualty and property insurance brokers. To determine whether you need such coverage, how much to buy, and what it will cost, you should consult your insurance agent. *(See also: Insurance, Property Insurance)*

Fire Insurance *(See: Insurance, Property Insurance)*

Fire Prevention

Few disasters are as drastic or as costly as a fire, and most such disasters can be prevented by following safety precautions. Consider not only that a fire can pose a serious threat to your life and the lives of those who live or work with you but that it can destroy your life's work, your prized possessions, your business records, your means to earn a living.

The following recommendations for safety in five major areas of fire danger are based on information from the National Fire Protection Association.

Fire Hazards

Smoking Hazards

This is one of the most common causes of fires, especially around vapors and dusty areas. Post No Smoking signs in potential danger areas, and be sure the signs are observed.

If you must smoke, be sure to use an ashtray. Do not rest cigarettes on windowsills, the edges of your workbench, or on other surfaces. Do not throw matches or cigarettes into wastebaskets even if you think they're out.

Of all the fire hazards, those caused by smoking are the easiest to prevent if proper precautions are taken.

Electrical Hazards

Never hang electrical wiring over nails, around metal pipes, near heat or oil, across passageways, or across the floor. Frayed insulation, broken plugs, loose connections, and defective switches or outlets must be repaired promptly. Keep hot bulbs away from liquids.

Overloading electrical equipment or bypassing the safe amperage of the fuse box creates a real fire danger. If a motor emits sparks or gets wet, it needs attention. A spark can cause a fire. The pennies saved on delay or skimping can easily become thousands of dollars spent to recover from fire loss.

If you must use electrical equipment near flammable liquids, gas, or dust, be sure that proper ventilation is maintained at all times and that the equipment is designed for that purpose—that it's explosionproof.

Cutting and Welding Hazards

All torch cutting and welding should be done in a safe place, away from flammable materials or explosives. Walls, ceilings, and floors can also catch fire from flying sparks. It is always best to have someone on hand to extinguish flying sparks that land in cracks or crevices. Don't walk away when you're through; examine your work area and stand watch for a while to be certain no sparks are smoldering anywhere. Use covers and shields to contain sparks and protect yourself.

Flammable Liquid Hazards

Don't ever allow flammable liquids to accumulate. Use them only outdoors or in a well-ventilated area. Always clean up spilled liquids immediately, and keep only a small amount in a clearly marked metal safety container— never glass—near your work area.

Using gasoline as a cleaning fluid is one of the most dangerous things you can do. Don't take the chance. Gasoline is a fuel, not a cleaner.

Keep flammable liquids away from all sources of flame or sparks (kilns, torches, heaters, electric tools). If oil-soaked rags must be kept, store them only in tightly covered metal containers; get rid of them as soon as you can. And if you have a cigarette dangling from your mouth while working with flammable liquids, you should work in front of a mirror so that you can watch a fool go up in smoke.

Housekeeping Hazards

Neatness counts! If your work area is littered with cartons and scraps and leftover materials, you're inviting a fire. Ditto with accumulations of chips, cuttings, oil drippings, dust, and other trash. Keep such stuff in covered metal containers and dispose of it regularly and properly.

Be sure that exit doors, stairways, and fire escapes are not blocked and that your sprinkler system, if any, is in good working order at all times. Establish a fire-escape plan and have a fire drill once in a while. Be sure that all family members or employees know the fire-escape procedures. A fire-safety fact sheet is available (see Appendix C).

Fire Prevention

Fire Extinguishers

Every workplace and home should have at least one fire extinguisher, depending on the size of the premises and the potential nature of a fire.

Different types of fire require different types of fire extinguishers.

1. Type A (water type) is used for ordinary combustible fires such as paper, cloth, wood, or trash fires;

2. Type B (dry chemical or foam type) is used for flammable-liquid fires such as from gasoline, paint, or oil;

3. Type C (carbon-dioxide type) is used for electrical-equipment fires such as those that result from fautly motors or wiring;

4. Type D (dry powder type) is used for combustible metal fires, such as from certain chips and shavings;

5. Type A-B-C (multipurpose chemical type) can be used for any of the various types of fire created by combustible materials, flammable liquid, or electrical equipment.

Never use a fire extinguisher on a fire for which it is not intended. Using

Type A (water) on an electrical fire, for example, can cause an electric shock.

Carefully read the instructions on the fire extinguisher. Also be sure you know how to use it and that it is placed in a strategic location so that it's accessible. Getting acquainted with the fire extinguisher after a fire starts may be too late.

What to Do if a Fire Starts

The whole point is to stop a fire from starting, and if one does start, you must keep it from spreading.

If you see smoke or fire, first turn in a fire alarm. If the fire is small, fight it while you wait for the firemen; but stay low and be sure you have an escape route available. If the fire grows and gets out of hand, get out fast! Close doors behind you to retard the spread of the fire. *(See also: Work Area)*

First Nation Arts

First Nation Arts is a nongovernmental organization formed to promote Native American art and crafts. Its goal is to assist Native American artists in achieving financial independence from the government. The organization provides seminars for Native American artists and collectors of Native American art and has assisted Native American artists in participating in numerous crafts shows (see Appendix C).

Free on Board (F.O.B.)

The term indicates to which point the seller of a product will deliver it and bear all the risks of loss and at which point the buyer takes over. F.O.B. is most commonly followed by the words *factory* or *seller's place of business*, which means the seller will get the goods packed and ready for pickup by the buyer or the buyer's agent—such as a freight carrier—at the seller's place of business. In practice this means the buyer pays the shipping charges, makes the shipping arrangements, and assumes the risk of loss during shipment.

Sometimes the initials F.O.B. are followed by the name of a location other than the factory. This means the seller is responsible for delivering the goods to that pickup point, whereupon the buyer takes over. If, for example, you are located in Los Angeles and buy a heavy piece of equipment from a manufacturer who has a factory in Philadelphia and a warehouse in San Francisco, then the difference between *F.O.B. factory* and *F.O.B. San Francisco* can become a significant factor in shipping and insurance costs. *F.O.B. factory* means you pay the shipping costs from Philadelphia to Los Angeles. *F.O.B. San Francisco* means the manufacturer pays for shipping from Philadelphia to the West Coast, and you pay the shipping costs only from San Francisco to Los Angeles.

The term F.O.B. involves another important consideration, especially when claims for damage in transit are involved. Title to the goods changes hands the moment the goods are picked up at the F.O.B. point. From that moment the buyer owns them, even if they have not yet been delivered.

Foreclosure *(See: Mortgage)*

Franchise Tax *(See: Income Tax—Business)*

Freight Allowance

With shipping costs going through the roof, most producers of merchandise add the cost of shipping to the cost of the items themselves. In certain cases they make a freight allowance; that is, the freight charges will be paid by the shipper. This is usually based on two considerations: the size of the order and the distance it has to travel. For example, all orders of more than a five-hundred-dollar value may have the freight paid by the shipper. The freight allowance is important to craftspeople both as purchasers of equipment and supplies and as suppliers themselves. In both cases the question is: Do you pay the freight charges or does the other party?

Some shippers make a freight allowance for deliveries within a limited area, such as within one hundred miles if they have their own truck delivering to that area anyway. In other instances, a freight allowance may be made to distant locations if the supplier wants to build customers in that area but can't compete if the freight charges are added.

A freight allowance need not be 100 percent. It can be graduated: a 10 percent charge if the order is less than two hundred dollars, 20 percent if it is between two hundred dollars and five hundred dollars.

As a supplier, a crafts producer should not offer freight allowances unless they are necessary to make the sale. As a buyer of equipment and supplies, on the other hand, craftspeople should try to get whatever freight allowance is possible.

Any freight you pay for—coming in or going out—is an expense item that eats into profits. *(See also: Free on Board, Shipping)*

Freight Collect

This means the recipient of the shipment pays the freight costs when the shipment is received. The delivering carrier will not leave the shipment unless those costs are paid.

If this situation applies, it should be stated on all price lists, order forms, and so on. *(See also: Free on Board, Freight Allowance, Freight Prepaid, Shipping)*

Freight Forwarders *(See: Shipping)*

Freight Prepaid

This means the shipper prepays the costs of shipment even if those costs are ultimately added to the bill. If so, it should be stated clearly on all price lists, order forms, and so on. *(See also: Free on Board, Freight Allowance, Freight Collect, Shipping)*

Gallery

A gallery is a retail sales outlet for craftwork, painting, or sculpture, with some important features that distinguish it from other outlets we call stores or shops. Those distinctions are traceable to the original meaning of the word, whose definitions included: a walkway, a promenade, a place where the audience sits at a performance. In other words, a room with a view. The upper balcony of an opera house, the spectator section at a golf match, and exhibition halls at museums are still known as galleries.

A gallery that sells craftwork is still a room with a view, since its selling activity is based on exhibitions rather than simple store display. Such galleries generally specialize in works of unusual or innovative design and technique and appeal more to the collector who is interested in buying one-of-a-kind aesthetic objects than multiply produced or mass-produced functional objects.

Whether a particular piece of work is unique is usually a major factor in a gallery owner's decision to accept and display the work. If something similar can be bought at a shop around the corner or in the local department store, it is not likely to find its way into a gallery. Galleries do not depend primarily on walk-in customers who are attracted by a window display or a big ad in the papers but, rather, on a carefully developed list of clients who respond to invitations to an exhibition. To build such response, a gallery owner must offer customers something that is unusually artistic, unique, or innovative. To accomplish this, many galleries build their reputations and clientele by specializing in certain types of work, certain artists, certain periods, certain schools, and so forth.

From a crafts artist's point of view, a gallery show includes many benefits beyond the possibility of selling the work. Since competition for gallery acceptance is keen, a great deal of prestige attaches to having such a show, even at a nonselling gallery in a museum. Many gallery exhibitions are reviewed in the press, and this can become an important asset in the crafts artist's portfolio when trying to sell to retail stores, obtaining special commissions or assignments, or qualifying for a teaching position—not to mention what it does for the ego.

When it comes to selling work with a high price tag—such as a large wall hanging or an expensive piece of sculptured jewelry—gallery selling often is the most effective way to find the customer who has both the appreciation for fine work and the money to spend on it. Once a good gallery connection has been established, it is easier for a crafts artist to find customers for important works in the future.

This background is by way of introducing the methods of approaching a gallery and the specific arrangements that should be made. First, determine whether your work is really suited to gallery selling according to some of the standards outlined above. Visit some galleries in your area or whenever you are on a trip. Walk in as a spectator and try to visualize your work in that setting. Does the gallery's general approach appeal to the kind of customers who might be interested in your work? Does the price structure seem compatible with yours? Do you like the way the gallery exhibits the work and prepares the show catalog? Can you find some reason why that particular gallery should be interested in handling your work?

The initial approach to a gallery, unless you know the owner or have a personal introduction, is to send a letter, enclosing a brief résumé that outlines your background, describes your experience, and includes some reference to exhibition or competition experience. Indicate in the letter that you will call in a week or so for an appointment to show slides or samples of your work.

Don't be discouraged if gallery owners don't fall all over themselves to see you and sign you up. They often have contracts and commitments for many months in advance. Unlike retail-shop owners, they don't work under intense daily pressure, and their concern is not how many units of a given item they can sell tomorrow. On the other hand, they are in business to make a profit, and anything you can tell them that would lead them to believe in the possibility of a profitable connection if they handle your work is an obvious advantage. For example, if you already have a list of potential customers who came to another exhibition of yours and could be invited to an opening, you are more likely to attract a gallery owner's interest.

The basic decision, of course, will be made on the quality of your work. When you finally do meet with the gallery owner, have a good set of slides or a representative group of pieces to show. No need to bring a slide projector; most galleries have their own. If your presentation is made by mail to a gallery in a distant city, then superb slides are even more important. It is best to start locally until you have some experience and credentials under your belt.

Be prepared, also, to discuss price. The overwhelming bulk of gallery work is sold on consignment, especially in the higher price levels. Some work, however, is bought outright, depending on a gallery's financial capabilities and its experience with a particular crafts artist.

In a consignment arrangement, you determine the ultimate retail price and get a percentage of the sale after it is made. The percentage generally runs between 50 and 60 percent. Galleries occasionally expect the artist to help defray some of the costs of a reception for an opening or of advertising for an exhibition. In that case, the percentage the artist receives should be around 60 percent since the artist has made an investment in his own show. If the gallery is responsible for all the costs, then it generally keeps between 40 and 50 percent of the ultimate selling price.

The concept of artists or craftspeople paying for some of the costs of an exhibition—also known as charge backs—is a subject of considerable controversy. What control, for example, do artists have over the quality and cost of the activity to which they are expected to contribute a share of the expense? Should such expenses more properly be a responsibility of the gallery as part of its normal operating expenses?

If you are approached with such a proposition as a condition for selling your work, ask yourself whether the gallery is really convinced that your work will sell or whether you are just being used to bring people into the gallery where they will be exposed to other artists' work as well as your own. Each situation should be evaluated on its own. Sometimes this arrangement can benefit the crafts artist, especially for a first show that establishes your credentials. If you do agree to share some of the costs, be sure everything is spelled out in detail and is in writing, especially the amount of money involved and what control you have over how it is spent.

Other points should be kept in mind about pricing. First, it should be clearly understood that the gallery cannot change the price of consignment items downward without your prior agreement. In addition, pricing one-of-a-kind objects differs somewhat from pricing production crafts. Raw materials, labor, and overhead must be calculated, of course. The elements of originality, exclusiveness, and artistry, however, are much more important in selling gallery items than in the kind of work that might be sold at a crafts fair or department store. The price can, therefore, be relatively higher to compensate you for these intangible elements.

Since it may take longer to sell a major work in a gallery than to sell production crafts items to a store, the price should reflect that your time and money are tied up for longer periods in an unsold work. The price must, of course, still be competitive, although the nature of the competition may have changed. Unless you are a big star, the market and the price range of the particular gallery must be considered if you hope to sell your work. These are subjects you can discuss with the gallery owner, who knows what type of work his clients will buy and what kind of price they'll pay.

The question of how long a gallery can keep your pieces if they remain unsold is a matter of negotiation. If the gallery spends considerable sums to mount an exhibition and pay for the promotion, then it will want the opportunity to recoup its investment. The most common time frames are between six months and a year.

Another important question is insurance. Is the gallery properly insured to cover consigned work that is on its premises but is still your property until it is sold? Who is responsible for damage or theft? Who is responsible for taking the work to the gallery and returning unsold work to you? This is particularly important when objects have to be shipped rather than hand delivered locally.

You may want to ask yourself and the gallery owner a few other questions: Do you have any say in the manner in which your work is displayed or what is shown near yours? What happens if you and the gallery owner don't agree about something? How are you protected if the gallery goes bankrupt? Does the gallery have the right to put your work out on loan? Does the gallery's sales contract with its customer include a clause that gives you a share in any increased value if the work is later resold by the customer at a higher price? Does the gallery want your work exclusively, or can you sell to and through anyone? When and how does the gallery pay you, and what kind of records does it keep?

Whatever arrangements you make about consignment, contributing to expenses, manner of payment, insurance, time, and so on should be put in writing to avoid future misunderstandings and controversies. A book that discusses the legal issues unique to art galleries and crafts retailers is *The Law (In Plain English)® for Art & Craft Galleries* (see Appendix C). *(See also: Consignment, Fine-Arts Floater, Insurance, Portfolio, Production Crafts, Résumé, Retailing)*

Government Activities

Many crafts-related activities and sponsorships are hidden in federal government agencies and departments.

Perhaps the best known of these are the programs of the National Endowment for the Arts (NEA). Although the NEA in recent years has focused its support on the organizational infrastructure of the arts, there are still some major programs available to individual crafts artists. Crafts categories for which fellowships are available include craftspeople-in-residence, artists-in-schools, craftspeople's fellowships, crafts workshops, master craftspeople, apprenticeships, and others. (See *Guide to the NEA Visual Arts Fellowship Program*, Appendix C.)

Equally active, though not engaged in funding, is the Craft Development Program of the United States Department of Agriculture. This, too, is conducted by a crafts specialist and is engaged primarily in helping local and regional groups expand the economic development of crafts and craftspeople in their areas. The crafts specialist helps in the establishment of craft groups, cooperatives, and other associations and in providing management and technical advice, educational materials, marketing information, and other assistance (see Appendix D).

Other divisions of the Department of Agriculture include a variety of crafts activities in their programs: the Extension Service through community-resource development and 4-H youth programs, the Farmer's Home Administration through loans for industrial and business development and community facilities under the Rural Development Act, the Rural Electrification Administration, and various research and education programs of the Forest Service.

The activities of the Small Business Administration, though not specifically oriented toward crafts, have had an immense impact on crafts producers through direct small business loans or guaranteed loans and through their publications on a wide range of business subjects.

Other government agencies involved in art and crafts activities are the Department of Health and Human Services, Department of Education, Commerce Department, Interior Department, Department of Justice (through its Prison Arts Program), the armed forces, Smithsonian Institution, Tennessee Valley Authority, National Park Service, and the State Department (through its Art in the Embassies and Graduate Study Abroad programs).

Many of the programs do not deal with individual craftspeople—the Small Business Administration and the NEA are the major exceptions—but are more involved with institutions or organizations. Of course, in most of these agencies the art and crafts interest is a minor one, but the programs provide opportunities, directly and indirectly, for economic support to crafts.

Complete details about federal funds and services available to the arts or crafts can be found in the *Cultural Directory* published by the American Council for the Arts. This volume can probably be found in most good libraries and should also be on the shelves of well-informed crafts organizations. Single copies can be ordered from the American Craft Council (see Appendix D). *(See also: National Endowment for the Arts, Small Business Administration)*

Grants

A grant is a specific sum of money given to an individual, organization, or institution for a specific project that has a useful purpose and requires more money than the recipient has available.

The major sources for grants are:

1. Government agencies such as the National Endowment for the Arts and state arts councils;
2. Private organizations or institutions, such as museums or foundations;
3. The business community, such as major corporations.

The largest single source for grants in the crafts field is probably the National Endowment for the Arts, which has a separate visual-arts department with a crafts coordinator. Its annual "Guide to Programs," published in August, gives details of the eligibility requirements for various grants. Fifteen categories involve grants of interest to craftspeople.

The other major source for grants are state arts councils or arts commissions. They can usually be located in each state capital. Both the size and the nature of grants vary from state to state. Some major cities, it should be noted, have their own arts councils or arts commissions that also have funds for grant purposes.

A number of federal agencies, notably the Department of Education, give grants for specific educational purposes. A complete list of federal funds for cultural activities is found in the *Cultural Directory*, published by the American Council for the Arts, available from the American Craft Council (see Appendix D). A further source of information about private funding is the *Foundation Directory* (see Appendix C), which is available in most good libraries.

Scholarships and fellowships for elementary and advanced university study are closely related to the concept of grants. The best approach is to decide which university offers the most suitable curriculum, and then inquire what scholarship aid is available at that institution. A good source for information is the *College Blue Book*, a three-volume reference work revised every two years. It includes supplements on fellowships, grants, and loans for study at both the undergraduate and graduate level and is cross-referenced by institution and by subject matter. It is available in most libraries.

Various agencies of state and federal government make some money available for scholarships or underwrite student loans. Such programs are, of course, subject to fluctuations in the economy as well as the direction of the political winds that dictate the size of available budgets for such purposes. A good place to start looking for information is the Office of Student Financial Assistance (see Appendix D).

Every institution of higher learning also has its own student-financial-aid office. If you've already determined which institution you want to attend, consult with the financial-aid office to find out what kind of scholarship, fellowship, grant, or loan assistance is available at that institution.

There are no prescribed general rules about how to apply for a grant, although many grant-application forms outline in specific detail what type of information is required. Since, however, a grant always has a purpose, the information the applicant furnishes should emphasize how the use of the funds, if they are granted, will help accomplish the purpose of the grant. *(See also: National Endowment for the Arts, State Arts Agencies)*

Gross

This word has three meanings for craftspeople:

1. In poor taste, unrefined, ugly, coarse, garish;
2. Twelve dozen, 144 pieces;
3. As applied to financial terms, to indicate that deductions have not been taken. For example, gross income is the total amount of dollars received before deducting costs of production, materials, labor, and sales. Gross profit is the total profit before taxes are deducted.

Gross is distinguished from net, which is essentially gross profit less deductions. *(See also: Income, Net, Profit)*

Group Insurance

Life insurance, health and major medical insurance, dental, and disability-income insurance policies can be bought at comparatively lower rates when a single policy is issued to a group to cover members of that group. A group can be formed by a business firm, an organization of craftspeople, or any similar organized entity. Most such policies require that the group consist of at least ten members, though some permit as few as three, and that a certain percentage of all members participate in the group policy. The group pays one premium to the insurance company on behalf of the enrolled members. These premiums can be paid by the employer or the organization's treasury, or they can be paid by the members through the employer or the organization. Most major insurance companies offer group plans. Among the better known in the hospital and medical field are Blue Cross and Blue Shield, but there are many local and regional companies, such as Preferred Provider Organizations (PPO) and Health Maintenance Organizations (HMO), that can favorably compete.

Members generally need no physical examination to qualify, even for life insurance, though this is changing in light of the AIDS crisis. When a member leaves the group, he or she usually has the right to convert to an individual health and medical policy within a specified period, generally thirty days, again without physical examination.

Group-insurance policies do not accumulate cash values as other life-insurance policies do, members cannot select their own amount of coverage, and the insurance company cannot cancel an individual member's participation in a group policy.

Group insurance is used by many companies as an added form of compensation and to induce employees to remain with the firm; organizations offer it as a service to members and to attract new members. *(See also: Insurance, Life Insurance)*

Guarantee

A guarantee is a seller's promise to repair or replace a product if it is found defective. Guarantees are normally made in writing—though the law sometimes recognizes oral guarantees—and generally stipulate the conditions under which the guarantee will be performed. There may be a time limit, such as replacing defective parts during the first ninety days; or a condition imposed on the customer, such as not using the product improperly—plugging an AC motor, for example, into a DC outlet—or specific restrictions, such as guaranteeing the working parts but not the exterior finish of a product.

The words *guarantee* and *warranty* are often used interchangeably, but there are several important differences, both from the seller's and the buyer's point of view.

Distinguish guarantee from guaranty, which is an agreement by which one party assumes the responsibility of assuring payment or fulfillment of another party's debts or obligations. *(See also: Warranty)*

Health Hazards *(See: Safety)*

Import *(See: Customs)*

Income

The financial gain resulting from any business activity, investment, labor, personal service, or other source is known as income. Income includes:

1. *Wages* that are paid for labor performed on an hourly basis or on production output.

2. *Salaries* that are paid for services over a specific period of time or for a specified function, such as annual executive salaries or a movie star's salary for a particular film.

3. *Dividends* that are paid as a return on investments.

4. *Interest* that is paid as a return for the use of money.

5. *Rents* that are paid as a return on the use of property.

6. *Royalties* that are paid for the right to use the creative work or natural resources owned by others.

7. *Sales receipts* that result from the sale of products or services (also known as gross income).

8. *Commissions* that are paid on the basis of performance, such as sales commissions earned as a percentage of sales produced.

9. *Fees* that are paid for legal, accounting, medical, and other professional services.

10. *Gains* from the sale or exchange of property.

11. *Alimony* and separate maintenance payments.

12. *Income* from life insurance and endowment contracts, annuities, income in respect of a decedent, income from an interest in an estate or trust, or, more generally, money, property, or anything of value from whatever source derived.

Income Averaging

Prior to the 1986 Tax Reform Act, income averaging enabled the taxpayer who had low income in several years followed by high income in a particular year to offset the consequences of being taxed in a much higher tax bracket in the one good year. For example, a craftsperson who just happened to sell one or more expensive pieces in a given year, resulting in a higher than normal income for that year, could be faced with federal income taxes of 50 percent or even higher. The same amount of income spread over the three preceding lean years would be taxed in lower brackets, which would result in lower overall taxes and more accurately reflect the individual's economic status.

Income averaging entailed adherence to a rigid set of rules and eligibility criteria. Although reasonable in theory, in practice the benefits of income averaging were not always limited to those with uneven income—as originally envisioned. For example, individuals such as college graduates beginning a new career received an unintended benefit when their income suddenly increased, even though it continued at the higher level. Income averaging did nothing for people who found themselves earning far less after several good years, which was the case for those laid off from their employment.

The 1986 act eliminated income averaging altogether. This was done partly in compliance with the purpose of the act, which was to simplify the tax system, and partly because, with fewer tax brackets and lower rates, income averaging would not have continued to be the boon it had once been to that handful of individuals whose income came in infrequent spurts. *(See also: Income Tax—Business, Income Tax—Personal)*

Income Statement

A summary, figured at least once a year, of the income and expenses during a given period is known as an income statement. It lists various categories of income and various categories of expense. Net income for the period is determined by deducting the expense total from the income total. If expenses were larger than income, the statement will show a net loss.

An examination of the income statement and a comparison with income statements of previous years can be helpful in pinpointing improvements or shortcomings in specific areas of income and expense.

The following example is of an income statement for an imaginary crafts

POT LUCK POTTERY

INCOME STATEMENT

For the Year Ended December 31, 1992

INCOME

Retail Sales	$ 5,631.52	
Wholesale Sales	31,944.30	
Shows and Fairs	3,443.76	
	Total Income	$41,019,58

EXPENSES

Raw Materials	$ 6,036.22	
Wages	16,800.00	
Payroll Taxes	2,429.00	
Rent	1,200.00	
Utilities	793.48	
Insurance	480.00	
Telephone	285.36	
Depreciation	2,120.00	
Sales Expenses	630.92	
Miscellaneous	379.86	
	Total Expenses	$31,154.84
	Net Income	$ 9,864.74

business. The owner of the business put herself on the payroll for thirteen thousand dollars, which is part of the wages expense. Her total income for the year (wages plus net income) was therefore $22,864.74. *(See also: Balance Sheet, Expenses, Income, Statement)*

Income Tax—Business

The federal income-tax laws require different things from different types of business organizations. Sole proprietors, partnerships, S corporations, and limited liability companies do not pay a business income tax on their firm's or corporation's profits; instead, those profits are taxed on the owners' income-tax returns. Of course, in these instances information returns have to be prepared to declare the income and expenses of the business. The forms to be used by the taxpayers are Schedule C with Form 1040 for individual owners, Form 1065 for partnerships.

C corporations are another matter. For a number of years, these businesses were taxed by the federal government at the rate of 22 percent on their first twenty-five thousand dollars in profits and 48 percent on everything above twenty-five thousand dollars. Those rules were changed gradually to reduce the tax rates on the smaller profits. By 1982, the rates were 16 percent on the first twenty-five thousand dollars, 19 percent on the next twenty-five thousand dollars, 30 percent on the third twenty-five thousand dollars, 40 percent on the fourth twenty-five thousand dollars, and 46 percent on everything of more than one hundred thousand dollars in profits. In 1983, tax rates on the first two categories were reduced to 15 percent and 18 percent respectively.

The 1986 Tax Reform Act reduced the number of tax brackets for corporations. Today, corporate taxable income of up to fifty thousand dollars is taxed at 15 percent. That portion of taxable income of more than fifty thousand dollars but not more than seventy-five thousand dollars is taxed at 25 percent. That portion that exceeds seventy-five thousand dollars is taxed at 34 percent. If the corporation has taxable income exceeding one hundred thousand dollars, then there is an additional 5 percent tax levied on that amount. This additional increment of tax is limited, however, to $11,750.

The corporate tax is, in effect, a double tax. First the corporation's income is taxed. When the income has been distributed to stockholders as dividends, the income is taxed again on the stockholder's individual income-tax return.

All states and many cities impose their own taxes on corporate profits. Some even tax the incomes of unincorporated businesses. That tax is often called a franchise tax, though it goes by a variety of names. It is, in effect, a tax on the right to conduct a business. An accountant or the applicable taxing authorities should be consulted to determine the specific tax requirements in your area.

The Internal Revenue Service has published an unusually clear *Tax Guide for Small Businesses* (Publication 334), which is revised annually and is available without charge from the nearest IRS office (see telephone white pages under *United States Government, Internal Revenue Service*) or by writing to the IRS (see Appendix C). *(See also: Accounting, Estimated Tax, Income Tax— Personal)*

Income Tax—Personal

For tax purposes, almost everything you earn from any source is considered income: wages, fees, dividends, interest, rent, profits, pensions, annuities, alimony, prizes and awards, jury-duty payment, tips, profit from the sale of real estate, and so on.

Income that does not have to be reported includes Veterans Administration benefits and disability payments, social-security benefits, life-insurance payments received by an individual at a person's death, workers' compensation or other benefits paid for injury or sickness, interest on certain state and municipal bonds, and money or other property that is inherited.

Who Must File?

Federal income-tax returns must be filed on or before April 15 each year by everyone whose income in the preceding year exceeded a certain minimum, depending on the taxpayer's status. The Internal Revenue Service publishes an annual list of minimum gross-income figures that require the filing of a tax return. Even if you are not required to file an income-tax return according to those figures, it is necessary to file if you were employed during the year and want to get a refund of income tax that was withheld.

Long Form or Short Form?

If you have taxable income of less than fifty thousand dollars and your income was solely from wages and you have no itemized deductions, you will generally find it easier to file the short Form 1040A as your federal income-tax return. If you also happen to be filing as single, under 65, not blind, and claiming no dependents, you may file the simpler Form 1040EZ. All you need do is record the amount of income paid and tax withheld as shown on the W-2 forms that are provided by the employer to every wage earner in January of the following year. The Internal Revenue Service allows a standard 16 percent deduction and calculates the tax due or the tax refund based on the number of dependent exemptions claimed.

Persons with larger incomes, self-employed income, or deductions beyond the standard 16 percent allowance must file Form 1040, calculate their tax, and send a check for the payment due or claim a refund.

Estimated-Tax Declaration

Taxpayers who have income from sources other than wages subject to payroll deduction must file a declaration of estimated tax when they file their income-tax return. Estimated taxes have to be paid in equal quarterly installments on April 15, June 15, September 15, and January 15. There are several ways to calculate the estimated tax, the most convenient being the use of the previous year's self-employed income as the basis for estimating the current year's tax obligations.

Telling the Truth

Intentional falsification of tax returns or even negligence can lead to severe penalties. Unintentional errors or deductions subject to interpretation may lead to a tax audit by the Internal Revenue Service (IRS). If you're not trying to defraud the government, the worst that can happen in such circumstances is that you'll be required to pay the shortage plus a penalty. The best that could happen is that the IRS tax examiner would agree that your tax return is correct.

The secret here is to have all the documents available to prove the claims you make. The initial examination of a federal tax return is usually made by a computer. If the computer finds something unusual, it refers the return to a pair of human eyes. For example, if you claim five thousand dollars in medical expenses and only eight thousand dollars in income, the computer will frown. That doesn't sound right. But if you have the receipts to prove that you really spent five thousand dollars on doctor bills, all will be well.

Hold on to every scrap of paper that supports your deductions for at least three years after the date of filing your tax return. Thereafter, you are not likely to be confronted with a tax examination or a need for those papers except in cases of fraud or if you omitted more than 25 percent of your gross income.

Where to Get Help
In most other cases, taxpayers will find that the cost of professional help in filling out the income-tax return often represents a saving in tax payments because professional tax preparers are more familiar with the latest regulations, what may be deducted and what may not be, and other intricacies of the tax laws. Be sure that whoever helps you knows his or her business. A fifteen-dollar tax preparer may be worth no more than that. Taxpayers can also get free help and advice from the nearest office of the Internal Revenue Service. *(See also: Accounting, Income, Income Averaging, Income Tax—Business, Tax)*

Industrial Design
Industrial design is nothing new. No matter what kind of product, it had to be designed before it could be produced by industry. But with the resurgence of consumer demand for mass-produced items that also incorporate some element of good design, major manufacturers have begun to seek industrial designers who are also thoroughly grounded in art and design. This has opened up numerous opportunities for craftspeople.

The pure crafts artist may find it unacceptable to design a refrigerator or a bath towel or a cookie cutter for mass production because the production process often imposes a need to adapt or compromise. Some believe, however, that by upgrading the appreciation for good design and good taste in such products—limited as the possibilities may sometimes seem—new customers will be developed for truly handcrafted design work. Besides, the fees for industrial design work often help a crafts artist to pursue his or her other craftwork under less economic pressure.

Schools such as Parson's Institute of Design, Pratt Institute, and Fashion Institute of Technology, all in New York City, offer courses in industrial design with special emphasis on textiles and similar consumer goods.

Finding a job or a commission in this field requires a considerable amount of digging and perseverance. If you think you are professionally and emotionally suited to do this kind of work, make a list of manufacturers of consumer goods in your area. Until you have a reputation, it is easiest to start locally, which does not require you to spend a large amount of time and money traveling around the country to introduce yourself.

Send your résumé with some slides or photographs of your work to these companies. Study what they are now producing so that your introductory letter can give them some indication of what you think you can do for them. Be sure that any original sketches you send out bear a copyright notice (such as © 1993 by John Doe). But if you contact a firm that makes dinnerware, for example, indicate that your experience includes both designing dinnerware that has sold successfully and an understanding of the production problems and processes.

The smaller the firm, the better your chance for an interview. Don't start with the likes of General Motors or Burlington Mills. They either have their own staffs of industrial and textile designers or deal with larger, established design firms.

An industrial-design commission should always be put into writing to avoid misunderstandings. The contract should specify what you are expected to do, when you are expected to do it, how much and when you will be paid (a flat fee or a royalty), who owns your design after you've completed it (usually the company that commissioned it, unless you're famous), and any other details that are important to the particular relationship. Have your lawyer look over the contract; you can be sure the company's lawyers will study it to protect their client. *(See also: Commission)*

Inland Marine Insurance *(See: Property Insurance)*

Installment
An installment is, by definition, a part of the whole. Thus, in an installment purchase or an installment loan, the whole amount is paid off in parts. Interest charges are added to the face amount, and the total is then divided into equal payments, usually on a monthly basis for one or more years.

In an installment purchase the buyer does not have full legal title to the property until the last installment has been paid. The seller can take the property back (repossess it), give no credit for what's already been paid, and sometimes claim the entire balance due as well.

Mortgages, automobile loans, and other long-term borrowing for major purchases are, in effect, installment loans, although they're not called that. The real estate, the car, or the equipment serves as security for the repayment of the loan and can be repossessed if the borrower fails to pay installments when they are due.

Interest rates on installment purchases are usually much higher than on bank loans. In many states such interest can reach 20 percent or more per year on short-term installment purchases. Many buyers find it more economical to borrow the money from a bank, pay off the installment-loan purchase in one lump sum, and repay the bank in monthly payments at the lower bank-loan rate.

Laws and regulations covering installment selling vary from state to state, but it is always wise to read the fine print on installment contracts before signing. *(See also: Contracts, Loans, Mortgage, Revolving Credit, Uniform Commercial Code)*

Installment Sales

Installment sales can also have important tax implications for the seller. An installment sale is any sale of property for which the payment is to be made over time in separate parts.

For tax purposes, if payments extend beyond a single tax year, then the installment method of taxation may be used. The installment method allows the taxable income resulting from the sale—which is equal to the selling price minus the seller's cost basis in the property sold—to be prorated over each payment received in the same proportion as the gross profit bears to the selling price. Thus, the tax is spread over the period of payments rather than all paid in the year of the sale.

For example, after a few years of service you sell the kiln you purchased. You agree to sell it for five hundred dollars; your basis in it is three hundred dollars. You sell it on an installment contract, taking one hundred dollars down and one hundred dollars per year for the next four years. Your gross profit is two hundred dollars, which is 40 percent of the total price. Thus, under the installment method, 40 percent of each installment payment is taxable income in the year that payment is received. The benefit, of course, is that you avoid having to pay all the tax in the year of the sale on the whole two hundred dollars, instead spreading your tax liability out over the full period of the installment contract.

You are entitled to make an irrevocable election out of installment-sales-tax treatment, but only if you do so in the year of the sale. This might be advantageous if, for example, you were expecting to be in a low tax bracket this year but a higher bracket in later years or if you had certain one-time losses to offset this year or if you simply did not want to be bothered with the paperwork for the next four years. Although, in the last instance, if the sale is large enough—such as a sale of real estate—the tax savings associated with installment-sales treatment can easily take the sting out of a little extra paperwork.

There are exceptions to installment-sales treatment. Dealer sales and sales of inventory of personal property are excluded. Dealer sales include sales of property by a person, such as a used-car dealer, who regularly sells property of the same type on installment contracts, and sales of real property that is held for resale to customers in the ordinary course of the taxpayer's trade or business.

As with all complicated tax issues, prior consultation with a qualified accountant or tax attorney is recommended if you are contemplating the use of, or election out of, installment-sales-tax treatment. *(See also: Depreciation)*

Insufficient Funds

When there is not enough money in a checking account to pay a check drawn against it, the bank marks the check *insufficient funds* or *NSF* (not sufficient funds) and returns it to the recipient who presented it for payment through the recipient's bank. For example, you take a check at a crafts fair in payment for a wall hanging. You deposit the check at your bank. Your bank sends it through to your customer's bank for collection. However, your customer doesn't have enough money on deposit to pay the check. Your customer's bank rubber-stamps the check *insufficient funds* or *no funds* or *no account*, as the case may be), and sends it back to your bank, which, in turn, sends it back to you. There's some colorful language to describe such checks. Since they've come right back to their starting point, they have bounced and are known as rubber checks. Your bank may add a nominal service charge to your monthly statement for handling such a check.

That's why it is so important to know the person from whom you accept a check. Usually it is an unintentional error. The person who gave you the check may have written it before a deposit had cleared. In that case you'll be told to deposit the check again, and it will usually clear the second time. If it does not, there's no third chance. Most banks will not handle such a check more than twice.

If the customer offers to write a new check, be sure it includes a reimbursement for the service charge your bank levied against you.

When the shoe is on the other foot—a check you wrote is returned to the recipient marked *insufficient funds*—you may get an angry phone call even though your intentions were honorable. Make sure you have enough money on deposit to tell the recipient to redeposit the check. If need be, tell him or her to redeposit it in three days or next week or whenever you know you can cover it.

Intentionally writing a check for which there are not sufficient funds on deposit can bring on a lawsuit. Keeping an accurate checkbook can avoid such difficulties. *(See also: Checking Account, Collection Problems, Overdrawn)*

Insurance

Everything in life is a risk, and insurance exists to reduce the consequences of some risks. An insurance policy is a transfer of some of the risk from your shoulders to those of the insurance company, in return for which you pay them a fee known as a premium.

It isn't quite that simple, of course. Some risks cannot be insured, some risks are not worth insuring, and some risks must be insured. To cite three examples: Betting on a horse is a risk that cannot be insured; throwing a pot that may turn out lopsided is a risk hardly worth insuring; driving a car is considered by many states a sufficiently high risk to require insurance by law.

There are some basic things that should be understood about insurance in order to buy wisely. These include the nature of risk, the types of insurance, insurable interest, what to insure, how much to buy, deductibles, telling the truth, and from whom to buy.

The Nature of Risk

Risks fall into two basic categories: pure risks, which can be insured, and speculative risks, which cannot. With a pure risk you have no choice in the outcome. If you own a building and a fire breaks out, there is a loss. Pure risks don't allow any other result but a loss.

With a speculative risk, on the other hand, you have a choice. You have a hand in controlling the risk and can, therefore, make a decision whether you want to take it. Going into business is itself a speculative risk. You might make money or you might not.

Types of Insurance

There are two general categories of insurance: personal and property. Personal includes life, accident, medical and hospital, public liability, and a few others. Property covers fire, theft, title, automobile, and minor types of insurance of little consequence in a crafts business.

Many of these are discussed in detail in this book under their appropriate alphabetical entries.

Insurable Interest

You cannot insure anything in which you have "no insurable interest"; that is, from which you would suffer no loss. You can insure a building you own against loss through fire, but you cannot insure the Empire State Building—unless you happen to own that too. You have no insurable interest in the Empire State Building. Similarly, you can insure the life of your family's breadwinner, but you cannot insure the life of the king of England—unless you are the queen of England. Again, you have no insurable interest.

The real test of insurable interest is whether you or the beneficiary of the insurance policy would suffer a loss if the risk covered by the policy came to pass. You need not even own a piece of property to have an insurable interest in it. The holder of a mortgage certainly has such an interest in a building on which he's made the mortgage loan. Nor need you be related to the person on whose life you take out a policy. An employer, for example, has an insurable interest in a key employee whose death might seriously damage the earning capability of the business.

The insurable interest must exist not only at the time the policy goes into effect but also at the time a claim is made. If you have a fire policy on a building that you subsequently sell and it then burns to the ground, you no longer have an insurable interest, even if you paid the premiums.

The exception is life insurance, for which the insurable interest needs to exist only at the time the policy is written. If, for example, you take out a policy on a key employee who subsequently leaves your employment, you can still collect in the event of his or her death, even many years later, as long as you continue to pay the premiums. Or if a big fight with your spouse leads to divorce and you remarry and live happily—almost—ever after, spouse number one can still collect on your life insurance if you have not instructed the insurance company to change the beneficiary on your policy.

It is sound judgment, therefore, to examine your policies periodically to determine what should remain in effect, what should be added, what can be canceled, and whether any of the beneficiaries should be changed.

What to Insure

On the assumption that craftspeople don't have unlimited funds to spend on insurance premiums, certain priorities must be established when you sit down to determine what to insure.

The first consideration has to be the risk in relation to your capability to survive it. Fire insurance is clearly a top priority. A serious fire can put you out of business. Even a minor fire can pose a serious loss if your productive activities are interrupted for any length of time.

With automobile insurance, liability takes precedence over collision. If a ten-thousand-dollar car is totally destroyed, you've lost ten thousand dollars. If, however, that same car gets into an accident without proper liability coverage, it could cost you one million dollars. Saving on the latter to pay for the former can be penny-wise and pound-foolish.

If you work at home, even if it's a totally separate shop or studio in your home, be sure you are properly covered. The ordinary homeowner policy does not include commercial or professional activities in its coverage. You can usually add your crafts activities to the homeowner policy at a fairly small premium.

If the worst anyone can steal from you is a few hundred dollars' worth of tools, you may not want to buy theft insurance. But if you're a jeweler with a tempting supply of gold and silver on hand, theft insurance may be essential. You have to make a list of priorities. If there are some items you can't afford to insure now, perhaps they can be insured later.

How Much to Buy

A big question always is, How much insurance do I need? In regard to property insurance, that depends to a large extent on the value of the property, how much of a loss you can sustain without insurance, and how much money is available for premium payments.

Underinsuring serves little purpose and can be expensive if trouble develops. Consider, for example, that you own the building where your pottery is located and that the building's current cash value is $125,000. Most fire-insurance policies require that you insure at least 80 percent of the fair market value or else you assume some of the risk yourself.

If you were to insure that $125,000 building for only seventy-five thousand dollars, that's 60 percent of the value. But it doesn't mean that the insurance company will pay your losses up to seventy-five thousand dollars and that you will pay the rest. If the particular policy requires 80 percent coverage and you buy only 60 percent, then the insurance company will pay only 60 percent of a claim. The rest is your responsibility. That's also known as coinsurance because you are, in effect, insuring yourself for part of the loss. It's rarely worth the risk. Expensive as fire insurance may be, few craftspeople can afford the chance of underinsuring or coinsuring.

Overinsuring is wasteful, because property-insurance policies do not pay off the face value of the policy, only the actual loss up to the face value. Again, the $125,000 shop—only now it is insured for $250,000 and you are paying a higher premium for the higher coverage. Even if the shop were totally destroyed, you would still collect only $125,000.

The major exception to this rule is life insurance. Since no one can place a dollar value on a human life, the purchaser of life insurance is entitled to determine how much insurance is desirable or necessary, and the entire amount is paid to the beneficiaries when the insured dies.

It is essential that property-insurance policies be reviewed periodically to determine whether the face value is still appropriate. You may have installed an expensive piece of equipment, or the property itself may have increased in value, in which case the policy should be increased. If the property has decreased in value, you can save some money in premiums by reducing the coverage.

But whatever you do, don't buy a particular policy simply because it seems cheap. Many factors enter into the determination of premiums, including not only fine-print inclusions and exclusions of coverage but also the insurance company's strictness in claims settlements, its financial condition, and so on. Know exactly what you are buying, and compare apples with apples.

Deductibles

Many insurance policies have a deductible clause. This is particularly true in automobile-collision insurance and in many medical plans. It means that the policyholder pays part of the claim—say the first fifty dollars or 10 percent of the total—or it establishes a waiting period after which benefits go into effect. Insurance companies do this to weed out the numerous small claims that cost more in paperwork than they are worth. In return, the difference in premium costs makes it worthwhile. If it costs you fifty dollars extra in premiums to get full coverage and remove a one-hundred-dollar deductible, you are paying a premium rate of 50 percent on that one hundred dollars worth of insurance, which is very high.

Telling the Truth

A key ingredient of every insurance policy is that the applicant tells the truth in the application. It's not only what you include in the truth but, even more important, what you leave out. In official language these are known as representations. The premise is that the insurance company is prepared to shoulder the risk, based on information you furnish. If you leave out anything that could affect their decision, one of two serious consequences can result: The policy can be canceled or, if the false or misleading statements are discovered after a claim is made, the claim may be denied.

For example, if you apply for fire insurance and tell the insurance company you've had no fires in the past ten years, they will assume that you take proper safety precautions and are a good risk. So they write the policy. But then you have a fire, and in the course of the investigation it is discovered that you had three fires in the last two years. Had the insurance company known that, it might never have issued the policy, or it might have set a much higher premium. It will fight your claim and probably win.

Similarly, even if you are in perfect health, the insurance company still has a right to know that your hobby is skydiving. It could affect the premiums it will charge or whether it will write a policy at all. It's better to tell all up front than run into a losing argument after the fact.

Where to Buy Insurance

Insurance is available through three sources: independent agents, brokers, or directly from the insurance company.

The bulk of property insurance is written by independent agents and brokers. Since they represent a number of insurance companies, they can provide you with the best coverage suited to your needs. They are in a position to issue a binder on your property the moment you telephone them, and you are insured from that moment on. Since they are usually also your neighbors, they can sit down with you and analyze your insurance needs, and they are nearby when a claim has to be settled.

A great deal of life insurance is written directly by the insurance companies through their own salesmen. Obviously, they sell only their product and, therefore, are not in a position to give you impartial advice on the merits and demerits of the policies issued by different companies. But settling a claim is a fairly uncomplicated matter. The insured either has or has not passed away.

Automobile and medical insurance can often be bought through the mail—without salesmen. This may save some money in premiums since there are no commissions to pay, but it removes the personal touch, especially when there's a claim to settle.

Selecting an insurance broker or independent agent should be done with the same care as choosing a lawyer or an accountant. It should be a professional relationship. The stakes can be very high. Consult other craftspeople or businesspeople whose judgment you respect. Settle on one agent or broker to handle all your insurance business. He or she will have a greater interest in you, and you're likely to get better service.

Craftspeople who want to dig more deeply into insurance matters can send for an excellent, nontechnical booklet published by the Small Business Administration (SBA): *Insurance and Risk Management for Small Business* (see Appendix C). In addition, *Insurance Checklist for Small Business* is available without charge from the SBA (see Appendix C), or from SBA field offices in major cities.

Not included in this discussion of insurance matters are personal insurance policies such as automobile policies and medical and hospital policies. It should be remembered that some insurance is compulsory, such as automobile insurance in most states; some, such as medical insurance, is voluntary. Almost anything can be insured. You can even buy insurance against bad weather at a crafts show, but the premiums are high because the risk is great. *(See also: Disability Income Insurance, Fine-Arts Floater, Group Insurance, Liability Insurance, Life Insurance, Product-Liability Insurance, Property Insurance, Unemployment Insurance, Workers' Compensation)*

Intellectual Property

Intellectual property is the collective term used to identify the ownership rights in various types of intangible property, including copyright, which protects original expression when reduced to a tangible form; patent, which protects new, useful, and nonobvious technological innovations, such as for inventions and functional design; trademark, which protects symbolic information used to identify particular goods and services; and trade secret, which protects any formula, pattern, or compilation of information used in one's business to obtain an advantage over one's competitors who do not know or use it. In recent years, the right of publicity has developed to enable individuals such as sports figures and actors to protect and exploit the economic value of their celebrity status. *(See also: Copyright, Patent, Trademark, Trade Secret)*

Interest

This word has both legal and financial meanings.

In legal terms it means that you have some claim to a certain property. For example, if you and a partner each invest one thousand dollars in a crafts business, you each have a half-interest in the business.

In financial terms, interest is money earned in exchange for the use of money. If you think of money as a product that you rent—much as you might rent a car—the interest is the price you pay for the use of that product.

If you borrow one hundred dollars from a bank at 8 percent annual interest, you are, in effect, paying the bank eight dollars rent for the use of its money for one year. Similarly, if you put one hundred dollars in a savings account at 6 percent annual interest, the savings bank is paying you six dollars rent for the use of your money for one year. The same principle applies if you buy bonds. You are lending your money at a specified rate of interest.

Interest rates are usually quoted on an annual basis, even if the period to which they apply is shorter. The interest rate on a department store charge account, for instance, may be quoted at 18 percent per annum. However, if your balance is one hundred dollars and you pay it off at the end of the month, you will pay only $1.50 in interest (one-twelfth of the annual amount, which in this case would be eighteen dollars).

Maximum interest rates are often set by state law. The present trend among states, however, is to deregulate the amount or percentage of interest that can be charged, relying instead on laws requiring lenders to disclose the rate of interest charged and the total amount to be paid by the borrower.

The financial world uses a whole host of interest terminology. For small businesses such as crafts, two terms are of concern: simple interest and compound interest.

Simple interest is calculated on the amount of money involved in the loan and is either paid to the lender when the principal is repaid at the end of the loan period or is included in the calculation of the periodic payments due. It does not itself accrue interest. This form of interest is most common when you borrow money.

Compound interest is paid on the principal plus previously accrued interest. The previously accrued interest, in effect, keeps increasing the amount upon which later interest is calculated. Bank interest used to be calculated quarterly. With the introduction of computers, it is now usually calculated daily so that the amount on deposit grows every day, and interest is paid on a higher amount each day. That explains why an annual rate of 6 percent will return, or yield, not six dollars but approximately $6.18 on every one-hundred-dollar deposit.

Maneuvering your money to earn the best interest can make a contribution to your profit picture. You may be saving to buy a new piece of equipment, or you may have just earned a bundle at a crafts show. Keeping those funds in a non-interest checking account makes no sense. Even if you deposit them in a savings account for only a few months, the money grows. Five hundred dollars can earn more than twelve dollars in six months. It may not be much, but better in your pocket than theirs. You'd probably have to sell more than sixty dollars' worth of craftwork to clear twelve dollars.

The interest rate on charge accounts and credit cards can be deceptive because the monthly amount seems small. If you finance a one-thousand-dollar piece of equipment at 12 percent for one year and make monthly payments, your total finance charge will be $66.19. If you borrow the money from a bank at 8 percent, pay off the equipment in one lump sum, and repay the bank in twelve monthly installments, the finance charge amounts to only $43.86. *(See also: Banks, Checking Account, Credit Card, Loans, Mortgage)*

Interior Decorators and Designers

The two terms are interchangeable, although some people think there's more prestige attached to the word *designer* than to *decorator*. One interior designer said she likes to think of herself as an interior architect since she makes sketches and is consulted on structural situations as they affect interior planning. "Interior decorators," she said, "are suburban ladies who run to antique stores to buy things for their friends at a discount." That kind of snobbery, of course, does not alter the facts.

The facts for craftspeople are that the services of interior designers and decorators can be excellent marketing outlets for craftwork. They are particularly interested in textile design, fabrics, furniture, lamps, and decorative objects. For major projects they may specify particular dimensions, color schemes, materials, design concepts, and so on. In addition to the fee they receive from their clients, they usually get a discount on the materials they buy (craftwork included) of between 10 and 30 percent off the retail price.

Interior designers and decorators can be found in the yellow pages of the telephone book. It is best to contact them by letter, enclosing a résumé and several photographs of your work. A personal invitation to visit your shop or studio, to see an exhibition of your work, or to stop by your booth at a crafts show often produces interest that can ultimately lead to sales. Interior-design work ranges from small projects such as a living room in someone's home to elaborate assignments to decorate a large hotel or an office building. A good connection can, therefore, be lucrative.

Since their stock-in-trade is good taste and new ideas, decorators and designers are constantly on the lookout for imaginative craftwork and innovative design concepts, especially one-of-a-kind objects. *(See also: Architects, Commission, Orders)*

Inventory

In the truest sense, inventory means everything you own that's movable and the value of those things. That would include the tools you work with, the chair you sit on, even stationery and paper clips. For the purpose of this book, however, inventory consists of everything you own that ultimately becomes a salable product: raw materials, work in progress, and finished work ready for shipping.

Every item in your inventory started out as a business expense and will —hopefully—end up as business income. In between it's all part of your assets and has a significant bearing on your money supply and your tax situation.

Million-dollar companies have teetered on the brink of bankruptcy because their millions were tied up in inventories, and they couldn't pay their bills. It may seem right to buy a ton of clay because it's cheaper than buying a hundred pounds twenty times, but it's not if that leaves you short of cash to run your pottery business. It may save production costs to make a thousand rings at a time and put them on the shelf, but it saves nothing if there's no money left to go to crafts shows to sell the rings. Inventories at both ends—raw materials and finished goods—have to be balanced carefully against available money supply, production capacity, and sales potential.

Having an inventory of finished goods presents a particular set of opportunities and problems.

Some of the advantages are:

1. Craftwork is always ready to ship; no need to start production when an order comes in;

2. It is usually more economical to make up a quantity of a given item than to make up one or two;

3. You can be ready for a crafts show or some other opportunity on a moment's notice;

4. If you sell at retail, you have a wide variety of products from which your customers can choose.

Some of the problems are:

1. Inventory represents an investment of money;

2. You need considerable storage space;

3. If your type of craft requires a wide variety of sizes or colors or shapes, the inventory will have to be extremely large to be complete;

4. The slow sellers that stay on the shelf must be eliminated so that you can invest the money in something profitable.

It becomes fairly evident that a beginning craftsperson is ill-advised to build up a sizable inventory. After you have determined that certain items move well, perhaps you can get your feet wet by putting several dozen of these in inventory. But remember that tastes change, the public is fickle, and if it's a trendy object, be careful.

Turnover

The key to a successful inventory is turnover. This means how many times in a given period, usually a year, you sell and replenish your complete inventory—how often your investment in inventory turns over. It's important in relation to your money supply and the return you get on your investment. If you invest one thousand dollars in time and material for craftwork that is put on the shelf and everything sells, you get back your original one thousand dollars plus—for purposes of this example—$250 in profit. The original one thousand dollars goes right back into producing more inventory; no need for more capital. If your inventory turns over twice during the year, you will have made five hundred dollars. But suppose it turns over five times—in other words, you sell and replenish the stock five times during the year. You will realize $1,250 on that same one-thousand-dollar inventory investment. Obviously, profits aren't quite that sensational in real life, but the principle is clear.

Inventory Control

Keeping careful records of what goes in and out of inventory is necessary as a guide to your production operations and to weed out those items that move slowly and, therefore, retard turnover and put a drain on your money. Your system can be manual or computerized.

Since the dollar value of inventory is needed to determine your annual net income for tax purposes, a *physical inventory* should be taken at least once a year as close to the end of the taxable year as possible. That involves the actual counting of all the pieces that are in inventory and recording the count together with the value of the pieces at what it cost to produce them—not counting the potential profit if they are sold. In other words, the price tag you put on an item is usually not the determining factor since it is generally higher than the cost of producing that item. Only when you sell work below what it actually costs to produce, such as you do with seconds, can the market value be used.

While direct labor costs are part of the costs of production and even some management expenses can be included, selling expenses can never be counted as production costs for inventory purposes, although they are deductible as other expenses.

To keep abreast of your inventory from day to day or month to month, a *perpetual inventory* control system is extremely useful. This need not be a complicated affair. If your inventory consists of a variety of items, it is best to use a loose-leaf book with one page for each item or even for each color or size of an item that is produced in various colors and sizes. Divide the page into four columns with the headings: Date, In, Out, Balance. Whenever you put items into stock or take them out of stock, you list the quantity under the appropriate column and the new balance in the final column. This enables you to see at a glance how much is in stock at all times and how fast each item is moving. If you mark a reorder quantity at the top of the page, you can compare that number with the current balance and know whether it's time to make more of the same. This will help not only in controlling what type of item goes into stock but in determining if particular colors or sizes of one item move better than others.

Why take a physical inventory if you keep a careful perpetual inventory? Experience has show that the two almost never agree. Breakage, theft, and small errors in record keeping inevitably occur during the year. The physical inventory is the only one that comes close to 100 percent accuracy, and that's what's needed for tax purposes as well as your own business information.

Since inventory represents the cost of work that was not sold, it becomes part of your final gross profit and can therefore increase or decrease your tax liability. Suppose, for example, that your total receipts during the year were twenty thousand dollars. Your inventory at the beginning of the year was two thousand dollars and at the end of the year was twenty-five hundred dollars. Your cost of production during the year—raw materials, labor, overhead, and so on—totaled eight thousand dollars. Those figures appear in the following table:

Total Receipts		$20,000
Beginning Inventory	$ 2,000	
Cost of Production	8,000	
Total		$10,000
Less Year-End Inventory	2,500	
Net Cost		$ 7,500
Gross Profit		$12,500

By carefully controlling inventory you can change your tax liability by changing your gross profit. If, for example, all the other figures in the preceding problem remain the same but you decide to produce less during the latter part of the year to reduce your year-end inventory, you would then work with this set of figures:

Total Receipts		$20,000
Beginning Inventory	$ 2,000	
Cost of Production	8,000	
	Total	$10,000
Less Year-End Inventory	1,000	
	Net Cost	$ 9,000
	Gross Profit	$11,000

The lower your year-end inventory, the lower your gross profit—and, therefore, your tax liability. The actual physical count at the end of the year allows you to remove shopworn, broken, and pilfered items from inventory; write them off as a loss; and reduce your inventory even further in terms of dollars. This is also valuable to reduce taxes for craftspeople in states or localities that impose an inventory tax.

This can be a complicated business. It is wise to consult an accountant before the end of the year—while there's still time to do something about problems you have. (See also: Multiple Production, Production, Turnover)

Investment

The money you put into some property with the expectation of a financial return is called an investment. The return can take various forms: stock dividends, an increase in the value of real estate, profits from the use of equipment.

Investments are generally of a long-term nature, and they generally expect a reliable return at relatively low risk. Though it doesn't always work out that way—look at the stock market—that's the hope when the investment is made.

Speculation is the opposite of investment. Speculation can bring a high return but always at great risk of loss. Buying a racetrack is an investment; putting money on a horse is speculation—or is it the other way around?

The essential difference between investments and other ways of spending your money is that ordinary expenses are expected to produce satisfaction for some want or need, and investments are expected to produce more money. It is, in fact, how much money you make on every dollar you invest that determines the quality of an investment. An ordinary savings account may pay 6 percent, or bring a 6 percent rate of return. A corporate stock may bring 8 percent. A bigger kiln may enable you to make more pots and increase your profit by 10 percent. This is a simplistic way of stating the case, but it serves to illustrate the point. Calculating the actual return on investment is best left to an accountant.

A consideration when making an investment is how readily it can be reconverted into cash if the need arises—its *liquidity*. A savings account is easily convertible: Just take the money out of the bank. A publicly traded corporate stock may increase or decrease in value, and you may not be able to sell when you want to without taking a beating, but stock is still considered relatively liquid. Used equipment, however, is a difficult investment to convert into cash.

All of these factors influence whether you make a particular investment and, also, the rate of return. If you want to keep your cash position truly liquid, a savings account may be the best investment, even if it doesn't bring the best return. However, if you must invest in a new piece of equipment or go out of business, then other considerations such as risk, liquidity, or rate of return are laid aside.

Unfortunately, the investment of creative energy, artistic skill, devotion, and love that you make in your craftwork is never calculated by accountants—or you'd be rich.

Invoice

The invoice (also called bill) serves two purposes: It lists in detail what was sold, at what prices and under what conditions, and how and where it was shipped; and it is the official request for payment.

Whether you use an elaborate printed invoice form with many duplicate copies or simply your letterhead or a plain sheet of paper—with at least one copy—every invoice should contain the following information:

1. An invoice number. These should be numbered in sequence.

2. Your name, address, telephone number.

3. The date of the invoice.

4. The name and address of the customer. Be sure to follow instructions if an order specifies that an invoice be directed to a particular department, such as the accounting department of a large store.

5. Where the merchandise was shipped.

6. When and how the merchandise was shipped (United Parcel Service, parcel post, and so on).

7. Payment terms, such as 2/10-net 30.

8. Claims limitations, such as accepting damage claims only if made within ten days of receipt of the merchandise.

9. The quantity, exact description, unit price, and total price of each item shipped. Where the same item is shipped in different sizes or colors, listing each one separately.

10. The total price for all items.

11. Sales taxes if any.

12. Shipping charges if any.

13. The grand total.

The original copy of the invoice is sent to the customer. You keep at least one copy in numerical order in an unpaid file. Mark the date you receive payment on the bill and transfer it to the paid file when the bill has been paid. This provides an easy check on what bills are outstanding and which are past due.

If you have a large volume of business that is billed, you may want to keep two copies: one to file under unpaid or paid, the other to file in a separate folder for each customer. That provides you with a handy reference on the purchasing record of each customer. Checking such files periodically may also remind you that it's time to call about a reorder.

Some large stores often require a blind copy of the invoice to be included in the shipment as a packing slip so that the store's receiving department can check the shipment against the packing slip. Blind means that the packing slip copy of the invoice shows everything except the prices. When the shipment has been verified, the packing slip is sent along to the accounting department as proof that the merchandise was received in good order and payment can be made.

If numerous copies of an invoice have to be prepared, it is usually best to get the invoices in preprinted carbon or carbonless sets. These sets normally provide a different color for each copy and also block out the price area on the packing slip. They also indicate who gets each copy: customer, file, packing slip, and so on.

Numbering invoices is essential for many reasons. It makes it easy to identify the particular invoice when you need to speak to a customer about it. It enables you to match a check with the invoice that is being paid, because checks from stores or other business firms almost always indicate the invoice number for which the check is drawn. If a packing slip is used, it will enable the accounting department to coordinate the receiving-department report with its outstanding invoices and expedite payment to you.

The grand total should never reflect such discounts as a 2 percent allowance if the bill is paid within ten days. Mark your copy of the invoice when payment is received to indicate that the discount was taken.

This cash-discount policy is one you have to be tough about. If you allow 2 percent for payment within ten days, then that's it. Some customers try to take the discount even when they pay in thirty or more days. Money is too hard to come by to allow that sort of thing. A few daring souls may even add a 2 percent surcharge if the bill is paid later than thirty days, but that's not strictly legal unless both parties agreed to it as a condition of the sale.

There's an exception, however. If you have a regular store customer to whom you make shipments every month or so and it is that store's policy to pay bills on the fifth of every month, then you'll probably have to allow the 2 percent discount even if it isn't within ten days. You could, of course, send the bill on the twenty-fifth or thereabouts. But whenever you send it, as long as the customer sticks to his regular payment date, you have accomplished the same purpose.

The conditions you set for returns or damage claims protect you against an occasional wise-guy customer. Say a store buys four dozen appliqué pillows from you. Two weeks later, the buyer finds a source for pillows that is less expensive, so he or she returns your pillows with hardly an explanation. The returns-within-five-days clause protects you. Of course, if it's a good customer, you may not want to make a fuss and should just take the pillows back. Then again, you may tell him nothing doing, and you have the law on your side. If the customer has a legitimate gripe—that the pillows aren't the color he or she ordered, for example—the customer should be able to discover that within five days.

The reverse of this situation applies when you receive a bill from a supplier for materials you bought. Examine the merchandise right away. Read the invoice carefully to see what your claim and return privileges are and what kind of cash discounts you're entitled to. *(See also: Business Forms, Orders, Sales Tax, Sales Terms, Shipping, Statement)*

Job Ticket

The term *job ticket* comes from the printing craft and has been adapted to many activities for which a variety of items is produced for a variety of customers.

A numbered job ticket or production envelope is prepared for each order. It enables the crafts producer to keep track of all the details and expenses connected with that order. If you decide to make one hundred pots for inventory, treat that like an order as well. The front of the 9 × 12-inch manila envelope lists the customer's name, address, order number, shipping information, delivery date, and the specification of the order, such as thirty wooden bowls #12.

The job ticket travels with the order through all the stages of production right to the shipping table. The back of the envelope is used to record the materials as they are used, time as it is spent, and any other factors that influence the cost of filling that order. When the time comes to add up all the costs in both labor and materials, a glance at the job ticket brings all the cost factors into sharp focus.

Any papers connected with the production of that order can be stuffed into the envelope. Each job ticket has its own number, and that number is associated with the order from the moment it comes in until shipment is made. If the job tickets are filed in numerical sequence after the order is completed and the number is indicated on all other records such as invoices and shipping receipts, it is easy to trace the history of a specific order and to determine what was involved in filling that order.

A simplified version is to set up a loose-leaf notebook, with each page serving the same purpose as the job ticket. This may be useful in a small crafts business where it is not necessary to have the job ticket move through the shop or studio with the order or where it's unnecessary to keep papers in the envelope.

The point of this system is not to create more paperwork but to arrive at more accurate pricing through more accurate cost records. The system also reduces the amount of information you have to remember and search for and, therefore, clears your head for more creative and productive pursuits. *(See also: Production, Systems)*

Joint Venture

A joint venture is a partnership for a specific or restricted purpose. For example, a leather worker and a buckle maker might form a joint venture to produce complete belts. Generally, the rules governing joint ventures are the same as those governing partnerships. *(See also: Contracts, Corporation, Limited Liability Companies, Partnership, Sole Proprietorship)*

Journals *(See: Ledgers and Journals)*

Keogh Plan *(See: Pensions)*

Labeling *(See: Textile Fiber Products Identification Act, Wool Products Labeling Act)*

Labor *(See: Apprentice, Employees)*

Lawyers
"I want to see a lawyer!"
That plaintive cry is heard most often when someone gets into a peck of

trouble. But most lawyers are not Perry Mason, keeping people out of jail by dint of clairvoyant detective work and facile courtroom oration. And most people fortunately do not need lawyers for so serious a purpose.

However, it is a rare individual who can get through the complications of an entire twentieth-century lifetime without ever having a need for a lawyer, particularly if that person conducts business activities. Lawyers, like doctors, are needed not only to solve problems, but to prevent them.

Like doctors or craftspeople, lawyers specialize. Because the law has become so intricate, some handle only corporation law, others specialize in divorce, still others take only criminal cases, and a relatively small group of specialists excel in arts or crafts law. Yet there are still thousands of general practitioners who are well versed in the ordinary problems that many face sooner or later: buying a house, signing a contract, making a will, setting up a business venture.

Of course, you don't need a lawyer every time you sign something. A contract for a booth at a crafts fair, for example, is rarely worth the expense of legal advice. Instead you might do well to follow the rule the New York State Bar Association provides: Get a lawyer's advice whenever you run into serious problems concerning your freedom, your financial situation, your domestic affairs, or your property. *Serious* is the important word in that sentence.

Legal matters fall into two basic classifications: civil cases and criminal cases. Civil cases concern such disputes as breach of contract, product liability, and personal injury. A lawyer is necessary in such cases to protect your rights. In the proper conduct of your business and personal affairs, a lawyer helps to prevent complications that could result in a civil case and represents you in either bringing or defending a lawsuit when your legal interests are involved.

Criminal cases concern violations of the criminal law, such as murder, theft, and forgery. In such cases the government accuses a person of committing a specific crime. The United States Constitution presumes that a person is innocent until proved guilty and provides that every criminal defendant is entitled to a lawyer, even if the government has to pay the lawyer's fees in the event that the defendant does not have the resources to hire a lawyer.

If you are ever confronted with a criminal matter that could lead to loss of liberty or property, the first call you should make is to a lawyer. Don't ever plead guilty to anything—except perhaps a parking ticket—without first consulting a lawyer. What may seem like an insignificant situation could well lead to serious consequences if you don't have proper legal advice. This applies to civil matters as well. The wording of a long-term contract, for example, may seem plain enough, but do you know how a court would interpret it?

When you discuss a case with your lawyer, do not hesitate to discuss the fee as well. Fees depend generally upon the amount of time, research, and skills of your lawyer. On simple matters, such as incorporating a business or drawing up a will, the time element is well established, and a fee can easily be determined. For more complicated cases you may receive no more than an estimate of the possible costs. In this case it may be better to hire an experienced lawyer who charges more per hour than an inexperienced one who bills at a lower rate but may take more time to learn the area of law involved in your case.

Some lawsuits, especially those involving the recovery of money in accident cases, are often handled on a contingency-fee basis. This means the lawyer gets between 25 and 50 percent of the amount awarded if the case is won but nothing if the case is lost—court costs and filing fees must, however, be paid by the client.

Communications between a lawyer and a client are held by law to be confidential. A lawyer cannot be compelled—indeed, is not permitted—to reveal what you discuss unless you give your permission. But you should realize that this confidential relationship exists to enable your lawyer to get all the information, even such information as may be unfavorable to you. Be sure to tell your lawyer everything, even the sordid details. It's the only way your lawyer can properly prepare a case and best protect your interests.

Where Do You Find a Good Lawyer?

Since all lawyers are licensed, it is a matter of finding someone in whom you can have confidence, much as you would find a doctor or any other professional in whom you put trust. Ask your friends or business acquaintances to recommend someone they have found satisfactory. You may want to talk to several lawyers before you settle on someone with whom you can establish that special relationship of confidence. The local bar association may be able to recommend someone if you have a problem that requires specialized legal expertise. If your resources are limited, your local legal aid organization may be of help, although these services rarely assist with business matters.

The better part of wisdom is to have a lawyer before you need one because sooner or later you probably will.

For information—and possibly free legal service—on problems related specifically to your work as a crafts artist, contact a Volunteer Lawyers for the Arts (VLA) organization if one exists in your state (see Appendix A).

For a book that sensitizes you to many of the legal issues that you may encounter in your crafts business, see *The Law (In Plain English)® for Crafts-people* (see Appendix C).

Lease

Reading the fine print is never more important than when you sign a lease. It's harder to get out of than a marriage contract.

A lease is a contract between landlord and tenant, and as does any other contract it spells out the responsibilities of and benefits to both parties. If you are renting, it is good to remember that leases are generally drawn up by the landlord's lawyer. They are usually weighted heavily on the landlord's side.

Some clauses should be obvious: how much the rent is, when it has to be paid, a description of the premises you are renting, the term, or the length, of the lease.

The fine-print clauses are not as straightforward, however. Who is responsible for painting the place? What restrictions are there on remodeling? (Some leases don't even allow you to put a nail in the wall without the landlord's permission.) Who pays for heat and hot water? What type of sign will you be allowed to use?

As a crafts professional, it is important that you carefully inspect the premises you are renting before you sign the lease. A thorough look around the place should help to answer such questions as: Will the floor sustain the weight of heavy equipment you use in your work? Can the electric wiring carry the load of heavy-duty equipment such as kilns? If it can't, whose responsibility is it to install the proper wiring? Are there any zoning, pollution, noise, or other restrictions that would affect your use of the premises?

Such an inspection should also raise other questions. Don't take for granted, for example, that the air conditioners in the windows will stay there after you move in or that you won't be charged with an extra fee above the stated rent to keep them.

Inspect carefully to see that everything is in good repair: water supply, radiators, bathrooms, windows, floors, ceilings. The lease should specify whose responsibility it is to fix such things if they break during the course of your lease. A tenant must realize, however, that the more responsibility there is on the landlord's shoulder, the higher the rent is likely to be.

Remember also that every request for repairs or improvements carries the possibility of lengthy debate and argument with the landlord. He or she will obviously want to save the money. If the lease gives you the right and the responsibility to do such work, be certain that you do not need to obtain the landlord's permission for every dab of paint you put on the wall. If the landlord is unwilling to give carte blanche for painting without prior permission, at least try to get a provision that the landlord's permission will not be unreasonably withheld. That will give you some basis on which to argue when your creative instincts later demand specific decorating and remodeling changes.

If the lease specifies that you pay for your own utilities such as gas, water, and electricity, make certain that separate meters are installed for your premises. Sharing the landlord's meter almost always leads to arguments when the bill comes in.

The lease should specify as well the terms of any remodeling you might wish to do. If you want to fix up the place by putting in walls and partitions, for example, or new wiring or light fixtures, the lease should provide for such things, with the only stipulations being that the end result meets all legal standards such as fire and building regulations and that it doesn't lower the value of the landlord's property or increase the landlord's insurance rates.

If the lease does not otherwise specify it, any permanent installation by a tenant—new wiring, for example, or a new sink—usually becomes part of the premises. You can't just rip out the wiring when you move out. If you plan to install permanent fixtures that you want to take with you, make sure the lease allows it. Determine also whether everything you see on the premises before you sign the lease will still be there after you sign it; the previous tenant may not have removed all of his or her property. Verbal promises by the landlord mean nothing. Get it in writing in the lease.

One area of landlord responsibility that the tenant should rarely assume is the basic structural condition of the premises or other conditions required by law. If it rains through the roof, the landlord should fix it. If the fire department issues a structural violation, it is the landlord's responsibility to fix it, unless the tenant created the violation. The lease should be specific on this subject.

Some craftspeople have found themselves in lots of trouble when they opened workshops or studios in premises leased for residential purposes. If it's a small and quiet affair, there's usually no trouble. But if the lease or the zoning regulations prohibit such activities, you can run into difficulties on two counts: The landlord may want more rent for the commercial use of the space; and neighbors may complain if extensive noise, odor, refuse, or objectionable conditions are associated with the improper use of the premises.

The end of the lease is as important as the beginning. Every lease includes a clause that the tenants leave the premises in the same condition as when they moved in. The deposit required by most landlords is one way in which they make sure that you pay for repairs that have to be made after you move out to restore the place to its original condition.

A sublease clause is also important. If you find it necessary to move out before the lease expires, do you have the right to find a new tenant to fill the remaining term of your lease? If you have that right, does the landlord have veto power? Can the landlord, for example, determine that a certain type of tenant is undesirable?

If the lease expires and you do want to renew, that is something else again. Suppose you sign a two-year lease with an option to renew. Does it specify at what rent you renew? When do you have to exercise the option? What happens if you don't exercise the option? In some states, the law assumes that you have renewed the lease and all its terms if you have not notified the landlord otherwise in writing by a certain date. In other cases, your lease may have expired but you remain on a month-to-month basis. In the absence of a lease at that time, the landlord can charge you anything he or she wants, unless the original lease specifies otherwise.

It is necessary, therefore, to carefully read all the terms of the lease, taking nothing for granted. Think carefully, too, about the implications of everything you sign. Be wary of the so-called standard lease.

If the lease is of any extensive term, or if you intend to make a major investment in improvements, it is advisable to consult a lawyer. Tell your lawyer what your requirements are, what you want to do and don't want to do, and let the lawyer analyze the fine print to make sure that your interests are properly protected.

Ledgers and Journals

Ledgers and journals are bookkeeping records in which the various financial transactions of a business are recorded.

The journal is the initial method of keeping the records, and no extensive bookkeeping expertise is required. Many businesses keep several journals: one in which to list all sales, one for expenses, one for wages, one for accounts receivable, and so forth.

While some large firms with complicated financial dealings may also keep several ledgers for different purposes, a crafts business usually has only one: the general ledger. The information recorded in the general ledger is based on the entries in the journals and is listed side by side in columns marked *debit* (expenses or liabilities) and *credit* (income or assets). Although an experienced bookkeeper can maintain a satisfactory ledger for an uncomplicated business operation, it is usually wise for a small business to engage the services of an accountant to keep the ledger up-to-date, based on journal entries or other records that the owner maintains. *(See also: Accounting, Bookkeeping, Credit, Debit)*

Legality *(See: Lawyers)*

Letter of Credit

A letter of credit is a special bank document in which a bank notifies its agent or correspondent bank that funds are to be paid immediately to the person named in the letter upon proper identification and evidence that the purpose for which the funds are to be paid has been accomplished. A bill of lading, for example, would be shown to prove that shipment was made. A letter of credit replaces the use of a check for payment and makes the money immediately available. In effect, it establishes a credit line for the recipient upon which he can draw as soon as the specifications of the letter of credit are carried out. Letters of credit are used primarily for large transactions and for foreign payments. *(See also: Uniform Commercial Code)*

Liabilities

Liabilities are what you owe others in terms of money, goods, or services. Bills you haven't paid are liabilities. Goods you haven't shipped to customers when you've already been paid for them are liabilities as well.

There are basically two types of liabilities: current and long-term. Current liabilities include all obligations that are due in the current fiscal year. Long-term liabilities are obligations that stretch over a number of years: a mortgage, a bank loan, or the payout on a piece of equipment such as a car.

Liabilities and assets appear together on the balance sheet, which is prepared at least once a year. In a sound and healthy business, assets are larger than liabilities. The difference can be taken as profit, or, if it remains in the business, it becomes an addition to your investment. *(See also: Assets, Balance Sheet)*

Liability Insurance

Any injury for which you or your business can be sued can be covered by liability insurance. Such insurance also covers injury caused to others by the negligence of your employees, but it does not cover the employees themselves.

There are several forms of liability insurance of concern to craft producers:

1. *Personal Liability.* This can protect you as an individual if, for example, your dog bites the letter carrier or someone slips on the ice in front of your house.

2. *Public Liability.* This protects you as a business owner if, for example, a customer suffers an injury while visiting your studio or workshop.

3. *Product Liability.* This protects you if a defect in a crafts object you made causes injury to the user of the product.

Some craftspeople buy specific short-term liability insurance to cover themselves at a crafts show or fair in case a visitor is injured at their booth. *(See also: Insurance, Product-Liability Insurance)*

License

A license is a grant of authority or permission for one to engage in some activity in which he or she would not otherwise be legally able to participate absent such authority. For example, states grant drivers' licenses and business licenses, and municipalities grant licenses to pet owners. In these instances, the purpose for the license is, presumably, to protect the public from certain dangerous activities or unscrupulous practices. Sometimes the purpose of the license is to collect revenue. Most people comply—if not with the concept, at least with the requirements for licensing.

Another form of license of interest to the crafts businessperson is the private-license agreement. As with a license under government authority, a private license grants authority to engage in a certain activity. Here, though, the activity is usually the use for commercial purposes of the owner's, the licenser's, rights in some creative work, often referred to as intellectual property. Intellectual property includes trademarks, patents, and copyrights, as well as trade secrets and certain forms of trade dress.

For example, you have created a particular graphic design for use on your pottery. Under the copyright law, you own a copyright in your design as soon as your original creation is "fixed in any tangible medium of expression." Soon thereafter, selling under the trademark Patz Potz, your pottery bearing that graphic design becomes so successful that you are unable to produce it fast enough to keep up with the demand. One possible approach would be to lease more studio space, acquire additional tools and equipment, hire and train employees, and eventually begin to catch up with demand. By doing so, however, you would risk losing your market during the time it takes to gear up and respond.

A potentially quicker way to respond to increased demand would be to contract with an existing producer, such as Big Potter, Inc. (BPI), who already has the capacity in its shops to make your product. In this case, the way to protect your rights in the design, while still allowing BPI to use it, is to enter into a private-license agreement.

The license agreement may be fairly brief or quite detailed and lengthy, depending on which rights you are licensing and the scope of each, the numbers and types of products, size of anticipated market, duration, and many other factors. For example, you may license the use of your copyrighted design (the graphic), your trademark (Patz Potz); the secret formula and techniques you developed to make and apply the glaze; and your distinctive packaging of the finished products—the trade dress.

Other factors that you should consider and clearly specify in the license agreement—and this is by no means an exhaustive list—include the licensee's territory, sublicensing and assignment rights and rights in derivative products, nondisclosure provisions to protect your trade secrets, amounts and timing of royalties and other payments, auditing provisions, quality control measures, and termination provisions. For example, can BPI market the products throughout the world or only in specific regions or countries? Can BPI sublicense your design to Shirts by Schultz for use on a line of wearable art? If so, how will you get paid, and will you have access to Schultz's books or to BPI's books? How frequently are their books audited, and who pays for the audit? If BPI inadvertently or purposely discloses your trade secrets, are you entitled to damages? What controls do you have to ensure that BPI continues to produce quality products under your trademark? Do you or BPI have the right to terminate the license, and under what conditions can it be done? Can it be done for such causes as poor quality, lagging sales, and nonpayment or can it be done at will? Is the agreement automatically terminated or does it terminate on a specified date?

Production of a few dozen items may not justify the complexity and expense of such a license agreement. However, when a new product shows early signs of success, particularly if it can be produced in quantities responsive to the demand, licensing may provide an avenue to meeting that response and to reaping big personal rewards—even though you may be sharing the success with BPI and Schultz.

As with any agreement or transaction in which you must put significant property rights at risk, a condition that certainly may exist in the licensing-agreement context, appropriate legal and financial advice should be obtained before you enter into the agreement. *(See also: Copyright, Intellectual Property, Patent, Trade Dress, Trademark, Trade Secret)*

Lien

A lien is a legal device by which one person or an entity such as the bank, or the Internal Revenue Service places a claim or encumbrance on the property of another to secure payment of a debt or obligation. If the debt is not paid, the obligation can be foreclosed, that is, the property can be sold for the benefit of the debtor. In that respect, it is similar to a mortgage.

Two types of liens follow:

1. *Mechanic's Lien.* If you hire a carpenter to erect an addition to your pottery shop and a plumber to connect the gas pipes for your new kiln but you don't pay them, they can file a lien against your property in the county clerk's office. A mechanic's lien usually takes precedence over all other obligations the property may have, including a mortgage but excluding tax liens. Banks and other mortgage lenders find out about such liens quickly, and you'll hear from them just as quickly because their loan is endangered if the lien leads to a foreclosure.

2. *Judgment Lien.* If someone sues you and wins a judgment for damages, they can also place a lien on your property, even though the cause of the

lawsuit is unrelated to the property—unlike a mortgage or a mechanic's lien. The same procedure and results apply as in a mechanic's lien.

Liens fall into two general categories: possessory and nonpossessory. In the case of a possessory lien such as a mechanic's lien, an auto mechanic may retain possession of your vehicle until he is paid for the work he performed on it. In the case of a nonpossessory lien, the lien is perfected when a document is filed in the appropriate government office. Article 9 of the Uniform Commercial Code (UCC) provides the procedure for perfecting a security interest in order to protect a lien. *(See also: Mortgage, Uniform Commercial Code)*

Life Insurance

Life insurance, unfortunately, doesn't guarantee that you'll live, only that the financial impact of your death on your survivors will be lessened. Life insurance is not based on the same kind of risk as property insurance. Medical examinations weed out the poor risks, but once a policy is issued, the probability that the insured will die is 100 percent. The risk to the insurance company is in how soon death will occur. Premiums, therefore, are related to risk. If you are twenty years old, the probability of your dying anytime soon is substantially less than if you are eighty. Statisticians—called actuaries in the insurance world—have figured out those probabilities and have calculated the premiums so that, on the average, you're paid up by the time you die.

Life insurance differs from property insurance in several other important respects:

1. The amount of coverage is not related to the value of the insured item since no dollar value can be placed on a human life. Everyone can choose his or her own dollar value—which is, of course, how much money becomes available to the beneficiaries. That value is reflected in the premium payments.

2. Most insurance policies have two parties: the insured and the insurance company. Life insurance has a third one: the beneficiary. The insured usually has the right to change beneficiaries at any time through proper notice to the insurance company. There are exceptions, such as with a business that carries life insurance on a key employee and that business is the beneficiary. There, the insured employee cannot change the beneficiary.

3. Most life-insurance policies cannot be canceled by the insurance company after a stated period of time, generally two years, except when the premiums are not paid or misrepresentations were made as to age or other important factors at the time the policy was issued.

4. Whole-life insurance policies have a cash value that increases over the years. This cash value belongs to and is paid to the insured if the policy is canceled or lapses for nonpayment of premiums. The cash value can also

be borrowed by the insured. If a loan is outstanding at the time the insured dies, the loan is subtracted from the benefits, and the balance is then paid to the beneficiaries.

5. Most whole-life insurance policies pay annual dividends based on the cash value of the policy and the earnings of the insurance company. They, therefore, represent not only protection but investment.

There are literally dozens of varieties of life insurance, but they fall into four major categories: ordinary, also known as straight; limited payment; endowment; and term.

1. Ordinary (straight) life insurance is a policy on which the premiums remain constant over the life of the policy, that is, for the life of the insured. The face value of the policy is paid to the beneficiaries at the death of the insured.

2. Limited payment is a policy under which premium payments are made for a specified period. Thereafter, the premiums stop, but the policy remains in full force and payable to the beneficiaries at the death of the insured. It is more expensive than ordinary life insurance in terms of the individual premium payments, but it may be less expensive in terms of total premiums paid, especially if the insured is young when the policy goes into effect.

3. Endowment policies are really savings plans with life insurance added, or vice versa. You pay premiums for a stated period of years. If you are still alive at the end of that time, you are your beneficiary. The face value of the policy is paid to you. If you die before the stated time, your beneficiaries collect.

4. Term insurance is pure life insurance for a specified period of time—generally no more than five or ten years, although some policies provide guaranteed renewal for longer periods. Then coverage ends. Term policies have no cash or loan value, but their premium rates are generally lower than those of other types of life insurance. Term insurance is used primarily to protect unusually heavy responsibilities during a limited period of time. For example, if you have teenagers, a five- or ten-year term policy ensures that money is available to get them through college in case you're not around to pay the tuition. Mortgage insurance is, in effect, a form of term insurance on the life of the mortgagor—the borrower—for the unexpired portion of the mortgage. If you die before the mortgage is paid off, the insurance policy pays the rest. There are no other benefits.

Life-insurance policies cannot be bought in the names of other people unless there is an insurable interest. A husband and wife can insure each other. Two business partners can insure each other, as well. A corporation can insure the lives of its executives, and a baseball club can insure the lives of its players. In all these instances there would be a demonstrable loss if the insured died, and, therefore, an insurable interest exists.

Unlike property insurance, for which the insurable interest must exist both when the policy is issued and when the claim is made, in life insurance that interest must exist only when the policy is issued. It becomes important, therefore, to examine your life-insurance policies periodically to see if the beneficiary needs to be changed. Such instances occur when the beneficiary dies before you do, when there's a divorce, when a partnership is dissolved, or whenever some other reason for which the beneficiary was named ceases to exist. *(See also: Group Insurance, Insurance)*

Limited Liability Companies

Limited liability companies (LLC) are new business forms first developed in Wyoming to entitle individuals who desire to do business through an entity providing limited liability—like a corporation—and achieve the tax pass-through features of a partnership, without the restrictions imposed on S corporations. Only a relatively small number of states have limited liability company laws or recognize this business form, though most states are studying them. Unlike S corporations, LLCs may have an unlimited number of owners, who need not be individuals or United States citizens. In addition, there may be more than one class of stock. The LLC is treated exactly like a partnership for tax purposes; that is, the company is not taxed and the owners must pay tax on their distributable shares of business profits and may deduct their pro rata share of business losses. *(See also: Limited Partnership, Tax)*

Limited Partnership

Limited partnership is defined in the Uniform Limited Partnership Act as a partnership with one or more general partners who have full personal liability—like the general partnership—and one or more limited partners, who have limited liability—like shareholders in a corporation. The Uniform Limited Partnership Act has been adopted in its original or a revised form in the vast majority of states. This form of partnership may be created only by filing Articles of Limited Partnership with the appropriate state or county office, customarily the same office in which corporations' articles of incorporation are filed. The limited partnership is not a taxable entity; the general and limited partners must personally pay tax on their pro rata share of distributable profits and may personally deduct their pro rata share of partnership losses.

The business of the limited partnership must be run by the general partners; limited partners who become actively involved in running the partnership's business will lose their limited liability.

The creation of limited partnerships is quite technical, and you should consult with your attorney before considering doing business in this business form.

For more information, see *The Law (In Plain English)® for Small Businesses* (Appendix C). *(See also: Corporation, Joint Venture, Limited Liability Companies, Partnership, Sole Proprietorship)*

Loans

Few people and even fewer businesses get through life without finding the need to borrow money sooner or later: It may be for a car loan, a mortgage to buy a house, funds for expansion of a business, an installment purchase of a piece of equipment for craft production, or cash to tide a business over until sales pick up again.

Loans can come from a variety of sources: friends and relatives who have confidence in you or share your crafts enthusiasm, your own life-insurance policies (if they have loan values), and lending institutions such as banks and credit unions. Even the credit extended by your suppliers is, in effect, a form of loan. The basic characteristics of any of these loans are that they must be repaid at some specified time or in periodic installments, and interest is charged for the use of the money.

The major source of money that is not a loan is the equity capital that investors put into a business. Unlike all other sources of funds, equity is never paid back unless the business is dissolved. It serves, rather, as the basis on which the investor is paid a share of the profits.

The first question that will go through a lender's head is whether the borrower can pay back the loan. This is determined by many other questions. A bank may want to know why you need the money; what you plan to do with it; how and when the loan will be repaid; what your credit rating is— that is, how you've repaid previous loans—whether you can put up collateral such as real estate, equipment, or inventory as a guarantee; and so forth. These are not idle questions on the bank's part. When a bank lends money, it has to be as sure as possible that the loan will be repaid. The answers to questions such as these determine not only whether the loan will be granted but how much interest will be charged. The greater the risk, the higher the interest.

To sum up, there are three basic sources of funds other than your own:

1. *Equity Capital:* the money that investors provide. This does not have to be repaid. The equity capital is the basis on which investors share in the profits. Equity capital may also be raised by issuing and selling securities— stock or investment contracts—to family, friends, close associates, and even the public. It is necessary for you to have an experienced attorney review any of these transactions in order to assist you in complying with the federal or state securities laws.

2. *Trade Credit:* the terms on which you are able to buy supplies without

paying cash. You are, in effect, borrowing money for a short term until you pay your bill.

3. *Loans:* the money provided by friends, relatives, or outside lending institutions, such as banks, with a specific understanding of how and when the loan will be repaid and what interest charges it is subject to.

There are two basic types of loans:

1. *Short Term.* These are loans for a period of between one and twelve months. It is expected that they will be repaid from the proceeds of the activity for which the money is needed. Suppose, for example, that you suddenly received a large order that necessitated the purchase of three thousand dollars' worth of raw materials. If you didn't have the three thousand dollars, you could borrow it for a period of a few months because the bank would expect that you would repay the loan as soon as you had been paid for the order.

2. *Long Term.* These are loans that you expect to repay from your profits over a fairly long period of time, usually in monthly or quarterly installments. Such loans are made for major expenditures such as the purchase of equipment or real estate, not for immediate operating cash needs.

A short-term loan can often be made as unsecured loans, which means that your signature and your credit reputation are sufficient. A long-term loan, on the other hand, usually requires some sort of collateral, the pledge of some asset that the bank can claim and sell if you, the borrower, fail to repay the loan. The most familiar of these is a real-estate mortgage in which the real estate itself is the collateral. Other forms of collateral may include stocks and bonds, life-insurance policies, accounts receivable, and signatures of comakers or endorsers who agree to be personally responsible and to pledge their assets as collateral if you default.

A bank does not really lend you its own money but the money that its depositors have placed in the bank's trust. To safeguard those deposits, a bank asks many questions, as noted above. It must be remembered that a bank is not in business to turn down loan applications—its profits are primarily from lending money.

What the bank wants to know, therefore, includes some or all of these points:

1. How solvent are you?

2. Are your books and records up-to-date and in good order?

3. How much do the owners take out of the business in salaries, dividends, and the like?

4. How many employees do you have?

5. How much insurance coverage do you have?

6. How large are your accounts receivable?

7. How large is your inventory?

8. What is the age and value of your fixed assets such as equipment? How are they depreciated?

9. What are your plans for the future?

For a business loan, the balance sheet and the profit-and-loss statements are the most important documents the bank usually requires, especially for long-term loans. They indicate your financial condition and your profit picture. A series of such statements covering several years will indicate your business growth and will demonstrate to the bank how much of a risk it is taking by lending the money.

That's why it is so difficult for brand-new enterprises to raise funds through borrowing. It's the age-old chicken-or-the-egg theory: You want to start a business but can't without the necessary capital. To get those funds, however, you must be able to demonstrate the soundness of your business. Securing a loan is easiest, ironically, if you are already established or if you already owe money or have paid back previous loans. It is much easier to borrow more money.

How much money to borrow is another important consideration both for the borrower and the lender. Here again your financial statements are a key factor because they reveal, if they are up-to-date, what your financial capacity to repay the loan is likely to be.

Suppose you have been successful as a potter, and you want to expand: buy another wheel, a larger kiln; remodel to make a bigger workshop; and hire someone to help you. If you can prove to the bank that your past financial performance is sound, that you have established some good connections with major retail outlets that bear great promise for the future if you expand, then the likelihood of getting the loan is good.

On the other hand, if you've done well in your own little workshop, you've sold well at crafts fairs, and now you want to hire a dozen potters and spend fifty thousand dollars on equipment because you feel the magic spell of success in your bones, the bank will think twice—or three times— and may suggest that a smaller loan for more modest expansion is more in order for your particular situation. You may hate the bank for being so tight with its money. But since a bank lends money on facts, not enthusiasm, it may even be doing you a favor by turning down an application that, on strictly financial terms, is not likely to succeed.

Another factor that a bank takes into account is your willingness to invest in your own business. If you make a long-range plan for expansion that will require a bank loan, it is wise to save up some money of your own. Then when you go to the bank with your loan application, you can indicate that you are ready to invest four thousand dollars but need another six thousand dollars. You'll probably get much more sympathetic attention. The bank will be more inclined to take the risk if it knows that you are also taking a risk.

Planning ahead through saving is itself an indication of good management that will impress the bank.

The limitations a bank sets on its borrowers, the size of interest it charges, and the terms of repayment are all related to the bank's interpretation of how great a risk it takes. That does not mean, however, that every bank interprets the same set of facts the same way. Some are more conservative than others. Some have had good experience with small-business loans or may have a policy of encouraging small local business to develop. Some may consider a particular type of collateral secure, while others may frown on it.

All of this influences your experience with a particular lender, and if the first approach does not succeed or the limitations and interest rates are not acceptable, it is perfectly reasonable to approach another bank.

An example of how easy it is to obtain a loan when the risk is low is the passbook loan, offered by many savings banks. The bank lends you any amount up to the balance in your bankbook. It also takes possession of the bankbook, however, and you can touch only that amount of money in excess of your loan balance. You pay your loan back regularly, the interest rate generally being only 1 to 2 percent above the interest the bank pays you on your savings (including the frozen funds, which continue to earn interest). If you don't repay the loan, the bank simply takes the money out of your savings account. Since the risk to the bank in this transaction is zero (there's no way to lose), you need show no financial statements, provide no documents of your credit worthiness: Just sign the loan papers that authorize the bank to take the money it already has in its possession to repay the loan if you fail to do so.

This is a good borrowing device if you have some cash in a savings account but don't want to use it because you fear that you don't have the self-control to repay yourself as regularly as you would the bank. And since interest charges are minimal, you might consider the cost worthwhile.

In addition to the financial documents that the bank will want to see, a carefully thought-out loan proposal also contributes a great deal to the application. The proposal should indicate how you expect the loan to perform the functions for which it is being sought, what the conditions in your own enterprise and in the crafts field in general are, how you foresee your own production and sales plans, what new products you plan to develop, how your business is managed, and so forth. Here again, the loan proposal not only provides the bank with a picture of how safe the loan might be but of how thoroughly you have considered the need for the money and how competent your own understanding of your business situation is. Readying these documents in order to complete the application is, of course, your responsibility. The financial documents should be prepared by an accountant.

Ultimately, discussion of your financial needs and the many borrowing opportunities with your accountant or your bank often provides valuable information that can't be covered in the scope of this overview. In addition, two excellent booklets about loans are available without charge from the Small Business Administration (SBA): "ABCs of Borrowing" and "Sound Cash Management and Borrowing" (see Appendix C). For more information about SBA business-development programs and services, call the SBA Small Business Answer Desk (see Appendix D). *(See also: Banks, Capital, Credit Card, Mortgage, Trade Credit)*

Loss Leader
An item that is sold below cost in order to attract customers to buy profitable merchandise is known as a loss leader. *(See also: Pricing)*

Magazines *(See: Periodicals)*

Mailing Lists
Whether you use the mails to make announcements that will bring customers to your store or studio or you use them to generate mail-order purchases of your craftwork, the mailing list is the most important ingredient.

Mailing lists come from two sources: lists you have compiled over the years of customers or prospects, and lists that you can buy from list brokers whose names you will find in the yellow pages of the telephone book.

Your own list is, of course, the most effective. Since the quality of a list is measured by how many names on it can be expected to buy from you, a list of your former customers or others who have seen your work is one of your most valuable possessions.

Keep that list up-to-date. A card file maintained in alphabetical order is convenient. Also available are a variety of data-base software for use on your personal computer and specialized mailing-list programs that print mailing labels and phone lists and that can even be programmed to sort based on eye color and sexual preference. Whenever you have a new customer, whenever you come across an interested name, add it to the list.

That list may be sufficient for your purposes. Invitations to a gallery opening that are culled from just such a list, for example, may produce a healthy turnout. However, there are occasions when you want to make a large mailing. There are literally hundreds upon hundreds of specialized lists available. The usual procedure is to buy the onetime use of such a list. The cost depends on the nature of the list and always includes a complete set of mailing labels. Prices generally run between thirty-five dollars and fifty dollars a thousand, though some are higher.

There are lists of doctors, society matrons, plumbers, and business executives. A list of business executives is often broken down by their titles or the size of their businesses. You can buy lists of art patrons, museum trustees, members of particular organizations, and many others.

Discuss your list needs with a large, reliable list broker. He or she will usually be able to give you good advice and obtain special lists for you. If you can't find a satisfactory list broker locally, however, you can contact any of the brokers in Appendix D.

If you want to make a mailing to the members of a specific organization or the subscribers of a specific publication, a direct inquiry may be useful. For a fee, some of them make their lists available to reputable firms. You might also exchange lists with other craftspeople who are not competing directly with you.

The size and nature of a list is not the only consideration, however. How clean a list is—how many names will actually be reached by your mailing piece—must also be considered. People move or die or change jobs, so from a list that has not been used and cleaned in a year you can expect as much as 20 percent or more of the mail to be undeliverable. That's an expensive proposition when you consider that even a simple mailing piece can cost fifty cents or more.

Ask a list broker how recently a list has been used. If it wasn't recently, ask for a refund on any undeliverable returns of more than 5 percent. Of course, the only refund you'll get is on the cost of the names you rented, but that's better than nothing. Most reputable brokers will stand behind their promises of clean lists.

Before you make a commitment to rent a large list, test it. Suppose a broker has four lists, each of which has ten thousand names. All four look good to you, but you can never be sure. Instead of buying forty thousand names and discovering that some of the lists are not suited to your purpose, buy only a representative sample of each list at first—say, one thousand names. You then have a mailing of four thousand pieces that will cost much less than taking a chance on forty thousand.

There's another use for testing as well. Suppose you have two kinds of possible offers to make in a mailing piece. Buy a representative sample of the list, and mail one offer to half the list and the other offer to the other half. If one pulls better than the other, you know which to send to the whole list.

Careful record keeping is necessary when you test or when you do any sort of mail promotion. There's too much money tied up in using the mails to skimp on tracking down the results.

What kind of response can you expect from a list? That depends on the quality of the list and the nature of the offer. Under normal circumstances, a list user considers 2 percent a satisfactory response. In other words, if you sent out ten thousand pieces, two hundred sales or inquiries would be considered acceptable. A response of 10 percent or more could be expected from an unusually good list, such as your own customer list.

In addition to the response received, however, the total costs must be figured to determine the actual success of the mailing. To send out ten thousand pieces at a total cost of twenty-five hundred dollars, for example, and wind up with a 2 percent response or two hundred orders of ten dollars each doesn't even pay for the cost of the mailing. On the other hand, if the orders are fifty dollars each, you take in ten thousand dollars on a 2 percent response. That should leave a nice profit if you've priced your work properly.

You may never see the names on the original list since most list owners will make labels available directly to your printer for mailing purposes only, but you do have the names of people who respond. Add them to your own customer list for future mailings. *(See also: Advertising, Calatog, Mail Order, Post Office)*

Mail Order

Mail-order selling is a hazardous exercise that only the most persistent and hardheaded businesspeople survive. It's not as easy as it looks, and it requires a combination of marketing skill, media selection, and a considerable sum of cash. When that combination works, it can be extremely successful. When it doesn't: disaster.

A profitable mail-order program is built on two operations that work in tandem: getting the customers' names through the sale of a single item and following up those names with catalog mailings for future business.

Except for rare hits, a single-item mail-order campaign rarely pays off. The cost of advertising and shipping normally eats up most of the income. Unless it is an item with an unusually high markup, don't be disappointed if the first order merely pays for itself. The real profits come when those customers order other merchandise from a catalog. That's why the initial mail-order ad is often known as a list builder.

The major components of initial mail-order selling include how to choose, how to price, where to advertise, and the follow-up.

How to Choose Items for Mail Order

Almost all mail-order items have several things in common. They cannot be bought in the usual retail store. They are familiar types of objects. They can be bought sight unseen. They can be produced in quantity and shipped easily. And they are easily described and illustrated in advertising or sales literature.

A pendant is a perfect example of these characteristics. It can be unique and not sold at retail. It can be crafted in quantity if the advertising results require it. It can be clearly illustrated, and because everybody knows what a pendant is, the description need only state the actual size and the material of which it is made. Finally, it is unbreakable and lightweight and, therefore, easy and inexpensive to ship.

As any of these components become complicated, the problems multiply. A fragile crafts object, for example, will increase the shipping costs. An object that comes in seven sizes and ten colors presents considerable inventory and ordering difficulties. An object so strange that it requires reams of explanation does not generally produce good mail-order response. And if you're not ready, willing, and able to produce in quantity, forget about mail order altogether.

This is an appropriate point at which to mention a federal regulation designed to prevent abuses in mail-order selling. The Federal Trade Commission requires that all mail orders be shipped within thirty days or customers are entitled to a refund. Mail-order sellers must notify customers if an order cannot be shipped within thirty days or another specified time period, and they must furnish customers with postcards on which the customer can indicate whether the order should be canceled. This rule applies only to orders accompanied by payment, which is the most common procedure in mail-order selling. Inventory and production capabilities become even more important in order to comply with this rule.

How to Price Items for Mail Order

The public is naturally reluctant to send a large sum of money to an unknown firm in response to a small ad in a newspaper or magazine. This is particularly true when there is a post office box number instead of an address. The initial mail-order item, therefore, has to be priced fairly low and must give the impression of being a good buy. Mail-order specialists consider between ten dollars and twenty-five dollars to be the range that will produce best results.

Depending on the costs of advertising space and the expected response in orders, a mail-order item should be priced at at least five times what it costs in materials and labor to produce. A leather belt that will be advertised for $19.95 should not cost more than four dollars to make. Yet the price has to remain competitive with retail prices. Though they may not be as unique or as beautiful as yours, if other belts can be bought in a local department store for $9.95, it will be difficult to convince many readers that the advertised belt is truly worth twice as much. Pricing, therefore, immediately rules out various types of craftwork that cannot compete with that kind of markup unless you are to skimp on the quality of raw materials or on the labor involved in creating a handcrafted piece.

The high markup is also necessary to meet substantial increases in overhead: handling the orders; packing, shipping, postage; maintaining the lists;

returns of damaged goods; answering complaints, correspondence about lost shipments; and so forth.

Where to Advertise

Picking the right medium for mail-order selling is often the key to whether even a good product at the right price makes it. An item that appeals especially to women or that is bought as a gift can do very well in the women's magazines, many of which have special shopping-mart sections full of mail-order offerings. Select the magazines or newspapers carefully so that your advertisement reaches the most likely prospects for your craftwork. Indeed, determine what kind of audience you want to reach, and then find the publication that reaches it.

Advertising in national magazines can be expensive. It is worthwhile, therefore, to get professional advertising help, both to select the right publications and to prepare an effective advertising message.

An essential ingredient of any mail-order ad is to key it; that is, to identify it in some manner so that you can keep track of the source of the returns. If it is a coupon ad, place a number or letter in some inconspicuous place in the coupon. That way the letter *A* will identify an ad that ran in one publication; the letter *B* an ad in another publication.

This can be refined even further by adding a number or two. You might identify the magazine by A22, the issue of February 1993 by *A*.

This technique works even if you don't use a coupon. You can simply add a *Dept. A* or *Dept. B* identification to your name and address and keep track of the source that way.

Keying the ads is also important if you want to test some variables in the same publication. Does one type of headline produce better results than another? Does one type of product outsell another? Does $9.95 bring in sufficiently more business than $10.49 and make the lower price more profitable? If you're trying to build a list, these tests take on even greater importance than the dollars-and-cents results alone.

When you test, change only one ingredient at a time. If you change both the headline and the price, for example, you can never know for sure what might have caused the difference in the results.

Finally, keeping accurate records of the results is the only way you can know whether one type of ad produces more than another, whether one publication pulls better than another, which publication produces results for what kind of product. With accurate records you can put your money where the best results are.

The Follow-up

It isn't often that a mail-order campaign is successful solely on the basis of offering a single item in a magazine ad. The real payoff comes through building a list of customers who respond to the ad and then producing additional orders from those same customers via catalogs or other sales literature. Many craftspeople don't start their mail-order efforts until they have a list or know where they can buy an outside list that has been tested and found productive. This avoids the huge gamble of investing in magazine advertising.

If you are able to afford to produce a catalog or sales brochure, you can offer many items rather than staking all on a single item. Illustrations can be larger, descriptions more extensive, and price ranges higher. The assumption is that the recipients of the catalog already know you—maybe they have bought from you before or signed their name to a guest book at your crafts-show booth.

The cost of preparing a catalog depends on how large the catalog is; whether it is a simple black-and-white printing job or an elegant full-color production; what kind of paper is used; and, most important, the size of the pressrun. The initial costs of preparing sales literature is the same whether you run one thousand copies or a million. On small quantities the initial cost is usually the largest ingredient of the whole job. If you have a list of only five thousand names, for example, a color catalog is usually out of the question because the setup and printing costs will usually be too high; a four-page black-and-white brochure would probably fit into your budget since it will necessitate only one printed sheet to be folded. But you might be able to join forces with another noncompetitive craftsperson and produce a joint catalog that saves each of you some money. It also offers the recipient a wider choice of items from which to choose—always an advantage in selling.

A mail-order catalog provides one other advantage that few other forms of advertising have: You can enclose an order envelope that makes it easier for the customer to respond and order. This is especially useful since you expect payment with the order, and because billing is a complicated procedure in mail-order selling and is rarely done.

When you get ready to prepare a catalog or other sales material, talk to your printer first. He or she may be helpful in finding the most economical way to publish. Consider the weight of the piece also. Trimming a quarter inch off the size of a catalog before you design it may bring the total weight into a lower postage category. Have the printer make a sample, called a dummy. Take it to a post office to be weighed on their scale. Your postmaster may have some suggestions on how to mail the material most economically.

There are additional points that are absolutely essential in mail-order selling. The specifications have to be spelled out in minute detail: sizes, colors, shapes, materials. Also, are shipping costs included, or how are they to be calculated? What sales taxes, if any, are due? And the order form—

there's no point in sending a mail-order promotion without one—must provide space in which the customer can note all the specifications. Finally, a money-back guarantee is also almost universal in mail-order selling. It serves to reassure the customer, who, after all, cannot examine the merchandise until after it is bought and delivered.

If much of this section sounds discouraging to craftspeople, it is designed that way. Mail-order selling looks simple, but it's a tough business. If the warnings have alerted you to the dangers, if you have examined them carefully and found them worth the risk, then your chances of success are improved.

There are certain rules that must be complied with when engaging in a mail-order business. These are promulgated by the Federal Trade Commission (FTC), and you should confer with the FTC before commencing such a business (see Appendix D). *(See also: Advertising, Catalog, Direct Mail, Mailing Lists, Post Office)*

Manufacturers' Representatives *(See: Sales Representatives)*

Margin

Margin is often confused with markup, particularly since both can be expressed in similar percentages. Margin and markup both represent the difference between the cost of products and their selling price. Out of this difference come all other expenses plus the profit.

Although markup is simply a percentage figure designed to determine a selling price, margin is the actual percentage realized on sales. Margin has to take into account a variety of factors that don't concern markup at all: defective pieces, unsold items, a disappointing crafts show, loss through damage or theft, and so on.

Thus, in theory, margin and markup percentages would be identical if every last piece were sold. In real life it rarely happens that way, certainly not over a period of time.

It may be easier to understand this difference if it is expressed in dollars. Suppose you make one hundred pots that cost five dollars apiece to produce and are marked up to sell for ten dollars each. If every last one were sold, you would realize five hundred dollars. That would also be your margin. But more than likely a few would break or come out of the kiln in unsalable condition. You might then sell only ninety. You would clear $450 after the cost of production. That's your real margin, and it is lower than the intended markup.

To think of markup in the same breath as margin can be misleading if you consider them both in terms of profit. Craftspeople often work on two kinds of margin if they sell at wholesale to stores and galleries and also sell at retail directly to the consumer. The first margin is the difference between the cost of production and the wholesale price; the second margin is the difference between the wholesale price and the retail price. The two margins need not be the same. Much depends on what's needed for expense and profit in each case.

Suppose your wholesale margin covers all your overhead and wholesale profit and is set at 50 percent (half the wholesale price). The second margin may need to cover only your show expenses and selling time. That margin could well be 30 percent or 40 percent and still turn a fine retail profit.

Margin must be calculated carefully. Your accountant can tell you at what point your margin is too low to make money. You may be doing a record business, the money rolls in, everything looks rosy. But if the margin isn't right, you may find yourself out of business in no time at all. *(See also: Markup, Pricing, Profit)*

Markdown

There comes a time when you have some items on hand that you have to sell below the regular price. This is called a markdown.

Markdowns are taken for many reasons. Sometimes a product is simply overpriced, and you want to move the stock out of inventory. Markdowns are occasionally made toward the end of a show to avoid the need for carting unsold merchandise home. Seasonal items are often marked down at the end of the season in order to clean out inventory and raise cash. Sometimes a specific item is marked down as a loss leader to bring customers to your store or booth where they can then see and hopefully buy other items at regular prices.

Markdowns are a legitimate business practice if they are taken for legitimate reasons. If everything is constantly marked down from the regular price, then there is, in truth, no regular price at all; your business becomes simply a discount or price-cutting operation. Advertising regular prices that never existed may even become deceptive or fraudulent advertising. *(See also: Loss Leader, Markup, Pricing, Profit)*

Marketability

A line of hand-built ceramic hanging pots was displayed at a New England crafts show recently. The craftsmanship was superb, the colors interesting, the glazes impeccable, and the price rational. Such pots were popular at the time, and this particular line was shown in various shapes and sizes in an attractive display.

Yet only one pot was sold during the two days of the show. What was wrong?

Each pot was designed as a face that could only be described as either a death mask or a gargoyle. From an artistic point of view the design may have been superb. From a marketing point of view it was a disaster. Gargoyles to ward off demons in the upper reaches of a cathedral wall are one thing; as planters hanging in a living room they are quite another.

Marketability, then, is the simple question of whether a given object or product can be sold to its intended customer.

The most common thought—sometimes the only one—that occurs to a seller is price. But this can be misleading, since price is not the only concern. Indeed, price is rarely the first concern. Before a customer asks how much, a tentative decision has already been made that it might be nice to have the particular crafts object. If a customer has absolutely no interest in buying a ring, he or she is not likely to ask what a particular ring costs. In that case it doesn't matter whether it's ten dollars or one hundred dollars or if the price is reduced from ten dollars to five dollars. Price follows the determination of need or desire except on certain occasions such as Christmas, when a customer might say: "I want to spend ten dollars on Aunt Susie's gift. Let's see what I can get for her." Which is not to suggest that price is not an important factor in marketability but that it is not the only factor.

Before a product can be sold to a customer—and this applies to all products, including craftwork—it must fill a need. The need may be functional, as in a chair to sit on; or emotional, as with an earring that makes the personal appearance more attractive; or prestige, as with a one-of-a-kind wall hanging that the customer's friends can admire; or any number of other reasons.

The next question is how the product or object meets that need. This is where such intangible elements as style, design, color, shape, and even current fads or trends become important. Tastes differ among people and change from one year to the next, one generation to the next. Craftspeople worth the calling need not compromise their artistic integrity for the sake of popular appeal, but to survive economically it is essential to tune a fine ear to what is marketable, what can be sold, what the customers are buying, what they're not buying—and why not? Is it a problem of style or price or variety or being behind or ahead of the times?

Don't play follow the leader, but don't ignore what successful craftspeople are doing. At most crafts shows there are always a few booths that have heavier traffic than others. See what's happening there. What's being sold? What's the appeal that draws customers to those booths? What are the prices?

Listen carefully to what's happening at your own booth. What are shoppers particularly interested in? What are they buying and not buying? What are they asking for? Do they want a round pillow when you only have square pillows? Do they want it in green when you have it only in blue? Is price a problem? Don't be shy about asking them directly what's on their mind. It's the only way you can find out what you're doing right, what you're doing wrong, and where you can improve.

Keep an ear tuned also to the popular mood and the current trends. In the mid-1970s, when tennis enjoyed a resurgence of popularity, a New York craftsman produced a finely crafted, tastefully designed line of pendants based on abstract interpretations of a tennis racket. They were advertised as available in silver and gold, and they sold quite well at various prices to tennis enthusiasts. During the Persian Gulf War, there was a resurgence of the anti-war movement, and the inverted-Y peace symbol was again incorporated as a design element in a wide variety of crafts objects, ranging from jewelry to stained glass to quilts.

No matter how marketable something is, it will never appeal to everyone. Some people like Beethoven. Some like country music. Some like rock. From an economic point of view, the importance of being concerned with marketability is to determine whether your work appeals to a sufficient number of customers to enable you to earn a living. *(See also: Design, Marketing, Market Research, Market Planning, Product Research)*

Marketing

Ask ten marketing experts to explain the term, and you're likely to get eleven answers. One that comes closest, in my view, was formulated by Norbert N. Nelson in his introduction to *Selling Your Crafts* (see Appendix C). Marketing, he said, is "the method of converting merchandise into money."

Note the word *method*. Marketing is not a single activity. Marketing and selling are often used interchangeably, but selling is only one part of the process. Other elements of the total marketing operation include publicity, advertising, timing, pricing, the image of the stores or shows through which you sell, and design as it relates to market acceptability—a fancy term for "Will people buy it?" Marketing, then, refers to all the things that happen to your craftwork between the time that it is finished in your shop or studio and the time the customer buys it. *(See also: Advertising, Marketability, Market Planning, Pricing, Publicity, Public Relations, Sale)*

Market Planning

This term is commonly used in the offices of huge corporations, but the principles can apply to even the most modest craftwork producer. No matter to what scale it is drawn, a market plan is your guide to what you hope to accomplish in selling your craftwork, how you hope to accomplish it, when and where you need to accomplish it, and how much it will cost.

It is possible to succeed on a hit-or-miss basis, but the chances for earning a living in this fashion are much less secure. It is not simply a matter of taking advantage of opportunities that come along—even a good market plan allows for unexpected opportunities—but whether you even know where to find those opportunities and how to fit them into your overall plan once you find them.

A sound market plan can influence what you produce. If your craft is batik, for example, do you want to concentrate exclusively on the creation of large pieces that sell through galleries for hundreds of dollars, or do you want to sell smaller—and therefore, less expensive—but equally artistic pieces through a boutique in a major department store?

Assume for a moment that your income in either instance would be the same. The question in that case is whether you can afford to wait six or twelve months to sell a few large pieces or whether you need the cash immediately and, therefore, want to sell a larger quantity of the smaller pieces as soon as possible. You may even decide that you can do both.

The marketing plan serves the same purpose as a road map. You may want to take all sorts of detours to see the sights, but you must know where you're going, have the itinerary mapped in rough outlines, and have some idea of how many miles you want to drive each day and where you'll stay each night.

Following are ten major considerations in drawing up a marketing plan:

1. How much can I produce?
2. At what price range?
3. Is it of limited or general interest?
4. In order of importance, what are the most logical outlets or combination of outlets, to include stores, galleries, co-ops, crafts shows, exhibits, and interior decorators?
5. Can I produce enough to satisfy the outlets I consider most likely?
6. What will it cost to reach those outlets?
7. Will my creative needs and artistic inclinations be satisfied?
8. Will my plan satisfy my cash-flow needs and production capabilities, or what changes are needed to amend my decisions in those areas?
9. Does my plan include enough flexibility to change if decisions prove ineffective? Do I have the will and resources to change?
10. Will this whole plan provide the kind of income and profit I want?

To implement the plan, it is well to draw up a twelve-month outline for the year ahead. This outline should be carefully reviewed at least every three to six months, particularly in the beginning, and should be updated for the following twelve months.

The plan should note whatever specific events or activities are planned, with dates and locations. What, for example, are the major shows at which you want to exhibit? When do you want to issue a brochure? If you produce specific items for a specific occasion—Christmas, for example—when do you have to make the sale to the stores? When do you have to deliver? What are the anticipated costs for each activity? What are the anticipated results? Only by noting these carefully and by keeping a diary of the events as they occur can you determine whether your marketing plan is effective or where it needs amending for the future.

Record keeping is all-important here. Don't trust everything to memory. A marketing plan is only as good as its implementation and analysis. A marketing plan can keep you from making the same mistake twice and helps you to prepare budgets and schedule purchases of equipment and supplies.

In addition, use your marketing plan to project the price ranges of craft-work you plan to produce. Keep a careful record of how these actually sell. Your plan may call for one hundred pieces to sell at twenty-five dollars and another one hundred at fifty dollars. Upon analyzing your records, you may find that the market for the twenty-five dollar item was rather slim and unprofitable considering the work you put into it. Such knowledge will help you to plan on a different price range in the future.

As another example, suppose that three days at a given crafts fair bring a profit of one hundred dollars. The show may not have produced loss, but if you could have spent those three days in your studio producing two hundred dollars' worth of profits through ultimate store sales, it may not pay to put that particular fair on your marketing calendar next year—unless the direct contact with the customer is the real reason you go.

Still another example: Last year you ran a special show and sale in your studio. You mailed one thousand invitations. One hundred people came and spent five hundred dollars. Not bad. But if your marketing plan projects a studio sale of $750 this year, it would stand to reason that you should have a mailing list of at least fifteen hundred names, that you should find some other way to attract more people, or that you should increase the price of your work. A carefully kept diary of last year's experience tells you exactly what went into producing the end result and what you need to do this year to improve that end result.

Still another function of the marketing plan is to pinpoint who your good customers are, which prospects merit further attention, and what types of items might be added to your line to expand sales to existing outlets that already buy your present line. It is always easier and more profitable to increase sales to existing clients than to develop new ones. If you can make a one-thousand-dollar sale on one trip to a retail outlet—making one shipment, writing one invoice—you are obviously better off than making four trips, four shipments, and four invoices to four customers who buy at $250 each. Of course, if you can do both, just do it. *(See also: Marketability, Marketing)*

Market Research

All the customers out there are the market. Finding out who they are, where they are, how to reach them, how to sell to them—that's the problem.

Big corporations call this market research. Call it what you will, the important thing is to find out when and where and how and to whom you can sell your craftwork.

Most craftspeople do this in an impromptu fashion, and it usually works out well. Since there are no million-dollar advertising budgets at stake or expensive tooling-up processes as in mass production, a small mistake need not spell disaster. But it pays to study which potential retail stores you want to approach to sell your craftwork: Do they cater to the kind of customer who might want to buy your work?

It also pays to study the shows and fairs at which you want to exhibit. Taking a line of five-hundred-dollar rosewood cabinets to a five-dollar and ten-dollar mall show would be approaching the wrong market.

Other questions present themselves. Can you reach enough customers through advertising? Does mail order offer selling opportunities that you can profitably exploit? Is your shop or studio in a high-traffic location that might justify selling at retail to walk-in customers? Or would that interfere with production to the point of being unprofitable?

Do you have any specific customers in mind when you design a particular crafts object? What are their tastes? Their ages? Their interests? Their needs and desires?

Marketing opportunities can also be developed among very specialized customers: architects, industrial designers, interior decorators. In such markets you work on a commission, which means that you create a craftwork to particular specifications at a predetermined fee.

Market research in a formal way is probably neither necessary nor feasible for most craftspeople. But in an informal way—by discussing the problems with others; by reading the crafts publications; by studying different shows, stores, galleries; by keeping your eyes and ears open—you can develop approaches to the market that will produce greater selling opportunities at lower selling costs. (*See also: Architects, Buyers, Customer, Industrial Design, Interior Decorators and Designers, Marketability, Marketing, Marketing Plan, Product Line, Product Research*)

Markup

Markup is the term used to describe the difference between the cost of merchandise and its selling price. It is usually expressed in percentages. A great deal of confusion exists in the use of this word because markup can be calculated either from the cost price or the selling price. The percentage results are different, although the dollars remain the same.

For example, you sell a ring to a jewelry store for ten dollars. The store puts a twenty-dollar price tag on it. If the store figures the markup on its cost price, then it is 100 percent (double the ten-dollar cost price). If the markup is figured on the basis of the retail selling price, then it is 50 percent (half the twenty-dollar retail price).

There's a logical reason for the two different methods. One or the other figure must always serve as a starting point, either the product cost or its retail price. If a store wants to put in a line of rings to sell for twenty dollars at a 50 percent markup, then it must find a source of rings at ten dollars each. On the other hand, if the store is out shopping for rings with no specific retail price in mind, then it knows that a ten-dollar ring must be retailed for twenty dollars in order to take a 100 percent markup.

The same principle is used by many craftspeople in pricing their own craft objects. If you know you can't sell a belt for more than ten dollars and you want to mark it up 50 percent, then you must find a way to produce that belt for five dollars. If your production cost is the first figure you know, you arrive at the retail price by adding the appropriate markup to the cost. In this example, the five-dollar belt must sell for ten dollars if it is marked up 100 percent.

If you know you can't sell belts for more than eight dollars, you either have to find a less expensive way to produce them or take a smaller markup.

You may tell another craftsperson that you work on a 100 percent markup, and she will think you're making a lot of money. After all, she's working on only a 60 percent markup. But then you discover that she's talking about 60 percent of the retail price, which means she spends only 40 percent on the cost of producing or buying the merchandise. You're talking about 100 percent added to the cost of the product, which means you're spending 50 percent of the selling price on the cost of the merchandise. So it turns out that she's actually making more money than you are.

Markup is critical because it has to cover all operating costs plus profit. It does not include the cost of the merchandise itself. Every store and every craft producer should know how much markup is needed in order to remain solvent and operate profitably. (See also: Margin, Markdown, Pricing, Profit)

Mass Production

This term applies to factory procedures in which many copies of the same product are produced by machines, usually on an assembly-line basis.

When craftspeople produce a number of copies from the same design, it is called multiple production rather than mass production as long as each piece is handmade—even if machinery is used at some points in the process. Being handmade, no two pieces are ever identical. Each has its own individual characteristics, which is what distinguishes such work from mass production. That a mass-produced item may be made in various sizes and colors does not invest it with sufficient distinction to be called handcrafted, since the basic design is stamped out by machines from a blueprint. *(See also: Multiple Production, One-of-a-Kind)*

Materials *(See: Suppliers)*

Media *(See: Advertising)*

Memo
Shipping on memo is one way of avoiding what metal and jewelry craftsman Ron Pearson of Maine calls the consignment quagmire.

Shipping on memo means that work is sent on an invoice with a 30- or 60-day return privilege. It is, in effect, on loan. Any unsold work is returned after that period, along with payment for work that is sold. The paperwork may be simpler than it is in consignment selling. The invoice states that the unsold work can be returned after the specified period and that the merchandise that is sold—or that the store wants to retain for future sales—is paid for at the stated price.

Pearson does this type of order only with established customers and only on specific occasions. "If an outlet is featuring our work and perhaps advertising the event," Pearson explains, "it can help them to produce sales if they have a broader range of pieces that includes higher-priced work."

With the 30- or 60-day return privilege, a retail outlet will be more inclined to take such higher-priced work and stock more than it usually would to produce more sales and more profits for both the craftsperson and the retailer. While the net legal effect is not any different from consignment selling, such matters as ownership, insurance, bookkeeping hassles, and other consignment problems might be avoided.

A variation of this method is to send samples of new items to established retail outlets *on approval* with a 10-day return privilege. For many craftspeople, this can be an inexpensive way of introducing a customer to a new item. Pearson does this almost daily (shipping the approval item along with a customer's order) and says that "it has proved to be a remarkably good method for generating sales." *(See also: Consignment, On Approval, Retailing, Salesmanship, Wholesaling)*

Merchandising *(See: Marketability, Marketing, Marketing Plan)*

Metric System
Things are measured in a language all its own. Everything in this world—and outside it—is measured in terms of time, distance, weight, mass,

and so on. Indeed, there are many people who are quite adept at calculating pounds, inches, dollars, and hours even though they can barely read and write.

The measuring system most common in the world today is the metric system and is based on units of ten. The United States is the only major industrial nation still using the difficult fractions of ounces and pounds, inches and feet, pints and quarts. Others use the metric system not only because it is easier and more efficient but also because it requires no translation across national boundaries.

It may seem unfamiliar at first glance, but you already use many metric measurements in your daily life. Your money—one hundred cents to the dollar—is the best example. Others in common use are the thirty-five-millimeter camera, the one-hundred-meter dash, kilowatt hours of electricity, the dosages of most medicines.

The United States Congress, whose constitutional duty it is to set standards of weights and measures, determined after lengthy investigation and study that the United States should change over to the metric system, just as Great Britain, Canada, and other holdovers of the old system had done. A ten-year changeover period was initially proposed, but delays—mainly in the heavy industrial sector where the changeover would have the largest economic impact—have pushed back full metrification in the United States until the late 1990s or until the turn of the century.

Many trades and professions, especially the sciences, already use the international metric language. Packages have begun to appear on supermarket shelves marked in both the old weights and their metric equivalents. Weather forecasters have started to announce the day's temperature in both the familiar Fahrenheit and the less familiar Celsius. The United States is slowly beginning to think metric.

For craftspeople this will require some rethinking of familiar terms and even some retooling of familiar sizes. A potter will no longer make a one-pint mug but a mug that holds half a liter. A weaver won't measure by square feet but by square meters. Instead of buying an ounce of silver, a jeweler will buy twenty-eight grams. All this may seem strange at first, but other countries have found that the initial difficulties of conversion were worth the eventual convenience of the much easier metric system.

The following table indicates the method by which approximate conversions can be calculated to metric and vice versa:

UNITED STATES WEIGHTS AND MEASURES AND THE METRIC SYSTEM

	When you know:	*You can find:*	*If you multiply by:*
LENGTH	inches	millimeters	25
	feet	centimeters	30
	yards	meters	0.9
	miles	kilometers	1.6
	millimeters	inches	0.04
	centimeters	inches	0.4
	meters	yards	1.1
	kilometers	miles	0.6
AREA	square inches	square centimeters	6.5
	square feet	square meters	0.09
	square yards	square meters	0.8
	square miles	square kilometers	2.6
	acres	square hectometers (hectares)	0.4
	square centimeters	square inches	0.16
	square meters	square yards	1.2
	square kilometers	square miles	0.4
	square hectometers (hectares)	acres	2.5
MASS	ounces	grams	28
	pounds	kilograms	0.45
	short tons	megagrams (metric tons)	0.9
	grams	ounces	0.035
	kilograms	pounds	2.2
	megagrams (metric tons)	short tons	1.1

UNITED STATES WEIGHTS AND MEASURES AND THE METRIC SYSTEM (*cont.*)

	When you know:	You can find:	If you multiply by:
LIQUID	ounces	milliliters	30
VOLUME	pints	liters	0.47
	quarts	liters	0.95
	gallons	liters	3.8
	milliliters	ounces	0.034
	liters	pints	2.1
	liters	quarts	1.06
	liters	gallons	0.26

Converting temperatures is slightly different. When, for example, you know Fahrenheit, you can find Celsius by subtracting thirty-two; dividing by nine, and multiplying by five. When you know Celsius, you can find Fahrenheit by dividing by five; multiplying by nine, and adding thirty-two.

Minimum Orders

A certain amount of cost is involved in filling an order, no matter how big or how small the order is. There is a point at which it doesn't pay to ship an order; indeed, it may be a losing proposition.

If you are confronted with many small orders that have to be shipped, it is worthwhile to calculate exactly how much it costs in time and materials for billing, packing, shipping, running to the post office, and all the other steps needed to fill an order. If you find that it costs an average of two dollars per order to do all this, then a two-dollar order is a total loss. You aren't being paid for the cost of materials and your work in making the item—not to speak of the loss of profit. Establishing a minimum-order policy can, therefore, be an important influence on your profits.

There is no magic formula to determine what that minimum order should be. Simply find what it costs you to fill an average order. Do this by keeping careful records on the next forty or fifty orders. Include the time you spend as well as the costs of the shipping materials. When these costs of filling an order are the same as your profits, you have determined your break-even point. For example, if your rate of profit is 20 percent of the sales price, and it costs two dollars to ship an average order, then you need a ten-dollar minimum order to break even. The minimum order should be at least double this break-even point. In the preceding example, therefore, the sales price should be not less than twenty dollars and ideally would be twenty-five dollars or thirty dollars.

Be sure to indicate the minimum-order requirement in all sales literature, catalogs, and conversations with customers.

Another solution to this problem is to add a service charge to all orders that fall below a certain minimum. That way you can fill such orders and still keep your costs covered. Such a charge may also induce customers to increase their orders to meet the minimum requirement.

There are always exceptions, of course. We can't be hidebound. If a good customer who usually buys in large amounts needs one particular item, ship it, even if it's below the minimum. Count it as an investment in goodwill and customer satisfaction. *(See also: Break-Even Point, Orders, Pricing)*

Minimum Wage

The federal minimum wage law, known as the Fair Labor Standards Act, was established in the 1930s for a number of reasons:

1. To create a floor below which wages cannot fall;
2. To raise the buying power of the lowest-paid workers;
3. To create a higher standard of living;
4. To protect employers who pay a fair wage from unfair competition by employers who would not voluntarily pay such a wage.

The law was last amended in 1974 and covers the entire country. Many states also have their own minimum-wage laws that apply in some areas of work not included in the federal law, such as working papers for minors. In states where both state and federal minimum-wage laws exist, the higher rates and standards apply.

As of 1993, the minimum hourly wage is $4.75. With some exceptions specifically stated in the law, no one can be employed for less than that.

Overtime must be paid at a rate of one and a half times the employee's regular hourly rate for all hours beyond forty hours per week. Overtime cannot be averaged over more than one week; in other words, if an employee works thirty-eight hours one week and forty-four hours the next, he is entitled to four hours of overtime pay for the second week. Furthermore, the workweek cannot be capriciously changed from week to week as a way of avoiding overtime obligations. A change can be made only if it is intended to be permament.

There are several important exceptions to the minimum-wage law that could affect craftspeople:

1. The spouse or children under twenty-one of an individual owner of a crafts business need not be paid the minimum wage or overtime.
2. Employees of an individual retail store are not covered by the minimum wage or overtime requirements when all three of the following conditions

exist: the total sales volume is less than $250,000 a year; at least half the annual sales volume is made within the state where the store is located; and 75 percent of the annual dollar sales volume is for goods that are sold directly to the ultimate consumer and are not sold for resale.

3. Executive, administrative, and professional personnel are exempt from being paid minimum wages or overtime. The law specifically includes in the category of professional employees those whose work is original and creative in the artistic field. Thus, an employee who helps load the kiln is not a professional employee, since the work is not original or creative. A potter who is expected to create his or her own designs and execute them could very well be considered professional within the meaning of the law. The important thing is not by what title the employee is known but what the employee actually does. When there is a question of qualifying for exemptions in this category, the basis on which the Labor Department determines eligibility is outlined in the secretary of labor's regulations, Code of Federal Regulations (C.F.R.) Part 541.

4. Salespeople who work away from the employer's premises on a commission basis are also exempt from both the minimum-wage and overtime provisions. But this exemption applies only to people who sell, not to those who do other work off the employer's premises.

5. Under certain circumstances and with special certificates from the Labor Department, students can be employed at wage rates below the minimum on a part-time basis or during school vacations. This also applies to learners in vocational-education programs and to people with handicaps.

Where piecework rates exist, they must be so constructed that an employee can, under reasonable circumstances, earn the equivalent of the minimum hourly wage.

The federal law also requires that no differentials in wages are allowed if they are based on the employee's sex, color, or other extraneous reason. Wage differentials are permitted when they are based on seniority, merit, or any other job-related factor.

The Labor Department is quite strict in the enforcement of this law. Failure to pay minimum wages or overtime is a federal offense. Not only can the secretary of labor or the employees themselves go to court to recover unpaid wages, but serious violations may also be subject to civil or criminal prosecution.

The law requires employers to keep accurate records on wages, hours, and other information. Such records must be kept for at least three years (two years for time cards, piecework tickets, and so on).

Questions on wages, overtime, hours, sex discrimination, and other subjects covered by the Fair Labor Standards Act can be directed by both employers and employees to any of the 350 offices maintained throughout the country by the Wage and Hour Division of the United States Labor Department. The telephone-book white pages lists them under *United States Government, Department of Labor, Employment Standards Administration.* *(See also: Apprentice, Employees)*

Model Release *(See: Photographs)*

Money Order

Money Order

If you have a checking account, you can write your own checks. If you have a savings account you can receive cashier's checks. If you have no bank accounts at all, you can buy money orders when you need to send money to a distant point.

Money orders are available from a variety of agencies such as banks, the United States Post Office, American Express, and others. They are written in specific amounts and are sold to anyone with the cash to buy them. A fee is charged based on the amount of the money order.

Money orders can be cashed, upon proper identification, at any office of the agency that issued them—at any post office, for example, in the case of postal money orders—or they can be deposited like checks in a bank account.

Mortgage

A mortgage is a conveyance of a conditional fee of a borrower to his creditor as security for the repayment of a loan, usually made for the purchase or refinancing of property. In effect, the borrower (mortgagor) grants to the lender (mortgagee) a conditional transfer of title (ownership) to the property even though he is still in possession of it and can pretty much do with it as he pleases, including selling it. In the case of a sale, of course, the loan obligation secured by the mortgage must be transferred to the new owner or paid off. When the loan is paid off, the mortgage, by its terms, becomes null and void. That is, the lien or fee in the property automatically revests in (returns to) the borrower (owner).

Mortgages, including interest charges, are usually paid off in monthly installments over a period of years—as many as thirty years in many cases. If the borrower fails to make his payments, the entire balance is due. If he fails to pay that, the lender can exercise his conditional right to the title. This is known as a foreclosure. The lender then sells the property for as much as he can. If he sells it for more than the balance on the mortgage, the borrower gets the difference.

Mortgages, even more so than most financial transactions, require careful consideration and examination of all the details. Most important among these is the rate of interest. Although the differences between various lending institutions may seem small, the dollars can be significant. Suppose one bank charges 10.0 percent interest, and another charges 10.75 percent. That three quarters of one percent may not seem like much of a difference, but look at the end result: A thirty-year, one-hundred-thousand-dollar mortgage will cost a whopping $20,120 more in interest at 10.75 percent than at 10.0 percent.

A few other questions: Does the bank allow the mortgage to be taken over by a buyer if you sell the property? That's important because an assumable mortgage makes it easier to sell a property.

Are there any penalties if you are late with a payment or want to prepay the balance of the mortgage before it is due? Are you required to pay into an escrow account at the bank from which the bank pays your annual or semiannual real-estate taxes, insurance premiums, and so on—but on which it pays you no interest—or can you put the money in your own savings account, earn interest, and pay the taxes and other bills yourself? Are you prohibited from getting a second mortgage?

A second mortgage—or third, fourth, and so on—is given to secure any additional loans on the property. For example, suppose that the total price of the property you want to buy is ninety thousand dollars. You make a down payment of ten thousand dollars and obtain a first-mortgage loan of seventy thousand dollars. That leaves a gap of ten thousand dollars, which could be raised by your getting a second mortgage on the property. A second mortgage can also be used to raise cash on a piece of property you already own if you have an old first mortgage at a low rate of interest that you don't want to disturb by refinancing that first mortgage at a higher interest rate.

First mortgages are generally granted to a bank or other institution for the basic financing of a property. Second mortgages are more often given to private lenders. In the event of a foreclosure, the first mortgage has a claim ahead of the second mortgage if there are not sufficient funds to pay off both. Since the risk is greater to a second mortgagee, the interest rate on a second mortgage is generally higher than on a first, and the term is generally not more than fifteen years.

Lending institutions such as banks and insurance companies normally require that the property be insured against loss from fire and the like.

A loan on a piece of personal property—property other than real estate, such as an automobile—is often secured by a *chattel mortgage*, now known as a security interest, which is perfected by filing a Uniform Commercial Code (UCC) financing statement in the appropriate governmental office and otherwise complying with Article 9 of the UCC. The basic principles of payment, interest, insurance, and foreclosure apply in such mortgages as well. *(See also: Interest, Lien, Loans, Uniform Commercial Code)*

Multiple Production

This term defines crafts objects of which more than one piece is made from the same basic design. Since all the pieces are crafted by hand, each differs in some detail, however slightly, from the others. Multiple production is distinguished from mass production, in which large numbers of absolutely identical pieces are turned out by machines, even though the original design may have been created by a skilled crafts artist.

Most craftspeople work in multiple production, since this is the most effective way to survive economically without becoming a mass-production factory or without having to rely on the occasional sale of expensive one-of-a-kind pieces.

Multiple production provides a number of advantages:

1. Savings in the purchase of raw materials and supplies since they can be bought in larger quantities;

2. More effective use of production time;

3. The development of a line of crafts products that increases sales potential;

4. Ability of retail stores to reorder items that sell well, based on the knowledge that you are in a position to furnish more of the same item. *(See also: Inventory, Job Ticket, Mass Production, One-of-a-Kind, Overhead, Pricing, Production, Wages)*

Museum

Traditionally museums have been scholarly institutions, collecting works of historic or artistic significance and often displaying such work for public viewing. Museums were generally, however, more interested in acquisition than in education or participation.

This approach has changed significantly in recent years with the advent of museums that not only mount a great many exhibitions and change them frequently but that also conduct lectures, tours, demonstrations, concerts, and other activities for the public. An even more recent innovation is the actual participation by the public in museum activities, such as through art classes and workshops. Many museums also operate shops in which crafts objects and fine reproductions of paintings can be rented or purchased.

The likelihood of having craftwork purchased by a museum is comparatively rare. Museums are certainly not a major market for most craftspeople, though museum shops may be. Participation in temporary exhibitions, however, and in invitational museum shows can provide important exposure of your work to the public. There may be little money in it—except for prizes and purchase awards in some instances—but the prestige of having your work shown in a reputable museum may add considerably to a crafts artist's future selling potential.

When you lend your work to a museum for exhibition purposes, a written form should clearly outline the length of time involved, who is responsible for shipping and insurance, an accurate description of the objects you are lending, and the conditions under which your work will be exhibited. Be sure that each object is properly identified as your property. Such a written form should also safeguard your rights in the work in the event the museum wants to reproduce it in some form for sale in its shop, even if that reproduction is only pictorial.

Museums will occasionally ask craftspeople to donate work to the museum's collections. Whether you wish to make such a donation is a business decision, although, if the museum has funds with which it buys other works, you should certainly try to have the museum buy your work. While art collectors can count their contribution to a museum as a tax deduction, the tax laws may not permit the artist who created the work to enjoy this same tax advantage. In fact, for purposes of federal income tax, the artist may deduct only the cost of materials used in creating that work and only in the tax year in which the work was donated. Oregon, Maryland, Arkansas, Michigan, and Kansas provide additional state-tax benefits for artists' donations to museums and other qualified charities.

Contributions of craftwork to a museum, therefore, make sense only if you have a special feeling for the particular museum and that museum is really strapped for funds. Possibly, the fact that your work is in a museum's collection is a point of pride and something that you feel is important on your résumé.

If you make such a contribution, be sure that the conditions of the gift are specified in writing. Especially note whether the museum has the right to put the piece in storage or to sell it and whether the piece must be returned to you if there is no further interest in exhibiting it. For more information about artists' donations of their work, see *Art Law in a Nutshell, 2nd Ed.* and *The Deskbook of Art Law, 2nd Ed.* (see Appendix C). *(See also: Purchase Award)*

National Endowment for the Arts (NEA)

The National Endowment for the Arts (NEA) is an independent agency of the federal government created by Congress to encourage and support American arts and artists. It pursues its mission by awarding grants to individuals and organizations concerned with the arts throughout the United States.

The endowment describes its mission thus: "to foster the excellence, diversity and vitality of the arts in the United States; and to help broaden the availability and appreciation of such excellence, diversity and vitality."

Crafts activities are an important ingredient of the endowment's visual-arts program. Grants, therefore, are available in numerous categories that involve crafts as well as other arts projects. Some grants are made to non-profit organizations on a matching-fund basis, and some are made directly to individual craftspeople.

Specific details about each grant—application deadlines and so on—are spelled out in the endowment's "Guide to the NEA" (see Appendix C). *(See also: Government Activities, Grants)*

Net

When this word precedes another word, such as *price, profit, income, worth,* or *weight,* it means that specified deductions have been taken and that the described subject is free and clear.

When used as a verb, it usually indicates the final, true income or profit after all expenses and taxes have been deducted from the selling price, as in: "I should net ten dollars on each of these leather bags."

Net should be distinguished from *gross. (See also: Gross)*

Net Price

The price after allowing for discounts. If an item retails for one hundred dollars and wholesales at 50 percent off, the net price to the retailer is fifty dollars.

Net Profit

The profit that remains after deducting taxes and expenses. *(See also: Profit)*

Net Weight

The weight of a shipment after the weight of the packing materials has been deducted; that is, the actual weight of the product being shipped.

This can become a cost factor because shipping charges are based on gross weight, which includes the content as well as the packing materials. The development of new, lightweight packing materials has been an important influence in keeping shipping costs in line even while the per-pound rates have gone steadily upward.

If you ship a two-pound glass object in a five-pound crate, you wind up paying more for sending wood than for sending glass. Craftspeople who do any sizable amount of shipping of crafts products may find that a study of the various packing materials can save them quite a bit of money. *(See also: Packing, Post Office, Shipping, United Parcel Service)*

Net Worth

The equity held by the owners of a business on a specific date after all liabilities have been deducted from all assets. It could be said that this is the true book value of the business on that date. Net worth is not related to the market value, which would take into account such intangibles as goodwill and future potential. *(See also: Balance Sheet, Equity)*

On Approval

Shipping on approval is a practice in which the crafts artist sends work to a prospective purchaser with the understanding that the recipient may examine the item for a limited period of time, which is usually specified, and either return it within that period of time without obligation or approve the transaction and pay for the work. The period for such an examination usually ranges from ten to thirty days. The Uniform Commercial Code (UCC) section on consignment distinguishes "on approval" from "sale or return," which is defined by the law as an actual sale unless the work is returned. Under the UCC, sale on approval is really a form of conditional possession and not ownership until the recipient agrees. *(See also: Consignment, Memo, Uniform Commercial Code)*

One-of-a-Kind

One-of-a-kind means exactly that. There is no other craft object like it, not even a copy by the same crafts artist. Concentrating exclusively on this kind of production is viable only for the most successful crafts artists who can command the generally high prices for their distinctive one-of-a-kind work.

However, many craftspeople create one-of-a-kind pieces in addition to their multiple production for several reasons. First, there is the need for creative expression that can occasionally be satisfied only by creating a large or unusual piece in which the possibility of sale does not determine the investment of time, labor, and materials. In addtion, an elaborate one-of-a-kind object can serve as a centerpiece for the display of the crafts artist's line of multiple-production items. It can thus help sell the line even if the big piece itself is not sold.

An elaborate glass chandelier, for example, can create an aura of prestige and artistry for the display of smaller glass objects made by the same crafts-person. This method can be used in a store or gallery setting or in the presentation of a line to a retail-store buyer. In either case, it serves to create a dramatic impression on the potential customer.

One-of-a-kind pieces are also suitable for publicity purposes, particularly if they incorporate some innovative or unusual design features. This is especially true for exhibitions or gallery shows that might attract press coverage. *(See also: Multiple Production)*

Orders

The next best thing to actual money is an order. The order can be translated into money but not until you've satisfied the customer. To avoid hassles and disputes, it is important that all orders clearly specify at least three basic conditions:

1. Exactly what is ordered (by catalog number or description, size, color, material, quantity, and so on);

2. The price per piece, the total price, payment terms, and sales-tax exemptions where applicable;

3. When the merchandise is to be delivered, where it is to be shipped, and who pays the shipping charges.

Depending on the nature of the object and the relationship with the customer, various other specifications may be necessary. In some instances, especially where a heavy investment in materials is needed, it may be advisable to specify a partial payment with the order if you don't know the customer well. You should certainly check credit references.

An order can take many forms. It can be as simple as a letter from a customer. Whenever you get a verbal order, be sure to acknowledge it in writing with all the details mentioned so that there can be no misunderstanding later.

You can enter orders on your own order forms, printed either specifically for you or on a stock form on which you can rubber-stamp your name and address. Such stock forms are available from suppliers in most major cities (look under *Business Forms* in the yellow pages).

Many institutions and stores have preprinted purchase-order forms that include a lot of fine-print conditions. Read them carefully. You'll often find specific billing addresses that differ from shipping addresses. Note also such important requirements as confirming the order and sending duplicate copies of invoices.

When an order has been accepted, it is implied between you and the customer that all the conditions are acceptable. To violate a condition and then plead ignorance because you didn't read it won't stand up in court if your customer won't accept shipment or refuses to pay for the merchandise.

Turn the tables for a moment. If you order blue yarn and the shipment is green or if you want delivery by March 15 and don't get it until May 1, you have every right to return the yarn and refuse to pay.

If you receive an order with unacceptable terms and conditions, notify the customer at once. Holding onto the order implies acceptance. In most cases, an unacceptable condition—a delivery date you can't meet, for example—can be negotiated if you discuss it with the customer immediately. Don't wait until the day before you're due to ship the items. If the customer tells you not to bother, you've not only lost a customer but you've spent a lot of time and money producing objects that you then have to try to sell elsewhere. *(See also: Business Forms, Collection Problems, Credit)*

Organizations

Organizations of craftspeople exist on national, regional, state, and local levels. Some have full-time professional staffs and permanent headquarters. Others operate strictly through volunteer officers. A few are merely paper organizations. There are also many associations organized to benefit the various craft media, such as weaving, glass, pottery, embroidery, jewelry, metal, and woodworking.

Activities vary considerably. Some groups confine themselves to periodic meetings and perhaps an annual crafts show or exhibition. Some are also extensively involved in marketing programs, and some operate their own shops at which members' craftwork is sold—such as the League of New Hampshire Craftsmen, Piedmont Craftsmen, The Kentucky Guild of Artists & Craftsmen, Southern Highland Handicraft Guild, and Ohio Designer Craftsmen. Most organizations publish newsletters or magazines in varying degrees of regularity, with varying degrees of competence.

Some organizations offer their members help with collection problems and medical insurance, some publish directories, and some offer extensive educational programs, special prices on crafts books, and business advice. Quite a few crafts organizations, especially those that conduct marketing activities, admit members only after a screening process to determine technical and design proficiency. The one common denominator of all such organizations is that they provide their members with opportunities to share information and ideas, improve their professional competence, and upgrade their selling potential.

An extensive list of crafts organizations in all fifty states appears in the *International Directory of Resources for Artisans* (see Appendix C). This book, updated biennially, is also available in many libraries. *(See also: American Craft Council, National Endowment for the Arts, State Arts Agencies, World Crafts Council)*

Outstanding Check

Any check that you have written but that has not been paid by your bank is an outstanding check. Outstanding checks have to be calculated in the monthly reconciliation with the bank statement and should be closely monitored. If a check is outstanding for an unusually long time, it is wise to find out why it has not been cashed. Perhaps it was lost or stolen, in which case a stop payment order should be issued and a new check written. *(See also: Bank Statement, Stop Payment)*

Overdrawn

Overdrawn means you wrote more checks than you have money in the bank to cover. When such a check arrives at your bank for payment from your account, it is usually returned to the person or company to whom you issued it with the notation *insufficient funds*. This can be embarrassing. It sometimes happens when you think you have enough money in the bank to write a check because you recently made a deposit. However, a check you deposit is only a piece of paper until it has actually been collected by your bank. That takes between three and ten days, depending on the distance from the bank where the check was issued.

If your bank knows you well, it will sometimes honor the overdrawn check and add a service charge, especially if it happens rarely and they note that you have a deposit waiting to clear. That saves you embarrassment, but don't depend on it. It is much better to keep your checkbook in good order to avoid this difficulty.

Writing a check when you know there's not enough money in the bank to pay it is illegal. In addition, you could run into problems of fraud or theft if the check was in payment for goods or services you've already used. *(See also: Balance, Checking Account, Cleared Check, Deposit, Insufficient Funds)*

Overhead

A crafts business has three major areas of cost: raw materials, labor, and overhead. That's true whether the activity is conducted by a craftsperson all alone in a basement workshop or whether it's an extensive operation with employees, elaborate equipment, and a store.

Overhead consists of all the operating costs that are not directly related to the production of specific craftwork. The cost of raw materials and labor—including your own—changes in direct proportion to how much is produced. Overhead does not. It remains fairly constant, even if nothing is produced. That's why overhead is also known as a general or fixed expense.

Rent, insurance premiums, telephone bills, and utilities have to be paid every month whether you are away at a crafts show or burning the midnight oil to complete an order.

Overhead can mean a loss of profits if it isn't figured carefully into your pricing. Accountants have devised many ways to do this, but two seem most practical for a small crafts operation: Assign a certain dollar amount of overhead to each hour of production, or increase each dollar of production cost—for materials and labor—by a specific percentage to account for overhead.

Before developing a formula to calculate overhead, examine what ingredients go into it. If your crafts activities and your personal affairs are completely separate, that's not too difficult. All your bills and all your payments appear either on your personal account or on your business account. If you work at home, however, and have one telephone bill, one electric bill, and so forth, it is essential that you maintain careful records to know exactly how much of the rent, how much of the telephone, how much of your car expense, how much of the electric bill can be charged to your crafts activity and how much is a personal expense. It is too easy to overlook overhead items in such a situation. But overlooking them eats into your profits because if you don't list a cost item as a business expense, you cannot use it as a tax deduction. In addition, if you overlook a business expense, you cannot include it in your pricing.

Following are some of the major items to include in a list of overhead expenses:

Rent
Insurance premiums
Payroll taxes
Transportation (*car or van*)
Utilities (*electric, gas*)
Heat and hot water
Telephone
Maintenance and cleaning
Repairs
Shipping-and-packing materials
Freight and other delivery costs (*unless charged separately to customer*)
Office equipment and supplies
Show and sales costs
Nonproductive service time

There are some obvious items missing from this list: mortgage payments, loan payments, taxes. Since these are not related to the day-to-day operation of the business but to investment and profitability, they have to be calculated into profit, not overhead. A sizable crafts business with extensive sales costs may want to list those as a separate category, but for many craftspeople it is probably more practical to include them in overhead, especially when they are primarily for show and fair expenses.

One essential overhead ingredient that is often overlooked is the service time you spend on nonproduction work doing billing, shipping, bookkeeping, cleaning up, running to the post office, and so on. The time spent can add up and has to be included in overhead. Service time is described more fully in the section on wages.

Use the preceding list and add other categories you consider important in your operation in making a list of your major overhead items to determine overhead costs. Next to each item indicate the total amount you spend—or expect to spend—for that item in one year. Certain amounts are easy to identify, such as rent and insurance premiums. Others have to be estimated, based on previous experience or some specific plans you have made. If you went to only two crafts shows last year, for example, but plan an extensive tour this year, that item should be increased proportionately. Note that although you ultimately want to wind up with a monthly figure, you must start with an annual total because many items—insurance premiums, show and fair expenses, repairs—don't occur every month.

If the list you've made up has been calculated carefully, taking into account price increases for utilities and supplies, additional insurance, and so on, you have a total of your annual overhead expense. Suppose, for example, that your total overhead amounts to $3,816.60. Divide that by twelve to come up with a monthly figure: $318.05.

Two methods exist for figuring that overhead cost into the price of a specific craftwork.

1. Assign a certain dollar amount of overhead to each hour of production. For this method you have to determine how many hours you spend in actual production of your craftwork, not counting the hours spent on such activities as billing, shipping, and selling. If, for example, you average 140 hours a month actual work on your crafts objects, divide the 140 monthly hours into the $318.05 monthly overhead to get an hourly overhead figure of $2.27. That means a crafts object that takes an hour to produce must have $2.27 included in its price to account for overhead. If the object takes twenty minutes—one third of an hour—to make, seventy-six cents should be added to its price for overhead. And if it takes ten hours, then overhead of $22.70 must be included.

2. Increase each dollar of production cost—materials and labor—by a specific percentage to account for overhead. If, for example, your total cost of materials and labor in your crafts operation is expected to be around $13,600 this year, based on previous experience and future plans, divide that production-cost figure into the overhead figure from the previous example ($3,816). You find that overehead costs are equivalent to 28 percent of production costs.

All you need do is add twenty-eight cents for overhead to every dollar of production cost. If labor and materials for a specific item total eight dollars, you add $2.24 (8 × 28¢) for overhead. To find the percentage on odd amounts, just move the decimal point two notches to the left and multiply by twenty-eight. For example, if labor and materials costs are $12.46, you find the percentage this way:

$$
\begin{array}{r}
.1246 \\
\times \quad 28 \\
\hline
\$3.49
\end{array}
$$

If you want to simplify this and avoid the long division every time you try to calculate the cost, make up a chart that shows the overhead cost in relation to specific dollars of production. Taking the same 28 percent example, we would have a chart like this:

Production Cost	Overhead
0.25	.07
0.50	.14
1.00	.28
2.00	.56
3.00	.84
4.00	1.12
5.00	1.40
6.00	1.68
7.00	1.96
8.00	2.24
9.00	2.52
10.00	2.80

Using this chart, calculate the overhead costs on the example of $12.46 in production costs. In your head you can break down $12.46 into three units: ten dollars, two dollars, and fifty cents. Add up the amounts next to each of these figures on the chart ($2.80, fifty-six cents, and fourteen cents) and come up with a total of $3.50, only a penny off the true amount ($3.49), which was the figure you arrived at through long division.

All of this may seem like a lot of trouble, but once you've got it down on paper, you can save a lot of time when you price your craftwork, and you know that you've priced it accurately to reflect all your costs. Unless major items change significantly, you don't need to calculate your overhead again for another year.

The figures discussed here are used primarily for pricing. For tax purposes, your accountant will determine the actual overhead costs. That figure can be important to you in two ways: for comparison with the estimates you used, and as a basis for next year's estimates. (*See also: Expenses, Pricing, Profit, Wages*)

Packing

More is probably lost through improper packing for shipment than any other single cause—lost not only in terms of actual cash in broken objects but in terms of tarnished customer relations. The customer has to write a letter. You have to write a letter. Damage claims have to be filed. And if the item was destined to be a gift or to be sold at a special event, the occasion may have passed before the situation is straightened out.

The American Craft Council's valuable guide to packing and shipping puts the whole problem into focus: "Since shipments are inevitably subjected to shock and stress, the main concern is to pack in such a way that the container, rather than the object, will absorb the shocks inherent in transit. If the object inside the container moves, if the inner cushioning material shifts and the object hits the side of the container, or if one object hits another, shocks and damage result." (See "Packing/Shipping of Crafts," Appendix C.)

Fortunately, modern technology has provided a great variety of excellent packaging materials that overcome these problems. Bubble paper is one of the most economical and most versatile for protection against shock. Shredded or crumpled paper and various types of paper or plastic padding are also readily available. Unfortunately, many of these materials raise environmental issues and, thus, may not be desirable. As an alternative, you may wish to try popcorn (leave out the butter and salt and feed the birds when you're through), excelsior (a natural fibrous material), or other natural materials. Test the different materials by making several typical packages exactly as you would ship them. Give them a good workout—as if they were being handled under the roughest conditions. Then unpack them, and see what works best.

It is best to wrap small, breakable objects securely; to fill the insides of cups, glasses, and vases with crumpled paper; to wrap all pieces (lids and so on) separately; to protect exterior protuberances such as spouts and handles; and to pack in small boxes, which are then packed into a larger shipping carton.

Breakage is not the only concern, however. Some objects must be protected against moisture; others from extremes in temperature. The construction of the outer package should be related to the weight of the content so that a heavy pot is not shipped in a light, corrugated container.

Items that need protection against moisture, such as jewelry or fiber work, should be wrapped in tarnishproof paper and then placed inside sealed plastic bags. It is also advisable to line the carton with waterproof paper.

If you ship a number of breakable items in one carton, observing a few simple rules will go a long way in reducing breakage:

1. Wrap all items individually in paper at least two layers thick;

2. Place at least three inches of crumpled paper on the bottom of the box or carton;

3. Place larger or heavier items on the bottom of the carton;

4. Cushion well between layers, and if the pieces are fairly heavy and have to be packed in the same carton, corrugated dividers are advisable between the pieces in addition to cushioning material;

5. Start packing from the outside edge of the box and continue filling toward the center;

6. Place bowls, plates, platters on edge, never flat;

7. If only one item is being packed, place it in the center of the box with cushioning under, over, and around it;

8. Fill the box to within three inches of the top, then fill the last few inches with paper or cushioning material;

9. Mark the outside of all boxes or cartons containing breakables with the word *fragile* and, if necessary, *this side up* and *other side up*.

Every package should contain a packing slip. This is usually a carbon copy of the invoice, often with the prices blocked out so you don't announce your wholesale prices to unauthorized parties. The packing slip can be enclosed inside the package or, better yet, fastened securely to the outside in a separate envelope prominently marked *packing slip enclosed*. The packing slip enables the recipient to check the contents against the packing slip. This is especially important in shipments to stores where the receiving department verifies receipt of the shipment in good order and sends the packing slip on to the bookkeeping department to be paid.

It doesn't pay to cut corners on packaging of craftwork that can break or be otherwise damaged in transit. The few pennies saved may become many dollars spent if breakage occurs. But there is a way to save if you can afford the investment: Buy packaging materials in quantity from a wholesaler who specializes in such items. This may not prove a small initial outlay, but it saves money in the long run. Buying one hundred cartons at a time is a lot less expensive than buying five cartons twenty times.

A good packing-materials wholesaler can also be useful in helping you determine what kind of packing materials to buy for your specific needs. Since this person keeps up with the latest developments in the field and is aware of the experiences other shippers have had and how they have solved their problems, his or her advice can be important.

Another excellent source of information is United Parcel Service, which has done considerable research into the subject and has ideas and suggestions in print for its customers. *(See also: Shipping)*

Partnership

When two or more people own a business it can be organized as a partnership. This requires an agreement between the parties. It should be written but can be oral or even implied by their dealings. If you are forming a limited partnership, then you must file documents evidencing the partnership with the appropriate state or local office—usually the secretary of state but in some states, the county clerk.

The danger in a partnership is that each partner has full power to contract debts for the partnership, and each partner is personally liable for those debts, regardless of which partner incurred them. If the business goes under, the creditors can collect not only from the assets of the business but also from each partner's personal income and assets such as savings, homes, cars, and so on. The one exception is a limited partnership. This is never a do-it-yourself project, and even a regular partnership should have legal guidance.

It is important, therefore, to avoid becoming partners by accident. The laws of many states often interpret a close business relationship in which two or more people agree to work together in the same legal terms as a partnership. The absence of a written agreement doesn't make it any less binding. Any ongoing relationship of this nature should be specifically described in writing so that an unintentional partnership does not occur.

When a partnership is established, it is best to obtain legal advice and to have an agreement describing each partner's participation. Specify, for example, how much of a share each partner has, whether they are active or inactive (silent) partners, and what happens if one partner leaves.

If one partner dies, the law provides that the partnership is dissolved, and the business may have to be liquidated unless provisions are made in the contract for the remaining partners to carry on by buying the deceased partner's share from his or her heirs. Since that may involve a sizable sum of money that often is not readily available, partners can take out insurance on one another's lives. The policies should specify that the proceeds are to be used to pay the heirs for the deceased partner's share. *(See also: Contracts, Corporation, Joint Venture, Limited Partnership, Sole Proprietorship)*

Part-Time *(See: Expenses)*

Patent

A patent is a government document that certifies an inventor's claim to his or her invention and protects the rights in his or her discovery. Patents cover inventions of a mechanical or utilitarian nature, as distinguished from copyrights, which protect artistic creativity, or trademarks, which protect brand names.

But what exactly is an invention?

Raymond Lee, a former United States patent examiner and one of the nation's foremost authorities on patents, put it this way: "Suppose that while preparing a batch of dye, you accidentally dropped part of your breakfast into the vat and discovered, much to your surprise, that it improved the color coverage considerably. Would that make you an inventor? Absolutely—provided you remember what it was you dropped in."

A variety of inventions may be eligible for patent protection. The following are probably of most concern to craftspeople:

1. A *mechanical patent* is granted for an object whose mechanical construc-

tion is new and different. A new device for firing ceramics, for example, would be eligible for a mechanical patent.

2. A *process* or *method patent* is granted for new ways of producing an object. A new method of glazing, for example, could be eligible for a process or method patent.

3. A *composition-of-materials patent* is granted for a method by which existing materials are mixed or compounded to create new and different materials. This generally applies to such products as medicines, plastics, and other chemical formulations. It could also apply to a totally new mixture for ceramic glazes.

4. A *design patent* protects new and original designs or ornamentations for functional objects, not the way those objects are constructed. The design patent covers how an object looks, but the mechanical patent covers what the object does. If the object has no function at all but is purely decorative, then copyright laws apply.

The patent examiner Lee came up with this imaginative example: "If you invented a new kind of radio, you would apply for a mechanical patent. If that radio, in addition to being new inside, also looked like a grapefruit, you would need both a mechanical patent *and* a design patent. If you made a conventional radio look like a grapefruit, just a design patent would suffice. If you created a grapefruit sculpture with no radio inside, it would fall under copyright."

Unlike copyright protection, for which you simply submit two samples of the work with a fee, patent protection is much harder to come by. It requires careful documentation of your invention. Specific sketches and notes made at the earliest stages of discovery that are dated and witnessed help to document when you first dreamed your great idea.

A preliminary patent search will usually determine whether someone else already holds a patent on a discovery that is the same as or similar to yours. This can cost as little as two hundred fifty dollars or as much as several hundred, depending on problems encountered in the preliminary search.

Once your patent application has been filed, you are entitled to claim *patent pending* on the product of your invention. This affords a certain amount of protection and establishes a prior claim in case someone else comes up with a similar idea later on.

Filing such applications and the subsequent legal work that is usually required are best done through a patent agent or an attorney. You are permitted to apply for the patent yourself, but the complications are monumental. The assistance you receive must be from either a lawyer or patent agent who is registered to practice before the patent bar. At this point, extensive patent searches have to be conducted, drawings and specifications have to be prepared, forms have to be filled out, and filing fees have to be paid.

It is important to do this properly and speedily. Someone else may be thinking the same great thoughts at this very moment, and your rights may be lost through delay or improper handling of the application procedure.

The costs for such legal services are rarely below one thousand dollars and can run much higher. It's worth the effort and expense if your invention is likely to produce a sizable amount of money for you. Before you sign up with a patent attorney, ask about fees and what the attorney will do for you.

The address of the United States Patent Office is Washington, D.C. 20231. A detailed booklet of "General Information Concerning Patents" is available from the Superintendent of Documents, United States Government Printing Office, Washington, D.C. 20402. *(See also: Copyright, License, Trademark)*

Payroll Tax *(See: Withholding Tax)*

Pensions
Self-employed craftspeople and those who are employed by firms without pension plans can set up their own retirement funds at considerable tax advantages.

1. If you are self-employed, or an owner or partner in an unincorporated business, each year you can deposit up to 15 percent (but no more than seventy-five hundred dollars) of your self-employed income in a Keogh plan for your later years.

2. If you are employed by a firm that does not have a pension plan, you can start your own individual retirement account (IRA) with up to 15 percent (to a maximum of two thousand dollars) of your annual salary.

3. Dividends, rents, interest, and so on are not eligible for inclusion under either the Keogh or IRA plans.

4. The money you put into your Keogh or IRA plan is not taxable in the year you earned it. The deposits, as well as the interest they earn, are taxable when you withdraw them. The assumption is that you will be in a lower tax bracket when you are of retirement age and can take advantage of special retirement-tax benefits then. For example, if your self-employed income this year is twenty thousand dollars and you put three thousand dollars into your Keogh plan, you pay taxes on only seventeen thousand dollars. You are, in effect, postponing your tax obligation on the other three thousand dollars until you retire and presumably are in a lower tax bracket. If you are in the 28 percent bracket now, you save $840 this year.

5. You must leave the money in your Keogh plan until you are at least fifty-nine and a half years old. If you withdraw it earlier, you not only have to pay back taxes based on your tax rate in the year that you earned it, but you'll also face stiff penalties.

6. If you die before age fifty-nine and a half, your beneficiaries receive

immediate payment. If you are permanently disabled before age fifty-nine and a half, you receive your full amount at once, with no penalties.

7. If you have employees who work for you at least twenty hours a week, five months per year for three years, you *must* include them in your Keogh plan, if any, and contribute the same percentage of their earnings as you contribute of your own. Employees have full vested rights to all contributions made in their behalf.

How to Invest

There are a variety of ways to invest your Keogh plan: mutual funds, annuities, bank accounts, certificates of deposit, and so on. Whatever plan you choose, it must be one that is approved by the Internal Revenue Service.

If the amount you plan to invest each year is not substantial, you might put the funds into certificates of deposit at your bank, which are protected by the Federal Deposit Insurance Corporation (FDIC). The banks act as trustees and generally charge no fee.

Talk to your lawyer, accountant, or bank. One of them can give you advice about whether to start a plan and about choosing a Keogh plan that suits your particular circumstances. Remember, a Keogh plan means that you tie up your money for a number of years in exchange for significant tax benefits. Only you can decide whether that's worthwhile. You may never plan to retire, but hopefully you'll be fifty-nine and a half some day.

Periodicals

Since crafts are a creative process, a crafts artist's education never really stops. New ideas, new designs, new techniques are as constant as the morning's sunrise.

A great deal of information can be found in the plentiful supply of crafts periodicals that are published throughout the world. Some of these are elaborate magazines with full-color illustrations. Some deal with the whole gamut of crafts, others concentrate on only one craft. Whatever the source, most craftspeople who intend to stay abreast of developments and ideas in their craft read at least one or two publications regularly. *(See also: Books)*

Petty Cash

Proper bookkeeping and accounting methods require that all expenses be paid by check and entered on the books under the proper category.

There are always small expenses, however, such as local carfare or delivery tips, that are too petty to warrant the check-writing procedure. A petty-cash fund is established for this purpose and is usually small—perhaps between thirty dollars and fifty dollars, depending on the size of the operation. To start the petty-cash fund, a check is drawn and cashed. The cash is kept separate from all other monies. Whenever a payment is made from the petty-cash fund, a slip of paper—called a petty-cash voucher—is placed in the box or envelope along with the remaining petty-cash money. The petty-cash voucher should include the date, the amount, the purpose of the expenditure, the payee, and the signature of the person receiving the cash. The combination of cash on hand and vouchers should always total the original amount of the fund.

When the fund is almost depleted, all the vouchers are added up, and a new check is written in the amount of the vouchers. That puts the petty-cash fund back to its original amount.

Your accountant will want to break down the petty-cash vouchers into various types of expenditures to apportion them into the proper expense categories.

One warning about the petty-cash fund: Even though you may be the boss and it's your own money, be sure to put an IOU into the box or the envelope whenever you borrow a buck or two for personal use. Redeem the IOU as soon as you can. To take out the money without leaving a note, hoping you'll remember to put it back, can cause untold havoc. *(See also: Bookkeeping, Expenses)*

Photographs

Almost every photograph has one or more of these three purposes:

1. To record an event (vacation snapshots, wedding pictures, news photographs, and so on);

2. To serve as a sales tool (advertising or catalog illustration, publicity stills, slides of craftwork, and so on);

3. To serve as an art form.

This section concerns itself only with the use of photographs to help sell or publicize craftwork. The technical aspects of photography are covered in *Photographing Your Product, Photographing Crafts, Photography for Artists and Craftsmen,* and *Photographing Your Crafts* (see Appendix C). These books assume a basic understanding of photography on the part of the reader. Numerous other books and manuals on photographic techniques and the use of equipment, both elementary and advanced, are available in libraries, bookshops, and photographic supply stores.

Almost everyone has handled a camera at one time or another, but there is a big difference between snapshots and photographs of crafts objects. Norbert Nelson, author of *Photographing Your Product,* describes the difference as one of taking a picture or making a picture.

In snapshots, the amateur photographer has comparatively little control, except perhaps in the adjustment of the camera's timing and exposure. When you take a picture of the happy couple running down the church steps, you can't tell them to turn this way or stand that way. You shoot away with whatever light the sun provides, and let the shadows fall where they may. That's taking a picture.

But when you photograph a crafts object, you have complete control. You can arrange all sorts of lights, backgrounds, reflectors, positions, and other fancy footwork, and you can shoot the same subject over and over again with various exposures, shutter speeds, and lighting arrangements until you feel fairly secure that you have just the shot you want. That's making a picture.

This very control scares a lot of craftspeople. It seems complicated at first. But if you are a potter, try to remember the first time you centered a glob of clay on the wheel. It probably went every which way until you learned how to control your medium. That's true of every other crafts medium as well.

Photography itself is a craft and requires a certain amount of equipment: a fairly good camera and a tripod at the very least. Flash equipment is not very useful for crafts photography since you need better light control. But sunshine will do fine if you can't afford elaborate lighting equipment. Crafts photography presents special problems, such as capturing textures in pottery and weaving, avoiding reflection in jewelry and metalwork, and so forth.

Some reading, some practice, and some experimentation will provide most craftspeople with the basic skills to photograph their craftwork. But whether you take the pictures yourself or hire a professional photographer to do it for you—for a sales presentation or a juried show, for example—there are some basic principles.

For crafts objects, the most common photographs are 35mm color slides. They are comparatively inexpensive, can be mailed easily, and can be projected so that more than one person—such as a jury—can see them at a time. They also provide faithful color reproduction. Slides are also useful when you are asked to give a talk about your craft at a school or before a local club. A well-organized slide presentation contributes immensely to making your presentation lively and dramatic.

Slides that are used for selling or jurying purposes should be as simple in composition as possible so that nothing detracts from the crafts object. Backgrounds should be neutral—white, gray, or black—and uncluttered. Extraneous subjects should be used only if they play a key role, such as providing a comparison frame of reference. For example, the size of a huge wall hanging may be put into proper perspective by placing a simple chair next to it.

The same basic rules apply to black-and-white photographs to be used for advertising or catalog illustration. Remember that you are selling craftwork, not fancy photographs. The illustration serves to give visual support to the selling text and the specific details that are provided through words. You want the reader to see the crafts object, not the photograph.

Publicity Photos

The rules change a little bit with publicity pictures that you hope to have printed—without charge—as news in newspapers or magazines. Here a little human interest becomes important. Put some flowers in the vase, and place it on a table. Put the rings on a finger or the belt around a waist. But don't let the human interest overshadow your craftwork. Again, you're not publicizing fingers and waists but rings and belts.

Another form of publicity photograph is a picture of yourself doing your craftwork, getting an award, exhibiting at an important show, giving a lecture and demonstration, or participating in some other newsworthy event. You'd be surprised what editors consider newsworthy. If the photograph shows someone doing something visually interesting, it has a good chance of appearing in print. The law of averages is at work here too. You can't expect to see yourself in the papers every week, but if you submit photographs to editors periodically, you're bound to increase your opportunities for having something used. This is especially true of small-town newspapers that may not have their own staff photographers and that are always on the lookout for interesting pictures to spruce up their pages.

Competition being keen among editors, it is best not to send the same photograph to several newspapers in the same town at the same time. If you've taken several pictures, you can submit different ones to every editor, even if the subject matter is similar. Otherwise, they'll be sore at you.

A warning: If you hope to have your publicity photographs published, don't make them Polaroid snapshots. Avoid slides or color prints too; they lose a lot when they are converted to black and white. Editors almost universally prefer 8×10-inch black-and-white glossies, and it is wise to give editors what they want. These glossies are also relatively inexpensive to reproduce in quantity if you have a commercial processing laboratory in your area.

Identification

Be certain that all photographs are properly identified. Write your name and address on the cardboard frame of every slide and on the back of every print. Use a soft pencil on the back of prints; ballpoint pens press through to spoil the image.

Slides that are submitted for selling purposes should be coded to the price list or whatever information you send along.

Publicity photographs must have a caption securely attached. The best way to do this is to type the caption—the description of the photograph—

on a piece of paper with two or three inches of blank space at the top. Then tape the top of the sheet to the back of the photograph so that the caption sticks out below the photo. For mailing purposes you fold the part that sticks out over the front of the picture. When the editor opens it, he or she doesn't have to turn the picture over to see what it's all about. Be sure the caption also includes your name and address or phone number so that it can be easily identified with the accompanying press release.

Mailing

Having spent all that money on photography, a little protection is in order when you send the photos through the mail.

For slides, the best method is to wrap them securely and mail them in a padded envelope (available at most major stationery-supply stores). If that's not possible, surround them with corrugated or chipboard protection. If it's only a few slides, two pieces of chipboard in an envelope will usually work, but mark the envelope *hand cancel* so that it doesn't go through the canceling machines at the post office.

Prints should always be sent in an envelope large enough to hold them without folding them, and should be backed with a piece of chipboard. Mark the front of the envelope *Do Not Bend*. Address the envelope before you insert the photos to avoid possible damage from the pressure of a ballpoint pen.

If you want your slides or prints returned, be sure to enclose a self-addressed, stamped envelope of the proper size and with the proper postage.

Model Release

If an individual is recognizable in any photograph that is used for commercial purposes, it is necessary to obtain a model release, even if it's your best friend or someone who works for you. If the model is a child, get a release signed by the parent or guardian. The best time to have a release signed is at the time the picture is taken. This can get ticklish at times, but you can always say that your lawyer or your printer told you to get a release. If someone refuses to sign a release, don't use the picture under any circumstances. You'd only be inviting trouble.

The model release—a form available at major photography supply stores or in *The Photographer's Business and Legal Handbook* (see Appendix C)—is the legal means by which an individual whose likeness appears in a photograph gives permission to use that photograph for advertising or other commercial purposes. Such releases are not necessary for noncommercial use such as publicity photos. Most photographers, however, consider it advisable to obtain a model release for all purposes. You never know when you might want to use the picture for a brochure or some other commercial-promotion piece. *(See also: Portfolio, Press Release, Publicity)*

Politics

Many craftspeople pride themselves on being individualists by nature. The self-sufficiency that's built into crafts sometimes extends to your view of yourself, the artist, as separate from the rest of the community. The difficulty of gaining recognition as an artist further sets you apart from the rest of the world. You have your studios, your workshops, your clients, your families, your friends. And that's that.

The reasons for noninvolvement are many, but the results are always the same. The voice of the crafts artist is rarely heard in public, so the economic interests of working craftspeople are overlooked. Laws are passed, programs planned, grants and commissions awarded—all with little or no input from the crafts community.

Political clout is an unacceptable phrase to many craftspeople, but it is a concept whose time has come. Only by participating in or at least influencing the legislative and planning process can you hope to get a fair share of the action or the proper protection of your interests as a craftsperson.

The very least that you can do is to write a letter to a legislator or public official—local, state, or national—when a matter of direct concern to craftspeople is on the agenda. The involvement might seem like an unattractive distraction from the creative life, but lack of involvement costs the crafts community too much in the long run.

Portfolio

A portfolio is you reduced to two dimensions. A good portfolio puts your best foot forward in terms of your craftwork; what you've done; where you've sold, exhibited, studied; and what others say about your work.

The portfolio consists essentially of three ingredients: your résumé, clippings or reviews, slides or photos of your craftwork. The latter two are considered here.

To show clippings to best advantage, cut them carefully out of the newspaper or magazine and mount them flat under two-sided acetate sheets, available in most good stationery-supply stores. Do the same thing with gallery programs or other prestige documents in which your name is listed.

Black-and-white or color prints can also be mounted under two-sided acetate sheets. For 8×10-inch prints, 10×12-inch sheets are most suitable since they allow you to show prints either vertically or horizontally without turning the portfolio binder around.

For color slides, photo-supply stores have plastic sheets that are clear on one side and frosted on the other to diffuse light. They can accommodate a dozen 2¼ × 2¼-inch transparencies, or twenty 35mm slides that can be easily removed for showing in a slide projector. Arrrange the slides or prints in some logical sequence, if possible, so that the person who looks at them doesn't have to jump from one idea to another.

If you plan to make a sizable number of presentations to galleries and store buyers, have a few of your best slides converted into color prints. It's much easier to examine them, especially if a slide projector or viewer is not readily available. But be sure it's a good shot to begin with; every defect is magnified when a poor slide or negative is blown up.

The portfolio itself can be one or more ordinary loose-leaf binders carried around in a case, or it can be a zippered case that has the three-ring binder feature built in. Don't skimp on this. It's the first impression a prospect gets of your work and your attitude.

Another suggestion, this one from a craft photographer, Doug Long: "Please assign a safe, cool place for your portfolio. I cringe every time I see one lying next to a kiln, on the corner of a worktable, or some other imminently disastrous spot. Slides and prints get dirty and warped easily, so unless that's the way you feel about your work, protect your investment."

Long also observes that "showing pictures is a sadly lacking level away from handling the real thing, but it doesn't have to be a necessary evil. There is room for your own expression in a portfolio. There are no rules, no limits. Just the reaches of your imagination." (*See also: Photographs, Résumé*)

Post Office

The government activity that touches most of us on a daily basis is the post office—officially the United States Postal Service. A great deal of cynicism exists with regard to the efficiency and cost of postal service, but since it's the only post office there is in this country—except for parcel post—you can make the best of it by understanding the variety of services it offers.

Mail is transported in four basic categories (postal rates quoted are 1991 figures):

First Class

All handwritten or typewritten letters, bills, and other individualized material must be sent via first-class mail, although almost anything else may be sent first class. First-class mail is completely private and may not be opened for postal inspection.

If you move, the post office will forward first-class mail to your new address at no extra charge for one year, provided you notify your old post office of your new mailing address when you move. Thereafter for six months the post office will return the mail to the sender with the correct address noted. First-class mail for which no new address is available is returned to the sender as undeliverable.

First-class mail of less than twelve ounces and in a standard letter-sized envelope travels airmail. If your mail is larger than standard and is not clearly marked "first class" or "airmail," it may not receive first-class treatment even though it has first-class postage.

The maximum weight for first-class mail is seventy pounds; the maximum size is 108 inches in length and girth combined.

First-class postage for mail weighing less than thirteen ounces costs twenty-nine cents for the first ounce and twenty-three cents for each additional ounce. Postcards, which are handled as first-class mail, cost nineteen cents each. Rates vary based on weight for first-class mail weighing more than eleven ounces—priority mail—and up to five pounds. Rates for mail of more than five pounds and up to seventy pounds are based on weight and distance by zone. You should check with the post office for specific rates.

Second Class

This is a special category for newspapers and periodicals and is of importance to craftspeople who send catalogs or brochures. Second-class mail is never forwarded.

Third Class

This category may be used for single pieces of printed matter or merchandise weighing less than a pound or for large mailings of identical pieces sent under a special bulk rate.

Delivery time for third-class mail is unpredictable. It is not unusual for mail to take as long as two weeks to reach distant parts of the country, especially during heavy-mail-volume periods such as Christmas. I believe third-class mail usually waits until everything else moves and is customarily sent by surface transportation.

Third-class mail is neither forwarded nor returned to the sender unless it is marked *Return Postage Guaranteed* or *Forwarding and Return Postage Guaranteed*. That means the sender guarantees to pay the extra postage for the extra handling. The label *Return Postage Guaranteed* is often used by senders of third-class mail to get the undeliverable pieces back and clean up their mailing list to remove the names of people who have moved. Such mail can also be marked *Address Correction Requested*, in which case the post office will provide for a thirty-five-cent charge the new address—if it has one—and you can determine whether to retain the name on your list at the new address.

The single-piece rate for third-class mail is the same as for first class for each of the first four ounces. Above that it becomes considerably lower. In other words, there's no point in using slower third class for pieces that weigh less than five ounces. The rate increments for heavier third-class and first-class pieces are compared as follows:

	Third Class	First Class
to 6 ounces	$1.21	$1.44
to 8 ounces	1.33	1.90
to 10 ounces	1.44	2.36
to 12 ounces	1.56	2.82
to 14 ounces	1.67	2.90
to 15.9 ounces	1.79	2.90

For bulk mailings, an annual permit fee is required, in addition to a one-time application fee. The postal rates vary according to the nature of the material that is mailed, in some instances according to zone distance and whether the mailer is a nonprofit organization or a commercial enterprise. Third-class bulk rate is, however, the least expensive way of mailing large quantities of identical material.

For example, if you mail five thousand announcements to your customers twice a year, the maximum per-piece charge is 19.8¢. The annual bulk fee of seventy-five dollars spread over the total ten thousand pieces brings the per-piece postage to 20.6¢, which saves you more than 8¢ on each piece, or more than $800 in this example, as compared to first-class mail.

Third-class bulk-rate mail is governed by complex rules and regulations. If you plan to make such mailings and take advantage of the lower rate, consult your post office before you have anything printed. Some post offices have actually set up formal classes for businesses interested in bulk-mail rates.

Fourth Class

This is also known as parcel post, and here's where the post office has some competition from such organizations as United Parcel Service.

Rates depend on weight and distance. Special rates apply to books and some other materials. Packages sent over long distances get faster delivery by the use of priority mail or express mail, since those move by air. The cost, of course, is higher. A six-pound package mailed from New York to California costs $4.54 via fourth-class mail as compared to $7.53 via priority mail.

If a new address is available, fourth-class mail will be forwarded if additional postage is paid by the recipient. Fourth-class mail that is undeliverable will be returned to the sender if the sender pays the additional postage.

This extra postage is computed on the basis of the applicable fourth-class rates.

Express Mail

Express-mail service is available for mailable items up to seventy pounds in weight and 108 inches in combined length and girth. The post office even provides pick-up service for a single fee of $4.50, regardless of the number of items per pickup. Express mail has built-in insurance for up to five hundred dollars.

Express-mail rates are $4.95 for letters up to eight ounces and $13.95 up to two pounds for various express-mail services. Destination choices include post office to addressee, post office to post office, same-day airport service or custom-designed service. Consult your local post office for rates on packages between two pounds and up to the seventy-pound limit.

A six-pound New York-to-Seattle package would cost $12.70 from post office to post office and $23.50 from post office to addressee. The minimum charge to mail even a letter anywhere in the country is $9.50 from post office to post office; $9.95 from post office to addressee. The post office will leave a piece of express mail without obtaining a receipt if pre-authorized by the sender.

Business-Reply Mail

Mailing pieces that ask for an order or for payment of a bill often enclose a self-addressed envelope in which the recipient can send the order or the check. Experience has shown that such an envelope encourages recipients to respond. For many years, those envelopes almost always had the return postage included in the form of a business-reply permit number in the upper right corner. With the rapid increase in postage rates in recent years, more and more reply envelopes no longer include reply postage. The envelopes are simply self-addressed, and the recipient is expected to use his or her own stamps, especially on bill payments.

However, business-reply mail with return postage is still used when a mailer wants to produce a large number of replies and is willing to pay the postage to get them. The post office will supply the exact form and wording in which this permit must be shown on the reply envelope. The actual postage is paid when the letter carrier returns the reply envelopes, or it is paid through an account established at the delivering post office if the volume is large enough.

The postage for business-reply mail is calculated in one of two ways. If a mailer pays an annual account-maintenance fee of $185, the cost per piece is nine cents in addition to first-class postage, or thirty-eight cents for a letter and twenty-eight cents for a postcard. Mailers using the Business Reply Mail

Accounting System (BRMAS) bar code and nine-digit zip code pay only two cents in addition to first-class postage. In the absence of the annual account-maintenance fee, the cost is forty cents per piece in addition to first-class postage or sixty-nine cents for the regular letter. Anyone who expects to receive at least seven hundred pieces of business-reply mail a year is ahead of the game by paying the $185 fee. In all cases, an annual fee of seventy-five dollars must be paid for the use of a business-reply permit number.

The post office performs the following various services for its clients in connection with the delivery of mail:

1. *Registered Mail.* This provides insurance protection for domestic first-class mail valued up to twenty-five thousand dollars and ensures that it is handled with special precautions. Rates vary according to value. The minimum one hundred dollars of insurance costs $4.50; one thousand dollars costs $5.25. For higher values, consult your postmaster.

2. *Insured Mail.* This provides insurance of up to five hundred dollars for domestic third-class, fourth-class, and priority mail containing printed matter or merchandise. Rates range from a minimum of seventy-five cents for value up to fifty dollars to $6.20 for value between five hundred dollars and six hundred dollars.

3. *Certified Mail.* This provides only a receipt and record of delivery at the post office. Certified mail travels no faster than first-class mail and provides no extra security. The fee is one dollar in addition to the postage.

4. *Return Receipt.* A receipt showing when, where, and to whom the mail was delivered is available for registered, insured, or certified mail. When requested at the time of mailing, it can show when and to whom it was delivered for one dollar and the address where it was delivered for an additional thirty-five cents. If the return receipt is requested after mailing, it costs six dollars and will show only when it was delivered and who signed for it.

5. *Cash-on-Delivery (COD) Mail.* Payment for merchandise ordered by the addressee will be collected by the post office and remitted to the sender by postal money order. The maximum amount that can be collected is six hundred dollars. The fees for COD service range from $2.50 to seven dollars and include collection of the postage and money-order fee from the addressee. COD fees include insurance protection against loss or damage. COD mail may also be sent as registered mail.

6. *Special Delivery.* This service ensures prompt delivery of mail when it arrives at the delivering post office, including arrival on Sundays and holidays. Costs range from $7.65 to $9.30, depending on weight and class. The normal special-delivery charge for a letter is $7.65 in addition to the postage. With the increase in express mail use, this service is becoming obsolete.

7. *Special Handling.* This service is available only for third- and fourth-class mail. It is difficult to determine exactly what special handling means, except perhaps that the post office will take special care not to run over the package with a truck. The fees in addition to postage are $1.80 for up to ten pounds and $2.50 for an item of more than ten pounds.

8. *Money Order.* If you can't send a check, you can buy a postal money order for a maximum amount of seven hundred dollars, which the recipient with proper identification can cash at any post office or deposit in his or her bank like a check. The fee is seventy-five cents for any amount up to seven hundred dollars.

Following are five points to observe to help speed your mail through the laborious machinery of the United States Postal Service:

1. *Zip Code.* This identifies the precise post office to which your mail is destined. It is required for all but first-class mail and is strongly recommended for first-class mail as well. Every post office has a zip-code directory that you can consult. Be sure your own zip code is included wherever your address is printed: on stationery, envelopes, labels, advertising, catalogs, and so forth. The so-called ZIP + 4 identifies the specific address (house, building, suite number, and the like) to which mail is to be delivered and may speed delivery. It is required for some postal services.

2. *Stampless Mail.* Mail without stamps is no longer being delivered with postage due to be paid by the recipient. If you don't put stamps on the mail, it is returned to you. If your mail goes out without postage and a return address, it winds up in the dead-letter office.

3. *Proper Packing.* Wrap all parcels carefully, and place the name and address of the recipient inside the package for extra precaution in case the wrapping comes undone. Improper packing, especially of packages, is a major problem for the post office. While the post office does not prohibit the use of string, rope, masking tape, duct tape, or the like, they encourage the use of strapping tape, which is less likely to tear on the automatic sorting machines and conveyors.

4. *Clear Handwriting.* Names and addresses that cannot be deciphered cause delays in the post office. Some scrawls require the expertise of a hieroglyphics decoder and consequently wind up in the dead-letter office.

5. *Change of Address.* If you move, the post office provides postcard forms on which you can notify publishers of newspapers or magazines to which you subscribe of your new address. Most publications require thirty to sixty days to change their records, and most publishers generally request that you send their mailing label with your new address for better identification on their computerized mailing lists.

The change-of-address forms are free except for postage. You can also use them to notify friends, relatives, department stores, insurance companies, and others who have occasion to write to you. It will get the mail to you more quickly. Unfortunately, it will get the bills to you more quickly too. *(See also: Shipping, United Parcel Service)*

Press Release

A press release is a particular means by which you get information to newspapers, magazines, radio stations, and television news programs with the hope of having it made public. The content is different for every release, but the format is quite fixed.

A few basic rules:

1. A press release should always be typed, double-spaced and on one side of the sheet only. If the release runs to more than one page, type *more* at the bottom of each page except the last, where you type *end*.

2. The press release should be typed on 8½ × 11-inch, letter-size white paper with plenty of margin space on all sides so that the editor can make notations, corrections, or changes.

3. If the press release is not typed on stationery, the name and address of the sender should be typed at the top, centered on the page. Skip a few spaces and, at the left margin, type the date the release is sent and, immediately below it, type the earliest date it is to be used. If it can be used any time, type *for immediate release*. Otherwise type *for release on . . .*

On the same line as the date line but far to the right, type the name of the individual who can be contacted for further information. Immediately below that, give the person's telephone number with area code.

When you write the press release, remember a few basic rules of newspaper writing. First of all, get all of the important information into the first paragraph. That includes the five Ws of journalism—when, where, who, what, and why—and how. Not all six apply to every story, but where they do, they should lead off the release.

Look how it's done in the sample press release: *An exhibition of welded sculpture (what) by John Hammer (who) will open on Sunday, March 2 (when), at the Louisville Gallery, 617 Main Street, Penfield (where), in observance of National Welded-Sculpture Week (why).*

Subsequent paragraphs in a press release should be written in descending order of importance so that the least important information comes at the end. When an editor makes up a newspaper page, he or she cuts from the end if everything doesn't fit. If the important information appears at the end of the release, it is more likely to disappear when the newspaper is printed.

What will tickle an editor's fancy and what will wind up in the wastebasket are unpredictable. But one type of press release is almost sure to be ignored: a release that sounds like nothing more than a sales pitch. Editors are

THE VILLAGE SMITHY
138 EAST MAIN STREET
Penfield, Missouri 27359

February 29, 1993   Contact: John Hammer
For Immediate Release   (627) 355-0846

EXHIBIT TO CELEBRATE
WELDED-SCULPTURE WEEK

An exhibition of welded sculpture by John Hammer will open on
Sunday, March 2, at the Louisville Gallery, 617 Main Street, Penfield,
in observance of National Welded-Sculpture Week.

Hammer's unusual work has received national acclaim and has
been shown in many major museums and galleries. The Louisville
exhibit will be open daily from 10:00 A.M. to 4:00 P.M. until March 15.
Admission is free.

Welded sculpture is one of the newest art forms based on one of
the oldest crafts: blacksmithing. The Hammer exhibit will be the first
public view of this unusual new technique in the Louisville area,
according to gallery director Simon Simple.

John Hammer, now seventy-two, began to work on the anvil at
age thirteen, when he apprenticed in his uncle's blacksmith shop in
Fairfax County, Missouri. Horses were still being shod then, Hammer
explains, and it was a busy shop. But with the appearance of the
automobile, blacksmithing became a dying art. Hammer estimates

(more)

interested in news and features; sales messages belong in the advertising
columns.

Study newspaper-writing style by reading the papers from that point of
view. Sentences are short. So are paragraphs. Good stories are written to
appeal to readers, not the egos of writers. Fancy words with obscure meanings may impress your in-laws, but they'll turn off most readers—and most
editors. The simpler and more direct the press release, the better its chance
of being printed.

If the editor thinks there may be a feature story in the activity announced
in the press release, he or she will assign a reporter to contact you. An editor
who has never heard of National Welded-Sculpture Week may want to know
more about it for a possible feature. Anything in your release that might
intrigue an editor is a bonus.

If you send the sample release to the weekly in sculptor Hammer's hometown as well as to the big cities' dailies, you might want to add a postscript to alert the hometown editor that Hammer lives in the neighborhood. That may produce interest or even a feature story in the weekly.

Timing is an extremely important factor. A daily newspaper can process a release for print overnight if it wants to. A weekly newspaper often has deadlines a week ahead of publication date. Monthly magazines usually require information two and even three months ahead of time to get it into print.

Most newspapers and magazines, even small weeklies, have special editors for special departments. A general news release can go to the city editor. A release on a gallery opening could also go to the arts editor. A release on a new line of earrings should go to the features-section editor. Since these are busy people, sending a release to the wrong department could be a total waste. The few phone calls to determine the name of the appropriate editor are usually worth the time.

Photos are also important when issuing a press release. Don't, however, bother with Polaroid shots, fuzzy candids, or color slides. Most editors want 8×10-inch black-and-white glossies with the picture caption—an explanation of the picture—and your name and address securely taped or glued to the back. Some papers will take 5×7-inch shots, but the bigger size stands a better chance of being reproduced. Getting a picture into the papers is worth the investment of having a good one taken. If it's a picture of a crafts object, be sure to mark which end is the top.

Two tips on mailing photos:

1. Never fold the picture. Get a large enough envelope, and use a piece of cardboard for protection.

2. Address the envelope before you enclose the picture. Addressing the envelope later may find the ballpoint pen pressing through and defacing the photograph. For that same reason, write on the back of a photo only very lightly and only with soft pencil or crayon. *(See also: Advertising, Photographs, Publicity, Public Relations)*

Price *(See: Pricing)*

Price-Cutting

Reducing prices under competitive pressure or because of customer insistence is a temptation that may produce a few dollars immediately but that can be costly in the long run.

There are some obvious dangers. Suppose a customer finds out that another customer bought the identical item under the same circumstances but at a lower price. You've earned nothing but bad feelings.

Price-cutting also undermines the confidence your customers can have in the real value of your work. If the price tag was fifty dollars yesterday and twenty-five dollars today, there had better be a good reason.

Cutting the price may seem the easiest way of overcoming competition, but it may prevent a serious examination of the real reason why you're not selling more. Price may have nothing to do with it. Cutting the price may not solve the problem but create new ones.

Price-cutting is not to be confused with normal and accepted price reductions such as clearance sales of incomplete sets, limited selections of discontinued items, seconds, and so forth. Pricing procedures such as wholesaling and quantity discounts are also not to be confused with price-cutting. In all these cases, there are legitimate reasons why the price has been reduced. If the original price for a given crafts objects has been reasonably determined—taking into account the costs of production, the market conditions, and the profit—then it is both dangerous and costly to engage in random price-cutting.

Situations may arise in which craftspeople may not even consider that they are cutting the price. This happens when you take a booth at a crafts show and sell your work at prices below those that are charged by nearby retail stores that stock your crafts objects. Undermining the retailer's established price for your work when you are, in effect, in direct competition with him is ill-advised. You're in town for only a few days. The retail store will—you hope—sell your work all year long and reorder from you in the future. Though the temptation is there for a quick dollar, you can undermine your profitability if you do any substantial volume through retail stores. Once you get a reputation for undercutting your own retail-store customers—they do talk to one another—it will be more difficult to sell to retail outlets in the future. *(See also: Pricing)*

Pricing

You are now in what may be the most important part of this book and of your economic success in crafts.

Pricing can make you or break you. If your price is wrong, it hardly matters whether you do everything else right. The old joke that you lose a nickel on every sale but you make it up in volume doesn't work here.

Before learning the methods for determining the price you charge for your craftwork, it is useful to understand the various ingredients that enter into the determination of price.

There are four major elements to be considered:
1. How much does it cost to produce the product?
2. How much does it cost to operate the business that creates the product?
3. How much profit do you want to make?
4. Will the customer buy it at the price?

These four are all interrelated. None can stand alone, and none can stand without all the others.

The cost of production, the cost of overhead and sales, and your profit margin can all be determined with a fair amount of accuracy. Suppose, for example, that an object costs five dollars in labor and materials to produce, that the overhead apportioned to that object is three dollars, and that you want to make a 25 percent profit—two dollars on eight dollars. You charge ten dollars. That takes care of the first three items in the preceding list of considerations.

Number four is the tricky one. It doesn't matter how rational you think the price is: If there are no customers who'll buy it at that price, forget it!

Customer acceptance of a price is based on both economic and psychological reasons. First, of course, there's the question of want or need. It is unlikely, for example, that many people would buy this book if it had been priced at one hundred dollars a copy. There simply aren't many craftspeople who see the need for so expensive a book. Conversely, if this book had been priced at thirty-nine cents, many craftspeople might ask, "If it's so cheap, can it be any good?" Therefore, the customer's perception of the value of a product to fill a need affects price.

The customer's desire for prestige and recognition also affects the price. Some people will pay ten times the amount for a Dior original than they will for a mass-produced imitation. They pay the price so that they can be the first or the only people wearing that particular garment.

The same principle applies to one-of-a-kind objects created by a crafts artist. A vase created by a well-known potter will fetch a better price at a gallery than a vase created by an unknown potter will get at a crafts fair even though the cost of the clay is the same and the vases may both be beautiful. This has been true in the field of fine art for many years. It is beginning to be a factor in the field of crafts.

There's also the customer's pocketbook to consider. If you can only afford a Plymouth, it doesn't matter how rational the price of a Cadillac is; you simply can't buy it. Translated into crafts, this means that a one-thousand-dollar tapestry won't sell at the average crafts fair, not because it isn't worth every penny but because the customers simply don't bring that kind of money.

Finally, there's the competitive situation. If you offer a line of jewelry at one price and a similar line is offered at a lower price, you must be ready with some good reasons why your price is higher or lose customers to the competitor. That doesn't mean your price should be based solely on what the competition charges, but the marketplace is such that this factor must be included in your calculations if you're both after the same customer. The fact that you pay a higher rent or want to make a better profit couldn't interest your customer less. If you use better materials or your craftsmanship is obviously superior, then you have a reasonable claim to a higher price. If, on the other hand, your competitor is simply more efficient and can therefore charge less for the same product, then he or she is going to make the sale. Price, in the last analysis, is simply a way of expressing the value of a product in terms of money.

There are two basic ways to calculate your selling price: Determine the ultimate selling price and then work backward to establish materials costs, production procedures, and other steps necessary to meet that price; or find out how much everything costs and set a price on the basis of those figures.

Experienced craftspeople probably know by instinct in what general price range a particular crafts object should fall. They proceed accordingly. In actual practice, however, the pricing procedure usually starts from the other end: Calculate the cost of production, materials, labor, overhead, and profit to arrive at a price; and perhaps make adjustments if the price is not right.

Every business activity involves two types of costs that are figured into this pricing procedure: fixed costs and variable costs. Fixed costs are those that remain constant, regardless of how much you produce. These are almost always included in overhead. Your rent, for example, goes on month after month, even when you go on vacation and produce nothing. Variable costs, however, are those that relate directly to production. Making one hundred belts requires ten times as much leather as making ten belts. If you reduce production and let a helper go, you also reduce your labor cost.

With both types of costs there may be slight variations. The telephone bill, generally a fixed cost, is likely to be somewhat lower, for example, when you're on vacation, although there's still a monthly minimum. Increasing production, too, may enable you to achieve a slightly lower cost per unit for raw materials if you get a better deal for buying a larger quantity.

Determining price requires a certain amount of record keeping during the course of production. Crafts artists who produce one-of-a-kind objects find this much simpler than production craftspeople. They need to maintain cost records only for the one object they're working on at a given time.

Craft producers, however, must be much more careful. Following are some of the major categories of expense. In all cases the dollar amounts for each expense item must be apportioned to the individual crafts objects that are produced. This is done either by fixing the actual cost of time or materials related to the item or by converting expenses into hourly averages and then applying them to the time it takes to produce a given item.

Production Costs
Raw materials
Wages (your own included)

Selling Costs
Advertising
Shows and fairs
Operating a store or showroom
Commissions to outside sales staff
Wages (your own included)
Photography
Samples

Overhead
Rent
Utilities
Water

Telephone
Stationery and supplies
Packaging materials
Maintenance
Repairs
Transportation
Taxes
Insurance
Bad debts
Loss through breakage and theft

Financial Considerations
Profit
Loan payments
Depreciation
Value of inventory

Not every craftsperson itemizes every one of these expense factors. Selling costs are often included in overhead, for example. On the other hand, a potter, being a heavy user of fuel to fire the kiln, may want to apportion some of the fuel bill directly to production costs.

Overhead is most easily totaled into a weekly or monthly figure, which is reduced to a per-hour overhead cost and then applied to the cost of the various items according to the time it takes to make them. Thus, if your overhead is three dollars per hour and you produce five stained-glass owls per hour, the price for each owl must include sixty cents for overhead.

With experience, some craftspeople have even arrived at a pricing formula based on some specific element of the production process. If you discover, after several years of careful record keeping, that the ultimate wholesale price always turns out to be ten times the cost of raw materials used in making the item, then it becomes a simple matter of keeping track of the cost of materials and multiplying by ten. But that's risky unless you're on sure ground, and even then it has to be constantly examined to determine whether other factors have changed sufficiently in cost to affect the formula. If your rent doubles, for example, it could throw the whole calculation out of whack.

It is usually safest—especially for craftspeople just getting started—to pin down every last expense item and add it into the total.

Revising the Price

Suppose you've done all your calculations and you discover, to your chagrin, that the price comes out too high. You aimed for twenty dollars, and it came out twenty-two dollars. If your calculations are based on a prototype, a first piece, you'll undoubtedly find savings in the production process when you begin to make a dozen at a time.

The normal tendency, unfortunately, is to simply cut two dollars off the price and let it go at that. So you've simply cut into your profit, perhaps even demolished it. Much better to go over all of your expenses to see where you can save.

As an example, suppose you've designed a belt that's two inches wide. The leather for the belt represents 25 percent of the ultimate wholesale price. If you can make the belt one and three quarters inches wide without affecting its aesthetic quality, you have saved 12½ percent of the raw materials cost, or just more than 3 percent of the total wholesale cost. At the same time, you're talking to several suppliers and find one who will sell leather to you at 12 percent less than you've been paying. That's another 3 percent on the wholesale price. You've now saved 6 percent. Not much, you say? Well, if your net profit was 10 percent before the savings, you've just increased it by 6 points, or 60 percent. Nothing to sneeze at. On top of that you've found a way to make six belts an hour instead of five, so your labor cost per belt has gone down approximately 20 percent.

Use this sort of careful examination in different areas of your crafts activity. You will find that you can either produce at a better price or realize a bigger profit at the same price.

Odd Pricing

It is a common retail practice to price products at a fraction below the next highest round-number price. Thus a pound of bananas costs nineteen cents instead of twenty cents, a radio costs $49.95 instead of fifty dollars, and a car costs $8,995 instead of nine thousand dollars.

This is known as odd pricing and is done on the assumption that customers think the price is much lower than it actually is. Marketing experts have questioned whether that's true, and many marketers agree that it has little bearing on such products as craftwork for which prestige, originality, creativity, and similar attributes are as much a part of the product as the material of which it is made or the use to which it is put.

Off pricing, therefore, seems to be of little or no consequence in determining what price you can put on your craftwork. Indeed, it may have an undesirable effect by creating a bargain-basement atmosphere around your price tag.

Trading Up

A basic objective in selling is to build up the ticket, to have each retail customer spend more. That is often based on prices that establish an advantage in buying a larger quantity. This is not about wholesale prices but about establishing prices that are slightly lower for sets than they would be for a similar number of single pieces. Not all craftwork lends itself to this kind of pricing, but it's worth considering.

For example, if the price tag on a pillow is nine dollars, sell three of them for twenty-five dollars. In addition to selling mugs at a dollar each, offer them at ten dollars a dozen. It may appear at first that you're cutting into your profit, but many of the basic costs—rent, telephone, the booth at a crafts show—remain constant whether your sales are one hundred dollars or one thousand dollars. It may, therefore, turn out to be more profitable to induce customers to buy in logical quantities at special prices. You thus build up your total dollar volume.

Pricing for Profit

As long as your costs are covered, you can set prices according to the biggest profit return you can get. Sometimes a lower price will bring a bigger profit: If you price an item at ten dollars, which includes a two-dollar profit, you will earn four hundred dollars if two hundred of those items are sold. If you reduce the price to nine dollars, your profit will be only one dollar per piece. But suppose you can sell five hundred pieces at the lower price. You've earned five hundred dollars in profits. Indeed, the larger volume may bring even greater returns, because you can buy the raw materials more economically in large quantities.

This is not to suggest that if the price is lower, the volume will necessarily be larger. You may not even want to produce a larger volume. But it is a consideration that should be included in your calculations.

Finally, if you've figured your wholesale price properly, it will include a decent wage for your production time and a decent profit for your creativity, management skills, capital investment, and so on. No need to cry over the retail store's selling your work to the consumer at double what you got for it. The store is performing a legitimate function for you—unless you already have more customers than you can handle.

When you are both a crafts producer and a crafts retailer—opening your own shop or selling at a crafts fair—your retail price should be established exactly as any other retailer might. In effect, you are buying from yourself at wholesale and adding a markup to cover your operating expenses, wages, and profits. The temptation may be great to go into retailing whole hog, but don't do it before you've calculated whether your time is spent more profitably producing the craftwork or selling it. If you can price for a profit margin of 25 percent at wholesale and a profit margin of 10 percent at retail, stick to producing the craftwork. You'll make more money. (See also: Advertising; Cost Accounting; Debts, Bad; Insurance; Inventory; Lease; Loss Leader;

Margin; Markup; Overhead; Profit; Retailing; Samples; Shipping; Shows and Fairs; Supplies; Tax; Telephone; Wages)

Printed Materials

Letterheads, envelopes, business cards, order forms, brochures, catalogs, tags, labels, invoices—the list of printed materials needed by even the smallest business with the simplest procedures may seem endless.

Although your craftwork is your most important medium of communication, your printed material often precedes it. What you send to customers or prospects in the form of letters or sales literature is often their first introduction to you and helps to establish the initial impression—positive or negative. So you should consider that it costs no more to have something printed that is well designed and expresses your individual style or personality than to print a jumble of pedestrian type. A basic design for your name or your company name, used on all your printed materials, gives each item greater impact and value as an extension of your crafts business.

A friend in the advertising business or a helpful printer can often provide valuable suggestions on how to produce your printed materials at the lowest possible cost. They could also suggest how to print several different pieces at the same time to get more for your printing dollar—even how you might take advantage of special colors or papers to make your printed material uniquely yours. *(See also: Advertising, Business Forms, Catalog, Direct Mail, Portfolio)*

Production

Production is the general term given to all the steps involved in making a crafts object, from the first contact with the raw material to the finished product ready for packing and shipping.

In the crafts field, the term production craftsman distinguishes the craftsperson who makes a number of copies, or multiples, of the same design from the craftsperson who makes one-of-a-kind pieces. Each of these multiple pieces is, of course, a fully handcrafted item with its own unique characteristics. It is not, as in factory production, stamped from the same mold.

The production process influences both the amount of satisfaction crafts producers get from their time at the bench or wheel or loom and the amount of money they make from their work. No two craftspeople will use the same production procedures. Individuality, after all, is the hallmark of craftwork. There are, however, a few basic considerations that can help make the work more satisfying and more profitable.

1. Get organized! Keep raw materials in one place, properly identified and easily accessible, so that you don't spend useless and frustrating time looking for things. Shelving for storing new materials, Peg-Boards for tools,

and jars or cans for small bits and pieces make life much easier. Raw materials that can spoil or soil easily should be properly protected so that time isn't wasted in getting them back into shape and money isn't wasted in throwing them away because they're unusable.

2. You've got to have rhythm! The secret of the well-organized crafts producer is that the production steps follow in logical sequence. The very nature of the craft dictates much of this. A piece of pottery, obviously, can't go into the kiln until it's been glazed, and it can't be glazed until it comes off the wheel. But in production crafts, the important question becomes one of how many steps should be performed at the same time. Who would dream, for example, of making a single mug, glazing it, and then firing it? That would be a clear waste of time and money. It would also seem laborious to make a mug and attach a handle, make a mug and attach a handle, make a mug and attach a handle. Getting two dozen mugs off the wheel and then attaching two dozen handles expedites the process, reduces the production time, and thereby increases the profit.

Care must be taken, of course, to avoid the boredom and thereby the potential decline in craftsmanship that can result from repeating the same step too many times before going on to something else. Achieving the right combination is a matter of individual style and experience. *(See also: Inventory, Job Ticket, Multiple Production, One-of-a-Kind, Overhead, Pricing, Turnover, Wages, Work Area)*

Production Crafts

Production crafts are works designed by a crafts artist and executed by hand, though replicated in multiples. It is quite common, for example, for potters to produce sets of dishes or mugs that are mass-produced even though individually handmade.

Product-Liability Insurance

You make a beautiful chair and find an enthusiastic customer. Then you get a call to tell you that the chair collapsed when the customer sat down in it, and the customer's back is sprained. The customer threatens to sue. If the person can prove that the chair collapsed because of defective workmanship, he or she might win the lawsuit.

Product-liability insurance is available to protect you in case of a lawsuit based either on some defect in the product for which you are responsible or on some characteristic about which you should have warned the customer. It doesn't matter whether you sold the item directly to the customer or whether it was sold through a retail store: The maker of the product can be held responsible.

The best product-liability insurance, of course, is to make the product as safe as possible and to alert the customer if special precautions have to be taken. If you inform the customer not to put the glassware in a dishwasher but the person cuts two fingers taking the broken glass out of the dishwasher, you have met your responsibility. If, however, the glass breaks and spills hot liquid on someone because you were careless in the production of the item, watch out.

For those who make objects that could cause accidents or injuries due to product defects, it is especially important to price and obtain such liability coverage. There are a number of guilds through which product-liability coverage is now available at reasonable rates. An example is the Montclair Crafts Council, Montclair, New Jersey.

Product Line

An essential truth in merchandising is that a line of products tends to increase the sale of each item in the line. If Campbell's, for example, made only tomato soup, it would not be nearly as successful—even with its tomato soup—as it is with a line that includes chowder, vegetable soup, onion soup, and a variety of other soups. Similarly, a potter who makes only drinking mugs will most likely find that sales go up if plates, platters, and other related items are added to the line. A jeweler who makes only pins often increases sales when earrings and other related items are added to the line and the whole line is displayed together.

A line is also enhanced if the same crafts object is produced in a variety of colors, shapes, or sizes. A group of pillows, all of which are red and square, will not sell nearly as well as a group of pillows that offers the customer a selection of colors and shapes.

A product line, then, is a group of related items, easily identifiable as coming from the same source and having similar characteristics. Related does not mean that they look alike, only that they have something in common with one another.

A product line succeeds when it accomplishes one or both of two purposes:

1. It offers the customer a choice. If the customer doesn't like the red pillow, he or she can buy one in blue or green or yellow—or three pillows in three different colors. If you have only red pillows, the customer may not buy any.

2. The line increases the sale. If the customer likes the mugs, sell him or her the plates as well. If you carry only the mugs, the customer will either buy plates elsewhere or won't buy from you at all if matching mugs and plates can be bought from another potter.

Developing a product line requires a bit of experimentation; items are added, others are dropped, based on the experience in the marketplace.

Customers themselves are often the best source of inspiration for a new item in your line. Listen carefully to what they ask for. Big business calls this market research; you can call it keeping your ears open. If you detect a trend for a particular item your customers want in your particular style or design, make a few and test them. If they sell, add them to your line on a regular basis.

Some crafts artists have two product lines bearing different names. This is because a jeweler, for example, selling eighteen-karat-gold jewelry with precious stones will be catering to a different market than will a jeweler who sells costume jewelry made of base metal and glass beads. The buyers in these different markets may be put off if it is obvious that the same crafts artist has two grades of work. *(See also: Product Research)*

Product Research

Product research is something most craftspeople do automatically, even if they don't call it that. The decision to make a particular crafts object is the end result of having made others, having made mistakes, having learned from experience, having sold—or not having been able to sell—particular crafts objects, and so on.

A craft object must, of course, satisfy your own creative needs. But it must also satisfy a customer's needs or it won't sell. Those needs may be functional, emotional, psychological, aesthetic, or whatever.

To state the obvious: A batik blouse, in addition to being beautiful, must also meet some specific human proportions or it won't satisfy the customer's need for a blouse. A batik wall hanging with the identical design, on the other hand, can be of any shape or size and still satisfy the customer's need for something pleasing to hang on the wall.

Once you've determined that your crafts product can satisfy a need, the question is whether a large enough market exists to make it worthwhile. Making eighty-inch belts may fill a need for men who weigh more than 300 pounds, but how many such men are there, and where do you find them? But wait: A "big men's" shop or a specialty magazine may be just right to reach such a specialized market.

Next comes the question of uniqueness. Making a crafts object that is being made by everyone else will inevitably reduce your share of the market. Can you make it different enough to stand out among the competition? Is there something unique in the design or the material that you can point out to a customer to make it more salable?

Variety, or a line, is another consideration. How many different sizes should you produce? How many colors? And which colors? Does it make sense to produce only mugs, or can you increase your sales by having plates of the same design?

If you produce a wide range of craftwork, you may decide to make certain items because they will sell best at crafts shows, while others are more suited to exclusive shops in major cities. That doesn't make one better than the other, just different. Each serves a different need.

The end result of product research, by whatever name or means you conduct it, is to determine what you should produce that can be sold to sufficient numbers of customers who want it and can pay the price you ask for it. That applies even to one-of-a-kind craftwork. True, you need only one customer, but if that customer doesn't exist or cannot be found, then there's no sale. *(See also: Buyers, Customer, Marketability, Product Line)*

Profit

If making a profit were only as simple as defining it. . . . Profit is what's left over after all expenses are deducted from all income.

For accounting purposes, there is a whole variety of profits: *gross profit*, which is the sale of merchandise less the cost of that merchandise; *net profit*, which is total income less the cost of production and other expenses in running the business; *paper profits*, which are those profits not yet realized, as represented, for example, by crafts items in unsold inventory; and a number of others.

From the viewpoint of most craftspeople, the only significant profit is net profit. Some people call it the bottom line—the last line in the financial statement that indicates what's ultimately left over for the owner of the enterprise. Even that profit is subject to taxation.

It is a common misconception that the more you sell, the more profit you'll make. To sell three hundred dollars' worth of craftwork that costs one hundred dollars to produce is usually more profitable than to sell four hundred dollars' worth of craftwork that costs $250 to produce. In the first case you clear two hundred dollars above the cost of production; in the second only $150, even though sales dollars were higher.

Since profits are so directly tied to both sales and costs, any change in either of those factors affects the profit. To increase sales can increase profits as long as costs don't rise out of proportion. Profits can also be increased if costs are cut even if sales don't go up. The ideal situation, of course, is to increase sales while decreasing costs; that really makes the profit picture sparkle.

Unless you're independently wealthy and money is of little consequence, a constant analysis of all your operations is essential for maintaining a healthy net profit. Keep asking yourself questions: Are some items less profitable than others, and can they be discontinued? Can some operations be modified to reduce expenses? Can I increase my profit by increasing production and reducing the price or vice versa? Am I attending a particular crafts show out of habit, or because I know it is profitable for me? Where can I find more economical sources of raw materials? Are some of my orders so small that it costs more to pack them than I make from the sale? Does a promotion mailing in October bring better results than one in June?

The list is endless; the questions, without limit. Take nothing for granted. Profits are found not in always having a ready answer but in always asking questions and in keeping careful records that help you answer those questions. *(See also: Accounting, Expenses, Income, Minimum Orders, Overhead, Pricing, Selling, Wages)*

Profit-and-Loss Statement

This statement, prepared by an accountant once a year, is also known as an income statement. Essentially it lists the total income from sales and the total cost of producing the product. The difference is known as *gross profit*—or *deficit*, if there is a loss.

Operating expenses, sales costs, and taxes are deducted from the gross profit to determine the net profit. *(See also: Financial Statement, Income Statement)*

Promotion *(See: Advertising, Catalog, Direct Mail, Mail Order, Printed Materials, Publicity, Public Relations)*

Property *(See: Assets, Equity, Mortgage, Property Insurance, Property Tax)*

Property Insurance

A wide range of insurance coverage is available to protect you against loss by fire, damage, or property destruction.

The most common of these is known as comprehensive insurance, which covers a number of related risks at a premium rate lower than that covering those risks separately. Typical of such policies is a homeowner's-insurance policy, which is available in most states and includes protection against loss from fire, wind damage, vandalism, theft, and personal liability. Similar types of policies are available for business purposes.

Costs of property-insurance policies vary, depending on the potential risk. A frame building, for example, generally costs more to insure than a brick building. Hurricane insurance is almost impossible to get at any price in areas subject to frequent hurricane damage.

Specific policies to protect against theft, burglary, or damage can also be obtained. This is especially important to craftspeople who put their work out on consignment to galleries. Although galleries should, by rights, provide insurance protection for work that is on their premises, they often don't. Recent laws in some states, however, have increased the protection given to consignor-artists and craftspeople by making consignee-galleries liable for damage to or loss of consigned works.

The best protection a crafts artist can have is to provide his or her own insurance coverage. This may be done by adding a fine-arts floater to another policy or by purchasing an inland-marine policy with a personal-property floater.

Theft-and-burglary insurance also varies in cost, depending on the crime rate in the insured's area and the nature of the coverage. Premiums may be higher for a goldsmith, for example, than for a sculptor, simply because gold is more tempting and easier to steal.

Your property-insurance coverage should be tailor-made by your insurance agent or broker to suit your specific needs for coverage, the potential size of the loss, and the cost of the premiums. *(See also: Fine-Arts Floater, Insurance)*

Property Tax

Except for income tax, property tax is probably the most common form of taxation. Most towns, cities, and states use the property tax as the most important source of revenue for operating their governments.

Personal taxes fall into two categories: real estate and personal property. All real estate—with such exceptions as religious buildings—is taxed locally. A specific tax rate per dollar of value is determined, and each piece of property is then assessed according to its dollar value. The assessed valuation is not necessarily the same as the market value of the property. Thus taxes can be increased either by raising the tax rate or by reassessing the property at a higher value. In the worst scenario, both the tax rate and the assessment are increased.

Another form of property tax—state property tax—is the automobile license. An inventory tax, which exists in some states, is also a form of property tax.

Craftspeople in states where an inventory tax exists would do well, therefore, to plan their production schedules even more carefully in order to keep inventory at the lowest workable minimum. *(See also: Estimated Tax, Income Tax, Sales Tax, Withholding Tax)*

Prospect List *(See: Mailing Lists)*

Publicity

There are two ways to get your name in the papers—an old colloquialism that today includes magazines, radio, television, and any other medium for reaching the public in large numbers. One is to pay good money for advertising space; the other is to come up with a good story idea for free editorial space. Any mention you get in the public media without paying for it is publicity, and good publicity is usually the result of an effort on the part of the person being publicized.

You may think that what you do is not particularly newsworthy. After all, you're so familiar with it that you can hardly imagine why anyone else should give a damn. But editors do! If you read your local papers carefully, you'll notice that news is made not only by presidents, baseball players, movie stars, and criminals but by hundreds of people who are newsworthy simply because they do things that are not done by everyone else.

The fact that you drive a car is not newsworthy. Lots of folks do that. But if you drive a 1926 Model T, you can be sure the local papers would be interested. And if you're ready to drive the mayor around in your Model T for the next Saint Patrick's Day parade, even the television cameras may show up.

The same principle applies to crafts. You are unique since you are able to create things most people cannot. Someone who can hardly shape dough into a loaf of bread is sure to marvel at the skilled hands of a potter.

The first step toward getting publicity, then, is to get over the modesty, shyness, and concern that nobody else is really interested. Step two is to realize that editors without stories are like weavers without yarn. In newspaper jargon, your story is human interest, and editors are always on the lookout for human-interest stories to relieve the tedium of politics, wars, crime, and economic troubles.

From your point of view, publicity has two values. One benefit, of course, is to rub your ego the right way. It never hurts to see something nice about yourself in print. The other reward, even more important, is that publicity is a sales tool. It does not sell as directly as advertising and, therefore, doesn't put people off in the way that advertising can. People know that advertising is bought, but publicity is earned. If a reporter or an editor or a television newscaster—all exercising their independent judgment—say that your craftwork is worth a story, then the viewing and reading public is much more likely to take note.

To get the most out of publicity, a few basic principles should be observed:

1. *Timing.* Obviously, a Christmas item is not publicized in March, and you don't send out an announcement about your new line of lawn chairs in January if you're in a cold climate.

Also, don't waste valuable publicity to announce that you are planning to design a new line of jewelry. If a reader is interested, how can he or she buy it? Announce it when it's ready. Always keep the sales potential in mind.

2. *Directness.* Make your presentation to an editor as simple and as straightforward as possible. Editors can and often do rewrite and cut to suit their styles. If the editor thinks there's more to the story than your announcement, he or she may assign a reporter to interview you. Accommodate

yourself to the reporter's needs and deadlines. The story may be extremely beneficial.

3. *Angle.* Provide the editor with a news handle if possible. A new product line, a gallery opening, an award, moving into a new shop, a trip to Arizona to see the work of the Hopi Indians as inspiration for your own weaving—all news handles. The possibilities are limited only by your imagination.

4. *Press List.* Most of your publicity will be with newspapers and radio or television stations in your area, not with the national magazines. Occasionally your local emphasis may change if you are at a crafts fair in some other area or participate in an exhibition at a gallery or museum in a large city. In either case, compile a list of press contacts on 3 × 5-inch cards. If there is more than one contact at a given newspaper—city editor, arts editor, features-section editor—make up a separate card for each name. Keep a record on each card of the results of each contact. If you don't succeed on the first contact, it is good to know when to make another, and you can time it according to the dates shown on that card. Make a note of the reaction: Were they favorably impressed, polite or curt, enthusiastic or disinterested? Did they tell you to call again in May? Do they want photos? All of this is useful because the more you can tailor your publicity to the particular editor's need, the better your chance of getting it into print.

Which brings up another important point: Unless the subject is a general news announcement, such as a gallery opening, it is best not to give the same story to more than one editor at a time. Give the editor a few days or a week to make a decision on a feature story. If the first one isn't interested, then take it to the next. The worst thing that can happen is two editors running the same feature story. Both of them will put you on their thumbs-down list for the future.

5. *Approach.* Most craftspeople generally find that the best approach is a press release with a suitable photo. You can, however, approach an editor directly, which is not as difficult as you might imagine. Most of us have a movie-version impression of editors as some sort of demigod. Most of them are hardworking, shirtsleeve journalists. They may be a little harried when they're working against a deadline, but they are always interested in a good story. A simple telephone call is often all that's necessary to make an introduction. If the story sounds mildly interesting, the editor may ask you to send a brief outline. Don't write a story, that's his or her job. And if the presentation sounds exciting enough on the telephone, a reporter may be assigned.

Aside from the print and electronic media, there are numerous other publicity opportunities for craftspeople. An unusual interest in crafts has been shown recently by banks all over the country. Numerous banks have invited craftspeople to display their work in bank lobbies—where security is good. In addition, some new office buildings and hotels also have display cases in their lobbies. A guest appearance on a radio or television talk show is another good opportunity to reach large numbers of people. If you can demonstrate your craftwork on the air, your chances are much improved.

Finally, there is an afterglow to much of this publicity. Use it in your own promotional materials. Reprint some of the articles that have appeared about you in the newspapers or magazines. Make a list of the radio or television stations on which you've been mentioned or have appeared. Arrange all this neatly on an 8½ × 11-inch sheet of paper. Don't make a montage of all the headlines, one pasted over the other; people have difficulty reading such jumbled arrangements. Have the whole sheet reproduced. The new, inexpensive offset printing processes available in most cities can do it for between three dollars and five dollars for one hundred sheets. Use the reprints on every occasion: with promotional mailings, as enclosures with bills, at shows and fairs, and anywhere else where you're tying to make a sale or impress a customer. What others have said about you is more convincing than what you say about yourself. And remember to list your name and address somewhere on the reprint. *(See also: Photographs, Press Release, Public Relations)*

Public Relations

Public relations means exactly that: relations with the public. But that's easier said than done.

Public relations covers every aspect of your contact with the outside world: salesmanship, price, publicity, advertising, community involvement, display, even your own appearance and conduct when you encounter your public at shows and fairs or when you see a buyer for a department store. All add up to your image: what other people think of you and your work.

The image of a Cadillac, for example, is quite different from the image of a Volkswagen. That doesn't make one better than the other, but each has its own personality, which represents not only the inherent nature or quality of the product but how it is presented to the outside world. For example, if your pottery sells only in the gift shops of high-fashion stores, it will obviously have a different image from the same pottery sold only at flea markets.

Your image as a craftsperson is created in much the same way that you have created an image of yourself as an individual. People have certain impressions of you: stingy or generous, tactful or blunt, calm or excitable, talkative or quiet. There is no one trait and no one time when images take hold. They are the cumulative experience people have with you.

In your craftwork, for example, suppose that you make a fine product but pack it in a slapdash, helter-skelter manner and ship it off to a customer who just sent you a check for two hundred dollars. The piece may not break in transit, but the customer may well say, "If he thinks so little of his own craftwork to pack it this way, how much good can it be?" Do that a few times and your image in that customer's eyes will decline perceptibly. Neatness counts.

Reliability is important as well. If you get a reputation for always missing delivery dates or for great variations in the craftsmanship of your items, your reputation for reliability will suffer.

Price is another factor. The higher the price, the greater the public's perception of quality and vice versa. The story is told of a supermarket that installed carpeting. The public stayed away in droves. Carpeting was associated in the public's mind with high-priced stores. Not a single price had been changed in the supermarket, but the image had changed.

Nobody's perfect. It is, however, when the imperfections outweigh the credits that your public relations begin to suffer. If many customers complain, for example, that you don't ship on time, you know you have a weak spot that needs correcting, and it had better be done before those customers find a more reliable craftsperson. Analyze your activities constantly to find the defects, and then plan carefully how to change them.

One side of the public-relations coin, then, is how you conduct yourself as a craftsperson, as a professional, as the owner of a crafts business. The other side involves the many things you can do to get your name before the public. This needs not always be related directly to sales, although you would hope that your public relations ultimately produce more sales.

Demonstrating your craft on a local television program and discussing the history of weaving on a radio talk show and being interviewed by the local newspaper are all good public-relations activities. None will produce an immediate dollars-and-cents return, but when you show the clipping of the interview to a prospective store buyer or quote from it in an advertising brochure, a good impression will be made.

Many craftspeople are shy about making such public-relations contacts. "What's the big deal?" they might ask. Since they are so thoroughly familiar with their own work, they can't possibly conceive that others would find it interesting. But if you read the papers carefully, you'll find that the personal items that interest you because you find them novel are probably ordinary to the people who were being interviewed. A book called *A Day in the Life of a Fireman* might make interesting reading for you, although when approached, the fireman probably asked, "What's the big deal?"

Don't be shy. Go out and tell the world about your work and your skill and your art. And don't be discouraged if you don't succeed on every try at public relations. If you keep at it, sooner or later you'll find an opening. (*See also: Advertising, Display, Photographs, Press Release, Publicity, Salesmanship*)

Purchase Award

A purchase award is provided in competitions where the sponsor agrees to purchase, for a reasonable asking price, one or more of the items exhibited.

It is quite common for organizations to advertise that purchase awards and other prizes are available for certain exhibitions. *(See also: Exhibitions, Museum)*

Quality Control

Production craftspeople have to meet two objectives: quantity and quality. The question is not how many or how good but whether the objectives, whatever they may be, are fulfilled.

It is essential to establish definite quality standards in production crafts, espeically if some of the work is done by others. Defective or substandard craftwork is a waste of money and effort because it cannot be sold. If it is sold, it produces complaints, demands for replacements, lengthy paperwork, and tarnished reputations.

Crafts produced to fill a specific order require particularly careful inspection. To avoid rejection of all or part of the order and to maintain a reliable reputation, multiple items must meet the same standards as the sample from which they were ordereed, and they should be inspected before shipment.

Quality control begins at the beginning, when you purchase your raw materials. You can't bake a first-rate cake with second-rate ingredients. Quality-control steps should also be taken at various points along the production process. A whole batch of superbly shaped pots, for example, can be wasted if the glaze formula is defective. There is, however, no prescribed method for establishing quality control. The particular procedure must be suited to each individual's craft medium, work process, and quality standards.

Work that does not meet the standard established by the craftsperson need not always be a total waste. Some types of work can be sold as seconds to outlets that specialize in that type of merchandise, but it is usually best for the craftsperson not to identify his or her name with such products. *(See also: Seconds)*

Record Keeping

Keeping good and accurate records serves two purposes:

1. Many records are required by the government for tax purposes and other reasons. These records generally fall into the category of bookkeeping.

2. Records that contain useful information can produce useful information.

Keeping records is the best way to control your business rather than having it control you. Inventory records, for example, should indicate at a glance what's selling and what isn't. This in turn points to proper production planning. Records of advertising results can help pinpoint where your promotional dollars are being spent wisely and where they are being wasted.

Keeping records of show income and expenses can avoid costly errors.

Judging a show strictly on sales performance can be an illusion. Balanced against those sales dollars must be the expense dollars for booth space, travel, motels, and so on. The net result is the true picture. Only a careful recording of all factors will produce a realistic picture as well as provide the necessary documentation of business expenses for tax purposes.

Financial records must be maintained for tax purposes. They are also necessary in applying for some bank loans.

Crafts producers who sell to retail stores and other regular customers find it useful to keep accurate records on each customer: what was ordered, when the last sale was made, what the terms of the sale were, and so forth. This information, in turn, can provide important direction for the next sales approach to the same customer. Including payment performance on such records will also indicate how promptly the customer paid and how much credit you can afford to extend. Beginning a system such as a card index or computer data base puts all information about each customer in one place; the whole history is then available at a glance.

The law requires that some records be maintained for a specified period of time. Documentation for income tax forms, for example, must be retained for at least three years beyond the filing date in case of tax examination. Some payroll records have to be kept for as long as seven years. But aside from the legal requirements, it is good business practice to maintain files of correspondence, checks, accounts receivable, bills payable, orders, contracts, and most other records of business activities and transactions so that they can be easily located.

Memory plays all sorts of tricks. Record keeping is the only reliable way of keeping the facts about your business accessible so that you can avoid past mistakes and plan for the future. *(See also: Accounting, Advertising, Book-keeping, Budget, Collection Problems, Inventory, Loans, Systems)*

Refunds *(See: Returns)*

Release *(See: Photographs, Press Release)*

Rented Crafts

When a corporation buys equipment or other property, the tax laws allow depreciation as a tax deduction. This allowance, however, does not apply to works of art purchased by a corporation. Tax deductions, however, are often available to the corporation if the art or craftwork is rented rather than purchased. This approach can provide a good source of income for some craftspeople.

Various rental plans are currently being used. The most popular are rentals with an option to buy and lease-finance agreement. Before entering into either agreement you should consult a lawyer.

Rentals with an option to buy are normally short-term arrangements, sometimes for only a few months, after which the works are returned to the artists. The monthly fees are fairly modest, normally between 5 and 10 percent of the retail price. The firm that rents the piece can usually take the rental fee as a tax deduction. If the piece is not returned in good condition, the firm is required to buy it, which gives it no tax advantage.

A lease-finance contract often runs for several years and is renewed automatically. The artist sets an annual rental fee, which is tax deductible to the renter. The concept here is that the annual fees will have paid the equivalent of the retail price by the time the initial contract period is up. Thereafter, the contract is automatically extended at a fairly low annual rental, which continues to produce income for the crafts artist beyond the original retail price.

For example, suppose you have a one-thousand-dollar wall hanging. Under a rental-with-option-to-buy agreement you might rent that hanging for six months at sixty dollars per month. At the end of the period you have $360, and you have your wall hanging back.

Under the lease-finance agreement, you might sign a four-year contract at $250 a year for this wall hanging. At the end of the four years the entire price has been paid, but the wall hanging remains in the custody of the renting firm. You then receive one hundred dollars a year for as long as the firm wants to keep your work.

Renting *(See: Lease)*

Repossess *(See: Installment, Mortgage)*

Résumé

Your résumé is your biography, without the novelist's frills. It is, as *Dragnet's* Sergeant Friday used to say, "just the facts, please."

A résumé consists of several clearly defined sections, each of which should be identified and separated from the others:

1. *Personal Statistics.* Name, address, telephone number, and the crafts media in which you work.

2. *Work Experience.* Start with your most recent experience, including teaching positions, and work backward. Indicate what your job function was and include dates of employment and names of supervisors.

3. *Professional Experience.* Include exhibitions, gallery shows, awards and honors, workshops you've conducted, lectures you've given, articles you've had published, membership in crafts organizations, and so on.

4. *Educational Background.* A complete educational background that is related to crafts should be included if you're applying for a teaching position.

Résumé

FIBER ARTIST

Suzanne Smith
1529 East 19th Street
Middletown, SC   28764
(803) 555-0218

WORK EXPERIENCE

10/88 to date

Free-lance fiber artist

6/83 to 9/88

Textile Designer
Burlingame Mills
272 East Street
Charleston, SC   28167
John Peterson, Design Director

8/75 to 4/80

Weaving Instructor
The Shuttle School
226 Raleigh Road
Fairfield, NC   19862
Margaret Taylor, Owner

PROFESSIONAL EXPERIENCE

Second Award, National Weaving Design Competition, 1986;
Permanent Collection, Tapestry Gallery, Atlanta Museum of Art;
Guest Lecturer, Art Department, University of South Carolina;
Articles on Appalachian Design published in *The Crafts Report*, 1991

Member: American Craft Council, Southern Highland Handicraft
Guild, Association of Master Weavers

EDUCATION

BFA in Textile Design, University of Georgia, 1977
Studied privately with Henry Jones, The Weaver's Loft, 1978

REFERENCES

Personal: Rev. Sam Smith   Dr. Frank Hamill
               8633 Third Street   179 West Broadway
               Middletown, SC   28745   Charleston, SC   27693
               (803) 555-7692   (803) 555-4629

Professional: Terry Witherspoon
               President, Association of Master Weavers
               229 Lenox Road, St. Louis, MO   44598
               (314) 555-2831

               Robin Robinson, Boutique Buyer
               Kneeman Markers
               Dallas, TX   67219
               (214) 555-9551

5. *References.* Two personal references and two professional references from people not related to you are normally sufficient.

Résumés are used as a way of introducing yourself for a variety of purposes: when you approach a gallery, when you seek a job or teaching position, when you want to furnish background material for a newspaper interview.

If your professional and work experience is extensive and you've been showered with numerous awards, written numerous articles, and had numerous exhibitions, it may be wise to prepare two résumés. One should be a single page and list only the most important accomplishments; another could go on and on to list all of your accomplishments and activities. Busy gallery owners or personnel people may not have the time or interest to read through several pages of biographical material on the first go-around.

A résumé should be neatly typed on one side of the sheet only. Most offset printers can typeset and reproduce your résumé at fairly low cost. Major cities have specialty printers who can print them for you within an hour at less than five dollars for one hundred copies. Professional résumé services have become popular and relatively inexpensive. Modern laser printers connected to your personal computer also provide excellent quality for your résumé and may permit you to print your own at home.

A résumé should almost always be accompanied by a cover letter that explains why you are sending the résumé. Submit the letter even if you are sending the résumé in response to a specific request—in which case you should mention the request in the letter to remind the recipient.

False modesty has no place in a résumé. If you've won an award or have work on display in a museum's permanent collection, don't be shy about it. No need to brag, of course, but let the facts speak for themselves—and for you.

Retail Buyers *(See: Buyers)*

Retailing
Retailing means selling to the consumer in small quantities. Most craftspeople become involved in retailing at one time or another, generally by renting a booth at a crafts show. Others are more extensively involved by operating their own stores or galleries.

It is not the intention of this book to discuss how to operate your own retail store; that would require another book. Besides, the vast majority of craftspeople probably don't have the time, the inclination, the location, the money, or the interest to run a retail store. That doesn't mean you can't sell at retail out of your own shop or studio. But an examination of what a retail store offers will quickly make clear the many pitfalls that await a craftsperson who plans to open a full-fledged retail crafts outlet.

Nonetheless, many craftspeople become upset when they see that the work they sell to a store is resold for double the wholesale amount. They feel that, somehow, they are entitled to the higher price. After all, it's their work on which someone else is making a profit.

But retail stores perform numerous legitimate functions:

1. They find customers whom the craftsperson might not otherwise find;
2. They offer a wide variety of merchandise that itself attracts customers;
3. They advertise;
4. They display the merchandise attractively;
5. They extend credit to their customers;
6. They are located in areas convenient to shoppers and furnish parking space.

It has been estimated that the cost of performing these functions costs the average retail store approximately forty-five cents of every retail-sales dollar. When a store buys crafts products at fifty cents of the retail-sales dollar, that leaves about a nickel for profit.

On the assumption that an effective retail-sales operation conducted by a craftsperson would also cost approximately forty-five cents of every retail-sales dollar, the question of a retailer's markup takes on a new perspective. The question is whether it is more productive and profitable for you to work for the 5 percent retail profit or spend the same amount of time in your shop or studio producing craftwork at a better rate of profit. It is important to realize which would give you the greatest satisfaction, because if you have figured the wholesale price properly, it should reflect a decent wage for your actual labor and a decent profit for your craftsmanship, management skills, and investment return.

The assumption has to be made that you work in crafts because that's what you like to do and it's what you do best. If your creative and production time are more profitable than your retail selling time, there's nothing wrong with having someone else make a profit selling your work at retail. When that someone else is you, as at a crafts show, all the better. But when it's not, consider that you're making more money and enjoying it more when you're making things than when you're selling them.

Good relations with your retail outlets are a prime ingredient for continued success. The first sale is always the hardest. Once you have a store signed up to buy your work, do everything you can to keep that store satisfied. It brings reorders.

Following is a checklist for good retailer relations:

1. *Maintain Quality.* Every item you ship should be as good as the sample you showed.

2. *Maintain Price.* The same item should never be sold to different stores at different prices except when the quantities are different—aside from being

illegal under the Robinson-Patman Act, it's also poor business practice. A store won't stick with you long if it finds another store across town selling your work at a lower price because you cut your wholesale price.

In addition, it is poor practice to undercut your usual wholesale customers by selling cheaper at shows, especially when the show is in the vicinity of a store that sells your work. If customers get wise to being able to buy your work cheaper from you than from a store, your store-outlet markets will dry up. Why should they be in price competition with you? There are plenty of other craftspeople from whom they can buy.

The proper way to handle show pricing is as if you're buying from yourself at wholesale prices. Add your markup, and then sell at what should be near the usual retail price. After all, you are entitled to be paid for the time and expense you spend selling at shows just as the store in town is entitled to be paid for its time and expense.

3. *Maintain Delivery Schedules.* There's nothing worse than receiving a Christmas shipment on December 26. Make certain that delivery schedules are clearly stated when you get the written order. Many stores work on short deadlines. Be sure you can meet them, or discuss the problem with the store before you accept the order.

4. *Pick the Right Outlet.* Every store has its own personality. The public image of Saks Fifth Avenue is certainly different from that of a roadside discount store. Your quality, your price range, and the stores in which your work is sold have to be mutually compatible. A one-thousand-dollar wall hanging can go to Saks; and the dozen mugs that fired imperfectly can go to the discount store. But never the twain shall meet. Check the various stores in your area. Examine the kind of craftwork they sell, the quality, the price ranges. You'll soon get an idea of what type of retail outlet is best suited to sell your work and, therefore, most interested in buying it.

For a book covering the business and legal issues unique to crafts retailing, see *The Law (In Plain English)*® *for Art & Craft Galleries* (Appendix C). *(See also: Consignment, Contracts, Memo, Orders, Salesmanship, Shipping, Shows and Fairs, Wholesaling)*

Return on Sales *(See: Sales Cost)*

Returns
Your policy on returns must strike a delicate balance between two objectives:

1. It must be fair enough to allow customers to return damaged or defective merchandise and thus maintain your reputation for integrity in your work;

2. It must be stringent enough not to allow returns for unsupported reasons or after lengthy use, because returns are expensive both in terms of actual cost and in terms of objects that cannot be resold.

For example, if a retail store wants to return a broken pot three months after it was shipped, you can be fairly certain it wasn't broken when it arrived but was knocked off the shelf last week. The most common policy on a time period for the return of damaged goods is within five days after receipt. That should give even a busy store an opportunity to examine the merchandise.

The possibility also exists that a store may want to return goods it cannot sell. You should clearly specify under what conditions, if any, you will accept such returns; in what time period—perhaps thirty days at most—that nothing will be accepted without prior written authorization; and who pays for the return shipment.

Returns, or refunds, based on damage claims should never be accepted unless the recipient has made such claims to the proper party, which is usually the agency or freight company that handled the goods in transit. Don't be too free with refunds—it's your money you're giving away. If the claim is legitimate, the carrier's insurance company will cover it if it was damaged in transit.

As in most other business practices, you have to be flexible with your returns policy. If a good customer wants to return something, even if you think the reasons are not entirely legitimate, your goodwill and future sales are enhanced, even if your wallet is a few dollars shorter. If a customer does this consistently, perhaps it's time to say good-bye and find someone else who is more reasonable.

To condense all this into two sentences, your returns policy might be: All claims must be made within five days after receipt of merchandise. No returns will be accepted more than thirty days after delivery and without prior written authorization. This policy should be clearly stated on your price list and invoice forms. *(See also: Quality Control, Sales Terms)*

Revolving Credit

When a bank, supplier, or a store make credit available to you up to a certain maximum, the money can be withdrawn or purchases made up to the credit limit without negotiating each loan or purchase separately. The credit is replenished every time a payment is made. This is called revolving credit and is most common with credit cards, department-store charge accounts, and personal cash-advance and credit-line accounts.

If your credit line is five thousand dollars and you make a five-hundred-dollar purchase, the credit line has been reduced to four thousand five hundred dollars. When you make a one-hundred-dollar payment, the credit line is back up to four thousand six hundred dollars. There is always a minimum payment due on the total monthly withdrawals or purchases, generally in the neighborhood of 2 to 10 percent of the outstanding balance.

Since revolving-retail-credit accounts usually charge high interest rates, as much as 21 percent or more in some states, it is wise to pay off the total outstanding balance each month, even if the money to do that has to be borrowed from a bank at a lower interest rate. There is usually no charge for having a revolving credit line, only for using it. Interest generally applies only to the balance that is more than a month old. Thus, if you always pay off your total monthly balance, you can enjoy the benefit of having credit always available, and you have the use of the money interest free, sometimes for sixty days or more—from the date of the purchase to the date the payment is due. A MasterCard, for example, might have a billing date of the twelfth of the month and a payment-due date of the seventh of the following month. If you were to make a purchase on May 13, it would show up on the bill dated June 12 and would be due for payment July 7. Thus, you have used the credit-card company's money for fifty-five days without paying a penny of interest. All this takes some self-control, of course, because it is all too easy to fall into the trap of paying only some of the balance due and then being charged a high interest rate on the unpaid balance.

Robinson-Patman Act

This federal law was enacted by Congress in 1936 to prohibit any practice that would tend to stifle free competition in the marketplace. It protects competitive buyers by making it illegal for one customer to have an unreasonable advantage over another, whether at the wholesale or retail level. Among the law's major prohibitions is price discrimination between customers and other special concessions that are not justified by cost. Thus, it is unlawful to sell a dozen items to one store at a lower price than the identical items are sold to another store. Special concessions that affect the price are also illegal; you cannot charge one customer for shipping costs and pay the costs for an identical order to another customer. The shipping charges themselves can vary, of course, depending on the actual costs involved. You can also differentiate among various groups of customers, say, by making local delivery free but adding shipping charges to deliveries beyond one hundred miles. Differences in price based on quantity, however, are legal, such as a price based on an order for one hundred pieces can be lower than a price based on ten pieces.

The law also protects craftspeople when they buy raw materials and supplies. It is illegal for your supplier to charge you one price for one hundred pounds of clay and charge another potter in your area a lower price for the same quantity.

The law does not prohibit special sales or other price reductions as long as all customers buying the product under the special conditions are treated equally.

Royalty

Royalty is a per-unit method of payment for the use of a particular piece of property. The term originally described the amount of payment a king would receive for granting rights to the use of his lands. It is still used to determine payment for such land use as oil drilling, whereby the owner of the land is paid a specific amount per barrel of oil extracted from the land. It is also common in payment for the use of patented or copyrighted work.

For artists, craftspeople, writers, performers, and other creative talents, the royalty is generally a specified percentage of the per-unit sale of the person's creative work. This arrangement is most common in agreements between writers and publishers.

If you design a pendant that is then manufactured in quantity by a costume-jewelry house, you can either sell the design outright for one lump sum or you can agree on a royalty based on a specific amount of the price for each pendant sold. The determination has to be based on an estimate of the potential income of an outright sale versus a royalty arrangement. A royalty arrangement obviously entails a certain amount of risk, and if you're short of cash, receiving a payment outright may well be worth more than the possibility of royalties.

If the manufacturer who wants to buy your design pushes hard for an outright purchase, you can assume that he or she expects a good sale and considers royalties a more expensive alternative than paying you one lump sum. That manufacturer is also taking all the risks in case the thing flops. On the other hand, if the manufacturer insists on a royalty arrangement, you can assume that he's not so sure of the sales potential and wants you to share the risk—at least as far as your own income is concerned.

Royalties generally range anywhere between 5 and 15 percent. The agreements often provide for a step-up in percentages as the number of units sold increases. which could mean, for example, that you would earn 6 percent on the first five thousand, 8 percent on the next five thousand, and 10 percent on sales of more than ten thousand. If the sums are potentially high, it is wise to consult a lawyer before signing a royalty agreement. *(See also: License)*

Safety

Some safety precautions are obvious: You don't let young children play with sharp knives, and you don't smoke when you pump gasoline. But for many, the potential hazards in craftwork have not been readily recognized, in part because there has not been public awareness of the health and safety aspects of the work and also because artists and craftworkers have not received appropriate training or information about their materials and processes.

The art workplace is a factory and, just as in a factory, industrial hygiene and safety principles must be observed. Hazardous materials and processes must be recognized, evaluated, and controlled. The artist or craftworker must learn to identify materials, to read labels and material-safety-data sheets

(MSDSs), and to keep records of materials and processes used in the studio, whether it is a basement or a schoolroom or a production shop. If it is not clear whether the materials or processes can be harmful to your health, advice can be sought from numerous sources such as government agencies, artists' organizations and publications, as well as from industrial-hygiene and safety professionals. This latter group can provide help in controlling safety and health hazards in any workplace. They can recommend appropriate ventilation, machine guarding, and protective equipment, and the cost of their services is tax-deductible to a business and may be tax-deductible for certain individuals as well.

The following list of safety precautions is merely illustrative. Included at the end of this discussion is a list of agencies and individuals who can help you find additional information.

1. In any list of safety precautions, the first and most important rule is to read the labels of products you use. Public Law No. 10,695, passed by Congress in 1988 and effective as of November 1990, requires manufacturers to label art products that contain ingredients that may be chronic health hazards. The products include inks or paints that contain solvents that might not cause problems with occasional, short-duration use but that might cause nerve damage over a prolonged period of concentrated use. Of course, the law has some limitation in that it only applies to art materials, and many arts and crafts professionals use materials or processes that are not specifically identified as art materials and processes.

Because you work in the arts, you have an increased responsibility to learn about the materials you choose to employ. If you work with metals, know what happens when a metal is heated. If you work with resins, learn about the health effects of the resin components and how and when adverse effects are likely to be caused. If you work with fibers, know about the health effects of dyes and dusts. In craftwork, dangers such as these lurk in unexpected places. For example, in early 1976 it was discovered that certain imported yarns used by weavers contained fatally toxic substances.

2. Follow safety rules, use guarding devices, and wear appropriate protective equipment when using machine tools of any kind. Do not wear jewelry or loose-fitting garments such as ties.

3. Read instructions carefully and thoroughly, and follow them.

4. Have electrical wiring and tools checked periodically by a trained electrician to be sure connections are in good condition and tools are properly grounded.

5. Get acquainted with the many kinds of protective equipment that will help make your work easier and safer. Use it. Maintain it properly.

6. Have an emergency-response plan, and post it in the studio and near a phone. It should describe what to do in case of a spill, a splash in the eyes, a bad cut or puncture and who can handle the emergency.

7. Ventilate. Remember that for any system to work, the air that is exhausted from a space must be brought back in an equal amount to replace it. Be sure that your exhaust system does not interfere with existing furnace or other exhausts.

8. Don't eat in the workshop, and avoid working in your kitchen.

Following are agencies that provide information:
Occupational Safety and Health Administration (OSHA)
National Institute of Occupational Safety and Health (NIOSH)
  (see Appendix C)

Following are organizations and individuals who provide information:
Center for Safety in the Arts
Arts, Crafts, and Theater Safety (ACTS)
Gail Barazani, researcher and writer on occupational health in the arts.
  (See Appendix D for complete information on these organizations.)

The following books provide valuable safety information:
Ventilation: A Practical Guide
Artist Beware
The Artist's Complete Health and Safety Guide
Protecting Your Health in the Art and Craft Workplace (see Appendix C).
  (See also: Fire Prevention)

Sale

A sale is not a sale until one basic condition has been met: The goods have been delivered or at least shipped. Someone's ordering a dozen pots or sending you money for a wall hanging does not constitute a sale.

The sale is complete if you've shipped or delivered the goods, even if you haven't been paid. What the customer owes you becomes an account receivable.

When you have an order and haven't shipped the merchandise—even if you've already been paid—it's not a sale; it's simply an order. If you ship only part of the order, the undelivered part is called a back order and doesn't become a sale until it is shipped.

All this may sound like a silly semantic game, but it is important if a sale or an order becomes a subject of dispute. *(See also: Accounts Receivable, Orders, Sales Terms)*

Sales Cost

Since time is money, the time you spend selling or the money you pay for someone else's time to sell your work should be calculated carefully so that it doesn't eat into the profits you make in the production of craftwork. For craftspeople, the costs of selling fall into four major categories:

1. Selling to retail outlets, whether you do that yourself, hire someone to do it for you, or do it by mail;

2. Selling at crafts shows and fairs;

3. Operating your own retail store;

4. Paying for general sales expenses, such as advertising.

Some of these selling expenses are easily identifiable. If you print a brochure or make a set of slides or pay a sales representative a commission or rent a booth at a show, you know exactly how much you've spent for those purposes.

Opening your own retail store opens a Pandora's box of cost factors and selling problems. If you already have an established reputation and if you can sell from your shop or studio or home without hiring sales help, paying extra rent, or committing yourself to expensive advertising campaigns, the problems are substantially reduced. But if you're thinking of opening a full-fledged retail operation, selling not only your own craftwork but also the work of others, a little knowledge provides a better chance of money in the pocket. Doing a good job at retail-store operation requires some solid background and study in business skills just as doing a good job at craftwork requires some solid background and study in crafts skills. Retailing may seem easy from the customer's point of view, but many dangers lie in wait for the uninitiated.

Mail-order selling can be as expensive a proposition as retailing. But in mail order, at least, it is easier to pull in your horns if you find that the results don't justify the costs. The biggest cost here and the one that must be most closely monitored is advertising. It's not so much how expensive a particular ad is but how much it produces. An ad that costs two hundred dollars and brings in two thousand dollars is more productive and, therefore, less expensive than one which costs fifty dollars and brings in three hundred dollars.

If you are seriously considering opening a retail store or going into mail-order selling, you would do well to read a library book or two on the subject, perhaps take a course or two at a local college, consult with other retailers and the chamber of commerce, and get hold of some of the publications issued by the Small Business Administration (SBA). A list of SBA publications can be had from any of their SBA offices in major United States cities (see telephone white pages under *United States Government, Small Business Administration*) or can be requested by writing to SBA Publications (see Appendix D).

The biggest problem most craftspeople face is in the hidden sales costs. At a crafts fair, for example, the cost of the booth, of transportation, and of a motel and meals away from home are clearly defined sales expenses. But what about your time? This includes not only the time you actually spend at the show but the time spent packing up the craftwork the day before, loading the car, unloading and unpacking when you get back. What about breakage or theft, display materials, business cards, or other printed material you hand out at your booth—all are selling costs that must be included in your final accounting of a crafts fair to know whether it has been worth the effort.

The actual costs of selling to retail outlets must become part of the wholesale price. It doesn't matter whether you do it yourself and use your own car, whether you hire your own salespeople and pay salaries or commissions and expenses, or whether you engage the services of an independent sales representative who usually gets approximately 15 percent of the wholesale price but pays all his or her own expenses.

Include, too, your costs for sales literature, slides or photographs, order forms, samples, and all the other paraphernalia associated with the selling process, whether it's done in person or by mail.

The question is often asked, "What percentage of my gross should I spend for selling?" That's difficult to answer. If a half dozen good retail outlets keep you busy with orders and reorders, your selling costs will be quite low. If every order you sell is a new order, the selling costs will increase substantially. The cost of going on the road to attend crafts shows and fairs may seem relatively higher, but then you're selling at retail prices that may justify the higher dollar cost.

Without prescribing any rule, since each situation is different, it would probably be safe to say that sales cost at wholesale should not exceed between 10 and 15 percent; at retail, no more than 40 percent. In mail-order selling this may be quite a bit higher, but the assumption is that mail-order selling produces a large volume of business, so the profit on each transaction can be a little smaller and still show a healthy total.

One important thing to remember: The sales cost is part of the price you charge. That a retail store sells your work for twice the amount it paid you does not, however, make the store's markup part of your sales cost. You are selling it at wholesale, not retail. Their price is to compensate for their sales costs. That's why the percentage of sales cost on your own retail selling is so much higher. (See also: Advertising, Catalog, Display, Expense Accounts, Mailing Lists, Mail Order, Overhead, Photographs, Pricing, Public Relations, Retailing, Salesmanship, Sales Records, Sales Representatives, Sales Terms, Samples, Shows and Fairs, Wholesaling)

Salesmanship

The word *salesmanship* conjures up in many minds a vision of a late-night television commercial with an advertiser wearing a white vinyl belt and matching shoes, and promoting a set of kitchen knives. But selling, in truth, is nothing more than explaining the benefits of a product to a potential customer so that the customer can make a buying decision.

There are, of course, unethical salesmen just as there are unethical doctors, lawyers, and craftspeople. But that is a defect in the individual, not the process. While the seller obviously benefits from making a sale, the buyer also benefits through a better understanding of what he or she is buying.

The first principle of salesmanship, therefore, is a thorough understanding of the crafts object being sold, what makes it unique, how it can benefit the buyer, and so forth. In every transaction something is not only sold, something is also bought. The customer is trading money for something that is worth more to him or her than having the money.

In craftwork particularly, the necessity of a sales explanation is an important factor. It's not like buying a pound of apples or a can of soup. They sell themselves because the customer is fully aware of the benefits of eating regularly.

The next major concern is to know what motivates each particular customer. No two customers are ever alike. Each brings to the transaction a particular set of needs, wants, perceptions, and expectations based on prior life experience and circumstances. Try selling a pack of cigarettes to a nonsmoker, or a hard-rock record to a Beethoven fan. Selling a silk blouse, for example, to a man requires quite a different approach from selling the same garment to a woman. Is the man buying the clothing as a gift or to be thoughtful? Does he want to play the big spender? Is the woman buying it for herself to be fashionable or different or to match a scarf she just bought?

Although it is often believed that price is the foremost factor in any sale, that's not always so. Indeed, there are always some people who will ask how much without any intention of buying. But price usually does not come into play until some other decisions have been made. The old expression "You Can't Give Away Ice in Alaska" expresses this best. If there's more ice than you can ever hope to use, it doesn't matter how cheap it is.

Yes, the price does become a major factor when the buyer has already made a tentative decision to buy, and there are always products so familiar to the customer that price is the only deciding factor, but in crafts selling, the effectiveness of the sales presentation plays a big part in justifying the price tag. An effective presentation makes the object so desirable to the customer that he or she understands its value and will consider the price a fair one. This doesn't mean every potential customer will buy; there's competition and the pocketbook to be considered. But good salesmanship helps.

These principles apply not only to direct selling, as at crafts shows, but also to selling to retail stores or other outlets. The motivations are different, to be sure. The store buyer's concern is whether the crafts object can be resold at a profit, whether it suits the store's merchandising policy, whether it is sufficiently different from other products in the store, and whether the price is suitable.

In such situations it is much easier to prepare an effective sales presentation. Look around the store before you make an appointment to see the buyer. See what type of merchandise and craftwork are being sold. What are the price ranges? Does your craftwork fit into that store's pattern? Will it give the store a competitive advantage over another store down the street? Can you explain to the store buyer why you feel your particular craftwork will be a profitable addition to the store's inventory?

Selling to a store buyer usually requires a good portfolio in addition to some samples, unless the nature of your craft (jewelry, for example) allows you to carry a large selection with you.

At a show, of course, salesmanship combines with a little bit of showmanship. Demonstrating how your craftwork is made adds some life to your booth and perks up your relationship with your customer. If you're tuned in to what the customer is saying as you show various items, you'll quickly determine in what direction to move.

In both cases, closing the sale is an important crossroad in the process. This is where you actually ask the customer to buy. Experience and sensitivity will tell you at what point to ask for the order—a point that is unlikely to be the same for any two customers.

There's also something called a trial close. This comes when the customer may not be quite ready to make a decision, and you have to nudge the customer a little. At some point in the proceedings you may want to ask: "Do you think you'd prefer this in blue or brown?" or "This larger size suits you beautifully." With that the customer who's simply wasting time will disappear, and the serious customer will move a little closer to the moment of truth.

Consider here a major roadblock that many craftspeople find difficult to overcome. If you are not by nature an extrovert, the approach to customers may be awkward in the beginning. It is not necessary to be aggressive; indeed, that turns a lot of customers off. But an effective sales approach requires that the seller display some real interest in the customer. Sitting in the back of a booth at a crafts show, nose buried in a book, is not likely to produce much activity. The customer must at least get the impression that you are interested in selling something.

A few character traits are sure to interfere with a productive sales presentation as well: impatience, haughtiness, sloppiness, distraction. The attitude that comes across when you sell is as important as any of the words you speak—sometimes more so. Being positive and confident always works better than being negative and apologetic.

Finally, there is the problem of rejection. Since your craftwork is so important an extension of your personality, there is a tendency to consider a refusal to buy as a personal affront or a rejection. Many aspiring craftspeople have been crushed and emotionally drained when a customer didn't like their work sufficiently to buy. But perhaps they simply didn't need it or didn't have the cash.

Even Babe Ruth didn't bat a thousand. When a sale is not successfully completed, it doesn't mean the customer has rejected you personally. That probably never entered the customer's mind—unless you were rude or insulting. It is simply that the fundamental balance of needs and wants and money didn't jell.

If you know that you have a good and salable product and that knowledge comes across positively and cheerfully, then the little tricks of the trade of salesmanship will come with experience. *(See also: Buyers, Customer, Display, Marketability, Marketing Plan, Photographs, Portfolio, Publicity, Public Relations, Retailing, Shows and Fairs, Wholesaling)*

Salespeople *(See: Sales Representatives)*

Sales Promotion *(See: Advertising, Catalog, Direct Mail, Mail Order, Publicity, Public Relations)*

Sales Records *(See: Record Keeping, Sales Cost)*

Sales Representatives

The boom in craft marketing is a fairly new phenomenon, and not all is yet in place in the distribution process. In many established industries, one of the most common links in the chain of getting products from the manufacturer to the ultimate consumer is the sales representative. That person represents several small, noncompeting manufacturers who have neither the need nor the finances to hire their own sales force.

The majority of craftspeople do their own selling, either by contacting retail outlets or by exhibiting at crafts shows and fairs. Few produce in such quantity that the cost of a full-time salesperson could be justified.

More and more craftspeople, however, utilize the services of independent sales representatives—also known as reps or sales agents or manufacturers' representatives—especially to develop business in areas away from their immediate area. The rep is the contact between you, crafts producer, and the retail outlets.

Sales reps usually carry a line of related but noncompeting products, and they cover specific territories. In the case of crafts, for example, a sales rep may handle a potter, a woodworker, a silversmith. The rep calls on the stores in his territory, talk to the buyers he knows, and takes orders for the products he carries.

Sales representatives work strictly on commission, usually 15 percent of the wholesale price. This is an added selling expense for you, the crafts producer, but its two advantages are that payment is made only on the basis of what is sold and that a good sales representative can keep a crafts producer busy making crafts objects instead of running around trying to sell.

Of course 15 percent of the wholesale price is only 7½ percent of the retail price. In other words, if an item sells for ten dollars to the ultimate consumer, the retail store pays five dollars for it. The sales representative gets 15 percent of that five dollars, or seventy-five cents. That commission is a selling expense that has to be figured into the wholesale price when all the costs are calculated.

In addition to taking the order, the sales representative usually performs several other functions. Most important of these is the responsibility to check the customer's credit references. Since the rep normally gets the commission only after the bill is paid, it is in his or her own self-interest to make sure that the sale is paid for.

If you sell through a rep, you are still responsible for production, packing, shipping, billing, handling complaints, and so forth. Remember that the sales representative is not a customer. The salesperson represents you to the retailer but never buys anything from you.

You must furnish the rep with price lists, order forms, and samples of the crafts objects you want sold. And you must have a written understanding of the basis on which you are represented, the territory, the terms of sale, the commission structure, credit policy, and also how the relationship can be dissolved if either party is dissatisfied.

To justify having your own sales force requires a considerable amount of production and money. Your own salespeople would normally receive a salary or a draw against commission, they would be entitled to vacation and other benefits, you would have to pay them during a training period, and you would have to pay their expenses. Sales reps work for themselves, and if they are good, they will give you no management headaches—very few anyway.

Balanced against the advantages of a rep are two drawbacks. You do not have complete control over the rep as you would with your own sales force. In addition, if the relationship ends, the rep may take on a different line that competes with yours and sell it to the same people to whom he or she previously sold your merchandise.

If you already have more sales than you can handle, there's hardly a need to get someone to sell for you. But if you want to sell in parts of the country you can't reach easily or economically or you want to get into retail outlets you haven't been able to sell, then a rep who covers a given territory or is experienced in a particular type of retail market can be of considerable help.

The great difficulty, however, is how and where to find a sales rep. There aren't that many in the crafts field. The good reps are already busy and may not be able to carry another line—and you wouldn't want a lazy rep. Also, reps would naturally prefer to carry a line by someone who is already well-known as a crafts producer, which sometimes works against the newcomer who really needs a rep's help to get into the market effectively.

The best source of finding a rep is by asking questions of other noncompeting craftspeople, retail-store owners, department-store buyers, crafts organizations, and so forth. Sooner or later you will probably make a good contact.

The rep's first question after looking over your craftwork and deciding that it's salable will probably be how much of it you can produce. It won't do the rep any good to sell one hundred pieces on which he or she can earn a decent commission if you can only make ten.

The crafts producer's first question—after determining that the rep can do the job—is to determine the minimum volume that the rep will produce. To turn the table, what good is a rep who sells only ten pieces when you can produce one hundred?

Once you establish a business connection with a sales representative, the two of you should work closely. Let the rep know promptly when you have a new product or design. Let the rep know just as promptly if you run into a problem with delivery or collection. Hearing it from you when a delivery is going to be late, not from the retailer to whom the rep made the sale, is only common courtesy and good business practice.

Furthermore, unless it's specifically spelled out otherwise, don't invade the rep's territory. A rep usually works hard to make a living, doing what he does best—selling—just as you work hard at making fine crafts objects, which is what you do best. Going after the rep's customers yourself can sour an otherwise beautiful relationship and probably cost more in the long run.

The most important point to remember in selecting a sales representative, whether the person is on your payroll or working independently, is that this person is you in the eyes of the customer. That does not mean the sales rep has to be exactly like you; indeed, as a sales specialist, the person's interests and personality may be quite different from yours. But what the sales rep says, how the person presents your craftwork, what promises the rep makes, the rep's appearance and conduct—all reflect on you. A good sales rep can be a great help, a bad one a great hindrance.

If you have a good rep, you'll find that the person can be an excellent source of information about conditions in the market. Some reps have even come up with design suggestions or product ideas based on the demand they detect as they call on the retail stores. If a rep has a suggestion to make, don't brush it off. The rep's interest is the same as yours: to produce sales for your craftwork so that you can both make money. *(See also: Sale, Sales Cost, Salesmanship)*

Sales Tax

Many towns, cities, and states impose a tax on retail sales to consumers. The tax is collected at the point at which the sale is made and is based on a percentage of the price. The amount of the tax varies from one state or city to another and so does the type of product or service on which it is collected. In some areas, for example, restaurant meals are taxable; in others, they are not. Food bought at retail is almost never subject to sales tax, although nonfood items such as paper towels, matches, soap, and soft drinks may be taxed.

Craftspeople who sell at retail in an area where sales taxes apply must get a certificate from the local taxing authorities. This authorizes them to collect the sales tax. How, when, and where the sales taxes are then forwarded by the retailer to the taxing authorities varies, but it is always illegal to retain the collected sales tax as personal income. Records have to be kept to relate total sales to sales-tax collections. Sales receipts and invoices are usually sufficient for this purpose. The sales tax must always be shown as a separate item from the price.

A sales-tax situation peculiar to the crafts field involves selling at crafts shows and fairs in areas where a sales tax applies. In some cases, the show management is authorized to obtain one blanket sales-tax certificate and the exhibitors must then report their sales or handle their sales through the show management. In other cases for which the authorities do not permit this or where it is impractical, each exhibitor must obtain a temporary-sales-tax certificate for the period of the show. Where this is necessary, the show management will instruct all exhibitors how to go about it. *(See also: Sales-Tax Exemptions)*

Sales-Tax Exemptions

On the principle that a sales tax is paid only once—by the ultimate customer—the sales tax need not be paid on raw materials you buy for the purpose of making crafts objects that will later be resold. Nor do you have to collect sales taxes on crafts products you sell to a retailer who will then sell them to his or her customers. In both cases, a resale number or sales-tax-exemption number is needed. Different places call this document by different names, but it amounts to the same thing. Contact the appropriate sales-tax authorities in your area for information on how to get this document.

When you sell your work to a store for resale, either directly or through wholesale shows, the retailer will furnish you with its own resale number, which authorizes you to make the sale without charging the sales tax. This is important in the event that the tax collector looks at your books and wants to know on what basis you sold your work without collecting the sales tax. If you don't have the store's resale number, which is normally indicated on the store's order form, you will have to pay the sales tax, whether you collected it or not. It is for this reason that your records should reflect the resale number, quantity sold, and price.

Sales and shipments you make to customers outside your sales tax area are normally not subject to the sales tax. A New York craftsperson—where sales taxes apply—who ships merchandise to a state such as Oregon where there are no sales taxes does not have to collect the New York sales tax. However, if the out-of-state customer goes to the New York craftperson's studio or store, buys the crafts object there, and takes it home, the sales tax has to be collected.

Unlike the raw materials used in making your crafts objects, office supplies and equipment, such as a potter's wheel or kiln, that do not ultimately become part of your crafts product are subject to the sales tax when you buy them because you are the final consumer of those items *(See also: Sales Tax)*

Sales Terms

The logistics of making a direct sale to a customer, as at a crafts fair, are fairly uncomplicated: You take the money, hand over the merchandise, and the transaction is completed. Making a sale to a retail store or some other wholesale customer usually requires a more detailed set of specifications that are known as sales terms or conditions of sale.

The two basic ingredients of the sale terms—products and price—are the most important, of course. These are most prominent on your price list. But the fine print, which spells out a variety of conditions under which the craftwork and the money change hands, is also important. Among the more common terms and conditions that should appear on your price lists and invoices are these:

1. *Cash Discounts.* This is usually 2 percent if the bill is paid within ten days of invoice date, the total amount being due thirty days after the invoice date. This is generally written *2/10-net 30.*

2. *Quantity Discounts.* These apply if a total order either exceeds a certain dollar minimum or is based on specific quantities of a specific item.

3. *Shipping.* You must specify who pays the shipping charges. Are there freight allowances, and on what basis are they calculated? Is shipment made freight prepaid or freight collect? Do you make cash-on-delivery (COD) shipments?

4. *Minimum Orders.* Specify whether you have a minimum order. What are the extra charges if the order is below the minimum?

5. *Packing Charges.* Are packing costs included in the list price? If not, what is the extra charge? Does this charge apply to all shipments or only to shipments below a certain dollar minimum?

6. *Returns and Claims.* State your policy clearly on damage claims and other

returns. To whom should damage claims be made—usually to the carrier who moved the shipment—and what is the time period in which a claim will be accepted? Will you accept returns without prior authorization?

7. *Credit.* To ship to a brand-new customer on credit without first checking credit references is inviting trouble. Sales terms should indicate what kind of credit information is required on a first order. *(See also: Credit, Discounts, Free on Board, Minimum Orders, Orders, Returns, Shipping)*

Samples

In addition to seeing slides or photographs of your craftwork, gallery owners and store buyers often want to see actual samples of your work. If they are interested, they may ask you to leave the samples so that they can be discussed with other store personnel before an order is written. It seems superfluous to note here that a sample should be a perfect representation of your work, but craftspeople sometimes grab the nearest crafts object on the way downtown and discover that they should have taken a piece that better indicated their technique and design capability.

When it is necessary to ship a sample, take extra precautions that it is properly protected and packed to avoid damage in transit. A valuable sample should be insured. One that is unusually valuable—a piece of jewelry, for example—is best to have covered by insurance beyond the ordinary shipping insurance, and the store should be made aware of the item's value.

Before you ship a sample or leave it with a store buyer, reach some understanding about when and how you will get it back. In the case of a fragile or valuable sample, be sure the store understands that it must be properly packed and insured. If a sample is damaged or lost while in the store's possession, it should, of course, be paid for.

It is usually unwise to send a sample if it has not been requested. This is not a real problem with inexpensive pieces—the loss of one or two would not create a terrible disaster. But sending unsolicited samples of expensive or unusual work only invites trouble.

When you submit a sample on the hope of getting an order of multiples of that sample, be certain that you are in a position, both in terms of quality and price, to fill the order with craftwork of standards equal to the sample. *(See also: Buyers, Orders, Salesmanship, Sales Representatives)*

Self-Addressed Stamped Envelope (SASE)

A self-addressed stamped envelope is often referred to by its initials, *SASE.* Jury requirements or other situations in which slides or photos are submitted often specify *SASE* for the return of the slides. When special packing materials are used, such as cardboard to protect slides, it is best to include such material in the SASE.

Savings Bank

A saving bank's main function is to handle savings accounts on which it pays interest, although it also performs numerous other banking functions, most notably in mortgage lending. In many states, savings banks are not permitted to handle checking accounts. *(See also: Banking, Commercial Bank)*

Scholarships *(See: Grants)*

Schools *(See: Education, Grants)*

Seconds

Any item that is not up to the best standard is considered a second. This is distinguished from the term *secondhand*, which refers to something previously owned and used by someone else.

Seconds may have slight defects, such as a scratch in the surface of a glass or a poorly fired piece of pottery. Seconds may also be overstocks of discontinued items that are no longer available in a full range of sizes or colors or complete sets.

Seconds need not be thrown away. If you sell seconds in your shop or studio at half the normal retail cost, you still make the wholesale price. And even if you sell them below cost, you recover at least some of the investment in materials and time.

A sale of seconds may bring large numbers of customers to your shop or studio. There may even be customers who will buy from your first line of craft items at the full markup if it is properly displayed and clearly set apart from the seconds.

Security

A major expense item in business these days is loss through burglary and shoplifting. Thieves make no distinction between Tiffany and a small jewelry display at a crafts fair. If the opportunity presents itself, they go to work. If fact, they're less likely to tackle Tiffany because security there is tighter.

A large store can afford to install sophisticated burglar alarms and two-way mirrors, to hire store detectives and use police dogs at night. They might even attach to merchandise electronic price tags that emit a telltale shriek if they're not removed by a special device before they leave the store.

Most craftspeople don't need, don't want, and can't afford to engage in such sleuthing. But there are some simple, commonsense steps that can prevent losses of this kind.

Shoplifting

Shoplifters and magicians have at least two things in common: Both rely on sleight-of-hand and while magicians make rabbits disappear, shoplifters do the same to your profits.

Shoplifting is not confined to retail stores. How many crafts artists haven't had something stolen at a crafts fair, especially if their craftwork is small and valuable?

It is not likely that someone will make off with a heavy pot or a large wall hanging. But jewelry is a perfect target. Less valuable items are not immune either, because shoplifters are not all professionals who will only steal what they can easily sell for a worthwhile sum. Some people steal for kicks or on a dare. Others steal because they like the item and don't want to pay for it.

You can't keep everything locked up, however. One of the reasons people visit a crafts show or fair is to examine the craftwork—to touch it, feel it, handle it. There are two basic ways to reduce shoplifting losses under those circumstances.

1. Keep displays neat and arrange them so that you can easily keep an eye on everything. Keep valuable things such as gold jewelry under glass or behind you. If customers want to see the item, you can hand it to them and stick with them until the item is sold or safely back in its place.

2. Keep an eye on customers. Most are honest. But if someone is carrying an umbrella when it's not raining or is wearing a cape or coat when it's warm, be extra careful. Umbrellas, shopping bags, coats, even baby strollers are devices in which stolen goods can quickly be hidden.

In that connection, be careful before accusing someone of stealing. If you're wrong, you can be in trouble. Ask them to return what they took, if possible. A question such as "Did you pay me for the ring you took?" will often produce an apologetic return of the item or a denial that anything was taken. Calling the cops or the show's security force is not always feasible for craftspeople, especially at a crafts fair, because it takes time away from the booth. On the other hand, leniency only encourages thieves who will continue to rip off others and may even visit you again.

Burglary

Locking the barn door after the horse is gone is doing it too late to keep the horse thieves away. First of all, most burglars are never caught. Some statistics put the rate of unsolved burglaries at 80 percent. Even if the burglary is solved, the only satisfaction—such as it is—you're likely to have is revenge; you're not likely to get the stolen goods back.

Prevention is the better cure. Retail stores are prime targets for burglars, but workshops or storage areas are not immune either. Therefore, install a good lock and don't have too many keys floating around. That will deter the spur-of-the-moment burglar who tries doors and enters those that are easy to open.

You should remember that burglars prefer to work in the dark. Keep a few lights on inside the house or store or workshop, and keep the outside lit up too. Inexpensive automatic devices such as timers or photoelectric switches will turn on lights automatically when it gets dark. Keeping lights on all day when you're away so that they will also be on after dark is a dead giveaway to a sharp burglar casing his night's work. Outside lighting should cover dark areas and alleys.

If you are in an area where burglary is a particularly high risk, ask the local police department for suggestions on other methods for protecting your shop or store or home. And if you go away for the weekend to a crafts show or go on a longer trip, alert your neighbors so that they can keep an eye on things.

Finally, note that money is the prime target for thieves. It is small, easy to hide, nearly impossible to identify, and ready to use. Don't keep money out in the open. Keep it in your pockets or in a box under the counter or table. In addition, if toward the end of a successful crafts show you might have a wad of bills, don't count out change from a roll and don't cash checks for people you don't know.

No matter how carefully you protect yourself, it is an unfortunate fact that you can still be a victim of burglars or shoplifters. Though being suspicious of everyone and everything can drive you into paranoia, ignoring potential troubles can drive you into bankruptcy. Be alert and take some commonsense preventive measures to cut down on such losses *(See also: Collection Problems, Shows and Fairs)*

Selling *(See: Consignment, Memo, Retailing, Salesmanship, Shows and Fairs, Wholesaling)*

Seminars *(See: Education)*

Service Charge *(See: Minimum Orders)*

Service Time *(See: Pricing, Wages)*

Shipping

Shipments of products can be made in many ways: via local truck; the post office; United Parcel Service (UPS), Federal Express, and other private-delivery agencies; freight forwarders, bus companies, airlines, and motor carriers, or truckers. Each is suited to a particular need.

The post office, for example, delivers everywhere in the world, but UPS delivers packages only in the continental United States and Hawaii. The per-pound rate of UPS is lower than the post-office rate, and they pick up as well as deliver, but there is a weekly pick-up charge that boosts the price considerably if you make only one shipment per week. If you have one hundred shipments per week, UPS's weekly charge adds only a few pennies to each shipment, which brings the total cost below the post office's. Both UPS and the post office have size and weight limits, and there are some shipments, such as of flammable liquids, that they won't handle.

Shipments that weigh more than the fifty-pound UPS limit or the forty-pound post-office limit can either go via motor carriers or freight forwarders. Both pick up at your end and deliver at the other. Their basic difference is that motor carriers, using only trucks and generally charging more, get the shipment to its destination faster. Freight forwarders pick up your shipment; take it to a central point where it is consolidated with numerous other shipments into a large truck, railroad car, freighter, or cargo plane; and send it off to its destination where it is transshipped to local trucks for delivery. That takes more time but generally costs less.

Freight rates themselves are a complicated business and are subject to government approval through the Interstate Commerce Commission. The rates are divided into numerous classifications based on the type of merchandise being shipped, its density, fragility, gross weight, distance, and other factors. There is usually a minimum charge based on five hundred pounds, and insurance coverage is available. (Look in the yellow pages under *Freight Forwarders*.)

Companies such as Emery Air Freight and Federal Express guarantee overnight delivery anywhere in the United States and pick up as well as deliver. Shipping directly via an airline on a specific flight can get a package to its destination even faster, but it has to be delivered to the airport at your end and picked up at the airport at the other end. Since such shipments are always more expensive than normal ground transportation or UPS and postal-air service, the time element has to be balanced against the cost. Companies that handle air shipments are found in the yellow pages under *Air Cargo*.

Using a bus service for delivery to nearby areas can often be the fastest way to move a package. Again, it has to be delivered to the bus station at your end and picked up at the bus station at the other end, but a package from New York can get to Philadelphia in less than three hours, or not much longer than it takes the bus to travel the distance. You need only let the recipient know that the package is on the bus that arrives at 4:30 P.M. and he or she can be there waiting for the package when the bus pulls in.

For more complicated situations, such as shipping a fragile piece overseas, shipping agents will take care of all the details: packing, shipping, customs declarations, and so forth. It is an expense but is one worth taking if there are special circumstances.

The American Craft Council has published an informative brochure about shipping called "Packing/Shipping of Crafts" (see Appendix C). The booklet contains many practical suggestions for packing specific types of crafts objects for shipment and includes names and addresses of shippers, firms that specialize in packing supplies, and shipping agents. (*See also: Customs, Freight Allowance, Net Weight, Packing, Post Office, United Parcel Service*)

Shows and Fairs

One of the more remarkable phenomena in crafts retailing has been the blossoming of crafts shows and fairs all over the country. They range from little Sunday-afternoon events on the church lawn with perhaps a half dozen craftspeople as exhibitors to such major events as the Buyers Market of American Crafts' show in Philadelphia, where, in 1992, almost twelve hundred craftspeople displayed their works for wholesale buyers.

Crafts shows are held indoors and out, at street fairs and in exhibition halls, in school gyms and shopping malls. Some are open to all comers, including hobbyists, while others require a tough jury process. For example, the 1993 ACC Craftfare for Baltimore screened slides submitted by almost three thousand applicants to choose eleven hundred exhibitors.

Show organizers run the gamut from crafts organizations to commercial promoters to charitable organizations and local chambers of commerce. Among the most successful, from the craftsperson's point of view, have been the shows and fairs organized by such crafts groups as the American Craft Council, Southern Highland Handicraft Guild, Texas Artists and Craftsmen, Kentucky Guild of Artists and Craftsmen, and Pacific Northwest Arts and Crafts Association. Occasionally, a small group of craftspeople get together to stage their own show, as in China Lake, California, where seven artists and craftspeople have conducted an annual Christmas fair over a period of several weekends in a model home provided for the purpose by a local builder. Saturday Market in Portland, Oregon assembles a much larger group of crafts marketers on Saturdays and Sundays—despite its name—from early spring to Christmas each year.

From the customer's point of view, a crafts show is an excellent way to shop among a large variety of crafts objects in one place. It often offers the person an opportunity to watch craftspeople at work and admire their crafts objects. A good crafts show raises the level of appreciation among the attending public so that they will buy more crafts in the future.

For the craftsperson, a crafts show provides an excellent outlet for selling craftwork. Since most crafts artists work in comparative isolation, their participation at crafts shows also provides an opportunity to test new ideas and new designs through direct contact with customers and other craftspeople. This is a valuable experience for anyone who produces craftwork for sale— especially for craftspeople just getting started on a professional career. Even the most successful crafts artists exhibit at shows for this experience alone. Many consider it a vacation from their bench or loom or wheel.

Choosing a Show

Since there are excellent crafts shows, mediocre ones, and even poor experiences, picking the shows at which you want to sell is an important consideration. Other craftspeople can often provide you with leads to the best shows they've attended. Ask them about attendance figures, admission prices, and promotion.

But be careful. Attendance figures alone don't tell the whole story. A commercial promoter of a shopping-mall show, for example, may report attendance of 150,000, but that includes all the people who come to the mall for their normal shopping excursions. Some of those people may stop to buy a leather belt for ten dollars or twelve dollars, but they're not likely to buy a woven wall hanging for eight hundred dollars. Mall shows are a subject of controversy among some craftspeople who feel that their presence there serves primarily to draw crowds for the mall merchants. Many mall shows also restrict the type of craft that can be shown in order not to compete with regular mall merchants who sell similar products such as jewelry.

An established show that has been running for some years and enjoys a good reputation and following is obviously preferred. Such a show in a popular resort area, for example, where people are in a spending mood, is an ideal setting for a summer weekend of selling—especially if it is promoted as a cultural event rather than a commercial operation.

Flea markets, on the other hand, are avoided at all costs by most crafts professionals. The atmosphere at such events cheapens the value of fine crafts, and flea-market customers generally look for bargains rather than quality.

A clue to the integrity of a show can be found in the requirements stated by the show management. Most shows insist that the exhibitor be the person who produced the craftwork. In other words, no distributors or importers are allowed. Many shows also specify that nothing made from kits or molds is to be shown. Such requirements are good indicators that it is really a crafts show.

How to Find Shows

The best source for listings of forthcoming shows are the craft publications, particularly *Sunshine Artists U.S.A.*, which emphasizes and evaluates outdoor shows, especially southern ones; *The Crafts Report*, which provides considerable detail about major professional shows; *Westart*, which concentrates on West Coast events; *American Craft*; the *National Calendar of Indoor-Outdoor Art Fairs*; *Craftmaster News* and the *Craft Fair Guide* (see Appendix C). Numerous local and regional publications, craft organizations, arts commissions, and chambers of commerce can often be helpful in providing lists of nearby crafts shows.

What It Costs

Fees to rent space at a crafts show are generally modest, ranging between fifteen dollars and one hundred dollars. Only the most successful shows charge higher fees, and they are usually worth the price. In addition to the fee, numerous shows take a commission on sales, normally around 10 percent. This is particularly true when the rental fee is low. Outdoor shows are almost always less expensive than indoor ones, but they also offer less in terms of facilities. A crafts fair in a park, for example, may furnish only an 8 × 10-foot plot, with no protection against sun or rain. An indoor show may furnish the same size space, but it is under cover, is well lighted, and has rest rooms and other facilities nearby—hence the higher price.

It is important to determine what is included in the fee. Does the show management provide tables, chairs, overnight security, electric outlets, a printed program that includes your name and address? If it is an indoor show, are there any labor problems or extra costs connected with moving in and setting up your display? What rules and regulations does the show management impose on exhibitors?

A major expense factor in attending shows, often exceeding the cost of the booth itself, is the cost of travel, eating, and staying overnight if the show is some distance from home. Some outdoor shows in warm climates provide camping facilities at reasonable cost. Others are in high-priced areas, such as major cities, where hotel rooms can run between $50 and $150 a night—sometimes even more. All this expense must enter into the determination of whether a particular show can be a profitable selling experience.

All costs associated with show participation are, of course, tax-deductible business expenses. It is necessary, however, to keep accurate records. The Internal Revenue Service (IRS) requires that receipts be kept for all lodging, for all meals exceeding twenty-five dollars, and for any other expense for which a receipt can be obtained. Tollbooths on turnpikes give receipts, for example. Automobile expenses can be calculated at the rate the IRS allows for deduction on your taxes, which is 28¢ per mile, plus parking fees and tolls. When you go on a show trip away from home, it is best to take a little book in which to record all expenses as soon as they are incurred. Don't trust to memory; even the dimes and quarters for phone calls add up. Take along a manila envelope and place all receipts in that envelope. At the end of the trip, the little book and the envelope should provide an accurate record of every expense. Put these away in a safe place until it's time to fill out your tax returns.

Your Display

It is remarkable how many craftspeople—consummate artists in the creation of tasteful design—make a totally cluttered mess of their displays at a crafts show. Simplicity is the essence of selling. There is no need to pile everything you've made on the table. Variety is important, but when too much is offered, the customer doesn't know what to look at.

1. Keep table coverings and backgrounds simple. Plain colors enhance;

fancy prints detract. The drop on table coverings should fall neatly to the floor. It not only looks better but provides space under the table to store cartons and extra pieces.

2. Try to display your work in its natural habitat. Wall hangings should not lie flat on a table but hang from a wall such as a Peg-Board. Pottery should be displayed on a table or a shelf arrangement.

3. If you construct your own display unit, keep it simple so that it can be transported easily and assembled without elaborate tools. Study what others do—not to imitate but to learn.

4. If you go to an outdoor show, take a sun umbrella to protect yourself against the heat and a waterproof covering you can quickly throw over your display in case of a sudden downpour.

5. Display your work so that small, expensive pieces are not out in front where shoplifters—yes, they visit crafts fairs—can get their hands on them. This is particularly important for jewelers.

6. Have some kind of printed material available, even if it is only business cards. An illustrated piece of literature showing your work is even better. It need not be expensive, but your name, address, and telephone number should be included so that customers can find you after the show if they're not ready to buy right then or don't have the money with them. Many craftspeople find that the interest they generate at a show turns into sales afterward.

7. Demonstrate your work if you can. Nothing attracts attention as much as activity in your booth. If you're weaving or hammering or turning a blob of clay into a pot, the crowd will gather and, hopefully, buy. That way you also use your time to produce. Demonstrating generally requires prior arrangements with the show management, especially if you need electricity or water. But most show managements encourage demonstrations because they bring the show to life. It also requires more than one person in the booth so that one can sell while the other demonstrates. Having two people at a show is useful under many circumstances, especially at a long show, for rest breaks and other purposes.

8. By all means bring a chair, but don't sit on it too often. Nothing discourages a potential customer more than to see a craftsperson who's sitting in a chair and reading a book or looking bored. Hard sell is neither necessary nor appropriate, but a pleasant greeting and an offer to help and explain is the first step toward making a sale at a crafts show.

Wholesale Days

A prominent feature of some major shows is a day or two that is set aside exclusively for wholesale buyers from department stores, galleries, museums, and the like. Such a day is known as a wholesale day and is becoming more and more prevalent. The crowds at wholesale days may not be as large as retail days, but the sales volume can be incredible. Charley Gohn, a Pennsylvania metal craftsman, reported that he wrote nineteen thousand dollars' worth of business during the wholesale days at the Rhinebeck show one year and had to stop writing orders on the morning of the second wholesale day because there was no way he could fill those orders.

Wholesale days at a few major shows can provide the bulk of the annual income for many craftspeople. Orders are written for later delivery dates, and production is thus spread throughout the year. As in all other forms of wholesaling, the ability to deliver when promised is as important a consideration as the quality and the price of the crafts objects.

Wholesale buyers are experienced and careful. They may not buy from you the first time around, but after they've seen your exhibit at several successive shows, they will gain confidence. Shows such as the Buyers Market of American Crafts, which is held in a variety of cities including Baltimore, Philadelphia, Boston, and San Francisco, are for wholesale buyers only.

Pricing
If you normally sell wholesale at 50 percent of retail, you may be tempted to cut your retail price at a crafts show. After all, you might figure whatever you make above wholesale is gravy. But that's a dangerous proposition. First of all, the costs of attending the show must come out of the retail markup—the other 50 percent. Furthermore, the time spent at a show is time spent away from production, and the profit for that time must also come out of the retail markup. Finally, if you've sold your craftwork to retail outlets in the area where the show is held, it is a dangerous practice to undercut the price of those retail outlets by selling your work at a lower price yourself. It is intelligent merchandising, therefore, to maintain the retail price of your work even at a crafts show.

What to Expect From Show Management
In return for paying the necessary fee, you have a right to expect certain services from the show management. First, of course, are the things specifically promised in the show brochure: a space of the promised size, setup time when specified, equipment if included, proper promotion to bring a crowd, and so on.

Some show managers fall down even in those areas, but most keep their basic promises. Thereafter, however, management ranges from the superb to the abominable. Some show managers walk away as soon as the show has moved in. Others are constantly on the premises, alert to every problem and ready to solve it.

The first Annual Arts and Craft Show at Disney World in Florida, for example, provided hammers and wire for exhibitors who ran into difficulties in setting up their displays, furnished sitters for booths that had to be left temporarily unattended, and even accommodated pets at their kennels. Admittedly, this sort of service is rare. But show managers do have certain responsibilities beyond providing the promised facilities.

Are booths positioned so that the traffic pattern helps to bring visitors past every exhibit? Are aisles wide enough to enable customers to move around without knocking into displays or one another? Are rest-room facilities available? Are all instructions clear, and have they been furnished to exhibitors well in advance of the show so that exhibitors can properly prepare for the show?

If the show is juried, do applicants know who the jurors are and what criteria are used? Are rejected applicants given a reasonable explanation? Does the show management interrupt constantly with entertainment or other distractions that draw people away from the booths where craftspeople are trying to sell? Is a show program or catalog published with names and addresses of exhibitors? Does the management report to exhibitors on the success of the fair afterward?

Are promised awards actually given? Is the show well publicized? Does the show management listen to complaints or suggestions with some expression of concern? Above all, are craftspeople treated with respect or are they simply moved around like chess pieces on the show floor?

As an exhibitor you also have some responsibilities. The major one is to comply with all the rules that were provided in writing. Beyond that, be friendly and courteous, operate the booth in a professional manner, and be considerate of the exhibitor in the next booth.

If you've never exhibited at a show, it may be useful to attend a number of different shows as a visitor to get a feel for how they're run. Ask questions of visitors and exhibitors. Study all the details carefully.

If you're visiting a show you plan to enter next year, ask yourself some questions. How does your work compare with the work of other exhibitors? Is there already an overabundance of your craft so that competition is even keener? Do the prices at the show make your prices seem realistic? Can you produce enough work in advance to keep your exhibit well stocked for the entire run of the show?

Even if you answer all these questions affirmatively, there is still no guarantee that the show will be a success for you. Suppose it snows and nobody shows up? But at least you can try to avoid some serious mistakes by judging beforehand the prospects of a show at which you plan to take a booth. (*See also: Display, Marketing*)

Single Entry

This term refers to a bookkeeping and accounting method that uses one set of books to record all transactions. This requires only a journal in which you record receipts and expenditures on a daily basis and a ledger in which you or your accountant distributes expenditures and receipts under various columns to indicate their purpose or source.

A ledger for a crafts business, for example, may include separate columns to record receipts from cash sales, shows and fairs, wholesale volume, and consignment business. The expenditures columns may be divided to reflect what you spend on rent and utilities, wages, taxes, selling costs, raw materials, and so on.

This system is easy for a layman to understand and helps you to analyze where the money is coming from and where it is going. Important changes that may require attention are quickly recognized even by nonaccountants. The ledger is brought up-to-date once a month or at least quarterly. *(See also: Bookkeeping, Double Entry)*

Slides *(See: Photographs)*

Small Business Administration (SBA)

The Small Business Administration is a government agency whose interest in crafts is purely economic. The creative aspects have nothing to do with its functions, which are primarily in the field of making loans to small business.

The Small Business Administration funnels money into small business enterprises in three ways:

1. By guaranteeing 90 percent—up to five hundred thousand dollars—of a loan made by a local bank or other lending institution;

2. By direct loans in special circumstances in which local financing is not available or to low-income people whose credit might not meet strict local lending policies;

3. By granting loans to state and local development companies, profit or nonprofit, that contribute between 10 and 20 percent of the cost of a small-business project in their own area.

The SBA also makes loans to businesses that have suffered from natural disasters such as hurricanes or from economic injury caused by such activities as highway construction or from other reasons beyond their control.

In order to obtain a loan, a detailed application must be filed that explains the purposes of the loan; the prospects of success; the schedule of repayment; as well as specific information about the nature and size of the business, the experience of the owner, and so forth. Most craftspeople would probably approach their own bank or other lending institution first. The possibility of an SBA guarantee for a bank loan can be discussed with the appropriate bank officials. They will also know when and how to proceed to make application.

The Small Business Administration has literature available that explains its lending and guarantee functions in great detail. This information can be obtained from any of the SBA offices in major cities throughout the country (see telephone white pages under *United States Government, Small Business Administration*) or can be requested by writing to the Small Business Administration (see Appendix D).

Another significant service rendered by the SBA to small businesses is an extensive and expanding list of publications on a wide range of business subjects discussed in clear and easy terms. Topics include cost control, business life insurance, cash flow, sales agents, budgeting, and accounting procedures. Many of these publications are free; the cost for others is modest. A complete list is available at any SBA office or from the SBA in Washington, D.C. Ask for *The Small Business Directory. (See also: Government Activities)*

Small-Claims Court

If you are lucky enough that every customer pays you promptly and every supplier delivers exactly what you paid for, then you're probably not even reading this entry. But life is not like that. As its name implies, each state's small-claims court exists to help people settle small claims against each other. The term *small* means different things in different places. The amount of a claim generally ranges between five hundred dollars and twenty-five hundred dollars.

The concept of small-claims court is that it is hardly worth the money to hire a lawyer to collect so small an amount. That's why many states don't even permit lawyers in small-claims court unless they are representing themselves or a corporation. And if you oppose a lawyer in small-claims court, it is the judge's responsibility to make sure your interests are properly represented. The usual legal procedures and rules of evidence don't apply. The proceedings are informal, quick, and inexpensive. Staff members are often available to help people fill out the forms. Filing fees range from forty-five to one hundred dollars depending upon the state and amount in controversy.

Small-claims courts have what some—not all—might call a drawback: Most states do not allow for an appeal. The judge's decision is binding. *(See also: Collection Problems)*

Social Security

Social security is a federal program enacted in 1935 and has become the basic method of providing income to people after they retire or become severely disabled and to their survivors when they die.

Nine out of ten people who work for a living, including self-employed craftspeople, are paying into the social-security fund and earning protection. Nearly one out of seven Americans receives a social-security check each month. This number includes not only retirees but the disabled and the survivors as well, regardless of age.

About twenty-two million people over age sixty-five and another two million people under sixty-five who are severely disabled have health protection under medicare, which is administered by the Social Security Administration.

The basic idea of social security is simple. Employees, employers, and self-employed people pay social-security contributions into special funds during their working years. When these people retire, become disabled, or die, monthly cash benefits are paid to replace part of the earnings that are lost.

Employers and employees pay an equal share of social-security contributions. If you are self-employed, you pay contributions at a somewhat lower rate than the combined rate for an employee and an employer, but that does not reduce the ultimate benefits. As long as you have earnings from employment or self-employment, the contributions have to be paid, regardless of your age and even whether you are already receiving social-security benefits.

Social-security contributions are calculated on a combination of two factors: a tax rate and an annual-income base. These are established by Congress and change—upward—from year to year. The rates are different for people who are employed versus those who are self-employed. Currently contributions are divided between the social security trust fund and a medicare trust fund. Employees and employers each contribute 6.2 percent to social security and 1.45 percent to medicare. The self-employed contribute 12.4 percent to social security and 2.9 percent to medicare.

But these figures don't tell the whole story. The contribution is imposed on all income up to a certain maximum that also changes each year. The maximum on which social-security contributions was imposed in 1976 was $14,100; by 1984 it had risen to $37,800. For 1993, it is $57,600 for social security and $135,000 for medicare. In other words, even if the rate were to remain the same or go up only slightly, your total social-security contribution could increase substantially if the annual base were increased. For example, a person who earned twenty-five thousand dollars in 1975 paid $869 in social-security contributions—5.85 percent on the first $14,100. In 1984, the same twenty-five-thousand-dollar income was subject to $1,675 in social-security contributions—6.7 percent on twenty-five thousand dollars—even though the tax rate rose by less than 1 percent.

The rate in both 1983 and 1984, for example, was 6.7 percent. But in 1983 that was 6.7 percent of $35,700; in 1984 it was 6.7 percent of $37,800, a difference of $140.70. For the self-employed, contributing 11.3 percent in both years, the 1984 maximum meant $237.50 more in social-security payments.

Social-security payments are automatically deducted from wages every payday. The employer matches the employee's payment and sends the combined amount to the Internal Revenue Service, which is the collection agency for the Social Security Administration.

If you are self-employed and your net profit is more than four hundred dollars a year, you must include your social-security obligations when you calculate your estimated-tax payments and pay any difference when you file your individual income tax. This is required even if no income tax is owed.

Wages and self-employed income are entered on each individual's social-security record during his or her working years. This record is used to determine retirement benefits or cash benefits. A fairly complicated formula is used to determine the average annual income earned since 1950. For a worker who retired at age sixty-five in 1993, the maximum monthly benefit would have been $1,128.00. A worker who began collecting benefits in 1993 at age sixty-two would have received about 20 percent less than the age-sixty-five payments. The monthly checks are reduced proportionately for workers who retire sometime between sixty-two and sixty-five. Delaying retirement beyond sixty-five earns extra credits and increased monthly checks. There is also a minimum for people who have worked under social security at least twenty years but whose earnings were unusually low.

Social-security benefit checks are increased automatically each July if the cost of living in the previous year has risen by more than 3 percent over the previous year. Future benefits will also go up because they are based on the higher payments made into the fund.

If you work for more than one employer in the same year and pay social-security contributions on both incomes, you can get a refund on any payments in excess of the required maximum. In 1982, for example, when the annual base was $32,400, an employee who worked for two employers, earning twenty thousand dollars with each employer, would have earned a total of forty thousand dollars, or $7,600 above the maximum on which he or she was required to pay social-security contributions. That entitled the employee to a refund of $509.20—6.7 percent of $7,600. The two employers would not have received any refund.

For many years it was the practice to reduce social-security payments to people over age sixty-five who continued having some employment income. Payments were reduced by the exact amount of that income. That policy was changed. Starting in 1976, a taxpayer could earn $2,760 in a year without having any benefits withheld. By 1993, that figure had grown to $7,680 per year for those who are age sixty-five and $10,560 for those over sixty-five to age seventy and appears to be growing each year. On annual earnings above the maximum, social security withholds one dollar in benefits for each two dollars in earnings for those under age sixty-five and one dollar in benefits for each three dollars earned by those ages sixty-five to seventy. This rule applies to everyone under age seventy. Anyone over that age can earn any amount without reduction in benefits.

Income from savings, investments, pensions, or insurance policies is not counted toward the earnings on which social-security benefits are reduced. However, starting in 1984, some social-security benefits themselves became taxable under certain circumstances. To determine whether your social-security benefits may be taxed as income, add one-half of your annual benefit to your gross income. If the total is greater than $32,000 for married taxpayers or $25,000 for individual taxpayers, then one-half of the social-security benefits must be reported as gross income. Otherwise, social-security benefits are not subject to income tax. Persons who retire out of the country and receive benefits should contact the Social Security Administration to determine their tax liability on social-security benefits.

Social-security records are maintained by social-security number, and your number travels with you throughout your working life. It is also used for identification on income-tax returns and on many other official documents. A social-security card can be obtained at any social-security office—there are about thirteen hundred throughout the country, listed in the telephone book white pages under *United States Government, Health, Education and Welfare, Social Security Administration*—and must be shown to an employer before beginning to work so that the employer can remit the proper amount to the employee's account. The amount withheld from wages for social-security purposes is also reported to every employee on the W-2 form, which is furnished to all employees once a year for income-tax purposes.

Social-security benefits do not start automatically; you must apply for them. The Social Security Administration lists the following conditions under which you may apply for benefits:

1. If you are unable to work, regardless of age, because of an illness or injury that is expected to last a year or longer;

2. If you are age sixty-two or older and plan to retire;

3. When you are within two or three months of age sixty-five—even if you don't plan to retire—you are eligible for benefits including medicare;

4. If someone in your family dies.

All the information in your social-security file is confidential.

An excellent booklet titled *Your Social Security* is available without charge from any social-security office.

The most important thing to realize is that social security, contrary to popular opinion, is not restricted to the elderly or the retired. Many social-security benefits and medicare benefits are available to millions of other Americans under specific circumstances. *(See also: Pensions)*

Sole Proprietorship

This is the simplest method for organizing a business. Few formalities are needed. Most states require filing a certificate if you conduct the business under an assumed name instead of your own. The secretary of state's office in most states can tell you what and where to file.

Even a sole proprietorship is well advised, especially for tax purposes, to have a business checking account and a federal-taxpayer-identification number. Talk to your attorney, banker, or accountant about this.

If your business has employees other than yourself, the proprietor, it has to maintain and pay for workers' compensation insurance, social security, and the like for the employees. Avoiding workers' compensation insurance and other employee-related benefits is often regarded as a benefit of the sole-proprietorship form. On the other hand, the absence of such benefits to the owner when the need for them arises can be one of the disadvantages of this form of organization.

It is important to note that the sole proprietor is personally and fully liable for the debts of the business. If the business fails, its creditors can go after the owner's nonbusiness income and assets such as car, home, and savings. *(See also: Corporation, Joint Venture, Limited Liability Companies, Limited Partnership, Partnership)*

Special Markets *(See: Architects, Gallery, Interior Decorators and Designers)*

State Arts Agencies

Each state, as well as the District of Columbia and all United States possessions, has its own arts commission or council. Some major cities also have them. The councils are official or semiofficial government agencies that go by different names in different states and that are funded in various ways by the various states. Canada has arts councils in each of its eight provinces.

The purpose of these councils or commissions is to provide leadership and funding for the development of the arts in their areas. Most have offices in the state or provincial capital. A complete list of all state arts agencies, with addresses and telephone numbers, is available for two dollars from the American Council for the Arts (see Appendix D). *(See also: National Endowment for the Arts)*

Statement

A statement is a recapitulation of a set of financial transactions or conditions, such as bank statements, financial statements, income statements.

When the word *statement* is used alone, it generally refers to a statement of account. This is a recapitulation sent by a seller to a buyer, usually on a monthly basis, to indicate all purchases and payments made during the period.

The statement lists each purchase according to the invoice number—sales-slip reference in department store or credit card statements—and lists each payment received, either by date or by invoice number, against which the payment is credited. The final balance is what is owed by the buyer to the seller on the date the statement is prepared.

The difference between an invoice and a statement is twofold. A statement is not a request for payment, only a recapitulation of what is owed and what's been paid. In addition, a statement generally does not indicate why or for what the money is owed. That's why invoice numbers are used for reference. *(See also: Accounting, Banks, Checking Account, Financial Statement, Income Statement)*

Stock Control *(See: Inventory)*

Stop Payment

If you tell your bank not to pay a check that you have already issued, it's known as a stop-payment order. There is usually a service charge of between three and five dollars that appears on your monthly statement.

Proceed with caution. In most states it is against the law to stop payment on a check except for good reason. Such reasons include stopping payment on a check that was lost in the mail or on a check that was issued as a down payment and has not been returned for a contract that has since been canceled. To stop payment on a check for an otherwise valid transaction is illegal.

A valid stop-payment order must, of course, be given before the check has cleared your bank. In commercial transactions, this has to be done before midnight of the day following the day the check was issued. The stop-payment order can be telephoned in to the bank but must be issued in writing as soon thereafter as possible.

Be sure to correct your checkbook entry to indicate that a check has been stopped. It affects the balance shown in your checkbook. *(See also: Checking Account)*

Stores *(See: Retailing)*

Suppliers

Since the raw materials—clay, yarn, wool, metal, fabrics—and the tools and equipment you use are major expense factors in any craft producer's budget, the suppliers of these items are important sources with whom a wholesome relationship should be developed.

If you produce craftwork for sale, you are usually entitled to purchase your supplies at wholesale prices or at least at some discount from the regular retail price. A neighborhood crafts-supply store that buys its stock at wholesale prices for resale to hobbyists can't really be expected to sell at wholesale to professional crafts producers. What they offer is convenience and a selection of products from a variety of manufacturers. However, if you buy supplies in large quantities or purchase expensive pieces of professional equipment, often you can establish a business relationship with manufacturers or wholesale distributors. In states that have a sales tax, you are usually required by the manufacturer or the distributor to provide your resale number in order to qualify for the wholesale price.

The advantage of the lower price is sometimes offset by having to order the merchandise by mail and by being required to order minimum quantities. With good planning to meet the minimum requirements and to account for the time element, however, the savings can be considerable.

A continuing relationship with a supplier generally also provides credit to the crafts producer. This means that you needn't pay cash at the time of purchase, but in effect you borrow the money for the period of time between the purchase and when the bill has to be paid, which can be as many as sixty days on a monthly billing cycle. Credit is rarely available to new customers until they've established a track record through payment with order or a number of cash-on-delivery (COD) orders. Some suppliers and manufacturers also require a minimum monthly dollar volume in order to qualify for credit purchases.

It is occasionally feasible for several craftspeople to join together to buy supplies in large quantities and thus earn a better price. This is especially true of supplies such as packing materials, office supplies, and other items not specifically related to the crafts object being made. Similarly, by planning ahead it is possible for you to save money by making one large purchase instead of three or four small ones. Of course, that involves a somewhat larger initial outlay of money, but if you can afford it, the savings may be worth the planning.

In addition to extending credit and offering discounts, a reliable supply dealer or manufacturer also keeps its customers informed of new products, new equipment, new colors. A good relationship with a supply dealer also makes it much easier to return a defective product or to make exchanges.

Where do you find such supply dealers or manufacturers? That's always a touchy question. So much depends on the personalities involved; on the reputation of the supplier; on your needs in terms of delivery, selection, and so forth.

A steady reading of crafts publications provides information both on what's available and who has it. Other craftspeople, crafts schools, and crafts organizations can usually be helpful in making suggestions based on experience. Two excellent books are available: *National Guide to Craft Supplies* and *Craft Supplies Supermarket* (see Appendix C). The latter lists only those suppliers who sell by mail.

Manufacturers and suppliers who sell by mail furnish catalogs, price lists, and other ordering information. They sometimes charge a small fee for the catalog that usually can be applied to the first order. For orders of yarn, leather, and textiles, they will also furnish swatches or samples of material.

Finally, it is considered as poor a business practice to stick to only one supplier as it is to jump from one supplier to the next. If you develop two or three good, reliable sources of supply, you can usually be sure to get the best prices while at the same time protecting yourself against problems one supplier or another may run into. You never know when flood, fire, or other disasters may strike. If you have only one source and that source is incapacitated, you're in trouble. On the other hand, if you spread your business too thin among too many suppliers, none of them will consider you a good customer and none will exert themselves on your behalf. *(See also: Credit, Equipment, Tools, Trade Credit)*

Surplus

By definition, surplus is anything that is left over. In accounting, for example, the amount left over after deducting all expenses from all income is a surplus. In inventory control, having more stock on hand than your books show you should have is also a surplus. If you have an order for one hundred pieces and you make 110, the extra ten are considered surplus.

The opposite of surplus is deficit. *(See also: Deficit)*

Systems

At first glance, a system seems like a waste of time. Why do all that paperwork when you could spend your time more profitably at the wheel or the loom or the workbench. Right?

Wrong! A sensible system for keeping track of money, time, supplies, and inventory has saving you time as its central purpose. Such a system really is nothing more than an orderly procedure for getting things done.

Of course, there are people who get so involved with procedures that the system becomes and end in itself rather than the means toward an end. That is a waste of time. A good system should keep your affairs in order and enable you to plan ahead. Such systems save you both time and money.

A simple system for keeping track of orders, for example, helps you to fill the orders properly. Without a system, you either have to rummage all over the place to find the order or trust to memory that you'll ship the right things to the right place at the right time. If you end up shipping the wrong stuff to the wrong place at the wrong time, you'll spend a lot of effort and money to set it right. You might even lose a good customer. An order-control system could have avoided all that.

Don't let the word *system* scare you. You personal phone book or Rolodex is a perfect example of a system at work. Without the system there are three ways to keep track of names and telephone numbers. You could try to remember them, but that's a little risky unless you have total recall. You could jot them down on little slips of paper and throw them into the nearest drawer. That would require quite a search every time you wanted to make a call. Finally, you could—and probably do—put them all in one place in alphabetical order. That seems by far the best system.

Your checkbook is another example. It doesn't affect your supply of money one way or another; it just keeps track. There's no law that says you must enter all deposits or checks you write on the stub. But how would you ever know what's left in the bank, whether there's enough to cover the next check you write, and whether there's a surplus that should be transferred to a savings account where it can earn interest? Your checkbook is the system that helps you keep track.

The same system's principle applies to all your other management and production procedures. A system need not be complicated to be workable. In fact, the simpler the system the better. But a system is only as good as its execution. It is important that everyone involved with your operation— even if you're the only one—follow whatever system you devise in order that things run more smoothly and you have more time for your creative work. With the advent of computers, systems can easily be implemented and maintained. *(See also: Accounting, Bookkeeping, Computers, Cost Accounting, Inventory, Orders, Record Keeping)*

Tax

A tax is the compulsory payment of money, established and enforced by law, to a governmental body for purpose of meeting the general expenses of government. Taxes are normally based on a percentage of the value of the taxable subject, which includes income, property, sales. Taxes are not related, however, to a specific benefit enjoyed by a taxpayer; that is, your tax does not go up because you call the fire department.

Compulsory payments that relate to a specific benefit or service are not generally called taxes even though they are also established and enforced by law and paid to a governmental body. These costs, including license fees, highway tolls, and sewer assessments, are usually fixed amounts instead of percentages. *(See also: Accounting, Capital-Gains Tax, Estimated Tax, Excise Tax, Expenses, Income Tax, Property Tax, Sales Tax, Social Security, Unemployment Insurance, Withholding Tax)*

Taxpayer Identification Number *(See: Employees, Withholding Tax)*

Telephone

The telephone has become not only the major mode of modern communication but also one of the major items in the monthly overhead.

Most of us have used the phone since we were barely able to talk, clutching the receiver in our tight little fist and muttering "Hi, Grandma" without really knowing where Grandma's voice came from. As a result, most of us never learned, or have forgotten, how to use the telephone effectively and economically in our social and business activities.

Shop Around for the Best Buy

There may be only one telephone company in town, but there is aggressive competition for long-distance service. In addition, there are many other services available. Following are the four most common ones, depending on your location and your needs:

1. Individual-line message-rate or measured service with the usual monthly allowance of fifty message units or a maximum number of minutes;

2. Individual-line message-rate or measured service with no message-unit or minute allowance. This is most economical for telephones that are used primarily to receive incoming calls rather than make outgoing calls. Once the outgoing calls reach thirty or forty a month, this service is no longer economical.

3. Individual-line flat-rate service that allows an unlimited number of calls within a specified calling area.

4. Party-line flat-rate service. This is the least expensive but, if another party on your line is using the phone, you cannot receive incoming calls or make outgoing calls. This service is no longer available in some areas.

Message Units or Measured Service

In many parts of the country, especially in metropolitan areas, the message unit is the way telephone usage is measured and billed. One call is not necessarily one message unit. Distance and the duration of the call both determine how many message units the call will cost. The time of day when the call is made can also determine the cost of each message unit. In New York City, for example, each message unit costs 10.2¢ if the call is made between 9:00 A.M. and 9:00 P.M.; 7.2¢ if it is made between 9:00 P.M. and 9:00 A.M.

Thus, a call in New York City that is three message units in distance can cost almost thirty-one cents even if you speak for only a minute. If you talk for fifteen minutes, that call can mount up to more than seventy-eight cents—plus tax. The actual charges are different in different parts of the country, but the message-unit principle is the same wherever it applies. Read the front pages of your telephone book carefully to see how it works in your area.

The secret is to make calls as brief and to the point as possible without being abrupt. If a customer calls, be considerate. Don't interrupt yourself to conduct other business while the caller hangs on. Just waiting for you to come back on the line costs the caller money. That's common courtesy, even in areas where message units are not counted.

Convenience Services

There are numerous other services available from local phone companies. These may include call waiting, call forwarding, conference calling, automatic number redial, and the like. These are offered individually or in packages. You should check with your phone company to determine cost and availability.

Multiple Lines

It is quite common to have more than one phone line servicing a single location. Here, too, there are numerous options available, such as multi-line phones, cross-over or hunt features, and the like. Your phone company can tell you what options are available in your area.

Long Distance

Place as many calls as you can by direct dialing. Once you use the operator for such services as person-to-person, collect, and credit card calls, the cost goes up substantially.

Charges differ according to the time of day you place your call. Generally, rates between 8:00 A.M. and 5:00 P.M. on weekdays are highest. Charges drop significantly between 5:00 P.M. and 11:00 P.M., Sunday through Friday; between 11:00 P.M. and 8:00 A.M. every day, all day Saturday, and until 5:00 P.M. Sunday. Every day from 11:00 P.M. to 8:00 A.M. the rates are lowest.

The charge for a long-distance call is determined by the carrier, as well as the time the call originates—and, of course, the duration of the call—so take time differences into account. Placing a call from Los Angeles to New York City before 8:00 A.M. gets the call to New York City before 11:00 A.M. since there's a three-hour time difference. Conversely, if you place a call in New York City at 6:00 P.M., you can still reach a business office in Los Angeles at 3:00 P.M. It does not pay, therefore, to make a call at 4:55, because a five-minute wait can cut the cost of that call by a third or more.

In the front pages of your telephone directory you will find the long-distance rates to major points from your area. It is often worthwhile to dial direct and take a chance on reaching the person you want rather than placing an expensive person-to-person call. You can generally afford several direct calls during the bargain hours for the cost of one person-to-person call completed by the operator. And if you connect the first time, you're ahead.

On long-distance calls you place often, it helps to establish a regular calling time during the bargain hours, say every Tuesday at 6:00 P.M.

The operator-assistance charges do not apply if you need help because there's trouble on the line when you try to dial the call directly. But be sure to tell the operator about the problem you had.

There is fierce competition between long-distance carriers, so it is worthwhile to shop around for the one that best suits your needs.

Wrong Numbers

If you reach a wrong number, call the operator. Tell the operator you reached a wrong number, and ask for credit. That applies to local calls for which message units are counted as well as to long-distance calls.

Keeping Track

If your business phone and your home phone are the same, the business calls are a tax-deductible business expense. Long-distance calls are easy enough to identify—the telephone bill shows the number you called and the date and time you called it. For local business calls, keep a small index card taped to the desk or the wall next to your telephone. Every time you make a local call, make a mark on the index card. If you're in a message-rate area, estimate how many message units you used, based on the length of time and distance you talked, and make a check mark for each message unit. At the end of the month, it's easy enough to add up the business calls by counting the check marks.

Answering Machines and Services

Answering devices are almost universal today in both homes and businesses. The cost of answering machines has declined dramatically, and voice messages are available from private businesses as well as most phone companies. There are also answering services employing human operators.

The decision on which of these, if any, you select for your business depends on cost and personal preference. Whether you select a machine or voice messaging, your outgoing message should sound professional. Avoid lengthy messages and background music or noise; be sensitive to the image your message projects. In addition, let the caller know if there is a time limit for the incoming message.

Facsimile ("Fax") Machine

Popular in recent years and growing more so, facsimile machines—better known as fax machines—have made the phone even more invaluable to the successful business. By connection to a standard phone line in your home or business, a fax allows instant transmission and receipt of copies (facsimiles) of documents such as catalogs; orders; confirming memoranda; shipping instructions; even photographs, sketches, and diagrams. Usually within the time it takes to make a phone call or two, fax machines make it possible for two individuals a few miles or several states apart to work out the details of an order—quantities, styles, patterns, colors—and to receive confirmation of the order's written terms and conditions. Thus, your customers can have virtually instant access to your products. Likewise, you can have ready access to the products of your suppliers.

If you are placing or accepting even a small number of orders per month, the enhanced access to your products that a fax machine can provide may make it cost-effective for you to have a second phone line dedicated for use by your fax machine. It is possible, however, to get by with a single line, connecting the fax only when you are actually going to send or receive a document. Some fax machines are designed to recognize incoming fax signals and switch on automatically.

Modem

Another device that has enhanced telecommunication facilities for the small business in recent years is the modem. A modem (*modulator/demod-ulator*) is a device that converts the serial or asynchronous communications output of a computer into sound (and vice versa) so that it can be transmitted via the telecommunications network between distant computers.

Modems give their users access to an ever increasing number of data-base services, including electronic mail; hotel, travel, and airline reservations; home shopping; newswire services; periodicals; and legal, medical, and general information data bases.

Beep Tone

If you hear a beep tone every fifteen seconds while you're talking, it means that your conversation is being recorded.

Debt Collection

The law prohibits you from making harrassing or threatening telephone calls to obtain money that is owed (or for any other purpose). Don't make such calls. And if you get a call like that, contact your telephone company's business office.

Fraud

It is illegal for anyone to use a credit card or charge calls to another number without authorization. If you lose your telephone credit card or find calls on your bill that you did not make, contact your telephone company's business office.

Displaying Your Phone Number

It's good business to let your customers know how to get in touch with you. List your telephone number, including the area code, on all letterheads, business cards, invoices, promotional literature, and wherever you put your name in print.

Information, Please

The charge for directory assistance varies depending upon whether it is for a local or an interstate number, and is waived for the legally blind. It pays to look up numbers yourself. Where such information charges are in effect, the telephone company normally makes directories for areas other than your own available upon request. In New York State, for example, a telephone user may request more than one hundred directories published in the state. Area codes for the entire country are printed in the front section of all major telephone directories.

Courtesy

It's important to remember that the telephone is your most frequent contact with the outside world, which includes your customers. A cheerful hello works a lot better than a dour yeah, especially if someone is calling with a complaint. In addition, it is discourteous to engage in another activity while you're speaking to someone on the phone. If you must turn away to take care of something else, excuse yourself for a minute. That's what you'd do if the caller were sitting across the table from you. And because some of the nicest people can become monsters on the telephone, never, never slam the phone down on the hook, even if you're angry. You could break the telephone.

Terms of Sale *(See: Sales Terms)*

Textile Fiber Products Identification Act

The Textile Fiber Products Identification Act, a federal law enacted in 1960, is designed to protect consumers by requiring proper labeling of all textile products other than wool—which is covered by the Wool Products Labeling Act.

Enforcement of the act's provisions is a haphazard affair, but as far as the letter of the law is concerned, craftspeople who work with fibers and textiles are supposed to observe the act's following requirements:

1. Every item made of any textile or fiber—garments, rugs, stuffed toys, quilts, and so on—must carry a tag or label showing the percentage of each type of fiber used in the item;

2. The name of the maker or distributor of the item must appear on the tag, which must remain with the item until it has been sold to the ultimate consumer;

3. Imported products must show the country of origin on their tags. This includes the origin of imported yarns that are used in creating a piece in the United States.

The act requires that all natural or man-made fibers be labeled with their generic names. A generic name is the one given to a family of fiber all having similar chemical composition, such as acrylic, acetate, or rayon.

The law also allows the manufacturer to use a trademark or trade name along with the generic name. For example, a tag marked *Orlon acrylic* identifies *Orlon* as the trade name and *acrylic* as the generic name. Other well-known combinations are *Dacron polyester* and *Arnel acetate*. Once the two appear together, they must always be used together. That way a consumer can begin to learn what to expect from a specifically labeled textile or fiber product.

If more than one fiber is used, the tag or label must show the percentage of each fiber, for example: 80 percent Dacron polyester, 20 percent wool. *(See also: Wool Products Labeling Act)*

Theft Insurance *(See: Property Insurance)*

Tools

Do machine processes and power tools change a handcraft design? Should a craftsman use only hand tools? These questions are debated whenever craftspeople get together, and there is no consensus. In Williamsburg, Virginia, the colonial restoration where traditional crafts are demonstrated, machine tools had been used behind the scenes to facilitate handcraft demonstrations. More recently, it was determined that the use of modern equipment on eighteenth-century crafts was inappropriate and the practice was discontinued. Today, the Williamsburg crafts artists are slower and less efficient, but their demonstrations are truly authentic. *(See also: Equipment)*

Trade Credit

One of the sources of short-term financing of your business is the use of trade credit. This is the money you owe your suppliers until you pay your bill.

Once your credit reliability has been established, you can purchase equipment and supplies without paying cash at the time of purchase. At the end of the month you will get a bill that you usually must pay within thirty days. It is possible, therefore, to borrow that money for as long as sixty days without paying any interest. For example, you make a purchase for five hundred dollars on the second of the month. You are billed twenty-eight days later. Payment is due thirty days after that.

This sort of short-term borrowing may not be a major factor in your financing if you buy only a few dollars' worth of supplies each month. But suppose your regular monthly purchases total two thousand dollars, and you always have a two-thousand-dollar balance billed at the end of the month; you, in effect, borrow two thousand dollars all year long. At a normal interest rate of between 8 and 10 percent, you save around two hundred dollars a year in interest charges. And if you pay your bills within ten days after receipt, you often save another 2 percent that many suppliers give as a discount for prompt payment.

What you are doing, in effect, is having your supplier finance part of your operation. The supply dealer benefits from this arrangement because credit terms are extended only to steady, reliable customers. Credit is one of the services he offers to keep you as a good customer. *(See also: Capital, Credit, Credit Card, Loans, Revolving Credit)*

Trade Dress

This is a relatively new form of intellectual property protection that is available without registration on the nonfunctional "aspects" of certain items. Packaging is functional and, thus, not copyrightable, yet products are frequently identified by their distinctive packaging. Examples include Campbell's red-and-white soup cans and the deckle-edged heavy paper and romantic look of Blue Mountain Greeting Cards. The distinctive look and feel of an item are known as its trade dress, which is protectable. *(See also: Copyright, Intellectual Property, Patent, Trademark)*

Trademark

A trademark is described in the Trademark Act of 1946, as amended in 1989, as "any word, name, symbol, or device, or any combination thereof adopted and used by a manufacturer or merchant to identify his goods and distinguish them from those manufactured or sold by others."

A trademark serves not only to indicate who made the product but often to suggest a certain level of quality based on the manufacturer's past performance. Typical, well-known trademarks are the oval Ford symbol, the distinctive lettering of Coca-Cola, and the Nike swoosh.

When you use a unique symbol to mark your craftwork, it is a trademark. While trademarks need not be registered, registration helps to protect the owner's exclusive right to use the trademark.

The difference between trademarks and trade names is that a trademark identifies the product, while a trade name identifies the producer of the product. When a trade name is designed in a unique fashion and is used on the product, it can become a trademark and be registered as such.

Trademarks must appear on the merchandise or its container, or be associated with the goods at the point of sale. They also must be used regularly in interstate commerce to remain valid. Certain material may not be used in trademarks, such as the United States flag, the likeness of a living person without his or her permission, and several others.

Trademarks may be federally registered with the United States Patent and Trademark Office, Washington, D.C. 20231, by furnishing a written application, a drawing of the mark, three specimens or facsimiles of the mark as it is actually used, and a fee of two hundred ten dollars. The registration is valid for ten years and can be renewed for further ten-year terms. When a trademark is not used regularly on a product or its container, the registration lapses, even if the ten-year term isn't up.

After a mark has been federally registered, notice of the registration should accompany the mark wherever it is used. Various means are available to do this, the most common being ®, which is placed right next to the mark. Note that ® may be used only in connection with federally registered marks.

Variations of a trademark are service marks, which identify services rather than products; certification marks, which are not related to specific products or manufacturers but might indicate regional origin, method of manufacture, or union label; and collective marks, used by members of an association, a cooperative, or another organization. All can be registered in the same fashion as a trademark.

The Patent Office can neither give legal advice regarding trademarks nor can it respond to inquiries about whether certain trademarks have been registered. The Patent Office does maintain a file of registered marks that is arranged alphabetically if words are included and ordered by the classification of the goods or services in which they are used if a symbol is the registered mark. These files are open to the public in the Search Room of Trademark Operations in Washington, D.C. It is advisable to search files to determine whether the same or a similar trademark to yours has already been registered.

A detailed booklet, *General Information Concerning Trademarks*, is available from the Superintendent of Documents (see Appendix C).

During the period when the application for federal registration is pending, it is common to use the designation ^{TM} for trademarks and ^{SM} for service marks. These designations have no official status but merely give notice of a claimed property right in the mark.

There is also a state trademark registry in every state in the Union. State registration is beneficial only within the registering state and does not permit the use of ®. The remedies for infringement laws are often different from those available under the federal statute. *(See also: Copyright, Intellectual Property, Patent, Trade Dress, Trade Name)*

Trade Name or Assumed Business Name

Many businesses use a name for public identification that differs from the name of the owner. You may be Sam Jones, but the sign on your door reads Pot Luck Pottery. That's a trade or assumed business name. In some areas, this is known as a *fictitious business name*.

Since trade names can't be held legally responsible for anything, it is almost universally required that a trade name be registered with some governmental authority, often the secretary of state or the county clerk.

The initials *d/b/a*, doing business as, appear on such documents as legal papers and credit reports to tie the trade name to the owner, as in *Sam Jones, d/b/a Pot Luck Pottery*.

To protect a trade name from unauthorized use by others, it may be registered with the federal government as a trademark if certain conditions are met. *(See also: Intellectual Property, Trademark)*

Trade Secret

A trade secret is any information that is nonpublic and that provides a commercial advantage. It could include, for example, a formula for a pottery glaze or customer or supplier lists. Trade secrets are protectable only as long as they remain secret, and one who improperly discloses a trade secret may be liable for damages. It is as good idea to identify your trade secrets by labeling them as such and by making them available only on a need-to-know basis. Employees or others who are given access to them for valid business reasons should be required to sign an agreement not to use or disclose the secret without your express written permission. Because trade-secret law and trade-secret protection are quite complex, you should consult with an experienced intellectual-property lawyer in order to establish a trade-secret program if you feel your business has trade secrets. *(See also: Copyright, Intellectual Property, Patent, Trade Dress, Trademark)*

Transportation *(See: Freight Allowance, Post Office, Shipping, United Parcel Service)*

Travel *(See: Business Trips)*

Traveler's Checks

Craftspeople who spend quite a bit of time selling at crafts shows and fairs, especially in tourist areas, have encountered traveler's checks. Such checks are sold in units of ten dollars, twenty dollars, fifty dollars, and one hundred dollars by most banks and some other financial firms, such as American Express.

Traveler's checks are extremely popular because they are safe to carry and are recognized almost everywhere in the world. The safety factor exists because purchasers sign their checks once when they buy them and then again when they use them.

Two precautions to heed in dealing with traveler's checks:

1. Do not accept a traveler's check unless the person who offers it signs it in your presence. Compare the signatures and accept the check only if the signatures match.

2. A traveler's check with both signatures but no endorsement is as good as cash if it is lost or stolen. Don't let the hustle and bustle of a busy booth

distract you. Immediately upon receiving a traveler's check as payment, endorse it with your business name, the words *for deposit only*, and your checking-account number. Then handle it like any other check on your bank-deposit slip.

Turnover

In all forms of merchandising and selling, turnover is one of the most critical elements of success or failure. It means, essentially, how often your investment turns into cash and is reinvested, or turned over.

Note this simple example: You invest one thousand dollars to produce a certain number of crafts objects on which you make a 10 percent profit. When you sell that one thousand dollars' worth of craftwork your profit is one hundred dollars.

If it takes all year to sell that one thousand dollars' worth of work, your investment will return one hundred dollars. But suppose you can sell one thousand dollars' worth of work in one month, take your one-hundred-dollar profit, and reinvest the original one thousand dollars to make more craft objects—again producing one hundred dollars in profits. Do this every month and you'll have an annual profit of $1,200 over and above your original investment. You have turned over your initial investment twelve times a year.

Any successful retailer will tell you to watch your turnover rate as closely as you do your cash register. The smaller the per-unit profit, the larger the turnover has to be. Thus, a big supermarket can make it on a profit margin of between 1 and 2 percent because the goods on the shelves move in and out fast. Turning over one thousand dollars' worth of inventory once a day at 1 percent profit, which equals ten dollars a day or close to three hundred dollars a month, is three times as profitable as turning it over once a month at 10 percent to make one hundred dollars.

But the total turnover is not the only important consideration. Examine all the items in your line to see whether some turn over faster than others. If you find an item that stays in your inventory month after month, it may be putting a drain on your earnings by tying up the money you spent to make it. Perhaps it doesn't belong there at all, and it's time to get rid of it so that you can invest the money in making something more profitable.

There are exceptions, of course. The profit margin on a slow-moving piece may be so high that it is worth your while to continue making it even though it doesn't turn over fast. Another example may be the prestige piece that helps to sell your other work. A large five-hundred-dollar batik wall hanging may not turn over rapidly, but displaying it at a crafts show may help draw attention to the forty-dollar and fifty-dollar batiks that sell fast. That makes the expensive piece an integral part of your total merchandising operation, and its absence might slow down the sales of all your other work and thus retard your total turnover.

There's a simple formula for determining the turnover rate. Divide sales by investment. Thus, if your investment were one thousand dollars and your sales were five thousand dollars, the formula would read:

$$\$5,000 \div \$1,000 = 5$$

The turnover rate in this example, then, is five times.

If you apply this formula to the various crafts objects you produce, you may find to your surprise that the most profitable turnover is not necessarily in the items that sell best.

Suppose that you are a potter who makes mugs and vases. In a given period you sell one thousand dollars' worth of mugs and nine hundred dollars' worth of vases. The mugs cost you five hundred dollars to produce; the vases, three hundred dollars. Apply the preceding formula—sales divided by investment—and see where your better turnover is:

Mugs: $\$1,000 \div \$500 = 2$ times
Vases: $\$900 \div \$300 = 3$ times

Even though your total sales of vases brought in less than the total sales of mugs, your investment in making the vases was more profitable. This doesn't mean you stop making mugs, but it reveals that finding new outlets for vases will bring a better return than finding new outlets for mugs.

Watch your turnover carefully, item by item. It is an important ingredient of your production and merchandising decisions. The real key is not simply how much you sell but how much those sales bring back to you in earnings on the money you invest. That depends on how quickly and how often you turn over your investment and your inventory. *(See also: Inventory, Multiple Production, Production, Record Keeping, Systems)*

Unemployment Insurance

Unemployment insurance is a program administered on the state level to provide cash benefits to qualified unemployed people who are seeking work. Eligibility requirements and the size of weekly checks vary from state to state. Payments are made by employers in the form of a payroll tax. The weekly check received by the unemployed is based on the amount of money the individual earned during the qualification period.

Unemployment insurance is not relief or a handout. It is exactly what the name implies: insurance that provides benefits as a matter of right without regard to need for as long as the unemployed applicant meets the conditions of the law. Benefits such as these are a major benefit to society at large during recession periods in order to stimulate consumption, production, and employment by introducing dollars and purchasing power into the economy.

The specific rules and regulations that apply in the different states are available through each state's Department of Labor. *(See also: Employees, Insurance)*

Uniform Commercial Code (UCC)

The Uniform Commercial Code (UCC) is the evolutionary embodiment and codification of the law of commercial transactions. Begun in the 1940s as a joint project of the American Law Institute and the National Conference of Commissioners on Uniform State Laws, the code brought together in a single document many of the common law principles and a number of earlier uniform laws governing such transactions.

Since its enactment in Pennsylvania in 1953, effective July 1, 1954, the UCC has undergone a number of revisions with reissues of Official Text and Comments in 1958, 1962, 1966, 1972, 1977, and 1987. States adopted one or another version of the UCC, either in whole or in part, and many have adopted later amendments as they appeared. Some states have incorporated their own language and modifications while maintaining the basic UCC matrix.

The purpose of the Uniform Commercial Code has been to simplify, clarify, and modernize the law governing commercial transactions. Its underlying policy is to permit the continued expansion of commercial practices through custom, usage, and agreement of the parties. Both of these goals have been successfully achieved by making the law fairly uniform throughout the various jurisdictions that have adopted the UCC.

The UCC continues to deal comprehensively with the various statutes relating to commercial transactions. Its articles cover broadly and specifically many aspects of personal property and contracts and other documents concerning them, including Article 1–General Provisions (and definitions); Article 2–Sales; Article 3–Commercial Paper; Article 4–Bank Deposits and Collections; Article 5–Letters of Credit; Article 6–Bulk Transfers; Article 7–Warehouse Receipts, Bills of Lading, and Other Documents of Title; Article 8–Investment Securities; and Article 9–Secured Transactions, Sales of Accounts, and Chattel Paper.

Another section, Article 2A–Leases, was added in the 1987 edition of the UCC. Most states adopted Article 2A into their commercial codes, with effective dates that began in 1989. It is likely that other states will continue to follow suit. *(See also: Collection Problems, Consignment, Contracts, Lease, Letter of Credit, Lien, Sales Terms)*

Unions

Labor unions are organizations of employees who work for wages. They gain their strength from two principles:

1. An individual employee is not able to negotiate wages, fringe benefits,

hours, and working conditions as effectively alone as the workers are able to together, since the loss of one dissatisfied worker will not seriously hinder production;

2. The workers' ability to bargain collectively and, if necessary, withhold their labor, to strike, to exert pressure on the employer to meet their demands.

Few craftspeople are ever faced with a union situation in their shops or studios since they usually work alone or with only a few employees. However, if a crafts operation begins in a field in which a union already exists, such as in jewelry making or woodworking, the likelihood increases that an effort will be made to organize the workers and negotiate a contract with the employer. This is especially true if the employees are not themselves skilled crafts artists.

The success of such an organizing effort depends in large measure on the employees' satisfaction with their wages and working conditions and on their relationship with the employer. When a union can offer workers something they do not or cannot get from their employer, its chances of success are much greater. That's not always related to wages. Even if the pay scale is good, a union may be able to convince employers that benefits such as medical plans, pension programs, sick leave, job security, and holiday and vacation schedules can be obtained through negotiations and a union contract.

Although a union contract does, of course, impose numerous conditions on the employer, it can also serve to stabilize labor-management relations, reduce the possibility of friction between individual employees and the employer, and provide the employer with a more predictable annual labor cost.

Many employers go into a state of shock when they first glimpse the union organizer outside their door. A more reasonable reaction might be to call your lawyer, find out what you may or may not do under the law—beware of illegal labor practices—and approach the situation rationally. (*See also: Employees, Minimum Wage*)

United Parcel Service (UPS)

No, Virginia, the post office is not the only way to ship parcels from one place to another. Private firms such as United Parcel Service (UPS) have provided an alternative for many years—UPS since 1907—and with the steady deterioration of postal service accompanied by hefty increases in postal rates, these alternatives have become real competition. United Parcel Service makes delivery by truck to any place in the continental United States and Canada, and ships by air to major cities, Alaska, Hawaii, Puerto Rico, Canada, and more than 180 other countries and territories.

UPS provides a number of advantages over postal service:

1. Every parcel is automatically insured up to one hundred dollars, with additonal insurance available at thirty cents per one hundred dollars.

2. UPS's delivery charges are often cheaper than the post office's.

3. Delivery time is often faster than the post office's. It takes one day to deliver parcels locally via UPS. To send a package all the way across the country by truck takes five days. To send by air takes two days—guaranteed.

4. UPS will accept parcels larger than those accepted by the post office. UPS parcels can measure up to 130 inches in length and girth combined. The post-office maximum is 108 inches. (Measuring girth is like measuring someone's waist: Measure around the middle.)

5. UPS picks up as well as delivers. Furthermore, UPS will make delivery attempts three days in a row if no one is available to receive the parcel on the first try. The post office leaves a slip in the mailbox on the first day to notify you of their attempt to deliver. Then you have to pick up the package yourself or call the post office to have it redelivered.

Rates

UPS shipping rates are, like post-office rates, based on weight, distance, and manner of shipment—ground or air. On that basis alone, UPS is usually less expensive than the post office. However, there is a minimum weekly pick-up charge of five dollars that applies whether you make only one shipment or a thousand.

For only an occasional shipment, then, the post office may be less expensive. However, if you ship one hundred packages a week, then the cost of each shipment is increased by only four cents, which still keeps UPS costs way below post-office rates.

For example, a ten-pound package from Portland, Oregon, to Washington, D.C., via UPS costs $5.75 plus the five-dollar weekly pick-up charge. That's a total of $10.75 compared to $12.75 for the same package via the post office. However, if you shipped one hundred such packages over that distance, the UPS charge will be $5.75 × 100, or $575.00, plus the five-dollar weekly pick-up charge, for a total of $580—as compared to $1,275.00 for the same one hundred packages shipped via the post office. In addition to the savings, you don't have the bother of taking the packages to the post office, and minimum insurance is included.

Shipping by air is less expensive with the post office than with UPS. However, UPS guarantees second-day delivery while the post office can only estimate third-day delivery. To ship a ten-pound package with UPS second-day air from Portland, Oregon, to Washington, D.C., costs $13.50 plus the $5.00 pick-up charge: a total of $18.50. Compare this with the post-office charge of $12.80 for parcel post shipping.

For overnight delivery UPS charges $27.50 to ship a ten-pound package from Portland, Oregon, to Washington, D.C. Of course, the $5.00 pick-up charge must be added. For express mail service from the post office the charge is $27.60. Again, if you ship only one or two packages per week, the post office is the better buy. However, shipping one hundred such packages per week with UPS is less expensive than the post office. Compare the UPS charge of $2,755 (100 × $27.50 + $5.00) with the post office rate of $2,760. Don't forget UPS picks up the package so you don't have to wait in line at the post office.

Please note that these rates may have gone up by the time you read this, but the principle and the comparisons remain valid. Note also, UPS charges extra for packages weighing more than twenty-four pounds and particularly unwieldy packages (greater than 84 inches length plus girth).

Regular Accounts

Businesses that ship many parcels on a regular basis can establish an account with UPS. Account holders are supplied with a record book stamped with an individual account number, cost charts, and special shipping labels. You fill out a daily slip that lists and describes all the parcels being sent out that day. The UPS truck comes by regularly every day to pick up all the packages, and the UPS driver signs for them.

Rates for the regular-account service vary in different parts of the country, and billing is done once a week. The same weekly minimum pick-up charge applies to regular accounts as well but amounts to almost nothing when the two-dollar or four-dollar charge is distributed over hundreds of packages.

Tracing

Since every package is signed for, from pickup to delivery, it is simple enough to trace a UPS parcel that may have gone undelivered. In such cases, UPS furnishes a photocopy of a signed receipt within three days or handles the claim as if the package were lost.

Insurance

A package sent by ground may be insured for any amount, while parcels shipped by air may be insured up to twenty-five thousand dollars. Since UPS insurance may be limited—the post office will insure for any amount—it is not advisable to send irreplaceable or unusually valuable objects, such as one-of-a-kind craftwork, by air via UPS. Note that UPS may wish to inspect packages with high declared values.

Restrictions

UPS makes no Sunday pickups, but in many areas it makes Saturday deliveries for next-day air shipments to specific areas. UPS does not handle packages weighing more than seventy pounds or measuring more than one hundred and eight inches in length.

For craftspeople who ship many parcels, particularly for those who do a sizable mail-order business, United Parcel Service often provides a less costly and less bothersome alternative to the post office. For single pieces, or those that require considerable insurance coverage, the post office is the better way. *(See also: Post Office, Shipping, Transportation)*

United States Department of Agriculture *(See: Government Activities)*

United States Department of Commerce *(See: Government Activities)*

United States Department of Labor *(See: Government Activities)*

Utilities *(See: Overhead, Pricing)*

Vendor

A vendor is, simply, one who sells. This term is commonly used by lawyers, which is why you often find it in sales contracts and on order forms. It is also used by purchasing agents as a generic reference to any source of supply.

When you sell your craftwork to a department store, you are the vendor. When you buy raw materials from your supply dealer, the dealer is the vendor.

Wages

Since most craftspeople work by themselves, they often confuse wages and profits. Since they get both, it doesn't seem important to make a distinction.

But it is important. All wages, including your own, are part of the production costs that determine the price you will ultimately charge for your craftwork. They are as important as materials, equipment, overhead, shipping, and other costs. Profits are added afterward and represent your training, your investment, your management skills, even your creative talents. But the actual work you or others do must be calculated as wages. Since this is often the single largest ingredient in the cost of production, it must be handled with tender care.

The productive time you put into your craftwork covers the time you spend at the loom or the wheel or the workbench. But don't overlook the service time you spend repairing equipment, packing orders and taking them to the post office, doing the bookkeeping, designing a brochure, selling at shows, running to stores to make sales calls, and uncountable other functions.

How, then, can a crafts producer figure his or her own wages? It is impractical, in most cases, to keep a time sheet to record your time as a chemist at twenty-five dollars an hour, a laborer at six dollars an hour, a bookkeeper at ten dollars an hour, and so on. It is important, however, to keep a diary of labor time invested by yourself, family, friends, and employees in the production of various types of items. This helps not only to price objects properly but to determine whether the various objects bring the proper return and to project future pricing possibilities for similar objects.

For the many hats you wear you can determine your hourly or weekly salary based on answers to a few reasonable questions:

1. What would it or does it cost to hire someone to replace you in one or more of your functions?

2. What could you earn if you worked for someone else?

3. What do you need in terms of money, and will it fit into the price structure of the craftwork you produce?

There are a good many craftspeople who might find, on close examination, that they work for a dollar or two an hour. There's nothing wrong with that if you decide that's what you want to do or if you have some other source of income, such as teaching. But if you work at that salary level simply because you've never figured out what you're actually earning, it may be wise to analyze the situation a bit more carefully.

If one item takes an hour to produce and another item, selling for the same price, takes two hours, then you are obviously cutting your hourly pay in half every time you work on the second item.

You have three alternatives for solving that problem:

1. Find a more efficient production method that enables you to produce more of the second item every hour than you did before and, thus, give yourself a raise;

2. Perhaps you can increase the price of the second item to properly reflect the time you spend producing it;

3. You can cut back on producing the second item and concentrate on the more profitable items.

Your efficiency and experience are key elements in this situation. An obvious example: A potter can undoubtedly produce more finished pots per hour if the potter throws two dozen at a time, glazes them all, and then fires them all instead of making one pot, glazing it, firing it, and starting all over again with another pot.

The specific procedure you develop depends on a variety of circumstances: the nature of the work, how much room you have to work in, how many people you have working with you, the capacity of the equipment, and so on. There can be no ready-made blueprint for this sort of thing. Everyone has different problems, different purposes, different work styles. In general, it helps if you can organize the various stages of producing multiples of an object by repeating each step ten or twenty times before going on to the next step.

But how do you figure out the time cost for each piece if you make a dozen or more at a time, especially if you work on a variety of items during the same period? You simply keep a careful record of time spent on each type of item, and then divide the time into the total number of items produced. It doesn't matter whether the various steps occur consecutively or are carried out on different days. As long as you make a note on a time sheet or job ticket of all the time you spend on each group of items, it's a matter of simple addition.

Once you have the time elements down on paper, there are various ways to calculate the wages per piece that must be included in the final price. In understanding the simplest method, assume that you want to earn five dollars per hour and work forty hours per week. That's a total of two hundred dollars. If one week you work on a particular group of crafts objects and find that you need a total of four hours to produce twenty pieces, that averages five pieces per hour. The value of your productive time is, therefore, one dollar on each piece.

But note how changing your production procedure can dramatically affect your wages. If instead of four hours you need five hours to make those same twenty pieces, your production is down to four pieces per hour. The difference may not seem world-shaking, but your production time per piece then costs $1.25—five dollars divided by four. To compensate, you must increase the price of the finished object.

None of this is intended to offer an iron-clad formula. There are many methods of cost accounting to help you calculate such things. But the key factor is to apply every expense—production time, raw materials, overhead—item to a specific crafts product so that the price accurately reflects the cost. You must, therefore, examine and reexamine your production methods and cost factors on a regular basis. It is the only way you can determine whether you are paying yourself a decent wage or whether you get your money's worth for the wages you pay others. (See also: Cost Accounting, Employees, Income Tax, Job Ticket, Overhead, Pricing, Production, Social Security, Withholding Tax)

Warranty

Buyers have a right to expect that the products they buy will perform more or less as expected under normal conditions. The legal basis for that right is known as a warranty. A warranty always involves a provable fact. As both a buyer and a seller, you need to know precisely what rights and responsibilities the word *warranty* imposes.

Warranties need not be in writing. They can be made orally. The written warranty is, of course, preferable because it is easier to document if trouble develops.

There are two kinds of warranties: express and implied. An express warranty is one that states a specific fact. If you sell a set of glasses and tell the customer they can be washed in the dishwasher without danger of breakage, you have given an express warranty, whether you put it in writing or not. If the glasses break in the dishwasher, you are liable not only to return the customer's money but if the broken glass jams the dishwasher, you may have to pay other damages as well.

An implied warranty means that the product is made with all proper care and that it will perform as similar products of its kind will perform under normal conditions. A customer need not, for example, inspect each glass to make sure that there are no unfinished edges; he or she can rely on the implied warranty.

As a buyer, you rely on both express and implied warranties every day. When you buy a drill, you expect that it will work when you take it out of the box and plug it in. That's an implied warranty. If the manufacturer states that the drill will turn at eighteen hundred revolutions per minute, that's an express warranty. When you buy a can of tomatoes, you expect that they will not be contaminated. That's an implied warranty. If the label reads ten ounces, that's an express warranty.

Remember, however, that the important ingredient of a warranty is the provable-fact aspect. The glass either breaks or it doesn't. The drill turns or stands still. There are either ten ounces of tomatoes in the can or there are not.

Sales talk is quite another thing. If you tell your customer that yours are the most beautiful glasses ever made or if the hardware salesperson tells you the drill will make your life a lot easier, no warranties have either been implied or expressed. Those puff statements are not provable facts.

Warranties are also involved when you show a sample to a store buyer. If the store places an order, it expects that the items it eventually receives will be of the same quality and will perform the same way as the sample. That's your warranty—express or implied, written or oral. If you tell a store that it will sell a million of those, that's no warranty. That's just sales talk, and if it sells only half a million, it has no legal recourse.

If you sell crafts products you know to be defective in some way, be sure to mark them *seconds* or *as is*. Although this does not absolve you of all obligation, it does place on the customer some responsibility to either ask what the defect is or to inspect the product carefully. *(See also: Guarantee)*

Wholesale Days *(See: Shows and Fairs, Wholesaling)*

Wholesaling
There are three ways in which a crafts professional can sell his or her craftwork:
1. Sell directly to the ultimate customer (retailing);

2. Furnish your work to a store or gallery with the understanding that you are paid only if and when the work is sold to a customer (consignment);

3. Sell to a store or some other outlet that in turn sells your work to the ultimate customer (wholesaling).

The differences among the three involve both work and money. As an example, consider that you have a crafts object that is sold to the ultimate customer for ten dollars. If you retail it directly, you get the whole ten dollars, but you also have the work and expense of retailing, such as operating a store or taking a booth at a crafts show. In consignment selling, you generally receive about 60 percent of the retail price, approximately six dollars in this example. However, you are investing your time and money in the store's inventory, and there are other dangers and problems associated with consignment selling.

If you wholesale to a store that then resells the work, you generally get 50 percent of the retail price, or five dollars in this example. However, you have none of the work and problems of retailing. You can spend your time in producing more craftwork, and you can presumably sell a larger number of pieces. The store purchases your work outright, whether or not it then resells the work to its customers.

Some craftspeople do not understand, and even resent, the notion that a store doubles the price of craftwork it buys from them. Statistics show, however, that most of that markup is not profit but is spent for rent in expensive high-traffic locations, for payroll, advertising, delivery, and all the other costs associated with running a store. Most stores consider a 5 percent profit on the retail price an acceptable ratio. In other words, their profit on that ten-dollar crafts item might be around fifty cents. In food stores, the profit ratio is much smaller, generally between 1 and 2 percent. The small per-unit profit, of course, can turn into a handsome annual profit if the store succeeds in selling a large quantity of merchandise.

So much for why a store doubles the price of goods it buys for resale. If you have priced your work properly at the wholesale level, the wholesale price should bring you a satisfactory profit. What you lose—or think you lose—in retail markup is more than compensated by selling larger quantities of your craftwork through wholesale distribution.

What type of retail outlet you approach depends in large measure on how much you can produce. If your production is limited, stick to the smaller stores—boutiques, gift shops, and the like. Department stores and chain stores are demanding in terms of price and in terms of delivery.

To meet the price demands of department stores that are in a competitive situation, it is perfectly legitimate to have a schedule of wholesale prices that varies according to the quantity ordered. Ten or fewer pieces of a particular crafts object, for example, may be priced at $5.50 each. For between ten and one hundred pieces the price can be five dollars. For quantities of more than one hundred you might charge only $4.50. If you organize your production schedules and packing operations properly, you can probably save the difference in the price you charge for different quantities and come out with the same profit margin in the end.

Wholesale buyers normally use their store's order form to buy from you. Read all the conditions on the form carefully. Are you prepared, for example, to allow a 2 percent discount if the bill is paid within ten days? Can you meet the delivery date? Do you understand the billing procedure? Does the order form include the store's sales-tax-exemption number so that you don't have to collect the sales tax?

Big stores, like anything else, are bureaucracies. If the paperwork isn't done right, everything comes to a dead stop. On the other hand, having a big-store customer who keeps you profitably busy all year can be worth the extra effort to meet the bureaucratic requirements.

How do you approach wholesale buyers? In a small shop it's fairly simple: The owner does the buying. Telephone first to make an appointment. Don't just drop in, especially at a time when the owner is busy with a customer.

With department stores the problem is a bit more complicated. Different departments have different buyers, and most buyers have a specific day each week when they see suppliers. Depending on how the store's buying operation is organized and what craft you are selling, you may have to see the gift buyer, the jewelry buyer, the home furnishings buyer, or whoever is responsible for buying the particular type of item you have to offer. A phone call to the merchandise manager's office will generally tell you whom you have to see and when. If possible, try to make an appointment.

Buyers are busy people. Be prepared to state your case clearly and succinctly. Take samples, a price list, and any other information. Be prepared to leave all this material and information with the buyer if requested.

Try to acquaint yourself with the particular store's general merchandising approach and clientele so that you can discuss your crafts objects from the store's point of view—namely, how it will sell in that store. If the store has no jewelry department, for example, it is hardly worth the effort for a silversmith to try selling earrings to that store.

The other major area of investigation concerns the store's pricing. Does the store you want to approach already sell your type of craftwork? At what prices does it sell the craftwork, and are its price lines, in crafts or otherwise, compatible with yours? A quick trip through the store will reveal whether your work fits into the store's merchandising and pricing pattern.

This type of approach is fine for stores in your area, but finding stores elsewhere, assuming that your production capabilities are such that you can supply stores in various parts of the country, can be a difficult task because the crafts field is one of the few in which agents or manufacturers' representatives are not too common—and for good reason. Most crafts-people, even if their production is extensive, can neither keep a sales organization busy enough nor can they afford to pay the extra commission to salespeople or agents. However, there are a number of sales representatives in various parts of the country who handle noncompetitive crafts lines. They have the contacts with the store buyers, and craftspeople who can meet the volume demands often find the extra commission worth the extra volume.

Finally, in the enthusiasm of making a sale, don't overlook one important question: What is their credit rating? There's no point in making a sale if you don't get paid for it. Ask around. Talk to some other people who have sold to the same store. If it's a big sale out of town, your bank may be helpful in getting a credit report.

Once you've convinced the store buyer that your craftwork will sell, the price is right, its credit proved sound, everything is set, you should be aware that there are still four important questions rummaging around in the back of the buyer's mind:

1. Can you maintain the quality of the work according to the sample?
2. Can you maintain the price?
3. Can you meet production needs?
4. Can you meet delivery schedules?

The initital orders from wholesale buyers, especially buyers from department stores, may be small until the buyers are satisfied that you can meet all four of these requirements. Once you prove that you can perform, wholesaling can be a profitable experience. *(See also: Consignment, Credit Reference, Memo, Orders, Retailing, Salesmanship, Sales Representatives)*

Withholding Tax

Whether you're a million-dollar tycoon or a part-time cashier at the supermarket, some portion of your wages or salary is withheld whenever you get paid, to pay your income taxes. The employer, in effect, acts as the collection agent for the Internal Revenue Service and for state and local governments that impose income taxes.

If you are an employer, there are several specific procedures to follow:

1. You must obtain a taxpayer-employer-identification number by filing form SS-4 with the Internal Revenue Service.

2. The IRS then provides you with a number of copies of Form 501, a punch card that has to accompany the remittance of the tax money you withhold from your employees—including yourself, if you are incorporated and draw a salary.

3. You deposit the tax money in your bank with Form 501 according to the following schedule:

a. If the total social-security contribution (both employer and employee contributions) and federal withholding taxes are less than two hundred dollars at the end of a quarter (three months), you remit quarterly;

b. If at the end of a month it is between two hundred dollars and two thousand dollars, you must make the deposit within fifteen days after the end of the month; if it is more than two thousand dollars, you deposit within three banking days;

c. If the total is more than two thousand dollars on the seventh, fourteenth, twenty-first, and thirtieth of any month, you must make the deposit within three banking days after each of those dates. The bank gives you a receipt for the deposit and, in turn, deposits all the money and all the Forms 501 with the Internal Revenue Service.

4. Every three months you are required to file directly with the Internal Revenue Service Form 941, a summary of all the withholding-tax payments that were made on behalf of your employees during that quarter.

5. Between January 1 and January 31 of each year, you are required to furnish a W-2 form to all employees. This is a summary of all the income paid during the previous year and of all income taxes and social-security contributions withheld during the previous year. The W-2 form is needed by the employees to file with their income-tax returns. The form must be furnished to all employees who were on the payroll at any time during the previous year—even if they worked for only a day or are no longer employed by you. If an employee leaves any time before the end of the year, they may demand and you must promptly provide their W-2 form.

One important observation: When cash supply is short, some employers are tempted to use the tax money they withhold for other purposes, hoping to have the money available when it has to be deposited at the end of the week or month or quarter. That's a temptation that should be resisted. Failure to deposit the withholding taxes is a serious federal crime. *(See also: Estimated Tax, Income Tax)*

Wool Products Labeling Act (WPLA)

The Wool Products Labeling Act (WPLA) was passed by Congress in 1939 to protect everyone involved in some way—manufacturers, distributors, and consumers—with things made of wool. Every product made in whole or in part of wool must conform to this law, except for upholstery and floor coverings, which are covered by the Textile Fiber Products Identification Act.

Although enforcement of the WPLA is concentrated among large manufacturers of wool products, the act's provisions apply to craftspeople as well. While it is hard to imagine a government agent going after a one-of-a-kind wall hanging at a crafts fair, technically everyone creating items for sale that are made of wool or other fibers is expected to know the composition of the item and label it properly.

The act established three specific categories of wool that have to be identified according to the percentage—by weight—used in a particular product:

1. *Wool, new wool,* or *virgin wool* has never been used, and special names for fibers that fall into this category are *mohair, cashmere, camel hair,* and *alpaca;*

2. *Reprocessed wool* is wool fiber taken from wool already woven or felted but never used or worn;

3. *Reused wool* is precisely that: wool that was knitted or woven to make items that were once worn or used and is later used again to make other things.

The Wool Products Labeling Act makes no requirements about the quality or amount of wool used in each category, only that it be properly identified. This label must accompany the wool item through each step of manufacture, from yarn to finished product. The label must state, in order of amount, the types of wool used in the item, along with the percentage by weight of each fiber used.

If nonwoolen fibers are used in a product made of wool, they must also be identified. However, all nonwoolen fibers that do not separately exceed 5 percent of the total may be called *other fibers.* Thus a product made of 55 percent virgin wool, 33 percent reprocessed wool, and 4 percent each of rayon, linen, and cotton may be labeled:

55% virgin wool
33% reprocessed wool
12% other fibers

The same principle applies to ornamentation, such as buttons and handles. If the extra design features make up less than 5 percent of the total fiber weight of the item, the label must read "exclusive of ornamentation." If it is greater than 5 percent, it must be identified as part of the total fiber content.

Two other points to consider:

1. Get a complete fiber-content breakdown before you buy wool supplies. The information should be printed on tags or labels attached to the yarn or bolts of fabric. If you can't find it, ask your supplier. You are ultimately responsible for the correct labeling of any wool item you make and sell.

2. It is helpful to your customers to include specific instructions on cleaning, where applicable. If you attach a label anyway, you might as well add *dry-clean only* or *wash gently in lukewarm water* or some similar information. (*See also: Textile Fiber Products Identification Act*)

Work Area

Since craftspeople spend so much time in their workshops or studios, the manner in which these work areas are designed can contribute greatly to the satisfaction of working in them and to the efficiency in producing crafts for profit.

Following is a checklist of design points that should be helpful:

1. If you work at home, make the work space serve your craft exclusively. First of all, it helps to justify the tax deduction that you can claim as a business expense. In addition, it makes it so much easier to find things, to get down to work, and to protect the work you've produced. A family room where children play is rarely a safe place for your equipment or finished work nor is it one that allows you the concentration to create beautiful things. If you constantly have to set up and take down your tools and equipment, you'll spend more time getting ready to work than working.

2. Be comfortable. There's no reason why artists should suffer. Working in solitude and being creative can be difficult enough—although they have their exquisite rewards when your hands have produced an object of beauty. Consider whether the table is so low that you have to bend over unnecessarily. Is it, on the other hand, so high that your arms get tired too soon? Is the light good enough to avoid eye strain? Are your surroundings too hot, too cold, or too noisy to provide the proper attention to your creative work?

3. The physical layout of your work area is important for both safety and production. Electric outlets should be readily available wherever you use electric tools or equipment. Extension cords running all over the place are a prime source of fire danger. Equipment and workbenches should be located in some logical relationship to one another so that you don't have to drag your work from one end of the place to the other and back during the various stages of production. It makes sense, for example, to have the table where you pack orders located next to the area where you store the finished work.

4. Plenty of shelving, Peg-Boards, and other storage devices help to keep raw materials, supplies, tools, and finished craftwork easily accessible and in good condition. Small supplies can be kept in jars or cans that are properly labeled. Dangerous tools should be protected, and hazardous substances such as flammable liquids should be properly stored. This is important not only when there are small children around but for your own safety. (*See also: Production*)

Workers' Compensation

The law has always held an employer liable for injuries or death suffered by his or her employees if the condition arose from the employer's negligence in not providing safe working conditions.

Workers' compensation laws in every state now allow employees or their heirs to recover damages from the employer's workers' compensation insurance carrier for injuries or death suffered by employees while on the job, regardless of whose fault it was, unless it was self-inflicted or caused by intoxication. The laws vary from state to state and so does the extent of the insurer's liability but most employers are required to carry workers' compensation insurance.

Premiums are generally based on a percentage of the payroll as related to two factors: the hazard of the job and the claims history of the employer. Premiums may be reduced, therefore, by increasing safety precautions and preventing accidents.

Craftspeople need not carry workers' compensation insurance if they work alone. The moment you hire an employee, however, even a part-time person, the workers' compensation law of your state will likely apply. Before you put anyone on the payroll, talk to your insurance broker or contact your state labor department to find out what's required of you under your state's workers' compensation law. *(See also: Employees, Unemployment Insurance)*

Workshops *(See: Education)*

World Crafts Council (WCC)

The World Crafts Council (WCC) is a nongovernmental organization founded in 1964 that represents craftspeople in eighty countries. It is associated in an official consultative capacity with several United Nations agencies, including UNESCO, UNICEF, and ECOSOC. Membership is obtained through the WCC national committee (the American Craft Council in the United States) or the WCC representative in the various countries.

The WCC publishes a bulletin periodically and has also published *In Praise of Hands*, *Crafts of the Modern World*, and *World Crafts Directory*. The WCC is governed through a general assembly that has met biennially in Switzerland, the United States, Peru, Ireland, Canada, Mexico, Australia, and Japan. It is active in the development of marketing and technical assistance programs through an Office for Craft Development and an Office for Information and Research (see Appendix D).

Writing

Writing a letter, a press release, an article, a sales brochure, or any other form of written communication makes most people freeze. Perhaps our constant exposure to nonwritten communication such as television, radio, movies, and the telephone has made writing a dying art. But there is hardly anything more basic and important than being able to express oneself in clear, concise terms, especially if trying to sell anything via the written word.

One need not be a writer to write well. A few simple rules of communication will make it easier:

1. Before you sit down to write, even if it's a letter, make some notes of the major points you want to include and in what order you want to present them.

2. Make your most important points at the start, to be sure the reader gets the basic information even if he or she doesn't read beyond the first paragraph or two.

3. Note how a newspaper story is written, and study some letters that have impressed you to see how they are constructed. Try to analyze what makes them interesting or attention getting.

4. Use simple language. Even if you know how to speak clearly, you may get all fouled up in complicated words and complex sentence structures when you sit down to write.

5. Use short sentences and short paragraphs. They're easier to read, to understand, and to write.

6. Make a draft, especially if it's an important message. Read it carefully. Show it to someone else to see whether you've expressed yourself clearly.

7. Don't be afraid to rewrite if you think your thoughts should be reorganized or stated in some other fashion. Most of the words you read every day did not come out of their authors' typewriters right the first time.

(P.S. This section was rewritten three times.) *(See also: Press Release)*

Zoning

Most cities and towns impose regulations on the use to which various areas under their jurisdictions can be put. Thus, some sections or streets may be zoned for residential use only, others for retailing or light manufacturing or heavy industry. Zoning regulations sometimes specify the number or size of buildings in relation to land area. This is done to preserve the character of a community and to protect residential areas, for example, from the noise of heavy industry. By way of what's known as a grandfather clause, most zoning regulations permit activities that existed prior to the establishment of the regulations to continue. That's why you might find a gas station or a drugstore on a street otherwise zoned for residential use only.

Zoning regulations can sometimes have an important impact on the conduct of a crafts business. If you have a loom in the basement, for example, and you don't have heavy customer or truck traffic coming to your door, it is unlikely that you would be found in violation of residential-zoning regulations in most areas. If you install a large kiln or run a blacksmith's forge, or open a retail outlet, you can almost count on having the authorities on your back—especially if the neighbors complain.

Most zoning regulations have provisions for granting an exception, or a variance, as it's called. This normally happens after hearings are conducted at which you present your case and your neighbors or such agencies as health, building, or fire departments have an opportunity to state their objections. The fire department, for example, may consider an open-hearth forge at the end of a narrow dead-end residential street of frame houses an additional hazard. The neighbors may simply object to the noise.

Before you make major alterations in your workshop or building, be sure they conform with the zoning regulations. Violations can be an awfully expensive mistake to correct. *(See also: Lease)*

Volunteer Lawyer Organizations

CALIFORNIA
California Lawyers for the Arts (CLA)
Fort Mason Center
Building C, Room 255
San Francisco, California 94123
(415) 775-7200

California Lawyers for the Arts (CLA)
Los Angeles office:
1549 Eleventh Street,
Suite 200
Santa Monica, California 90401
(310) 395-8893

San Diego Lawyers for the Arts
Attention: Peter Karlen
1205 Prospect Street
Suite 400
La Jolla, California 92037
(619) 454-9696

COLORADO
Colorado Lawyers for the Arts (COLA)
208 Grant Street
Denver, Colorado 80203
(303) 722-7994

CONNECTICUT
Connecticut Commission
on the Arts (CTVLA)
227 Lawrence Street
Hartford, Connecticut 06106
(203) 566-4770

DISTRICT OF COLUMBIA
Washington Volunteer Lawyers
for the Arts
918 Sixteenth Street, N.W.,
Suite 503
Washington, D.C. 20006
(202) 429-0229

Washington Area Lawyers
for the Arts (WALA)
1325 G Street, NW—Lower Level
Washington, D.C. 20005
(202) 393-2826

FLORIDA
Volunteer Lawyers for the Arts/Broward
and Business Volunteer Lawyers
for the Arts/Broward, Inc.
5900 North Andrews Avenue, Suite 907
Fort Lauderdale, Florida 33309
(305) 771-4131

Business Volunteers
for the Arts/Miami (BVA)
150 West Flagler Street, Suite 2500
Miami, Florida 33130
(305) 789-3590

GEORGIA
Georgia Volunteer Lawyers
for the Arts (GVLA)
141 Pryor Street SW, Suite 2030
Atlanta, Georgia 30303
(404) 525-6046

ILLINOIS
Lawyers for the Creative Arts (LCA)
213 West Institute Place, Suite 411
Chicago, Illinois 60610
(312) 944-2787

KANSAS
Kansas Association of Non-profits
% Susan J. Whitfield-Lungren, Esq.
400 North Woodlawn
East Building, Suite 212
Post Office Box 780227
Wichita, Kansas 67278-0227
(316) 685-3790

LOUISIANA

Louisiana Volunteer Lawyers
for the Arts (LVLA)
% Arts Council of New Orleans
821 Gravier Street, Suite 600
New Orleans, Louisiana 70112
(504) 523-1465

MARYLAND

Maryland Lawyers for the Arts
Belvedere Hotel
1 East Chase Street, Suite 1118
Baltimore, Maryland 21202-2526
(410) 752-1633

MASSACHUSETTS

Lawyers for the Arts
The Artists Foundation, Inc.
8 Park Plaza
Boston, Massachusetts 02116
(617) 227-2787

MINNESOTA

Resources and Counseling, United Arts
429 Landmark Center
75 West 5th Street
St. Paul, Minnesota 55102
(612) 292-3206

MISSOURI

Saint Louis Volunteer Lawyers
and Accountants for the Arts (SLVLAA)
3540 Washington
Saint Louis, Missouri 63103
(314) 652-2410

Kansas City Attorneys for the Arts
% Rosalee M. McNamara
Gage & Tucker
2345 Grand Avenue
Kansas City, Missouri 64108
(816) 474-6460

MONTANA

Montana Volunteer Lawyers for the Arts
% Jean Jonkel, Esq.
P.O. Box 8687
Missoula, Montana 59807
(406) 721-1835

NEVADA

Mark G. Tratos
Quirk & Tratos
550 East Charleston Blvd.
Las Vegas, Nevada 89104
(702) 386-1778

NEW JERSEY

New Jersey Bar Committee
on Entertainment and The Arts
% Mathews, Woodbridge & Collins
Attention: Christopher Sidoti
100 Thanet Circle
Suite 306
Princeton, New Jersey 08540-3662
(609) 924-3773

NEW YORK

Volunteer Lawyers for the Arts Program
Albany/Schenectady League of Arts (ALA)
19 Clinton Avenue
Albany, New York 12207
(518) 449-5380

Volunteer Lawyers for the Arts (VLA)
One East 53rd Street
Sixth Floor
New York, New York 10022
(212) 319-2787

Arts Council in Buffalo and Erie County
% Karen Kosman, Program Coordinator
700 Main Street
Buffalo, New York 64141
(716) 856-7520

NORTH CAROLINA

North Carolina Volunteer Lawyers
for the Arts (NCVA)
% William F. Moore, Esquire
P.O. Box 26513
Raleigh, North Carolina 27611-6513
(919) 832-9661

OHIO

Volunteer Lawyers and Accountants
for the Arts (VLAA)
% The Cleveland Bar Association
113 Saint Clair Avenue
Suite 225
Cleveland, Ohio 44114-1253
(216) 696-3525

Toledo Volunteer Lawyers for the Arts
% Arnold Gottlieb
608 Madison Avenue
Toledo, Ohio 43604
(419) 255-3344

OKLAHOMA
Oklahoma Volunteer Lawyers
    and Accountants for the Arts
Post Office Box 266
Edmond, Oklahoma 73083
(405) 340-7988

PENNSYLVANIA
Philadelphia Volunteer Lawyers
    for the Arts (PVLA)
The Arts Alliance Building
251 South 18th Street
Philadelphia, Pennsylvania 19103
(215) 545-3385

RHODE ISLAND
Ocean State Lawyers for the Arts (OSLA)
P.O. Box 19
Saunderstown, Rhode Island 02874
(401) 789-5686

TENNESSEE
Tennessee Arts Commission
Bennett Tarleton
320 Sixth Avenue N.
Nashville, Tennessee 37243-0780
(615) 741-1701

TEXAS
Austin Lawyers and Accountants
    for the Arts (ALAA)
340 Executive Center Drive
Austin, Texas 78731
(512) 338-4458

Texas Accountants and Lawyers
    for the Arts/Dallas
% Katherine Wagner
2917 Swiss Avenue
Dallas, Texas 75204
(214) 821-2522

Texas Accountants and Lawyers
    for the Arts (TALA)
1540 Sul Ross
Houston, Texas 77006
(713) 526-4876

UTAH
Utah Lawyers for the Arts (ULA)
170 South Main Street, Suite 1500
Post Office Box 45444
Salt Lake City, Utah 84145-0444
(801) 521-3200

WASHINGTON
Washington Lawyers for the Arts (WLA)
219 First Avenue S., Suite 315-A
Seattle, Washington 98104
(206) 292-9171

**OTHER VOLUNTEER
LAWYERS GROUPS**

CANADA
Canadian Artists' Representation Ontario
    (CARO)
Artist's Legal Advice Services (ALAS—
    Ontario)
183 Bathurst St., First Floor
Toronto, Ontario M5T 2R7
Canada
(416) 360-0780

Canadian Artists' Representation Ontario
    (CARO)
Artist's Legal Advice Services (ALAS—
    Ottawa)
189 Laurier Avenue E.
Ottawa, Ontario K1N 6P1
Canada
(613) 235-6277

Canadian Artists' Representation
    Saskatchewan (CARFAC)
Artist's Legal Advice Services (ALAS—
    Saskatchewan)
210-1808 Smith Street
Regina, Saskatchewan S4P 2N3
Canada
(306) 522-9788

PUERTO RICO
Voluntarios Por Las Artes/Volunteers
    for the Arts
563 Trigo Street
El Dorado Blvd., Suite 5-B
Miramar, Puerto Rico 00907
(809) 724-0700

Appendix B

Artist/Gallery Consignment Laws and Significant Features of Those Laws (by State)

Alaska	Alaska Stat. §§ 45.65.200 to 45.65.250 (Michie 1989).
Arizona	Ariz. Rev. Stat. Ann. §§ 44-1771 to 44-1773 (West 1987).
Arkansas	Ark. Stat. Ann. §§ 4-73-201 to 4-73-207 (Michie 1987).
California	Cal. Civ. Code § 1738 (Derring 1991).
Colorado	Colo. Rev. Stat. §§ 6-15-101 to 6-15-104 (1990).
Connecticut	Conn. Gen. Stat. Ann. §§ 42-116k to 42-116m (West 1990).
Florida	Fla. Stat. §§ 686.501 to 686.503 (1989).
Idaho	Idaho Code §§ 28-11-101 to 28-11-106 (Michie 1990).
Illinois	Ill. Rev. Stat. Ch. 121-1/2, Para. 1401 to 1408 (1989).
Iowa	Iowa Code §§ 556D.1 to 556D.5 (1989).
Kentucky	Ky. Rev. Stat. Ann. §§ 365.850 to 365.875 (Baldwin 1991).
Maryland	Md. Com. Law Code Ann. §§ 11-8a-01 to 11-8a-04 (Michie 1983).
Massachusetts	Mass. Ann. Laws Ch. 104a, §§ 1 to 6 (Law. Co-op. 1990).
Michigan	Mich. Comp. Laws §§ 442.311 to 442.312a (1990).
Minnesota	Minn. Stat. §§ 324.01 to 324.05 (1990).
Missouri	Mo. Rev. Stat. §§ 407.900 to 407.910 (1989).
Montana	Mont. Code Ann. §§ 22-2-501 to 22-2-505 (1990).
New Hampshire	N.H. Rev. Stat. Ann. §§ 352:3 to 352:12 (1989).
New Jersey	N.J. Rev. Stat. § 12A:2-330 (1990).
New Mexico	N.M. Stat. Ann. §§ 56-11-1 to 56-11-3 (1989).
New York	N.Y. Arts & Cult. Aff. Law §§ 11.01, 12.01 (McKinney 1991).
North Carolina	N.C. Gen. Stat. §§ 25C-1 to 25C-5 (1990).
Ohio	Ohio Rev. Code Ann. §§ 1339.71 to 1339.78 (Baldwin 1991).
Oregon	Or. Rev. Stat. §§ 359.200 to 359.255 (1989).
Pennsylvania	73 Pa. Cons. Stat. §§ 2122 to 2130 (1989).
Tennessee	Tenn. Code Ann. §§ 47-25-1001 to 47-25-1007 (1990).
Texas	Tex. Rev. Civ. Stat. Ann. Art. 9018 (Vernon 1989).
Washington	Wash. Rev. Code Ann. § 18.110 (1990).
Wisconsin	Wis. Stat. Ann. §§ 129.01 to 129.08 (West 1989).

Art Sellers Covered by the Statutes:

Alaska:
"Art dealer" means a person engaged in the business of selling works of art, other than a person exclusively engaged in the business of selling goods at public auction.
Arizona:
"Art dealer" means a person engaged in the business of selling works of fine art, other than a person exclusively engaged in the business of selling goods at public auction.
Arkansas:
"Art dealer" means a person engaged in the business of selling works of art.

California:
"Art dealer" means a person engaged in the business of selling works of fine art, other than a person exclusively engaged in the business of selling goods at public auction.

Colorado:
"Art dealer" means a person engaged in the business of selling works of fine art, other than a person exclusively engaged in the business of selling goods at public auction.

Connecticut:
"Art dealer" means a person, partnership, firm, association or corporation other than a public auctioneer who undertakes to sell works of fine art.

Florida:
"Art dealer" means a person engaged in the business of selling works of art, a person who is a consignee of a work of art, or a person who, by occupation, holds himself out as having knowledge or skill peculiar to works of art or rare documents or prints, or to whom such knowledge or skill may be attributed by his employment of an agent or broker or other intermediary who, by occupation, holds himself out as having such knowledge or skill. The term "art dealer" includes an auctioneer who sells works of art, rare maps, rare documents, or rare prints at public auction as well as the auctioneer's consignor or principal. The term "art dealer" does not include a cooperative which is totally owned by artist members.

Idaho:
"Art dealer" means a person engaged in the business of selling works of fine art, other than a person exclusively engaged in the business of selling goods at public auction.

Illinois:
"Art dealer" means a person engaged in the business of selling works of fine art, other than a person exclusively engaged in the business of selling goods at public auction.

Iowa:
"Art dealer" means a person engaged in the business of selling works of fine art, in a shop or gallery devoted in the majority to works of fine art, other than a person engaged in the business of selling goods of general merchandise or at a public auction.

Kentucky:
"Art dealer" means a person engaged in the business of selling, as either a primary or supplemental source of income, works of fine art, other than a person exclusively engaged in the business of selling goods at public auction.

Maryland:
"Art dealer" means an individual, partnership, firm, association, or corporation, other than a public auctioneer, that undertakes to sell a work of fine art created by someone else.

Massachusetts:
"Art dealer" means a person engaged in the business of selling works of fine art, other than a person exclusively engaged in the business of selling goods at public auction.

Michigan:
"Art dealer" means a person engaged in the business of selling works of fine art, other than a person exclusively engaged in the business of selling goods at public auction.

Minnesota:
"Art dealer" means a person engaged in the business of selling works of fine art, other than a person exclusively engaged in the business of selling goods at public auction.

Missouri:
The term "art dealer" means a person engaged in the business of selling fine arts. The term "art dealer" does not include any person engaged exclusively in the business of selling goods at public auction.

Montana:
"Art dealer" means a person engaged in the business of selling works of fine art, other than a person exclusively engaged in the business of selling goods at public auction.

New Hampshire:

"Art dealer" means a person, including an individual, partnership, firm, association, or corporation, engaged in the business of selling works of art, other than a person exclusively engaged in the business of selling goods at a public auction.

New Jersey:

"Art dealer" means a person engaged in the business of selling crafts and works of fine art, other than a person exclusively engaged in the business of selling goods at public auction.

New Mexico:

"Art dealer" means a person primarily engaged in the business of selling works of art.

New York

"Art merchant" means a person who is in the business of dealing, exclusively or non-exclusively, in works of fine art or multiples, or a person who by his occupation holds himself out as having knowledge or skill peculiar to such works, or to whom such knowledge or skill may be attributed by his employment of an agent or other intermediary who by his occupation holds himself out as having such knowledge or skill. The term "art merchant" includes an auctioneer who sells such works at public auction, and except in the case of multiples, includes persons, not otherwise defined or treated as art merchants herein, who are consignors or principals of auctioneers.

North Carolina:

"Art dealer" means an individual, partnership, firm, association, or corporation that undertakes to sell a work of fine art created by someone else.

Ohio:

"Art dealer" means a person engaged in the business of selling works of art, other than a person exclusively engaged in the business of selling goods at public auction.

Oregon:

"Art dealer" means a person, other than a public auctioneer, who undertakes to sell a work of fine art created by another.

Pennsylvania:

"Art dealer." A person engaged in the business of selling crafts and works of fine art, other than a person exclusively engaged in the business of selling goods at public auction.

Tennessee:

"Art dealer" means a person engaged in the business of selling works of art, other than a person exclusively engaged in the business of selling goods at public auction.

Texas:

"Art dealer" means a person engaged in the business of selling works of art.

Washington:

"Art dealer" means a person, partnership, firm, association or corporation, other than a public auctioneer, which undertakes to sell a work of fine art created by another.

Wisconsin:

"Art dealer" means a person engaged in the business of selling works of fine art, other than a person exclusively engaged in the business of selling goods at public auction.

Artworks Protected by the Statutes:

Alaska:

"Work of art" means an original or multiple original art work including: (A) visual art such as a painting, sculpture, drawing, mosaic, or photograph; (B) calligraphy; (C) graphic art such as an etching, lithograph, offset print, or silk screen; (D) craft work in clay, textile, fiber, wood, metal, plastic, or glass materials; (E) mixed media such as a collage or any combination of art media in this paragraph; (F) art employing traditional native materials such as ivory, bone, grass, baleen, animal skins, wood and furs.

Arizona:

"Work of fine art" means an original or multiple original art work which is: (a) A visual rendition, including a painting, drawing, sculpture, mosaic or photograph. (b) A work of calligraphy. (c) A work of graphic art, including an etching, lithograph, offset print or silkscreen. (d) A craft work in materials, including clay, textile, fiber, wood, metal, plastic or glass. (e) A work in mixed media, including a collage or a work consisting of any combination of subdivisions (a) through (d).

Arkansas:

"Art" means a painting, sculpture, drawing, work of graphic art, pottery, weaving, batik, macrame, quilt, or other commonly recognized art form.

California:

"Fine art" means a painting, sculpture, drawing, work of graphic art (including an etching, lithograph, offset print, silk screen, or a work of graphic art of like nature), a work of calligraphy, or a work in mixed media (including a collage, assemblage, or any combination of the foregoing art media).

Colorado:

"Work of fine art" or "work" means: (a) A work of visual art such as a painting, sculpture, drawing, mosaic or photograph; (b) A work of calligraphy; (c) A work of graphic art such as an etching, a lithograph, an offset print, a silk screen, or any other work of similar nature; (d) A craft work in materials, including but not limited to clay, textile, fiber, wood, metal, plastic, or glass; (e) A work in mixed media such as a collage or any combination of the art media set forth in this subsection.

Connecticut:

"Fine art" means (1) a work of visual art such as a painting, sculpture, drawing, mosaic or photograph; (2) a work of calligraphy; (3) a work of graphic art such as an etching, lithograph, offset print, silk screen, or other work of graphic art of like nature; (4) crafts such as crafts in clay, textile, fiber, wood, metal, plastic, glass or similar materials; and (5) a work in mixed media such as a collage or any combination of the foregoing art media.

Florida:

"Art" means a painting, sculpture, drawing, work of graphic art, pottery, weaving, batik, macrame, quilt, print, photograph, or craft work executed in materials including, but not limited to, clay, textile, paper, fiber, wood, tile, metal, plastic, or glass. The term shall also include a rare map which is offered as a limited edition or a map 80 years old or older; or a rare document or rare print which includes, but is not limited to, a print, engraving, etching, woodcut, lithograph, or serigraph which is offered as a limited edition, or one 80 years old or older.

Idaho:

"Fine art" means a painting, sculpture, drawing, work of graphic art, including an etching, lithograph, signed limited edition offset print, silk screen, or a work of graphic art of like nature; a work of calligraphy, photographs, original works in ceramics, wood, metals, glass, plastic, wax, stone or leather or a work in mixed media, including a collage, assemblage, or any combination of the art media mentioned in this subsection.

Illinois:

"Work of fine art" means: (a) A visual rendition including, but not limited to, a painting, drawing, sculpture, mosaic, videotape, or photograph. (b) A work of calligraphy. (c) A work of graphic art including, but not limited to, an etching, lithogrpah, serigraph, or offset print. (d) A craft work in materials including, but not limited to, clay, textile, fiber, wood, metal, plastic, or glass. (e) A work in mixed media including, but not limited to, a collage, assemblage, or work consisting of any combination of paragraphs (a) through (d).

Iowa:

"Fine art" means a painting, sculpture, drawing, mosaic, photograph, work of graphic art, including an etching, lithograph, offset print, silk screen, or work of graphic art of like nature, a work of calligraphy, or a work in mixed media including a collage, assemblage, or any combination of these art media which is one of a kind or is available in a limited issue or series.

"Fine art" also means crafts which include work in clay, textiles, fiber, wood, metal, plastic, glass, or similar materials which is one of a kind or is available in a limited issue or series.

Kentucky:
"Fine art" shall include, but is not limited to, a painting, sculpture, drawing, work of graphic or photographic art, including an etching, lithograph, offset print, silk screen, or work of graphic art of like nature, a work of calligraphy, a work of folk art or craft, or a work in mixed media including a collage, assemblage, or any combination of the foregoing art media.

Maryland:
"Work of fine art" means an original art work which is: (1) A visual rendition including a painting, drawing, sculpture, mosaic, or photograph; (2) A work of calligraphy; (3) A work of graphic art including an etching, lithograph, offset print, or silk screen; (4) A craft work in materials including clay, textile, fiber, wood, metal, plastic, or glass; or (5) A work in mixed media including a collage or a work consisting of any combination of works included in this subsection.

Massachusetts:
"Fine art," a painting, sculpture, drawing, work of graphic art, including an etching, lithograph, offset print, silk screen, or work of graphic art of like nature, a work of calligraphy, or a work in mixed media including a collage, assemblage, or any combination of the foregoing art media.

Michigan:
"Art" means a painting, sculpture, drawing, work of graphic art, photograph, weaving, or work of craft art.

Minnesota:
"Art" means a painting, sculpture, drawing, work of graphic art, photograph, weaving, or work of craft art.

Missouri:
The term "fine arts" includes: (a) Visual art such as paintings, sculptures, drawings, mosaics, or photographs; (b) Calligraphy; (c) Graphic art such as etchings, lithographs, offset prints, silk screens, and other works of a similar nature; (d) Crafts, including any item made by an artist or craftsman through the use of clay, textiles, fibers, wood, metal, plastic, glass, ceramics, or similar materials; (e) Works in mixed media such as collages or any combination of the art forms or media listed in paragraph (a), (b), (c), or (d) of this subdivision.

Montana:
"Fine art" means a painting, sculpture, drawing, work of graphic art (including an etching, lithograph, signed limited edition offset print, silk screen, or work of graphic art of like nature), a work of calligraphy, photographs, original works in ceramics, wood, metals, glass, plastic, wax, stone, or leather, or a work in mixed media (including a collage, assemblage, or any combination of the art media mentioned in this subsection).

New Hampshire:
"Work of art" means an original art work that is any of the following: (a) A visual rendition including, but not limited to, a painting, drawing, sculpture, mosaic, or photograph. (b) A work of calligraphy. (c) A work of graphic art, including, but not limited to, an etching, lithograph, offset print, silk screen, or other work of similar materials. (d) A craft work in materials, including, but not limited to, clay, textile, fiber, wood, metal, plastic, glass, or similar materials. (e) A work in mixed media, including, but not limited to, a collage or a work consisting of any combination of the items listed in subparagraphs (a) through (d) of this paragraph.

New Jersey:
"Craft" means an artistic rendition created using any medium, including, but not limited to, a collage and other works consisting of any combination of painting, drawing, sculpture, photography and manual creation in clay, textile, fiber, wood, metal, plastic, glass, stone, leather or similar materials.

"Fine art" means an original work of visual or graphic art created using any medium, including but not limited to, a painting, drawing or sculpture.

New Mexico:
"Art" means a painting, sculpture, drawing, work of graphic art, pottery, weaving, batik, macrame or quilt containing the artist's original handwritten signature on the work of art.

New York:
"Craft" means a functional or non-functional work individually designed, and crafted by hand, in any medium including but not limited to textile, tile, paper, clay, glass, fiber, wood, metal or plastic; provided, however, that if produced in multiples, craft shall not include works mass produced or produced in other than a limited edition.

"Fine art" means a painting, sculpture, drawing, or work of graphic art, and print, but not multiples.

North Carolina:
"Work of fine art" means an original art work that is: (a) A visual rendition, including a painting, drawing, sculpture, mosaic, or photograph; (b) A work of calligraphy; (c) A work of graphic art, including an etching, lithograph, offset print, or silk screen; (d) A craft work in materials, including clay, textile, fiber, wood, metal, plastic, or glass; or (e) A work in mixed media, including a collage or a work consisting of any combination of works included in this subdivision.

Ohio:
"Work of art" means an original art work that is any of the following: (1) A visual rendition including, but not limited to, a painting, drawing, sculpture, mosaic, or photograph; (2) A work of calligraphy; (3) A work of graphic art, including, but not limited to, an etching, lithograph, offset print, or silk screen; (4) A craft work in materials, including, but not limited to, clay, textile, fiber, wood, metal, plastic, or glass; (5) A work in mixed media, including, but not limited to, a collage or a work consisting of any combination of the items listed in divisions (D)(1) to (4) of this section.

Oregon:
"Fine art" means: (a) An original work of visual art such as a painting, sculpture, drawing, mosaic or photograph; (b) A work in calligraphy; (c) A work of graphic art such as an etching, lithograph, offset print, silk screen or other work of similar nature; (d) A craft work in materials including but not limited to clay, textile, fiber, wood, metal, plastic, glass or similar materials; or (e) A work in mixed media such as a collage or any combination of the art media described in this subsection.

Pennsylvania:
"Craft." An artistic rendition, created using any medium, including, but not limited to, a collage and other works consisting of any combination of painting, drawing, sculpture, photography and manual creation in clay, textile, fiber, wood, metal, plastic, glass, stone, leather or similar materials.

"Fine art." An original work of visual or graphic art of recognized quality, created using any medium, including, but not limited to, a painting, drawing or sculpture.

Tennessee:
"Work of art" means an original art work which is: (A) A visual rendition, including a painting, drawing, sculpture, mosaic, or photograph; (B) A work of calligraphy; (C) A work of graphic art, including an etching, lithograph, offset print, or silk screen;

(D) A craft work in materials, including clay, textile, fiber, wood, metal, plastic, or glass; or (E) A work in mixed media, including a collage or a work consisting of any combination of subdivisions (6)(A) through (6)(D).

Texas:
"Art" means a painting, sculpture, drawing, work of graphic art, pottery, weaving, batik, macrame, quilt, or other commonly recognized art form.

Washington:
"Work of fine art" means an original art work which is: (a) A visual rendition including a painting, drawing, sculpture, mosaic, or photograph; (b) A work of calligraphy; (c) A work of graphic art including an etching, lithograph, offset print, or silk screen; (d) A craft work in materials including clay, textile, fiber, wood, metal, plastic, or glass; or (e) A work in mixed media including a collage or a work consisting of any combination of works included in this subsection.

Wisconsin:
"Work of fine art" means an original art work which is: (a) A visual rendition including, but not limited to, a painting, drawing, sculpture, mosaic, or photograph; (b) A work of calligraphy; (c) A work of graphic art, including, but not limited to, an etching, lithograph, offset print or silk screen; (d) A craft work in materials, including but not limited to clay, textile, fiber, wood, metal, plastic or glass; (e) A work in mixed media, including, but not limited to, a collage or a work consisting of any combination of pars. (a) to (d).

Special Provisions:

Alaska:
Artist-consignor may waive the right to trust-property protection, if such waiver is clear, conspicuous, and agreed to in writing by the artist. No waiver is valid with respect to proceeds from work initially placed on consignment but later purchased by the art dealer-consignee. Nor shall any waiver inure to the benefit of the consignee's creditors in a manner inconsistent with the artist's rights.

Arizona:
Any waiver by artist is void. An art dealer who violates the statute is liable to the artist for damages of $50 plus actual damages, including incidental and consequential damages, sustained by the artist, and reasonable attorney fees.

Arkansas:
Any waiver by artist is void. An art dealer who violates the statute is liable to the artist for a civil penalty of $50 plus actual damages, including incidental and consequential damages, sustained by the artist. Reasonable attorneys' fees and court cost shall be paid the prevailing party.

California:
Any waiver by artist is void.

Colorado:
Any waiver by artist is void. An art dealer who violates the statute is liable to the artist for a civil penalty of $50 plus actual damages, including incidental and consequential damages, sustained by the artist. Reasonable attorneys' fees and court cost shall be paid the prevailing party.

Connecticut:
Any waiver by artist is void. Artist-consignor is required to give notice to the public by placing a tag on the work stating that it is being sold under consignment or by posting a conspicuous sign in consignee's place of business giving notice that some works are being sold under consignment. Statute requires a written agreement covering (1) payment schedule for sale proceeds; (2) responsibility of gallery for loss or damage;

(3) written agreement as to retail prices; and (4) artist's written consent to displays and credit on displays.

Florida:

Any waiver by artist is void. Artist-consignor is required to give notice to the public by placing a tag on the work stating that it is being 'sold under consignment or by posting a conspicuous sign in consignee's place of business giving notice that some works are being sold under consignment.

Idaho:

The art dealer, after delivery of the work of fine art, is an agent of the artist for the purpose of sale or exhibition of the consigned work of fine art within the state of Idaho. This relationship shall be defined in writing and renewed at least every three (3) years by the art dealer and the artist. It is the responsibility of the artist to identify clearly the work of art by securely attaching identifying marking to or clearly signing the work of art.

Illinois:

If the sale of the work of fine art is on installment, the funds from the installment shall first be applied to pay any balance due to the artist on the sale, unless the parties expressly agree in writing that the proceeds on each installment shall be paid according to a percentage established by the consignment agreement. Customer deposits shall be used to pay the amounts due the artist within 30 days after such deposits become part of the payment for the work. Any agreement entered into pursuant to this subsection must be clear and conspicuous.

Iowa:

Any waiver by artist is void.

Kentucky:

None.

Maryland:

None.

Massachusetts:

Artist can give written waiver of right to have sale proceeds applied first to pay any balance due artist. If gallery buys artworks for its own account, proceeds shall be trust funds until artist is paid in full.

Michigan:

Artist may waive right to have sale proceeds in any twelve month period in excess of $2500 considered trust funds. If gallery buys the artwork, artist must be paid in full and no waiver of trust fund provision is permitted.

Minnesota:

None.

Missouri:

None.

Montana:

None.

New Hampshire:

None.

New Jersey:

None.

New Mexico:

None.

New York:

Artist-consignor may waive the right to trust-property protection of sale proceeds exceeding $2500 in any twelve month period beginning with the date of the waiver. To be valid, such waiver must be clear, conspicuous, in writing, and signed by the consignor. No waiver is valid with respect to proceeds from work initially placed on consignment but later purchased by the art dealer-consignee. Nor shall any waiver inure to the benefit of the consignee's creditors in a manner inconsistent with the artist's rights.

North Carolina:

None.

Ohio:

None.

Oregon:

The art dealer may accept a work of fine art on consignment only if the dealer and artist enter into a written contract establishing: (1) the retail value of the work; (2) the time within which the proceeds of the sale are to be paid to the artist; (3) the minimum price for the sale of the work; (4) the percentage of the proceeds to be retained by the dealer. Any provision of a contract or agreement whereby the consignor waives any of the statute is void.

Pennsylvania:

None.

Tennessee:

None.

Texas:

None.

Washington:

The art dealer may accept a work of fine art on consignment only if the art dealer enters into a written contract with the artist which states: (a) the value of the work; (b) the minimum price for the sale of the work; (c) the fee, commission, or other compensation basis of the art dealer. Any portion of a contract that waives any portion of this statute is void. The gallery can only display the work if notice is given that it is the work of the artist and artist gives prior written consent to the particular use or display. If the gallery violates the statute, it is liable to the artist for $50 plus actual damages, and the artist's obligation for compensation to the dealer is voidable. The court may award the artist reasonable attorney's fees.

Wisconsin:

Statute requires a written contract that establishes: (1) an agreed on value for the artwork; (2) the time after sale in which payments must be made to the artist; and (3) the minimum sale price for the consigned artworks. If the gallery fails to enter into such a written contract, a court can void the artist's obligations to the gallery. Also, the gallery can only display an artwork if it credits the artist as creator and has the artist's consent to the particular display. If the gallery violates the statute it must pay the artist $50 plus actual damages and attorney's fees.

Appendix C

Table of Resources

ABCs of Borrowing
Publication FM1
Small Business Administration Publications
Post Office Box 30
Denver, Colorado 80201-0030

American Craft
American Craft Council
401 Park Avenue, South
New York, New York 10016
(212) 274-0630

Apprenticeship in Craft
Edited by Gerry Williams
Daniel Clark Books, 1981
Post Office Box 65
Goffstown, New Hampshire 03045

Artist Beware
by Michael McCann
Lyons & Buford, Pubs., Inc.
31 West 21st Street
New York, New York 10010
(212) 620-9580
480 pages; $29.95, Softcover
(ISBN 1-55821-175-6)

The Artist's Complete Health
  and Safety Guide
by Monona Rossol
Allworth Press, 1990
10 E. 23rd Street, Suite 400
New York, New York 10010
(212) 777-8395
328 pages; $16.95, Softcover
(ISBN 0-927629-10-0)

An Artist's Handbook on Copyright
by Robert C. Lower and Jeffrey E. Young
Georgia Volunteer Lawyers for the Arts, 1987
141 Pryor Street, SW, Suite 2330
Atlanta, Georgia 30303
(404) 525-6046

Art Law in a Nutshell, 2nd Ed.
by Leonard D. DuBoff
West Publishing Co., 1993
Post Office Box 64526
Saint Paul, Minnesota 55164-0526
(612) 228-2778
350 pages; $16.95, Softcover
(ISBN 0-314-01335-0)

Be Your Own Boss: The Complete,
  Indispensable, Hands-On Guide to Starting
  and Running Your Own Business
Dana Schilling
Penguin, 1984
375 Hudson Street
New York, New York 10014-3657
(212) 366-2000; 1-800-331-4624

Business Forms & Contracts (In Plain
  English)® for Craftspeople, 2nd Ed.
by Leonard D. DuBoff
Foreword by Lammot duPont Copeland
Interweave Press, 1993
201 East Fourth Street
Loveland, Colorado 80537
(303) 669-7672; 1-800-272-2193
111 pages; $14.95, Softcover
(ISBN 0-934026-83-1)

Contemporary Crafts Marketplace
by The American Craft Council
Bowker Publishing Co.
121 Chanlon Road
New Providence, New Jersey 07974
(908) 464-6800; 1-800-521-8110

The Cooperative Approach to Crafts
(CIR 33)
Agricultural Cooperative Service
United States Department of Agriculture
Post Office Box 96576
Washington, D.C. 20090-6576

Cooperative Approach to Crafts
for Senior Citizens
(PA 1156)
Agricultural Cooperative Service
United States Department of Agriculture
Post Office Box 96576
Washington, D.C. 20090-6576

Craftmaster News
Attn: Marsha Reed
P.O. Box 39429
Downey, California 90239
(310) 869-5882
Fax (310) 904-0546

Craft Fair Guide
by Lee Spiegel
Post Office Box 262
Mill Valley, California 94941

Craft Supplies Supermarket
by Joseph Rosenbloom
Oliver Press
Willits, California 95490

The Craftsman's Survival Manual
by George and Nancy Wettlaufer

Crafts Marketing Success Secrets
by Barbara Brabec
Brabec Productions, 1988
Post Office Box 2137
Naperville, Illinois 60567
104 pages; $11.95, Softcover
(ISBN 0-9613909-1-3)

The Crafts Report
700 Orange Street
Wilmington, Delaware 19801

Creative Cash: How to Sell Your Crafts,
Needlework, Designs & Know-how
by Barbara Brabec
Aames-Allen, 1991
1106 Main Street
Huntington Beach, California 92648
(714) 375-4889
200 pages; $16.95, Hardcover
(ISBN 0-96113909-3-X)

The Deskbook of Art Law, 2nd Ed.
by Leonard D. DuBoff and Sally Holt Caplan
Oceana Press
75 Main Street
Dobbs Ferry, NY 10522
(914) 693-8100

2,000 pp; $250, Hardcover (two volumes)
(ISBN 0-379201-57-7)

Encouraging American Craftsmen
by Charles Counts
The Superintendent of Documents
United States Government Printing Office
Washington, D.C. 20402

Fire Safety Fact Sheet
Publications 91-41 and 3088
Occupational Safety and
   Health Administration Information
Room N-3647
United States Department of Labor
Washington, D.C. 20210

Foundation Directory
Columbia University Press
136 South Broadway
Irvington, New York 10533

General Information Concerning Patents
Superintendent of Documents
United States Government Printing Office
Washington, D.C. 20402
75¢

General Information Concerning Trademarks
Superintendent of Documents
United States Government Printing Office
Washington, DC 20402
50¢

Guide to the NEA Visual Arts
Fellowship Program
National Endowment for the Arts
Washington, D.C. 20506
(202) 682-5400; TDD: (202) 682-5496

The Handcraft Business
Small Business Reporter
Bank of America, 1972
Department 3120, Post Office Box 37000
San Francisco, CA 94137
16 pages; $1

How to Start a Cooperative
(CIR 33)
Agricultural Cooperative Service
United States Department of Agriculture
Post Office Box 96576
Washington, D.C. 20090-6576

Insurance and Risk Management
for Small Business, 2nd Ed.
Small Business Management Series No. 30
Superintendent of Documents

United States Government Printing Office
Washington, D.C. 20402

Insurance Checklist for Small Business
Small Marketer's Aid #148
Small Business Administration
Washington, D.C. 20416

International Directory of Resources for Artisans
by Caroline C. Ramsay;
ed. by Sheila Mooney
Crafts Center, 1992 Edition
1001 Connecticut Avenue, NW, Suite 1138
Washington, D.C. 20036
(202) 728-9603
181 pages; $49.95, Hardcover

*The Law (In Plain English)® for Art and
   Craft Galleries*
by Leonard D. DuBoff
Interweave Press, 1993
201 East Fourth Street
Loveland, CO 80537
(303) 669-7672; 1-800-272-2193
156 pp.; $14.95, Softcover
(ISBN 0-934026-87-4)

*The Law (In Plain English)® for Craftspeople,
3rd Ed.*
by Leonard D. DuBoff
Foreword by Jack Lenor Larsen and
Introduction by Sam Maloof
Interweave Press, 1992
201 East Fourth Street
Loveland, CO 80537
(303) 669-7672; 1-800-272-2193
148 pages; $12.95, Softcover
(ISBN 0-88179-032)

The Law (In Plain English)® for Small Businesses
by Leonard D. DuBoff
Wiley & Sons, 1991
605 Third Avenue
New York, New York 10158-0012
(212) 850-6000
240 pages; $29.95, Hardcover;
$14.95, Softcover
(ISBN 0-471-53617-2)
(ISBN 0-471-53616-4)

Legal Guide for the Visual Artist
by Tad Crawford
Allworth Press, 1989
10 East Twenty-third Street, Suite 400
New York, New York 10010
(212) 777-8395

224 pages; $18.95, Softcover
(ISBN 0-927629-00-3)

*Making It Legal: A Law Primer
   for Authors, Artists & Craftspeople*
by Martha Blue
Northland Publishing, 1988
Post Office Box 1389
Flagstaff, Arizona 86002

National Calendar of Indoor-Outdoor Art Fairs
by Henry Niles
5423 New Haven Avenue
Fort Wayne, Indiana 46803

*National Directory of
   Shops/Galleries/Shows/Fairs*
Edited by Sally Ann Davis
Writer's Digest Books,
1982–83 Annual Edition
1507 Dana Avenue
Cincinnati, Ohio 45207
(513) 531-2222; 1-800-289-0963

National Guide to Craft Supplies
by Judith Glassman
Van Nostrand-Reinhold Co., 1975
115 Fifth Avenue
New York, New York 10003
(212) 254-3232; 1-800-926-2665

Packing/Shipping of Crafts
American Craft Council
401 Park Avenue South
New York, New York 10016
(212) 274-0630
$3

*The Photographer's Business
   and Legal Handbook*
by Leonard D. DuBoff
Images Press, Inc., 1989
22 East 17th Street
New York, New York 10003
(212) 675-3707
156 pages; $18.95, Softcover
(ISBN 0-929667-02-6)

Photographing Crafts
by John C. Barsness
American Craft Council, 1974
401 Park Avenue, South
New York, New York 10016
(212) 274-0630

Photographing Your Craftwork
by Steve Meltzer
Madrona Pubs., 1986

Post Office Box 22667
Seattle, Washington 98122
(206) 325-3973; 1-800-367-8420
144 pages; $9.95, Softcover
(ISBN 0-88089-012-6)

*Photographing Your Product for
   Advertising & Promotion:
   A Handbook for Designers and Craftsmen*
by Norbert Nelson
Van Nostrand-Reinhold Co., 1971
115 Fifth Avenue
New York, New York 10003
(212) 254-3232; 1-800-926-2665

Photography for Artists and Craftsmen
by Claus-Peter Schmid
Van Nostrand-Reinhold Co., 1975
115 Fifth Avenue
New York, New York 10003
(212) 254-3232; 1-800-926-2665

*Protecting Your Health
   in the Art and Craft Workplace*
by Gail Barazani
Copeland Press, 1992
700 Orange Street
Post Office Box 1992
Wilmington, Delaware 19899

Sound Cash Management and Borrowing
Publication FM9
Small Business Administration Publications
Post Office Box 30
Denver, Colorado 80201-0030

Suhnshine Artists U.S.A.
Sun Country Enterprises

1700 Sunset Drive
Longwood, Florida 32750

Tax Guide for Small Business
Publication 334
Internal Revenue Service
United States Government Printing Office
Washington, D.C. 20402

This Business of Art
by Diane Cochrane
Watson-Guptill Publications, 1989
One Astor Plaza
1515 Broadway
New York, New York 10036
(212) 536-5121
240 pages; $19.95, Hardcover
(ISBN 0-8230-5361-X)

Ventilation: A Practical Guide
by Nancy Clark, Thomas Cutler,
Jean-Ann McGrane
Center for Occupational Hazards
Five Beekman Street
New York, New York 10038
(212) 227-6220
128 pages; $15.99, Hardcover;
$7.95, Softcover

Westart
Post Office Box 1396
Auburn, California 95603

Your Social Security
Social Security Office
See U.S. Government pages in phone book
   for local office

Appendix D

Resource Organizations

Agricultural Cooperative Service
United States Department of Agriculture
Post Office Box 96576
Washington, D.C. 20090-6576
(202) 245-5356

American Council for the Arts
570 Seventh Avenue
New York, New York 10018
(212) 274-0630

American Craft and Retailers Association
Post Office Box 9
Woodstock, Maryland 21163
(301) 484-1410

American Craft Council
72 Spring Street
New York, New York 10012
(212) 274-0630

American Craft Museum
40 West 53rd Street
New York, New York 10019

Arts, Crafts and Theater Safety (ACTS)
Director, Monona Rossol
181 Thompson Street, #23
New York, New York 10012
(Publishes *Arts Facts*, a monthly newsletter
   updating regulations and research
   affecting the arts.)

Gail Barazani
"Protecting Your Health"
The Crafts Report
87 Wall Street, Second Floor
Seattle, Washington 98121
   or
Gail Barazani
"Protecting Your Health"
The Crafts Report
5340 North Magnolia
Chicago, Illinois 60640

Center for Safety in the Arts
Director, Michael McCann
Five Beekman Street
New York, New York 10038
(212) 227-6220
(Publishes *Art Hazards News*,
   ten issues yearly.)

Craft Emergency Relief Fund (CERF)
Ex. Director Lois Ahrens
245 Main Street
Northampton, Massachusetts 01060-3114
(413) 625-9672; (413) 586-5898

Crafts Specialist
Agricultural Cooperative Service
USDA-ACS
Post Office Box 96576, 1
Washington, D.C. 20090-6576

Dome Publishing Co.
Providence, Rhode Island 02903

Federal Trade Commission
Pennsylvania at Sixteenth Street
Washington, D.C. 20580
(202) 326-2222

First Nation Arts
69 Kelly Road
Falmouth, Virginia 22405
(703) 371-5615

Ideal System Co.
Post Office Box 1568
Augusta, Georgia 30903

List Brokers:

   Dependable Lists, Inc.
   257 Park Avenue South
   New York, New York 10010

R.L. Polk & Co.
551 Fifth Avenue
New York, New York 10017

Fred Woolf List Co.
309 Fifth Avenue
New York, New York 10016

Alan Drey Co., Inc.
600 Third Avenue
New York, New York 10016

Fritz S. Hofheimer, Inc.
88 Third Avenue
Mineola, New York 11501

Noma List Services
2544 Chamberlain Road
Fairlawn, Ohio 44313

Names Unlimited, Inc.
183 Madison Avenue
New York, New York 10016

National Institute of Occupational Safety
& Health (NIOSH)
1 (800) 356-4674

Occupational Safety and Health
Administration (OSHA)
(202) 523-9667

Office of Student Financial Assistance
United States Department of Education
Washington, D.C. 20202

Small Business Administration
Washington, D.C. 20416

Small Business Administration Publications
Post Office Box 30
Denver, Colorado 80201-0030

Small Business Administration Answer Desk
1 (800) 368-5855
(202) 653-7561 in Washington, D.C.

United States Copyright Office
Library of Congress
Washington, D.C. 20559

United States Customs Service
1301 Constitution Avenue, NW
Washington, D.C. 20229

World Crafts Council
401 Park Avenue South
New York, New York 10016